Guide to Colorado Historic Places

SITES SUPPORTED BY THE COLORADO HISTORICAL SOCIETY'S STATE HISTORICAL FUND

by Thomas J. Noel

A PROGRAM OF THE
COLORADO HISTORICAL SOCIETY
STATE HISTORICAL FUND
GRANTS FOR
HISTORIC PRESERVATION

WESTCLIFFE PUBLISHERS
westcliffepublishers.com

ACKNOWLEDGMENTS

Mark S. Wolfe, director of the State Historical Fund (SHF), and Alyson McGee, SHF public outreach coordinator, made this book possible in many ways. Tom Carr, Lyle Miller, Rachel Simpson, James Stratis, and John Semple of the SHF office have also been indispensable. Thanks also to Dale Heckendorn, Chris Geddes, and Holly Wilson of the State Office of Archaeology and Historic Preservation. Susan Collins and Meg Van Ness were especially helpful about how to showcase archaeological treasures preserved and interpreted with the help of SHF grants. This book was also made possible by funding from the Colorado Historical Society's State Historical Fund.

John Fielder and Rick Wicker at Westcliffe Publishers, who have done so much to increase awareness of Colorado's natural landmarks, graciously agreed to publish this. Furthermore, Craig Keyzer, Martha Ripley Gray, Jenna Samelson Browning, Jennifer Jahner, and Barrett Webb at Westcliffe helped plan, refine, and illustrate this first-ever guide to Colorado's restored landmarks.

At the University of Colorado at Denver, Dr. Margaret Cozzens, vice chancellor for academic affairs, and Prof. Mark Gelernter both took a special interest in helping to fund this project. Thanks also to history chair Myra Rich as well as Dean Jim Smith, JoAnne Pugh, Steve Honda, and Sue Eddelman of the College of Liberal Arts and Sciences, and Dorothy Yates and Amy Gannon of Contracts and Grants. Georgianna Contiguglia, the president of the Colorado Historical Society (CHS) and State Historic Preservation Officer, has been supportive in various ways.

In the CHS Publications Office, David Wetzel, Ben Fogelberg, Steve Grinstead, and Larry Borowsky graciously shared their materials on various preservation projects and exhibits, which have greatly strengthened this book. CHS librarians Barbara Dey, Rebecca Lintz, Debbie Neiswonger, and Ruba Sadi as well as photo curator Eric Paddock also assisted. Another tip of the hat to the Denver Public Library Western History staff, especially Eleanor Gehres, Coi Drummond-Gehrig, Bruce Hanson, Joan Harms, James Jeffrey, Jim Kroll, Phil Panum, Barbara Walton, and Kay Wisnia.

CU Denver students did much of the preliminary legwork and research for this survey. Thanks to Holly C. Allen, Mary Katherine Allen, Shawn W. Collins, Celia Curtis, Kristen Egnes, Christine Falcon, Jamie Field, Greg Francis, Rick Gardner, Ryan Hanneman, Chuck Hanson, Natalie Hook, Simone Howell, Heather Lang, Michael Lee, Ted Misunius, Kara Miyagishima, Kathryn Ordway, Heather Petersen, David Richardson, Kevin Rucker, Darcy Schlicting, Julie Schlosser, Christie Smith, John Stewart, Heather Thorwald, Cheryl Seibert Waite, Brian Weiss, and Laura Ziemke. Amy Zimmer fact-checked and edited the manuscript.

Previous Page: *In Denver's Montclair neighborhood, the Baron Walter von Richthofen built his molkery (dairy) and sanitarium for tuberculars. The fresh air, sunshine, and warm milk right from the udder would cure, the baron promised, any and all ailments.*

A medical building from 1863 in Central City, now used by the Central City Opera House Association

We visited all 64 counties in the state, where locals often showed us their SHF-funded landmarks. Thanks to hundreds of other helpful Coloradans, especially Becky Anderson, Robert L. Atkinson, Kevin Bennett, Bart Berger, William J. Bertschy, Bill Bessesen, Hugh Bingham, Betsy and Geoff Blakeslee, Larry Bohning, Lew and Leslie Cady, Richard Carrillo, Gina Carter, Hap Channell, Julie Coleman, Dan Corson, Alan and Marcy Culpin, Rusty DeLucia, T. Ray Faulkner and Bob Perry of Perry-Mansfield Camp, Joann West Dodds, Janice Welborn Downing, Erik Dyce, Bill Fetcher, Rich Fike, Peggy Ford, Steve Friesen, Chet Gaede, Dennis Gallagher, Nancy Gauss, Barbara J. Gibson, Bishop José Gomez, Breck and Mary Lynn Grover, Colleen B. Hannon, Jim Hartmann, John W. Hickenlooper, Fabby Hillyard, Kathy Hoeft, Ann and Neal Hoffman, Grant Houston, Linda Jones, Patience Kemp, Bet Kettle, Ashley King, Steve Leonard, Karolyn Lestrud, David Lively, Gary Long, Jan MacKell, Don Mattivi, Esther McCrumb, Jay Mead, Chocolate Dan Monroe, John Moriarty, Ron Neely, Jim Noel, Vi Noel, Allen Nossaman, Bill Owens, Nancy Penfold, Ed, Martha, Abigail, and Columbine Quillen; Neil Reynolds, Bev Rich, Mark Rodman, Sandy, Bruce, and Buddy Schmaltz; Ed Simonich, Duane and Gay Smith, Jack Smith, Arianthé C. Stettner, Wayne Sundberg, Carol Svensen, Carol Tunner, Thayer Tutt, Rev. Pat Valdez, Rebecca Waugh, Rodd Wheaton, Jim White, Lynn Willcockson, and George Williams.

Special thanks to all fellow patrons of the Black Hawk, Central City, and Cripple Creek casinos, whose optimism makes this book and the good work it celebrates possible.

To my students, who are educating me.

CONTENTS

The Carver Power Plant in Steamboat Springs, built in 1901, is now known as Centennial Hall and houses city offices and a cafe.

FEATURED TOWNS

The numbers listed below are shown on the map on pages 6–7 and represent towns with historic sites featured in this book.

TOWNS WITH *SHF-FUNDED LANDMARKS*

Each number on this map represents a town featured in this book. For a complete list of numbered towns, see p. 5.

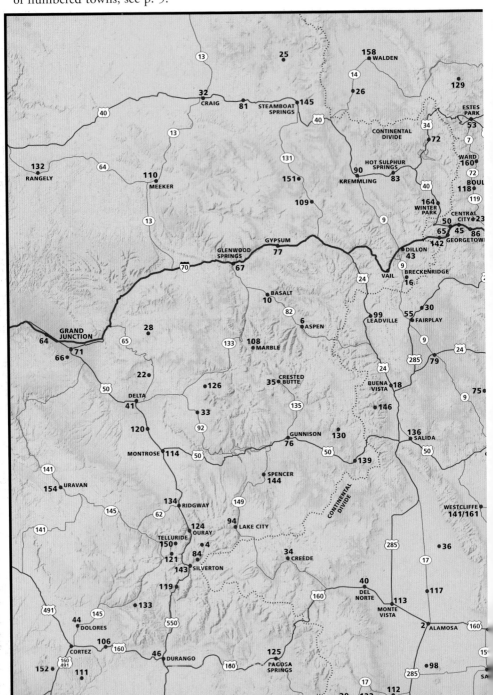

FEATURED IN THIS GUIDEBOOK

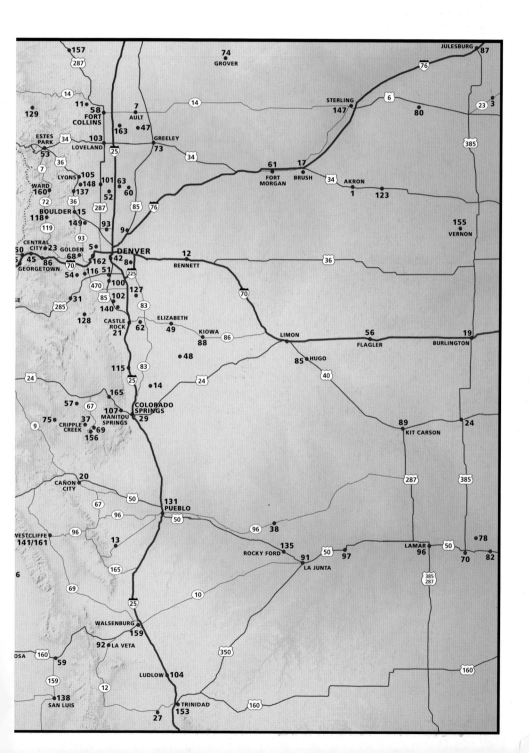

REFLECTIONS ON THE STATE HISTORICAL FUND

Former Colorado Governor Bill Owens:

"Investing in our past is just as important as investing in our future. We need to understand what our ancestors did to get us where we are today. And the hundreds of landmarks preserved all over Colorado by the State Historical Fund make a great roadmap to our past."

Georgianna Contiguglia, Colorado Historical Society President and State Historic Preservation Officer:

"Without a doubt, Colorado's most significant contribution to preservation has been the establishment of the State Historical Fund. In the past decade, the SHF has provided incentive, technical assistance, and hard cash for the identification and preservation of the state's historic and prehistoric built environment. Equally important, it has encouraged many communities to develop and adopt historic preservation ordinances and to integrate them into growth and economic development plans. For Coloradans, preservation is as much a matter of practical business as cultural heritage."

Mark S. Wolfe, director of the State Historical Fund and Deputy State Historic Preservation Officer:

"From little one-room schoolhouses to enormous power plants, from agricultural landscapes to archaeological studies, from the lighthouse on Monkey Island at the Pueblo Zoo to the monumental State Capitol, Colorado has awarded more than $160 million to hundreds of sites. Preservation partners in all 64 counties imagined what could be, and asked us to give them a hand at realizing their dreams. Their dreams become ours, and

their enthusiasm is contagious. We find ourselves cheering them on, trying to find ways to make their budgets stretch just a little bit further, and smiling as much as they do when ribbons are finally cut and people file in to see the reborn landmark. Preservation pays. For every $1 million in SHF rehabilitation grants, an additional $6 million has been spent by others to restore and preserve Colorado's treasures."

Most State Historical Fund support goes to the restoration of endangered public places: libraries, museums, parks, and schools. In the tiny Weld County town of Grover, for instance, the SHF helped the Pawnee Historical Society save this old railroad depot and rehabilitate it as a museum and birdwatchers' clubhouse.

Photo courtesy of Tom Noel

John Fielder, photographer and preservationist:

"Though I had been reading Colorado history books for years, I don't think my appreciation for our remarkable past matured until I stood in the same 300 places all over Colorado from which photographer W. H. Jackson recorded 19th-century Colorado on glass film plates. That project, Colorado 1870–2000, *produced three books, exhibits, and slide lectures, which collectively attracted thousands of people to the idea of historic preservation. The restored landmarks of our past provide us a sense of place and a pride in our communities. Thanks to the Colorado Historical Society's State Historical Fund, Colorado has set the pace nationally in preserving its cherished landmarks, as this book shows."*

Jim Hartmann, past president of the Colorado Historical Society and State Historic Preservation Officer when the SHF was established:

"Created by a vote of the people, the State Historical Fund has been an amazing success because the Colorado Historical Society, chosen by the Colorado General Assembly to administer it, wisely sought to make the people of Colorado partners in its planning and implementation. Colorado Preservation 2000, *a statewide preservation plan, resulted from a series of statewide meetings called to identify and address preservation issues and opportunities. The meetings generated new thinking and fresh possibilities, and clearly revealed that the preservation of Colorado was a shared value. Coloradans set a goal for themselves that, over the next 25 years, Coloradans will increasingly appreciate, respect, and protect their heritage and will embrace their role as its stewards. What we do day by day will shape how Colorado looks centuries from now. With this realization and vision, SHF resources can help point out and preserve Colorado's ever-increasing, ever-changing heritage as a legacy for the future."*

The former Carnegie Public Library in Colorado Springs, now the Penrose Public Library, was given a much-needed $3 million restoration, $794,699 of which came from the State Historical Fund.

WHERE DID THE $175 MILLION GO?

Colorado voters chose preservation in 1990, authorizing a change to the state constitution that would allow casinos in the three mountain mining towns of Black Hawk, Central City, and Cripple Creek.

Voters said "yes," hoping that gaming would economically revive these once booming, then busted, cities of gold. For broader, statewide benefits, the state would tax casinos to finance historic preservation in all 64 counties. Since that election, more than $175 million has been spent to restore endangered buildings in communities from Akron to Woodland Park.

The Colorado Historical Society's State Historical Fund works with local communities, which initiate the preservation of their historic resources. The SHF strives to rehabilitate and restore old buildings for continued use, keeping in mind the words of the father of historic preservation, Eugène-Emmanuel Viollet-le-Duc: "The best means of preserving a building is to find a use for it."

Where did that $175 million go? That is the story told in these pages, a story that will also guide you to more than 600 landmarks now restored for Coloradans and tourists to visit, use, and enjoy. While projects are constantly changing and not all could be included or updated, the locations profiled in this book offer a vital window into the dynamic and inspiring people and places keeping Colorado's past alive for current and future generations.

PRESERVATION TIMELINE

1879: Colorado Governor John L. Routt and the legislature create and fund the State Historical Society of Colorado to collect, preserve, and interpret state history and historic sites.

1906: President Theodore Roosevelt and Congress designate Mesa Verde as the first national park founded to preserve buildings.

1906: The National Antiquities Act makes it a federal crime to remove architectural or archaeological relics from federally owned public lands.

1930: Mrs. Margaret "Unsinkable Molly" Brown buys the Denver cottage of journalist and poet Eugene Field at 307 West Colfax Avenue in order to save it from demolition. She donates it to the Denver Public Library for installation in Washington Park as the Eugene Field Branch.

1932: Central City Opera House is restored by Anne Evans, Ida Kruse McFarlane, and others. This pioneering restoration inspires similar revivals in other fading Colorado mining towns, notably Aspen, Breckenridge, Crested Butte, Georgetown, Lake City, Ouray, Silverton, Steamboat Springs, and Telluride.

1933: The Historic American Building Survey is established in Washington to identify and document notable structures nationwide.

1935: The National Historic Sites & Buildings Act provides for identifying, acquiring, and interpreting significant historic sites.

1949: The Aspen Institute for Humanistic Studies undertakes to preserve and rejuvenate Aspen, a dying silver-mining town, as a center for arts and scholarship.

1949: The National Trust for Historic Preservation (NTHP) is chartered by Congress. With some 100,000 members and aggressive preservation lobbying, publications, and tour programs, as well as its Endangered Properties Fund, the National Trust spearheads preservation across the nation and forms alliances with other preservation groups. After federal funding ends in 1998, the Trust becomes self-sustaining.

1960s: Urban Renewal projects nationwide demolish much of America's heritage, giving rise to local preservation groups.

1960: The National Historic Landmarks program is established to celebrate the most important National Register sites with this most exalted designation.

1962: Grand Junction converts its Main Street to a shopping mall, setting an example followed by Aspen, Boulder, Denver, and other communities trying to restore their downtowns.

Photo courtesy Denver Public Library

In its haste to demolish old "blighted" buildings, the Denver Urban Renewal Authority used dynamite during the 1960s. This blast leveled the Cooper Building at 17th and Curtis to create a parking lot.

1965: Larimer Square Associates, spearheaded by Dana Crawford, saves one block of old Denver from the Urban Renewal Authority wrecking ball. Larimer Square emerges as one of the country's first historic district commercial rehabilitation projects. Its success inspires the 1989 designation of the Lower Downtown Historic District, a national model for using preservation to transform Skid Row into a prosperous residential, retail, art, and entertainment hub.

1966: The National Historic Preservation Act creates the Advisory Council on Historic Preservation to review any federally funded project to determine its impact on historic resources. This act establishes State Historic Preservation Offices (SHPOs) in each state to facilitate the development of nominations to the National Register of Historic Places. The act also provides assistance in developing and implementing statewide historic preservation plans and advising and assisting other agencies, such as town and county governments, in developing and conducting preservation programs. In addition, SHPOs provide public information, education, and training in preservation. Thanks to this act, the United States has more than 79,000 listings on the National Register, including more than 1,200 in Colorado.

1967: Colorado's first local landmark preservation agency is established. The Denver Landmark Preservation Commission has subsequently designated more than 313 individual landmarks and 45 historic districts.

1970: Historic Georgetown, Inc., one of Colorado's first small community preservation groups, helps make that town a national model for preservation. Since then, the town has not lost a single building in its historic district and even raises money to buy out developers.

1970: Historic Denver, Inc. (HDI), is founded to save the Molly Brown House, which it preserves and converts into one of Colorado's most popular house museums. HDI goes on to preserve Ninth Street Historic Park as the centerpiece of the Auraria Campus, Colorado's largest higher education center.

1973: The Colorado Historical Society establishes a Historic Preservation Department (now the Office of Archaeology and Historic Preservation) headed by Jim Hartmann, with Stephen Hart serving as the first state historic preservation officer.

1975: The Colorado State Register of Historic Properties is created, and grows to include more than 1,600 listings.

1976: The U.S. Bicentennial/Colorado Centennial celebration fosters preservation, restoration, and reuse of old buildings, such as railroad depots, schools, churches, and other landmarks. Along with other creative new uses, many landmarks are rehabilitated for use by local historical societies and museums.

1978: New York City's Grand Central Station decision by the U.S. Supreme Court stops Penn Central Railroad from demolishing this 1913 Beaux-Arts landmark. This decision pleases protesters, including the architect Philip Johnson, writer Brendan Gill, and Jacqueline Kennedy Onassis. The court decision affirms the power of local landmark commissions to block the destruction of a historic building if the decision does not deny the owner "all reasonable economic use of the property."

1990: The State Historical Fund (SHF) is created by a state constitutional amendment approved by Colorado voters to allow limited-stakes gaming in Black Hawk, Central City, and Cripple Creek.

1991: Colorado begins a State Historic Preservation Income Tax Credit of $5,000 to $50,000 for approved restoration projects on designated landmarks.

2003: The national convention of the National Trust for Historic Preservation is held in Denver, where Trust president Richard Moe calls Colorado a national pacesetter "for its preservation efforts and the State Historical Fund." The state receives an unprecedented four national awards for its spectacular restorations of Ouray's Beaumont Hotel, the Kit Carson County Carousel, the Central City Opera House, and Porcupine House in the Ute Mountain Ute Tribal Park.

Animas Forks, like more than 400 other Colorado ghost towns, is haunted by deteriorating buildings. Thanks to the San Juan County Historical Society and the SHF, the Duncan House (right) has been stabilized for tourists to enjoy.

PRESERVATION IN COLORADO

Have you ever gone back to your hometown and looked for your family house? Your childhood school? That old ranch or farm outside of town?

Prepare to be disappointed. The old ranches and farms outside of most Colorado cities are now gone, replaced by suburban sprawl. Schools are condemned as too small and too old and replaced with enormous new facilities. Old homes are regularly demolished to build bigger buildings for "higher use." Farms and forest lands often become vast parking lots and big-box stores, destroying open space and killing smaller main street businesses.

To foster a greater sense of place, to keep Colorado neighborhoods special and memorable, the Colorado Historical Society has been administering the State Historical Fund (SHF) since 1991. The previous year, Coloradans voted to amend the constitution to allow limited-stakes gaming in Black Hawk, Central City, and Cripple Creek, provided that a healthy share of gaming tax proceeds go to historic preservation. Gaming tax revenues are divided, with 28 percent going to the State Historical Fund, 22 percent to the gaming towns and counties, 49.8 percent to the General Fund, and 0.2 percent to the Colorado Tourism Promotion Fund. Of the 28 percent that goes to the SHF, one-fifth is returned to the gaming towns. The remaining 80 percent is used to support the operations of the Colorado Historical Society and to fund historic preservation projects around the state. This arrangement has given Colorado the largest state historic preservation funding program of its kind in the nation, and one entirely financed by gaming tax revenues.

Photo courtesy of Wayne Sundburg Collection

This Fort Collins Presbyterian church was demolished in 1974 despite the biblical warning: "Cursed be he that removes his neighbor's landmark. And all the people shall say, Amen."
                    —*King James Bible, Deuteronomy 27:1*

The SHF has funded the restoration of public schools, county court-houses, and town halls. It has helped resurrect many old churches, salvage ancient jails, and restore a priceless antique carousel. The fund was also used to help transform Denver's old Skid Row into the vibrant Lower Downtown Historic District (LoDo), America's showcase urban reincarnation.

Power generators at the restored Fall River Hydroelectric Plant in Estes Park

Long-closed and forlorn hotels such as the Central in Durango, the Tabor Grand in Leadville, and the Cliff House in Manitou Springs have been restored to glory. The Tabor Opera House in Leadville, the Golda Meir House on Denver's Auraria Campus, the Fall River Hydroelectric Plant in Estes Park, and rolling stock at the Colorado Railroad Museum in Golden have all been brought back to life.

Coloradans have been preservationists for more than a century. In the early 1900s, women's groups and private citizens fought to save such treasures as the cliff dwellings of Mesa Verde, Pike's Stockade in the San Luis Valley, the Hotel de Paris in Georgetown, and the Central City Opera House. A 1953 state law authorized the Colorado Historical Society to acquire significant properties such as the Georgetown Loop Railroad, the Baca and Bloom mansions in Trinidad, Fort Vasquez in Platteville, and the Healy House in Leadville.

The National Historic Preservation Act of 1966 launched a new era. After that act, lawmakers and civic leaders created a whole range of tools for preserving significant structures. The Colorado Historic Preservation Department (now the State Office of Archaeology and Historic Preservation) was established in 1973 to develop a statewide survey of historic resources and prevent the loss of significant properties. The legislature established a statewide tax credit of up to $50,000 for approved restoration of landmark homes and business buildings. Local organizations such as Historic Boulder, Inc., Historic Georgetown, Inc., and Historic Routt County! helped raise public awareness and rallied support to save jeopardized landmarks. Since the 1990 creation of the SHF, cities, towns, and counties throughout Colorado have found it a resource enabling them to make old places new again. Coloradans save landmarks not only for their physical presence but also for the meanings and associations they carry. Like Mom's jewelry, Dad's old watch, or that old family Bible, rescued buildings symbolize constancy and tradition in a rapidly changing world.

GAMBLING ON THE FUTURE

Central City, Black Hawk, and Cripple Creek have long been gambles—beginning with the gold rushes to Central City and Black Hawk back in 1859. Ever since, Coloradans have been taking their chances on striking it rich, whether in gold or silver, cattle or sugar beets, railroads or ski resorts, oil wells or cable television. Whatever the outcome, boom or bust, new players have always been eager to ante up for another deal.

Coloradans have generally preferred to wager on tomorrow, betting everything on the next draw from the deck. The State Historical Fund, though, operates from the premise that the best bets are often the cards you already hold in your hand. The fund helps communities to preserve the buildings, landscapes, and neighborhoods that have shaped their identity.

How has Colorado's bet on preservation paid off? Walk into the elegantly restored Montrose County Courthouse. Or take a ride on the Georgetown Loop Railroad. Enjoy a concert at Boulder's Chautauqua Auditorium. Or view *Los Caminos Antiguos*, a public-television documentary about a Scenic and Historic Byway in the San Luis Valley. Browse through the Denver Public Library's online collection of digitized historic photographs and decide for yourself.

As the largest state historic preservation program of its kind in the nation, the Colorado State Historical Fund helps communities make history a vital part of the present and future. The stakes couldn't be higher—for ourselves and for our descendants. Even during the economic slump of the early 2000s, gaming and preservation continue to thrive, leaving the future of the past looking bright.

SHF gaming funds have helped to restore Boulder's Chautauqua Auditorium (both at left) as well as once-elegant but fading hotels as low-income and senior housing. The Northern Hotel located in Fort Collins (below) is one of these old hotels now reborn.

Photo courtesy Tom Noel

ABBREVIATIONS AND SYMBOLS USED IN THIS BOOK

CHS   Colorado Historical Society
SHF   State Historical Fund

CO   Colorado highway (with number)
CR   County Road
FR   Forest Service Road
US   U.S. highway

H   Colorado Historical Society's annual Stephen H. Hart Award for excellence in historic preservation

LL   Local landmark, either city or county

LLD   Local landmark district, either city or county

NRD   National Register Historic District

NR   National Register of Historic Places

NHL   National Historic Landmark

NHLD   National Historic Landmark District

SR   State Register of Historic Properties

Cedaredge in western Colorado's Delta County celebrates its agricultural heritage with these 35-foot high, 9-sided silos. With new foundations and roofs, they are the centerpieces of their community's Pioneer Town Museum.

Akron

WASHINGTON COUNTY COURTHOUSE
150 Ash Ave. (SR)
Built: 1909; John J. Huddart, architect

Huddart, the designer of several Colorado courthouses, planned this $65,000 symmetrical, Neoclassical red-brick structure with a basement jail and a domed

cupola. Except for a rear jail addition, it was virtually unaltered—and little repaired—until the SHF came to the rescue with $109,880 in grants to assess the building, restore the exterior, and install an elevator and a bathroom providing accessibility to the disabled. Restoration was long overdue, according to architect David Wise, an Akron native whose mother worked at the courthouse during World War II. She and other women workers took breaks in the cupola, where they left graffiti that Wise has preserved. The graffiti includes a roster of those stationed to watch for enemy aircraft in the cupola of this tallest structure in Akron. Although Washington County's population has slipped from a peak of 11,208 in 1920 to 4,926 in 2000, they have continued to take pride in its fine courthouse.

Alamosa

The Denver & Rio Grande Railroad founded Alamosa in 1878 as the railhead for its San Luis Valley and San Juan Mountains operations. Alexander C. Hunt, who was president of the D&RG Construction Company and a former Colorado territorial governor, presided over the town's construction. His house survived at 1st and Colorado in Cole Park until 2004. The city park along the Rio Grande features a reconstructed depot and restored narrow-gauge train. SHF grants will enable the Alamosa Chamber of Commerce to resurrect the narrow-gauge locomotive, coach, and caboose in Cole Park as an operating train. Most of the town's once vast railyards have been demolished, although the freight and passenger depots survive.

Other SHF funds have helped Alamosa dress up its major landmarks. On the northern outskirts of town, the 97,000-acre Baca Ranch and 100,000-acre Zapata Ranch are being preserved and interpreted in partnership with the adjacent Great Sand Dunes National Park and Preserve, the SHF, and The Nature Conservancy. This complex includes a distinctive park headquarters, some of America's most important Folsom Culture archaeological sites, and other Native American and Hispanic sites, as well as America's largest and highest sand dunes.

ALAMOSA COUNTY COURTHOUSE
702 4th St. [NR]
Built: 1937; George C. Emery, architect; Works Progress
   Administration, builder

This U-shaped, Spanish Colonial Revival gem, according to renovation project manager Ken van Iwaarden, has been "restored to its original and unique charac-ter." Van Iwaarden noted the security challenges of getting workmen in and out of a facility with an operating jail. Workers replaced the leaky red-tile roof, repointed the brick masonry, restored the windows, made the arcade accessible to the disabled, and added wood-framed, custom-made storm windows to blend into the elegant façade. The 1937 cornerstone was taken out and its well-preserved con-tents catalogued and reinstalled along with new items such as the Alamosa County budget, the signatures of the court-house employees, and a list of county projects made possible by SHF grants that totaled $277,380 and county funds of $101,048.

ALAMOSA MASONIC LODGE No. 44
514 San Juan Ave. (SR)
Built: 1887; W. C. Brown, brick- and stonemason

Alamosa Masons dubbed No. 44 the "Narrow Gauge" Lodge because many members worked for the three-foot-gauge Denver & Rio Grande Railroad. The second-story hall is supported both physically and financially by street-level retail stores. The Alamosa Masonic Temple Association, with its own funds, city support, and SHF grants, installed emergency exit doors, replaced the roof, and repaired and repainted the windows.

The second story's cornice-and-cast-iron façade, with its elaborate Italianate trim, was badly damaged, weathered, and faded. It needed replacement finials, cornices, and parapet caps, all of modern zinc-coated steel and sheet aluminum. Larry Smith, the lodge member who led the restoration effort, calls it "awesome" and notes that "it all flowed together pretty easily" thanks to grants of $141,875 from the SHF and $50,000 raised by the Alamosa Masonic Temple Association.

AMERICAN NATIONAL BANK
500 State Ave., southeast corner of Main St. [NR]
Built: 1909

Ben and Alyce Fujii restored this stately structure, which was a bank until 1951. Some 50 years later, it is a bank again. Designed as a symmetrical, arcaded block, it elegantly reflects Alamosa's boom years. A 1930s flood stained the light brick and sandstone, which were cleaned and repaired during the restoration. Belinda Zink, the restoration architect, believes this structure would be landfill now if not for SHF grants of $109,964 and Alamosa Uptown & River Association's $33,000 match. These funds covered the masonry work, replacing the roof and parapets, and repairing and repainting the doors and recessed arched windows.

BAIN'S DEPARTMENT STORE / LA PUENTE HOUSING AND COMMUNITY THRIFT STORE
510 Main St., southwest corner of Hunt Ave. (SR)
Built: 1936; Victor Bain, builder

This Depression-era building opened as the largest department store in the San Luis Valley, offering groceries and clothes as well as household and farm goods. Builder Victor Bain was arrested in the late 1940s for selling meat from rustled cattle. On the day he was to go to court he killed himself, but the charges were later found to be untrue and were dropped. Bain's embittered son packed up and moved his department store to Pueblo.

The building was restored by La Puente Housing Authority, a nonprofit organization that aids the hungry, homeless, and disadvantaged of the San Luis Valley. The Bains' second-story living quarters were rehabilitated into six rental units, and the street level now houses a thrift shop. Every weight-bearing interior wall was shored up in order to keep the load off the exterior masonry walls. The roof, skylights, plumbing, and wiring were completely reconstructed. According to Steven Townsend of Faleide Architects, the project was "a labor of love, as engineers and architects alike tried to instill community spirit and beauty in affordable housing spaces." SHF grants also funded repointing brick and reconstructing the original storefront.

This $428,488 restoration was funded by $309,692 from the SHF, loans from the Colorado Housing and Finance Authority, $40,000 from the Johnson Fund, $65,000 from the Colorado Division of Housing, $11,400 from La Puente, and $127,000 from the community. The Coors, Gates, and Boettcher Foundations, as well as local volunteer groups, also helped rehabilitate the Bain structure as a demonstration project, showing how historic structures can be restored to meet critical housing needs.

DENVER & RIO GRANDE RAILROAD LOCOMOTIVE No. 169
Alamosa Visitor Center, north end of Hunt St. in Cole Park Ⓢ🅡
Built: 1883; Baldwin Locomotive Works, Philadelphia, Pennsylvania,
   builder

Baldwin built this 60-ton, narrow-gauge steam locomotive, a ten-wheeler engine previously restored for exhibition in the 1939 New York World's Fair. The D&RG donated it to Alamosa in 1941, and the Alamosa County Chamber of Commerce reconstructed the Queen Anne–style depot (the original had been destroyed by fire) for use as a visitor center. This locomotive has long been part of the town's lore and is decorated every Christmas.

A $99,985 SHF grant will enable craftpersons to disassemble and completely clean, repair, and restore No. 169. An ultrasound scanner has determined where the boiler needs to be patched and strengthened. Local funds of $442,200 will also facilitate restoration of the 1880 passenger car and caboose No. 0518, completing an operational train for rental and special excursions. In 2003, a train-shed pavilion funded by the Colorado Department of Transportation was built beside US 160 and the Rio Grande in Cole Park, with interpretive kiosks explaining Alamosa's glory days as a rail hub.

SACRED HEART CATHOLIC CHURCH
727 4th St., northeast corner of Edison Ave. [NR]
Built: 1928; Robert Willison, architect

Designed in the Mission Revival style by Robert Willison, who also designed St. Cajetan's in Denver, Sacred Heart was stuccoed over its original brick in 1953 to create a "Southwestern" look.  The church's restoration committee raised a match for SHF grants of $108,378 for stucco repairs and roof and downspout work on the church and rectory. The quatrefoil stained-glass windows were covered with a discreet yet protective covering. Chris Martinez, a church member who spearheaded the restoration, noted that the parish used both preservation and liturgical consultants. The ahead-of-schedule, on-budget exterior restoration has inspired the parish to continue with restoration of the interior, which contains murals by Joseph Steinhage.

Amherst

St. PAUL'S LUTHERAN CHURCH
300 Monmouth Ave. (SR)
Built: 1931; Eugene G. Groves, architect

The façade of this one-story brick edifice is distinguished by round-arched stained-glass windows. In what is thought to be his only ecclesiastical design, prominent Denver architect Eugene Groves framed the stained glass in cast stone and centered

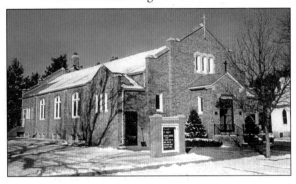

it above the entry gable. Inside, four exposed wooden trusses support a vaulted ceiling. The church matched the SHF's $25,000 to restore the glorious stained glass. This structure replaced the original white frame church next door, which is now used as a school.

Animas Forks

ANIMAS FORKS TOWNSITE
13 miles north of Silverton on CO 110 **H** [LL]
Built: 1873–1915

At an elevation of 11,200 feet and at the confluence of the North and West Forks of the Animas River, this mining town once boasted some 200 residents and a main street with several hotels, saloons, as well as the highest newspaper published in the United States, the *Animas Forks Pioneer.* The stout old jail (1882), featuring stacked two-by-six-foot board construction to create stronger walls, survives. So does the William D. Duncan House (also known, incorrectly, as the Thomas Walsh house),

with its prominent bay window, at the northwest end of Main Street (see p. 13). The San Juan County Historical Society, the Bureau of Land Management, and the SHF, which contributed $42,660 in grants, have undertaken to survey, stabilize, and, as resources allow, preserve Animas Forks and some of the surrounding mines and mills. One of Colorado's most picturesque ghost towns still boasts the remnants of about 30 buildings.

Arvada

Founded in the 1870s as a farming hub, Arvada has evolved into Colorado's sixth largest city. Despite tremendous growth, this preservation-conscious city and the Arvada Historical Society have created the Olde Town Historic District and have used more than $500,000 in SHF funds to restore landmarks and create a walking tour with interpretive plaques and brochures. The city and the Society have celebrated the 1850 Ralston Gold Discovery Site, the first known strike in what is now metro Denver, by building a park at West 56th Avenue and Fenton Street.

ARVADA FLOUR MILL
5590 Olde Wadsworth Blvd. NR
Built: 1925; Eugene Benjamin and Bert Wales, builders

Set in the historic district of Olde Town Arvada, the 30-foot-tall wooden mill originally ground Arva-Pride flour. Conveniently located along the railroad, it received, processed, packaged, stored, sold, and shipped flour. The mill is now clad in historic pressed-tin siding with a brick pattern to aid in the survival of this antique, which ceased its milling operations in 1950. The Arvada Historical Society acquired the mill in 1975 and matched $25,000 from the SHF to stabilize and rehabilitate it. Many volunteers and local businesses donated their services to make the mill an authentic, working museum.

Photo at left courtesy of Tom Noel

Photo below courtesy of Kim Grant, City of Arvada

Aspen

Founded in 1880, this silver city offers restored Victorian structures and a full range of modern architecture by nationally prominent architects. In Colorado's glitziest resort town, development pressures and the practice of knocking down million-dollar structures to build even more extravagant buildings have challenged efforts to create historic districts. The fairly well-preserved commercial area and many landmarks make Aspen a fascinating mix of the new and the old.

ASPEN ARMORY HALL/CITY HALL
130 S. Galena St. [LL] [NR]
Built: 1891

The State of Colorado built this National Guard armory with offices on the first floor and an upstairs hall. Over the years, the two-story hall housed military meetings and maneuvers, balls, concerts, and public meetings, while also serving as a roller rink, auditorium, and gymnasium. After

the city demolished its old City Hall on Durant Avenue in 1944, it acquired the armory and converted it into a new City Hall. The city received a $100,000 grant from the SHF to restore the red-brick exterior and install replica windows and a new roof.

HOLDEN MINING AND SMELTING CO. / HOLDEN/MAROLT MINING & RANCHING MUSEUM
1000 W. CO 82 on Castle Creek bike path [LL] [NR]
Built: 1891; Carl A. Stetefeld, Salkeld and Behr Architects

As one of America's largest silver producers from 1887 to 1893, Aspen also aspired to become an ore-processing center. The huge Holden Lixiviation Mill sprawled over 22 acres on either side of Castle Creek with a state-of-the-art ore-processing plant whose mill and smelter could process tons of ore a day to extract silver and other precious metals. But just 14 months after its completion, the federal government repealed the Sherman Silver Purchase Act, which had subsidized silver. The resulting 1893 silver crash shut this plant and doomed Aspen to an abrupt decline.

The mill, bankrupted along with hundreds of others, then sat largely idle until 1940 when Mike Marolt purchased the property for a dollar to add to his family

ranch. He recycled some of the buildings for ranching purposes but tore most of them down. With the help of a $38,000 grant from the SHF, the best-surviving building, the assay office, was restored by the Aspen Historical Society, from its stone foundation to its distinctive windowed cupola. Electricity, plumbing, and access for the disabled were added to what is now a museum, operated by the Aspen Historical Society, touting the town's mining and ranching heritage. Opened in 2003, this $500,000 restoration includes a working stamp mill, a vast collection of mining and ranching equipment, and a comprehensive narrow-gauge diorama of the Holden Works constructed by the Roaring Fork Valley Model Railroaders.

D. B. KOBEY & CO. BUILDING
423 E. Hyman Ave. [LL]
Built: 1888

When David Kobey started a men's clothing business in the 1880s, he commissioned an 11-by-22-foot, black-on-white sign with the words "D. B. Kobey & Co. Gents' Furnishers & Clothiers." The business remained for 50 years, but the sign eventually faded. In 2001, it was repainted, with the help of $3,750 from the SHF. By using the faded paint and historical photographs, Gaard Graphics returned the wall to the way it looked when Kobey first opened his haberdashery. Now home to the real-estate office for the upscale Ritz-Carlton Club, this three-story, red-brick building, with its revived wall sign, anchors the Hyman Avenue pedestrian mall.

UTE CEMETERY
East end of Ute Ave. in Ute Park [LL] [NR]
Established: 1880

After a pioneer prospector was buried here in June 1880, Ute Cemetery became the final resting place for numerous prospectors, Civil War veterans, and working-class Aspen residents. The city never officially named Ute Cemetery as a burial ground, but between 1880 and 1930 approximately 215 people were buried there

in random fashion, with only 79 in marked graves. With the help of the SHF's $99,500, the city preserved the surviving monuments and added a pedestrian path and interpretive information. The community raised an additional $60,000 and enlisted volunteers to rehabilitate what had been a derelict potter's field for the poor and unknown dead. The city's project manager and preservation historian, Ron Sladek, reports that the deceased are honored with two large boulders carved with the names of the people identified as buried at the site. Their biographies are on the City of Aspen website and in an interpretive brochure. Guarded by a quaint picket fence, this cemetery, now a city park, is overgrown by aspen trees and wildflowers and resembles the native-plants section of a botanical garden. It illustrates how useful, beautiful, and historically fascinating abandoned bone-yards can be.

Photo courtesy of Tom Noel

WHEELER-STALLARD HOUSE MUSEUM / ASPEN HISTORICAL
SOCIETY HEADQUARTERS
620 W. Bleeker St. [LL] [NR]
Built: 1888

When Jerome Wheeler began investing in Aspen, he especially fancied this large plot on the west end of Bleeker Street, where he built his large, three-story, Queen Anne–style home. Because his wife refused to move from Manitou Springs, Wheeler ended up renting the residence to numerous people, including his mother-in-law. In 1917, Edgar and Mary Ella Stallard acquired the house, where they lived for the next 40 years. In 1968, the Aspen Historical Society moved in, converting it into their offices and a museum.

In 1999 and 2000, retired contractor Bonnie Murry decided to try one last project. "Restoring the Wheeler-Stallard House was always a dream of mine," she says. So Murry started with a $150,225 SHF grant for interior and exterior restoration. Much of the mortar had to be repointed to stabilize the brickwork. To remedy water problems, Murry and her crew, including restoration architects Andrews & Anderson of Golden, designed a new patio, roof, and flashing. Landscape architects redesigned the grounds and planted historically consistent flowers, trees, and shrubs.

The Society replaced the plumbing, heating, electricity, and worn plank floors. The restoration crew came upon a few surprises along the way. While demolishing an upstairs wall, workers found an original doorway, boarded over, between two bedrooms. When the ceiling was taken down to install sprinkler lines, artifacts started falling to the ground. "They were like gifts from heaven," explains Murry. Among the items found were letters to the Stallards, newspaper cartoons, a hand-painted card, a ticket stub for "A Family Reunion," and several checks that were written by Edgar Stallard.

Ault

AULT HIGH SCHOOL
208 W. 1st St. (SR)
Built: 1921; Sidney G. Frazier, architect

Next to a city park on a grassy, tree-shaded site, this three-story brick-and-stucco school exemplifies the Craftsman-Mission style in its polychromatic brick-work, ornate roof brackets, and artistic details, including bas-relief entablatures. The town's sole high school from 1921 to 1976, the structure later housed Ault's junior high school until 1992. The SHF contributed $359,125 to Weld County School District RE-9 for interior and exterior rehabilitation to revive the Craftsman elements and replicate the historic windows. Today, Ault High School remains one of the town's finest architectural treasures and will still be used for educational purposes.

Aurora

Originally founded in 1891 as the town of Fletcher, Aurora is now Colorado's third largest city, with a population of more than 300,000. In a quest for community roots, the city created the Aurora Historical Commission in 1970 to establish the Aurora History Museum, which opened in 1979 on Florence Street near Colfax Avenue. In 1991, the museum relocated to a larger facility near Alameda and Chambers in what is now the City Center Complex. The Aurora Historic Preservation Commission, created in 1985, is charged with establishing historic landmarks in Aurora as well as preserving sites owned by the city. Today, Aurora boasts more than 20 historic landmarks.

CENTENNIAL HOUSE
1671 Galena St. LL NR
Built: 1890

Painted peaches-and-cream, this Queen Anne gem was one of Aurora's first homes. Town founder and real-estate broker Donald Fletcher built the home and sold it upon completion for $3,500. By the late 1890s, Donald Fletcher had left Colorado. During World War II this building became an apartment house. The house was purchased and restored by the City of Aurora in 1990 and opened as a museum in 1991, during Aurora's centennial year. Although the kitchen is still furnished in a 1950s style, the rest of the house is a trip back to the 1890s.

In 1995, a lawn sprinkler sprang a leak and damaged the foundation. To help the Aurora Parks and Open Space Department restore the foundation and basement, the SHF provided $20,000. Since 1991, volunteers of the Aurora Historical Society have supported and operated Centennial House. It is open, by appointment only, during the summer months and the Christmas season. Volunteer Helen Walters says, "The Centennial House Christmas tree is garnished with handmade ornaments from local schoolchildren. Many neighborhood kids whose families cannot afford a tree of their own make this their house and their holiday tree."

DeLANEY FARM ROUND BARN
170 S. Chambers Rd. H LL NR
Built: 1901

In 1862, John and Bridget (Gully) DeLaney emigrated from Ireland to Central City, where they operated the Central City Bakery. In 1868, John Gully, Bridget's father, built what is now the oldest structure in Aurora on his homestead, near the present-day intersection of Chambers and Mississippi. Around 1870, John and Bridget DeLaney relocated to a site along Toll Gate Creek to raise horses. John DeLaney became the toll collector at the gate where the old wagon road running to Denver crossed the creek, near where 6th Avenue crosses Chambers Road today.

The homestead on Toll Gate Creek eventually included a home constructed in 1892 for their son, John, and his wife, Mary, and several outbuildings. Around 1901, young John DeLaney had an unknown itinerant carpenter build one of Colorado's few surviving round barns, perhaps using a set of mail-order plans. The DeLaneys originally used it as a silo, but around 1908 they converted it into a cow barn.

The City of Aurora bought the DeLaney family farm in 1982 with plans to preserve the area as open space and a historic site. At that time, the city moved the house of John Gully to the site. The DeLaney round barn was restored in 1994 by Aurora with the help of the SHF. Funds totaling $63,875 were earmarked for stabilization and restoration. The city contributed $53,324 for planning, survey, and designation. Aurora subsequently did further restoration work on the barn and other farm buildings. All this work earned the City of Aurora and the Aurora History Museum a Colorado Historical Society Stephen H. Hart Award in 1994.

Today, the round barn is the showcase of this agricultural park. In the fall, a metro-wide festival, known as Pumpkinfest, includes a pumpkin toss and decorating the barn for Halloween. During the rest of the year, the DeLaney Farm hosts classes on beekeeping, gardening, composting, and blacksmithing. Denver Urban Gardens maintains a planting area on the northern part of the site. The restored farm also attracts wildlife watchers, hikers, and photography and painting clubs, who value this rural oasis amid Aurora's newer developments.

EISENHOWER SUITE, FITZSIMONS HOSPITAL
12101 E. Colfax Ave. LL SR
Built: 1941; T. Robert Wieger, architect

Suite dreams have become reality in Room 8002, from which President Dwight D. Eisenhower ran the country for seven weeks. In the fall of 1955, he was taken to Fitzsimons Army Medical Center following a heart attack suffered during a visit

Photo courtesy of Tom Noel

with his wife Mamie Dowd's family in Denver. The event focused worldwide attention on Fitzsimons and led to the 25th Amendment to the U.S. Constitution, which clarified the issue of presidential disability and succession.

Left vacant or used as an office for nearly 50 years, the Eisenhower Suite, as it came to be known, has been restored as a museum, thanks to a $67,100 SHF grant, a $10,000 donation from Wells Fargo, and matching funds from the University of Colorado. The restored suite, which opened in 2003, features Eisenhower-era details such as nurse-call buttons and glass ashtrays along with a Secret Service sitting room, nurses' station, and private dining room. "We were unable," says project historian John Stewart, "to duplicate all the personal touches of Mrs. Eisenhower, such as the pink toilet seat."

The former medical base, established in 1919, was named for Lieutenant William T. Fitzsimons, the first U.S. medical officer killed in World War I. The 10-story hospital itself was the largest building in Colorado when it was erected in 1941. To improve the health and spirits of recuperating military personnel, architect T. Robert Wieger used a stepped plan with open roof decks to capture sunshine, fresh air, and views of Denver and its Rocky Mountain backdrop.

The University of Colorado Health Sciences Center secured the site in 1995 for its relocation from the old Denver campus at East 9th Avenue and Colorado Boulevard. The old hospital building is the historic centerpiece of the new state-of-the-art medical campus.

LOWRY BUILDING 810, UNITED STATES AIR FORCE ACADEMY
710 Boston St. [LL]
Built: 1942

As part of the extension of Lowry Field during World War II, this H-shaped wood-frame building was constructed as offices and supply storage. From 1955 to 1958, Building 810 was the headquarters for the newly established United States Air Force Academy. The City of Aurora gained ownership of the building after the closure of Lowry Air Force Base on September 30, 1994. For a short time the Wings Over the Rockies Air and Space Museum used the building before moving to much larger quarters in Hangar No. 1. Using funds from a variety of sources, including $100,000 from the SHF, Aurora restored Building 810 as the Lowry Interdevelopmental Center. Combining a senior center with a preschool program, it promotes interaction between the old and young, who call this rejuvenated landmark the "Adopt-a-Grandma" building.

MELVIN SCHOOL
4950 S. Laredo St. [NR]
Built: 1922; Ren and Henry DeBoer, architects

Aurora's first municipally designated historic landmark, the Melvin School, was built in 1922 and operated as a school until 1949. In 1950, when the construction of Cherry Creek Dam flooded the old town of Melvin, the building was saved from destruction and relocated to the southwest corner of East Quincy Avenue and Parker Road, where it became the Emerald Isle Tavern. The Cherry Creek Valley Historical Society moved the building to its current site on the Laredo Middle School campus, where the community restored it in 1977–1978. The square bell tower, lost during the building's wild times as a tavern, has been reconstructed, and the linoleum flooring, kitchen, and other "improvements" have been removed to recreate the original school. In 2000, the SHF awarded $7,219 to repair the schoolhouse roof, which was completed in 2001.

B Barr Lake_____

BRUDERLIN HOUSE / ROCKY MOUNTAIN BIRD OBSERVATORY

19400 E. 152nd Ave. Ⓢ︎Ⓡ︎
Built: 1889–1890

Emil Bruderlin arrived in Denver in the early 1870s to work as a bookbinder for the Rocky Mountain News Printing Company before going into business for himself. Remembering stone houses in his native Switzerland, he ordered several railroad cars' worth of South Platte Canyon granite to build this 4,300-square-foot, two-and-a-half-story home for his growing family. Shortly after completing

this big country home, Bruderlin was killed in a train accident. His family subsequently had to sell the home, which became a boarding house until its abandonment in the 1960s.

"This house was a total disaster," says Joanne Carter, the restoration manager for the Rocky Mountain Bird Observatory (RMBO). "The whole building needed to be gutted. Kids had used it as a place to party and trashed the interior with graffiti." The SHF awarded $150,078 in grants to RMBO, which raised another $350,000 to restore the most prominent structure on the banks of Barr Lake. SHF grants helped restore and rehabilitate plumbing, heating, plaster, and paint, as well as make the facility accessible to the disabled. Today, the building houses the RMBO, which keeps an eye on some 330 different species of birds seen at Barr Lake, including resident bald eagles. In conjunction with Barr Lake State Park, RMBO also showcases natural history in its community services and classes for children and adults.

Photo courtesy of Tom Noel

Basalt

FRYING PAN KILNS
Arbaney Park LL
Built: 1882

The Town of Basalt received an SHF grant of $10,000 to stabilize the ruins of the old Frying Pan Kilns that once produced coke for Aspen and Leadville smelters.

These 25-foot-tall, beehive-shaped structures also provided winter shelter for the Arbaney family's livestock on what is now a part of Arbaney Park. Constructed of unfired brick, native stone, and mortar, the coke ovens suffered from damage and decay over the years. Basalt administrative assistant Kay Philips says the SHF grant "enabled us to bring in a mortar consultant and purchase materials to preserve Basalt's oldest existing structures."

Bellvue

ARROWHEAD LODGE
34500 Poudre Canyon Hwy. (CO 14) NR
Built: 1935–1946; Carl M. Brafford and Brye Gladstone, builders

After this Rustic-style inn of peeled logs and river rock closed in 1984, the U.S. Forest Service bought the main lodge and 12 tiny cabins for demolition. Locals Elyse Bliss, Stan Case, and others objected strenuously to the loss of the canyon's last historic resort. They persuaded the USFS to pursue a National Register designation. The Friends of Arrowhead Lodge and Conservators of Nature Society (FALCONS) agreed to maintain and staff the 13-acre property as an information center and museum during the summer months, with self-guided tours, exhibits, and interpretive programs. A $20,000 SHF grant helped install new roofs and restore interiors, most notably in the main lodge/interpretive center, with its open-beam ceiling and massive stone fireplace decked out with a large alabaster arrowhead.

B Bennett

MUEGGE HOUSE
401 S. 1st St. LL
Built: c. 1914; Ed Smith and Henry Dunbar, builders

The Harris family hired Smith and Dunbar to build this house, which Charles Muegge later purchased in the 1940s. The Muegge family used it as a bunkhouse

for hired farmhands before donating it to the Town of Bennett. The SHF granted $55,147 to the town, which procured local matching funds to rehabilitate the interior and exterior, repair the foundation and roof, add a wheelchair ramp, and install heating and air-conditioning—much needed in the town that set Colorado's all-time high-temperature record of 118 degrees. The upstairs of this restored residence houses the Bennett Historical Society and Bennett's Parks and Recreation Department, while the downstairs houses the I-70 Chamber of Commerce.

Beulah

PUEBLO MOUNTAIN PARK
9167 Pueblo Mountain Park Dr., 1 mile south of CR 220 NR
Built: c. 1926–1942, Civilian Conservation Corps; Arthur Carhart and Frank H. Culley, landscape architects

This 611-acre park and summer camp, owned by the City of Pueblo, features various Civilian Conservation Corps and Works Progress Administration structures.

Pueblo matched the SHF contribution of $393,500 to rehabilitate and restore structures including the stone Pavilion (1940), the Pueblo Revival–style Horseshoe Lodge (1942), and several Rustic-style picnic shelters. The outdoor porch along the horseshoe-shaped lodge has been restored, along with the ballfield bleachers.

Senior Pueblo planner Steven Meier observes, "We could not have restored the Mountain Park without the SHF and their technical staff. They helped us with the grant process and advised us wisely on the restoration-rehabilitation process, patiently guiding us through the learning curve." Meier hopes to restore more of the complex, which originally had wildlife-viewing areas, an archery range, an equestrian events arena, and a tennis court.

*Black Forest*_____

BLACK FOREST SCHOOL
6770 Shoup Rd. [NR]
Built: 1921

In 1921, the Black Forest community donated land, logs, and labor to construct this school. In 1997, citizens came together again to preserve what had become

a beloved social center for dances, ice-cream socials, church services, and meetings of the Black Forest Ladies' Club and the 4-H Club. After a consolidated school district closed the school in 1945, the building housed county maintenance staff for 30 years. By the 1990s, after many haphazard renovations and severe water damage, the school was a mess. Working through the Black Forest Fire Protection District, the community raised funds to augment the SHF's $33,113 to complete a $36,038 interior and exterior restoration. The school was moved to a temporary site so the old foundation and steps could be replaced. Black

Forest resident Carrie Robertson recalls that the move "did not disturb a thing inside!" Project supervisor Ted Robertson and some volunteers replaced damaged logs, installed a new roof, and reopened the school as a community and visitor center.

B TAYLOR MEMORIAL CHAPEL
6145 Shoup Rd. NR
Built: 1929; John Gaw Meem, architect

Noted Southwestern architect John Gaw Meem designed this Pueblo Revival masterpiece for Colorado Springs philanthropist Alice Bemis Taylor as a memorial to her husband. It sits on the Taylor family's summer estate, La Foret, named for the abundant ponderosa pine trees that frame awesome views of Pikes Peak. What is now Taylor Memorial Chapel served as Mrs. Taylor's private place of worship until she died in 1942. In 1944, the Bemis Taylor Foundation gave the chapel to the Rocky Mountain Conference of the United Church of Christ.

The SHF granted $120,000 for exterior restoration, overseen by SlaterPaull Architects, focusing on repairing damaged viga ends, stucco walls, and the sculpted wall enclosing the grounds. Interior restoration addressed deterioration of woodwork carved by Santa Fe artist Eugenie Shonnard, including the balcony railing, doors, windows, entry gate, and other ornamentation. The reborn chapel is once again a centerpiece of La Foret Conference and Retreat Center, which is open to both religious and nonreligious groups.

Boulder

Boulderites have protected the town's architectural heritage, mountain views, solar access, and small-town charms by creating the Pearl Street Pedestrian Mall, passing a height ordinance limiting buildings to 55 feet, and designating more than 139 landmarks and nine historic districts. Boulder County led other Colorado counties as the first to begin designating and protecting county landmarks. Concerned citizens formed Historic Boulder, Inc., in 1972 in response to the demolition of the 1873 Central School and proposed demolition of the Highland School and 1890 Union Pacific Depot. In 1974, Boulder passed a historic preservation ordinance and created the city's Landmarks

Photo courtesy of Tom Noel

Preservation Advisory Board. Boulder has also designated more than 65 Structures of Merit to recognize important buildings.

In 1994, at the urging of the Boulder Landmarks Board, the city council passed a demolition ordinance that required a Landmarks Board review before issuing demolition permits for any building more than 50 years old. If such a building meets the requirements for an individual landmark, alternatives for its continued use are explored with the building's owner. Such legislation, furthered by citizen activists and a large number of designated landmarks and historic districts, has made Boulder a statewide preservation pacesetter. Chris Meschuck, historic preservation planner for the City of Boulder, comments, "The legacy of preserving the buildings and neighborhoods has created a unique sense of place and community identity for Boulder."

B

BOULDER COUNTY COURTHOUSE / LIONS CLUB FOUNTAIN
1300 Pearl Street Mall [LL] [NRD]
Built: 1933, courthouse; 1935, fountain; Glen H. Huntington, architect

Most Colorado courthouses tend to be Neoclassical in style, but Boulder chose the Art Deco style for this replacement of the original Second Empire courthouse destroyed by fire in 1932. Considered shockingly ultra modern in 1933, this cubistic edifice glories in step-backs showcasing its sandstone blocks taken from bridge abutments of the dismantled Switzerland Trail Railroad. The SHF contributed $15,500 to the courthouse's exterior restoration, which inspired similar work on the courthouse plaza with its notable Lions Club fountain. This white terracotta fountain visually bridges Pearl Street Mall and the plaza by mimicking

the courthouse's terraced architectural style on a smaller scale. By the 1980s, however, the fountain had stopped functioning and was being used as a planter. Boulder County used a $34,825 SHF grant to repair and restore the beloved landmark with a match from Boulder County and the Boulder Lions Club.

The Boulder County Architects Division disassembled the fountain's terracotta blocks and numbered, measured, and drew each piece so that it could reassemble the structure after blocks were cleaned, repaired, and, in some cases, even replaced with replicas. The preservation architects used old photographs to restore the original spray pattern. A high-tech wind monitor adjusts water pressure and spray levels to make sure Boulder's notorious winds don't turn the fountain into a shower for passersby on the mall. The fountain reopened as the center-piece of a $400,000 renovation of the entire courthouse plaza.

Photo courtesy of Tom Noel

B

BOULDER THEATER
2032 14th St. LL NRD
Built: 1936; Robert Boller, architect

Historic Boulder, Inc., matched a $23,438 SHF grant to restore a marquee and canopy near collapse. Robert Boller, with his brother Carl, formed a Kansas City architecture firm that designed more than 90 theaters in Missouri, Kansas, Texas,

and Oklahoma, as well as now-demolished movie palaces in Pueblo and Colorado Springs. Their Art Deco theater for Boulder has a stucco façade, upper-level glass-brick windows, and floral panels of polychrome terracotta. The marquee is trimmed in bright bands of red and blue neon, and the theater incorporates brick from the demolished Curran Opera House (1906), which previously stood on the site. The interior retains some Art Deco murals of desert plants in pastel shades, under walls painted with Southwestern motifs. A balcony-level mahogany bar was put back into use when the movie house, closed in 1982, reopened as a cabaret with live concerts in 1988.

CARNEGIE BRANCH LIBRARY FOR LOCAL HISTORY
1125 Pine St. LL NR
Built: 1907; Thomas MacLaren, architect

Early Boulderites called their town the "Athens of the West" and built their first public library in the Greek Revival style with distinctive Ionic columns. Architect Thomas MacLaren of Colorado Springs supposedly modeled it after a small Greek temple unearthed in 1905 near Athens. This roomy sanctuary has golden oak tables and captain's chairs, oak ceiling beams, oak wainscoting, and a large, green marble fireplace. The little-altered interior even retains the portrait of Andrew Carnegie—looking like a well-trimmed Walt Whitman. After the opening of the new main library, this building became the local history branch.

A $36,200 SHF grant enabled repair of drainage systems and downspouts. Branch librarian Wendy Hall says that the library has more than 200,000 photos, 4,000 books, 1,000 oral history interviews, and thousands of other items concerning Boulder County history. "They are now protected, as we are finally waterproofed, thanks to the SHF."

Photo courtesy of Tom Noel

CENTRAL PARK NARROW-GAUGE TRAIN
Broadway and Canyon Blvd. (SR)
COLORADO & NORTHWESTERN RAILROAD LOCOMOTIVE No. 30
Built: 1898, Brooks Locomotive
D&RGW COACH No. 280
Built: 1881, Jackson & Sharp
D&RGW NARROW-GAUGE CABOOSE No. 04990
Built: 1919

Photo courtesy of Tom Noel

Prominently located in City Park at a major downtown intersection, this narrow-gauge train has been restored by the Boulder County Railway Historical Society, Inc., and Boulder Parks and Recreation (Parks) with the help of $64,390 from the SHF to restore the locomotive. Parks also used $125,000 from the SHF to help restore Denver & Rio Grande Western Coach No. 280, one of only two surviving unaltered

Jackson & Sharp–manufactured passenger coaches in Colorado. Parks used another $6,082 from the SHF to restore D&RGW Caboose No. 04990. Boulder historian, preservationist, and former city councilperson Dan Corson says, "This elegantly restored narrow-gauge train is an attractive and appropriate tribute to Boulder's railroading days." Colorado & Northwestern Railroad Locomotive No. 30 is being restored for service on the Georgetown Loop Railroad.

CHAUTAUQUA PARK HISTORIC DISTRICT
900 Baseline Rd. LLD NHLD
Built: 1898

Of some 300 Chautauquas established in the nation, this foothills campus is one of the best preserved and is still open to the public year-round. On July 4, 1898, more than 4,000 people gathered for opening day in Boulder. The idea had originated at Lake Chautauqua in upstate New York in 1876, where the first such educational institution still survives. At its peak in the 1920s, the Chautauqua movement attracted some 40 million people to sites throughout the country for music, drama, lectures, debates, and other educational, spiritual, and recreational activities. The Great Depression marked the end of the Chautauqua heyday, and most parks closed down.

Photo courtesy of Tom Noel

B

At the Colorado Chautauqua, many buildings fell into disrepair and by 1975 the City of Boulder considered demolition to build a convention center. Local preservationists rallied behind a cooperative effort with the Colorado Chautauqua Association (CCA) to revitalize the entire campus. The initial fund-raising campaign, including federal Community Development Block Grants, state funds, and private donations, focused on restoring the auditorium.

Encouraged by SHF funds of more than $650,000, the CCA raised $500,000 to restore aging landmarks on its 91-acre campus. "SHF funds," explains former Chautauqua executive director Bob D'Alessandro, "have enabled us to operate this place year-round for educational, recreational, and social use." Continuing in the spirit of its original mission, Colorado Chautauqua offers events throughout the summer, including music, dance, theater, a film series, and lectures. Since the 1990s, CCA has rehabilitated the Auditorium, Community House, Missions House, and nearly all of the 60 association-owned cottages.

With SHF help, the CCA has installed interpretive signage, issued free brochures, and conducted courses in historic preservation. The CCA has also worked with Boulder County Parks and Open Space to manage Chautauqua's distinctive landscape, nestled at the foot of the Flatirons. "We want to make our campus a seamless part of the Boulder park system," D'Alessandro says. SHF funding has helped in what restoration architect Kristen Lewis calls "a first-rate rehabilitation" and enabled Chautauqua to graduate to National Historic Landmark status in 2006.

CHAUTAUQUA AUDITORIUM
900 Baseline Rd., Chautauqua Park **H** **LL** **NHLD**
Built: 1898; Franklin E. Kidder and Eugene R. Rice, architects

The first structure of Chautauqua Park, this large, barnlike wooden building features unusual truss supports that are more common in bridge construction. Within the cavernous interior, slices of daylight are visible between ceiling planks, while the original 1898 wooden benches flank an amalgam of theater seats that were salvaged from other Boulder sites. The wooden stage has been stabilized and reconstruc-ted with ponderosa pine saved from an old gymnasium and laid down in the original, angled pattern. Besides its soft, warm look, the wood makes for fine acoustics. The SHF contributed $128,442 toward auditorium restoration projects, including roof rehabilitation, stage-floor reconstruc-tion, interior and exterior painting, trim and façade repairs, and re-erection of the original flagpole.

In 2002, a Chautauqua staff person noticed a bulge on the building's north and south angled walls and discovered that battens on those sides were stretched

B

to the breaking point. With SHF assistance, the Colorado Chautauqua Association successfully stabilized the exterior walls.

This unique space has hosted notables, including William Jennings Bryan, Victor Borge, Bobby McFerrin, and Emmylou Harris, who reportedly quipped, "Playing in this auditorium is like how it would be to perform inside my guitar."

CHAUTAUQUA COMMUNITY HOUSE
900 Baseline Rd. LLD NHLD
Built: 1918

In Chautauqua's earliest days, visitors rested in tents and only stayed for the summer. Soon they built simple cabins and cottages, without kitchens or baths. In 1918, residents constructed this building to be the "living room of Chautauqua." This two-story structure, made of local sandstone with grapevine mortar, has an unusual triangular fireplace inside. By the early 1990s, the ceiling and floors were sagging, the plaster was cracking, and the building was barely habitable. Chautauqua came up with $76,700 to match SHF grants of more than $97,000 to fix these problems, winterize the building, install a fire sprinkler system, bolster the structural elements, repair the floors and ceiling, create a larger kitchen, and make the building accessible to the disabled. Instead of removing the original single-pane windows, storm windows were installed, thereby marrying historic integrity to modern functionality. Many local groups now use this comfortable space year-round, enjoying a rehabilitated interior and restored exterior.

CHAUTAUQUA PARK COTTAGES
900 Baseline Rd. LLD NHLD
Built: 1899–1970s

In addition to the Chautauqua campus public buildings are 99 cottages, 39 of which are privately owned. Some still belong to descendants of the original schoolmarms who resided in them while attending summer school at the University of Colorado. Rental cottages include the Woman's Christian Temperance Union Rest Cottage at 401 Wildrose Road. Cottages range from one to six bedrooms, and most have been winterized. The SHF provided $152,000 and Chautauqua $159,300 to rehabilitate the interiors and restore the exteriors of six cottages.

B

COLUMBIA CEMETERY
8th St. to 9th St. between College and Pleasant [LL] [NR]
Established: 1870

Photo courtesy of Tom Noel

As of 2005, the SHF had invested $478,922 in grants, which were matched by Boulder Parks and Recreation funds, to restore Boulder's historic downtown burial ground. Columbia Cemetery Conservation Corps volunteers have worked over the past several years to conserve and restore the cemetery, resulting in restoration of the iron fence, professional conservation of 60 grave markers, erection of an entrance sign, and restoration of another

250 markers by volunteers. Columbia Cemetery became a statewide model for preservation of historic funeral grounds thanks to special training for professionals and volunteers, who went on to conduct how-to sessions in locations around Colorado.

Many residents see the cemetery as a vital part of Boulder's past and present. Archaeologist Jack E. Smith, a Boulder native and cemetery volunteer, observes, "Columbia Cemetery is like an encyclopedia of events and people who helped make Boulder what it is today. People can also enjoy the cemetery as a public park and in this way maintain emotional and psychological links with Boulder's past." Middle-school teacher Mary Jo Bode comments, "Recently my students, team teachers, and I went over to the Columbia Cemetery to study the history of early Boulder. What a pleasure it was to see all the fabulous work that has been done to improve the cemetery."

With 10.5 acres containing nearly 3,000 markers, and continual threats from vandals and environmental conditions, a lot of work is left to do. Utilizing a 1994 master plan, the city continues to pursue conservation projects that will resurrect this treasure trove of tombstones.

HARBECK-BERGHEIM HOUSE / BOULDER HISTORY MUSEUM
1206 Euclid Ave., in Beach Park [LL]
Built: 1899

The Harbeck-Bergheim House was first constructed as a summer home for wealthy New Yorkers Kate and John Harbeck. Clothier Milton Bergheim and his family owned the house from 1939 to 1969, when it was sold to the City of Boulder. Formerly called the Boulder Historical Society and Museum, the sandstone structure is prominently sited on a corner lot in what is now a one-block city park and features a Dutch-style front door and a 6-by-9-foot, Tiffany stained-glass window. Former director Thomas Meier notes that the Boulder History Museum received $46,175 in SHF grants for restoration, with additional funds from the Federal Community Development Block Grant program and Boulder's Parks & Recreation

Department. Work included repointing masonry, cleaning and repairing woodwork, and installing a protective covering on the stained-glass window. SHF funds also went toward a brochure and exhibition about the house's history. The museum is home to some 20,000 artifacts, such as the hunting dress and double-barreled shotgun belonging to famed Boulder naturalist Martha Dartt Maxwell.

HOLIDAY DRIVE-IN MARQUEE
US 36 near CO 93 and Lee Hill Rd. [LL]
Built: 1953 for the original 28th and Colorado drive-in site; relocated in 1969

The Holiday opened in 1953 with an upscale, two-story projection building, a huge 45-by-70-foot screen, and a distinctive marquee above an ornamental rock wall. In 1969, the Holiday moved to its new location and reopened as the Holiday Twin, updating the distinctive marquee for the new twin theater. Although the drive-in closed in 1988, that old marquee has come back for an encore performance as part of the Holiday neighborhood, a new mixed-income venture of Boulder Housing Partners (BHP). The 27-acre project includes 330 housing units, with 138 affordable units, in a collaboration among BHP, Habitat for Humanity, the Affordable Housing Alliance, four private developers, Naropa University staff and faculty housing, and Wonderland Hills cohousing. A smattering of office, retail, and gallery space has also been incorporated into this new north Boulder community. "The centerpiece will be a triangular park with an extra-large, outdoor video-screen reincarnation of the old drive-in theater," says former Boulder city councilperson Dan Corson. The SHF contributed $24,567 and Boulder Housing Partners $50,000 toward the restoration of the marquee as a celebration of this innovative $70 million project, which brought much-needed affordable housing to Boulder.

B

MOUNT St. GERTRUDE ACADEMY/RESIDENCES
970 Aurora St. LL NR
Built: 1892, Alexander Cazin and Luther Hixon, architects;
1919 addition, George H. Williamson, architect

Photo courtesy of Tom Noel

Originally a Catholic girls' day school run by the Sisters of Charity, and the first private school in Boulder, Mount St. Gertrude was a boarding school until declining numbers of nuns and students caused it to close in 1969. That year, the University of Colorado acquired the commanding Richardsonian Romanesque edifice and used it for a variety of offices, including extended education. But when a fire destroyed the fourth floor and bell tower in 1980, the university abandoned the structure to the weather and vandals.

In 1989, The Academy Group, a housing developer, undertook to redevelop the landmark as what architect Chris Shears terms "a service-enriched retirement community." As part of the ensuing 10-year project, Shears and others designed and constructed nine new Craftsman-style bungalows on the old school grounds. Encouraged by a $100,000 SHF grant, they also restored the old academy as residential units. The builders discovered that Boulder firefighters in 1980 had saved the original stones from the bell tower, stacking them in the chapel. Using the original drawings and the salvaged stones, the team then reconstructed the tower. "SHF partnership," says Shears, "reinforced the rigor and attention to historical detail that has garnered critical acclaim, including 10 local, state, and national awards."

UNIVERSITY OF COLORADO, NORLIN QUADRANGLE
Between Broadway, Baseline Rd., 28th St., and Arapahoe Ave. NRD
Built: c. 1885–1939; Charles Z. Klauder, Day & Klauder architects

A $30,848 SHF grant to the CU Foundation for restoration of buildings on the Quadrangle helped the campus to retain what the architect, Charles Klauder, called the "University of Colorado style." Although some buildings, such as Old Main and Mackey Auditorium, were already in place, Klauder master-planned the campus between 1917 and 1919 with the help of his partner, Frank M. Day, with Norlin Quad at its heart. Klauder used rough, locally quarried Lyons sandstone, aggressive symmetry, and architectural elements that he had admired in Tuscan hill towns. Klauder employed a formal Beaux-Arts plan for the campus and especially for the Quad. For trim, Klauder used limestone, for which more recent architects have substituted precast concrete. However, CU Campus Architect Emeritus Bill Deno says, "We continue to try to use the black wrought-iron ornament that Klauder designed in restoring his original entries." With SHF support, Deno continues, "We have restored the historic doors on the McKenna Language Building, Hellems

B

Hall, and the Guggenheim Building." Inspired by and learning from the SHF grant, CU has also independently restored other doors on the Education Building, the Economics Building, and Carlson Gymnasium. With SHF funds, Deno notes, CU was also able to rehabilitate the Rose Room, a women's lounge in McKenna and one of Klauder's most precious designs. "Thousands of students pass through these doors every day," Deno says. "They take quite a beating and desperately needed this restoration."

UNIVERSITY OF COLORADO, WOMEN'S COTTAGE NO. 1/ WOMEN'S STUDIES PROGRAM
East of Broadway NRD
Built: 1884; Frederick J. Sterner and Ernest P. Varian, architects

Cottage No. 1, the first women's dormitory on campus, is one of the oldest structures at CU and the first designed to accommodate female students. Although the exterior remained largely untouched, Anna Vayr, the Women's Studies Program advisor, explains that "the interior was not always treated with loving care." The cottage needed substantial structural, mechanical, and electrical work by the time the CU Foundation and a volunteer coalition came together to raise restoration funds. The SHF contributed $100,000 toward a $1 million restoration of the gardens as well as the cottage interior and exterior. The restored building now

houses CU's Women's Studies Program, thus fulfilling its original purpose which was supporting higher education for women in Colorado.

B

WALKER RANCH WHEAT BARN & PIG PEN
7701 Flagstaff Rd. [NRD]
Built: 1869–1940; James A. Walker, builder

James Walker filed an 1882 homestead claim on 160 acres on this site where he had squatted earlier. He kept buying additional land until his ranch encompassed more than 6,000 acres. Currently the Walker Ranch consists of 2,566 acres under the ownership of Boulder County Parks and Open Space. The wheat barn and pigpen are two of 13 ranch structures, which include an 1869 hewn-log cabin, an 1880 livestock barn, an 1881 house, an 1885 wagon barn and turkey house, and, at a safe distance, a 1914 "gas house" to store the family's automobile. Among the ruins are a sawmill, the Langridge cyanide mill, and Arapaho Indian sites.

A $37,895 SHF grant, with a $22,705 match from the Boulder County General Fund, restored the wheat barn and pigpen. The ranch is used for living-history programs, interpreting ranch life for school groups and anyone else wanting to savor a stroll into the past.

Breckenridge———————————

DEWERS-PASTORIUS HOUSE / RED, WHITE & BLUE FIREHOUSE MUSEUM
308 N. Main St. [NRD]
Built: 1887

Behind a white picket fence, this clapboard cottage housed Johnny B. Dewers, owner of the Corner Saloon. The popular Dewers was shot and killed in the middle of Main Street by Dr. Condon, the town physician, possibly over a woman they both admired. An active supporter and member of the Breckenridge Fire Department, Dewers would no doubt be pleased to see that his home is now a free museum operated by the Red, White & Blue Firehouse next door. Volunteers offer tours of the firehouse, which houses an American LaFrance hook-and-ladder truck, a hose cart, and other firefighting equipment and memorabilia.

The museum is for people who are interested in the history of Breckenridge and the fire department that kept it intact, says fire chief John Moles. The SHF provided $13,500 for the rehabilitation, including preservation planning, insulation, lighting, and plumbing. One of Colorado's best examples of boomtown log-and-frame architecture, the historic old house now has a new life.

EDWIN CARTER CABIN
111 N. Ridge St. [NRD]
Built: 1875

Concerned about the disappearance of native species during the gold-rush onslaught, pioneer naturalist Edwin Carter collected more than 3,000 specimens of wildlife. One of Colorado's first museum buildings, his cabin housed many of these creatures

that later ended up in the Denver Museum of Nature and Science. The Summit Historical Society and the Town of Breckenridge saved the house, which stood on a prime development site.

More than $600,000 was raised to purchase the land and recycle the cabin as a museum of history and natural history. SHF grants totaling $52,000 were used restoring the exterior. Rebecca Waugh, a preservationist with the Town of Breckenridge, says, "Edwin's house is now almost the same as a century ago. We have restored the original hand-hewn logs, installed a new drainage system, fixed up the front porch with four-leaf-clover posts, and saved the original wavy-glass windows."

HATTIE FINCHER HOUSE
111 N. Main St. [NRD]
Built: c. 1890

An August 2000 fire ravaged this one-story house with 18-inch-thick walls of hand-hewn native timber. Clapboard installed over the façade logs, Greek Revival window pediments, and a corrugated-metal roof distinguished this pioneer home of Hattie Fincher, editor of Breckenridge's *Summit County Journal.*

Mayor Sam Mamula and city preservationist Rebecca Waugh pleaded for assistance before winter snows collapsed the fire-damaged building. The SHF acted quickly on their emergency request for $9,750, matching town funding and $3,250 from the Lois G. Theobold family, who owns the site. A new roof, fascia, and façade, and other repairs have restored this mainstay of Breckenridge's downtown National Register Historic District.

B

Brush

ALL SAINTS LUTHERAN CHURCH OF EBEN-EZER CARE CENTER
120 Hospital Rd. [NR]
Built: 1916–1918; Baerresen Brothers, architects

All Saints Church is a splendid example of the architecture of the Danish-born
Baerresen Brothers of Denver. The Rev. Jens Madsen founded the Eben-Ezer
Sanitarium with his wife in 1903. He provided the preliminary design plans for
the church, including features he recalled from Danish churches. Eben-Ezer served
as a tubercular sanitarium that also cared for the indigent and aging in this rural
part of Colorado. Danish immigrants supplied the labor and equipment for a
1922 east-side church addition in the same style, which now houses the museum
and archives of Eben-Ezer. The $62,623 restoration included a cash match of
$17,126 from various individuals and $45,497 in SHF funds for exterior stabilization and restoration. The reborn church is used by the community for weddings,
chorale concerts, and Morgan Community College classes.

KNEARL SCHOOL
314 S. Clayton St. (H) [NR]
Built: 1910

Around 1900, many German-Russian immigrants settled in Brush to work in the
sugarbeet fields that supplied the Great Western Sugar factory. The population
increase necessitated the building of this one-story, red-brick, Craftsman-style
school. Named for William "Billy" Knearl, an early Brush merchant, postmaster,
and school-board president, the school remained open until 1971. After 25 years
of neglect, the old school received an $88,500 SHF grant, which, with matching
funds from various organizations and individuals, provided new plumbing, repaired
windows, doors, floors, and walls; and stabilized the structure in a $168,500
restoration. The rejuvenated structure again offers learning opportunities through
its use as a museum, exhibition gallery, community arts studio, and educational

facility. Lifetime Brush resident Evelyn King remarked,
"My memories of the first
and second grade at Knearl
have become more vivid since
our school has become a focal
point of preservation in Brush."
The reincarnated school shines
in a large city park complete
with bandstand, picnic pavilion,
playground, swimming pool,
and a CHS roadside sign that
encapsules the history of Brush.

Buena Vista

GRACE EPISCOPAL CHURCH
Main St. and Park Ave. [NR]
Built: 1889; Lannan Brothers, builders

Grace Episcopal Church sits prominently on Main Street in the center of town, where settlers of over a century ago entered through the same doors used today. This board-and-batten landmark is one of the state's best examples of Gothic Revival architecture, with its lancet windows, frame buttresses, and a Gothic-arched entry hood. Inside, the timber trusses are trimmed with pendants, and a Gothic arch frames the chancel.

In 2003, the congregation received a $79,692 SHF grant to restore the interior and exterior. To address foundation problems, the site was regraded to direct water away from the building. Deteriorated siding and trim were repaired and repainted in the historic color scheme. In the 1950s, an arched trifoil-type window had been removed from the south wall. The window frame was found in storage, reglazed in plain stained glass, and reinstalled. Today, the interior is bathed in cheerful tones of light that shine on a most appreciative congregation.

St. ROSE OF LIMA CATHOLIC CHURCH / BUENA VISTA
AREA CHAMBER OF COMMERCE
343 US 24 (SR)
Built: 1880

This Carpenter Gothic gem, the first church building in town, was moved to its present location on US 24 in downtown Buena Vista in 1969. Named for the first canonized saint in the New World, the rehabilitated church now houses the Buena Vista Chamber of Commerce Visitor Center. When the center's 40,000 annual visitors were endangered by an unstable roof, a preliminary SHF grant enabled the Chamber to consult a structural engineer, who termed the roof beyond repair.

The historic preservation committee obtained a second opinion and discovered that the old roof had the necessary structural integrity, as long as its trusses were shored up. On the roof, workmen cut a large hole in the south side, removed the shake shingles, crawled inside, and painstakingly reinforced the bowed rafters with new lumber. They then closed up the hole, reusing as many old square nails as they could. Kathy Perry of the Chamber says in-kind help came from the community, including stained-glass artistry from local artist Kim Heidemann. Work crews from the Buena Vista Correctional Facility used their sweat equity to help match the SHF's $42,021 and $9,812 from the Chamber. In May 2001, three feet of wet snow fell in Buena Vista, and the roof held. "It felt like a miracle," says Perry.

B

TURNER FARM
829 W. Main St. (SR)
Built: c. 1880, cabin; 1912, farmhouse

Gilbert Walker bought an 1880 homestead and in 1912 built a new main house with a stream running under it to keep dairy products and fresh produce cool. That same year, Walker sold the property to Clara Turner, who moved in with her husband and son, William. For 80 years, the Turner family ran a small dairy operation and sold Transparent and Wealthy apples and other produce from their orchards and gardens.

The Buena Vista Heritage Museum bought the farm in 1996, using $100,000 in acquisition funding from the SHF and $103,800 from museum funds. Subsequent SHF grants of $90,069, with a $67,500 cash match from the museum, covered

interior and exterior restoration work on this frame structure with open porches. The grounds include the 1880 homestead cabin, the 1912 farm-house, a two-story log barn built by the Turners in 1924, a blacksmith shop that has become a garage, as well as several other outbuildings.

The challenge, according to restoration architect Christina Brandenberg, is "to know how far back to go, how many layers to take off." In the tiny 1880 cabin, a new roof and flooring needed to be re-created, since only the outside shell was intact. Workers lifted up the old cabin, created a foundation, and reseated the building. A large 1915 log barn is to receive a new tin roof, plus a restored tack shed and chicken house. The goal is to make the site a working farm again to educate visiting school groups and to enhance the Turner Farm's annual Applefest, its main fundraiser.

*Burlington*_____

KIT CARSON COUNTY CAROUSEL
Kit Carson County Fairgrounds, Colorado Ave. and 15th St. **NHL**
Built: 1905; Philadelphia Toboggan Co., builder

Project supervisor Mary Jo Downey says, "Our carousel is unique—a wonderful spin back in time." This proud, prancing, ridable National Historic Landmark now also has its own enclosed carousel house to protect it from the elements. Downey believes it to be the world's best restored historic carousel.

The National Trust for Historic Preservation presented one of its coveted National Honor Awards to this carousel in 2003. This is the sixth of 74 carousels that were built by the Philadelphia Toboggan Company between 1904 and 1933. The carousel first spun at Denver's Elitch Gardens Amusement Park in 1905. Its 46 hand-carved wooden animals, which including a lion, giraffe, zebra, camel, tiger, deer, and even a seahorse, took riders of all ages on an enchanted journey that was enhanced by oil paintings, bright lights, and gold-leaf trim. The music was supplied by a big 220-pipe Wurlitzer Monster Military Band Organ.

In 1928, Elitch Gardens bought an updated model and sold this one to Kit Carson County, which installed it at the fairgrounds in Burlington. Residents there at first gave it a rude welcome, complaining loudly about the $1,250 price tag and

B

forcing the three county commissioners involved to resign. The Great Depression ensued, and Kit Carson County halted its annual fair and the carousel spent six years in a storage hangar, where rodents and birds took up residence and gnawed wounds into the wooden animals.

Colorado's centennial and the nation's bicentennial events brought a new appreciation for the carousel. The Kit Carson County Carousel Association was established in 1975 and restoration efforts began on it. The carousel was listed on the National Register of Historic Places in 1979, and in 1987 it received the nation's highest honor, being designated as a National Historic Landmark. The 25-year-old preservation effort was finally completed in 2005 when the carousel celebrated its 100th anniversary. Partners in the $2.75 million project have included Kit Carson County, the National Park Service, the Boettcher Foundation, the Gates Foundation, the National Carousel Association, the American Carousel Society, and also the State Historical Fund, which helped contribute nearly $500,000. Work has included total restoration of the 45 wooden figures and four chariots, reconstruction of decorative moldings, installation of a

fire suppression and alarm system, reconstruction of sweep valances that had been missing since 1928, restoration of the famous Wurlitzer Monster Military Band Organ, and restoration of the historic building that houses the carousel. The Carousel

Association's latest project is the development of a 3,000-square-foot museum to tell the story of the carousel, including hands-on exhibits that will help visitors to appreciate the craftsmanship, music, and artistry of this amazing structure. And best of all, the carousel remains open for business through the summer months, a major focus for heritage tourism on the Eastern Plains.

Cañon City

This city along the Arkansas River has preserved many of its gems, including the riverfront, which is now a major rafting and recreational resource. Downtown Cañon City boasts a National Register Historic District stretching from Main Street to Macon Avenue between 3rd and 9th Streets. The city set an early example for preservation by putting its courts and police into the renovated 1909 Denver & Rio Grande Depot. Cañon City has also restored the 1880 Clelland-Peabody Residence as a chamber of commerce and visitor center, and an old fire station has been converted into the Dinosaur Depot Museum.

With the help of $15,759 from the SHF, Fremont County and the U.S. Bureau of Land Management have created signage and interpretive programs that guide visitors to Fremont County's famed Phantom Canyon Road. Following the 1892 narrow-gauge roadbed of the Cripple Creek & Florence Railroad, this unpaved route is one of Colorado's most spectacular—and scary—drives.

CAÑON AUTO COMPANY
709–729 Main St. [NRD]
Built: 1918

Over the years, this two-story masonry building, originally an auto showroom and dealership, shifted from cars to other businesses, including a garage, offices, a thrift store, and Rich Gobin's office supply. Main Street USA of Cañon City used an $81,485 SHF grant and matching funds from the city to restore Gobin's building. With the help of old photos, they brought back the exterior and interior, removing false ceilings to reveal the beautiful wooden beams and skylights. This

textured masonry, Southwestern-style building is now fully occupied with various retail businesses. Gobin reports, "We have had a lot of compliments. And our work inspired restoration of the building next door!"

C

CAÑON CITY POST OFFICE AND FEDERAL BUILDING / FREMONT CENTER FOR THE ARTS
505 Macon Ave. [NR]
Built: 1931; James A. Wetmore, architect

When the U.S. Post Office moved out of this terracotta-trimmed, limestone-clad structure in 1990, city building restoration manager Becky Walker recalls, "There was a public outcry to continue the use of this beautiful building. Coincidentally, the Fremont Center for the Arts had needed a home for a long time." With $45,000 in SHF grants, the restoration and renovation helped make this a usable space for the center. "We maintained the original floor plan—even down to the post-office boxes," explains Walker. Donors "purchased" the boxes, which now display their names. The museum showcases local artists while preserving a cornerstone of Cañon City's past.

ELKS LODGE No. 610
404 Macon St. [NRD]
Built: 1911

In 2002, the Elks and Elkettes at Lodge No. 610 realized that their building, which still hosts 400 members, was falling into disrepair. The Elks restoration team worked with local historian Cara Fisher to get SHF grants totaling $22,975. These funds, in addition to money raised by the lodge, covered restoration of the north entrance, with its Doric columns and portico, along with new gutters and repairs to the yellow brickwork and the front railing. "Our lodge," says project director Jack Draman, "looks young again."

FIRE STATION / DINOSAUR DEPOT MUSEUM
330 Royal Gorge Blvd. **H** [NRD]
Built: 1938

The Garden Park Paleontology Society raised $32,778 and SHF grants of $38,700 to convert this two-story sandstone fire station into the Dinosaur Depot Museum, which opened in 1995 in partnership with the Bureau of Land Management and the Denver Museum of Nature and Science. This building interprets Cañon City's Garden Park, one of the largest Jurassic graveyards in the world. The museum includes numerous exhibits, a hands-on discovery room, and a lab where visitors can interact with volunteers working on dinosaur fossils. Although many of the fossils and skeletons have been removed and put on display in such prominent museums as the Smithsonian Institution, research and excavations continue. Trails have been built to view the quarries surrounding the center. New discoveries in the area ensure that Garden Park continues to be a hot spot for tourists, geologists, and paleontologists alike.

HOLY CROSS ABBEY
2951 Royal Gorge Blvd. (US 50) [NR]
Built: 1924; Joseph Dillon and L. A. Des Jardins, architects

Benedictine monks built this $500,000 abbey as the showpiece of their only preparatory school in Colorado. Built on a Latin Cross plan with a prominent bell tower, this church is sheathed in beige, gold, and brown bricks decorated with cast stone trim. With dwindling numbers of monks and students, Holy Cross used prayer and a $20,000 SHF grant to restore the roof and repair the masonry. The free museum in the basement of the abbey, opened in 1988, houses a Native American collection and religious materials associated with the abbey, including old vestments and the abbot's throne. The abbey's library also houses some rare medieval books. Since 2002, the abbey has also operated a winery, a traditional Benedictine business, in an adjacent building.

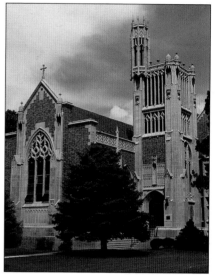

Photo courtesy of Tom Noel

MADISON EXPLORATORY SCHOOL
202 E. Douglas Ave. (SR)
Built: 1924; C. F. Ward, builder

Madison Exploratory opened in 1992 as a charter alternative school emphasizing hands-on community projects. Cañon City and Fremont RE-1 school district obtained a $100,000 SHF grant to acquire and restore the city's oldest surviving school building for this reuse. Refurbished floors, new walls, repaired brick and mortar, and new windows have rejuvenated this one-story, yellow-and-red-brick structure, with ornate brick trim flourishing in an entryway ogee arch and curvilinear parapet. Principal Molly Sasser considers the restoration a success: "The kids

Photo courtesy of Tom Noel

got to watch the renovation, instilling a sense of pride in their school." The students have constructed a historical display in the front lobby of the building.

C

RAYNOLDS BANK
330–332 Main St. NRD
Built: 1882–1883; L. A. Allen, builder

Fredrick A. Raynolds owned a chain of banks in Leadville, Rosita, Silver Cliff, Alpine, Buena Vista, and Saguache. None were as handsome as this one. The

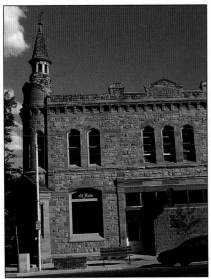

adjacent McGee Mercantile and Fraternal Order of Eagles were built of matching stone and style. By the 1990s, however, this once proud Gothic Revival edifice was losing its stone trim. Theresa Hamby Accountants and Cañon City procured a $62,377 SHF grant to hire expert stonemason John Hofmann of Cañon City to restore the façade. Two false ceilings were removed to access the original 18-foot-high, pressed-metal ceiling. Distinguished by its slender corner spire, this sandstone building with its restored trim is once again a safe landmark in the Cañon City Historic District. Converted into office space, it is also a stop on Cañon City's ghost walk tours.

Photo courtesy of Tom Noel

SANTA FE DEPOT
401 Water St. Ⓗ ⓈⓇ
Built: 1913; C. F. W. Pelt, builder

Although the Santa Fe Railroad lost the Royal Gorge Railroad War to the Denver & Rio Grande in the 1870s, it still built this red-brick Spanish Colonial Revival depot in Cañon City. In the 1970s, the city bought the abandoned depot and, with $121,460 in SHF grants, restored the site to its original grandeur. The depot is now a tourist and passenger hub once again, complete with a restaurant, lounge, and ticket office for the Royal Gorge Route Railroad. The Theodore Roosevelt Dining Car offers gourmet lunches and dinners. "The restored depot and train thrilled the community," says city project manager Becky Walker. "And the tourist response has been terrific. Cañon City now has a viable railroad station and a train again."

Castle Rock

Settled in 1871 as an agricultural community, Castle Rock soon became known for its rhyolite quarries. The volcanic stone, found in gray, pink, and purple shades, is showcased in many of the town's landmarks. After the Denver & Rio Grande Railroad arrived in 1871, Castle Rock began shipping its signature stone to construction sites in Denver and other boomtowns.

BENJAMIN HAMMAR HOUSE
203 Cantril St. LL NR
Built: 1887; Benjamin J. Hammar, builder

Benjamin Hammar, owner of the Santa Fe Quarry and Castle Rock Stone Company, built his own house with favorite rhyolite specimens from his quarry. Hammar

also built many of the stone buildings in and around Castle Rock, including the Denver & Rio Grande Railroad Depot, which is now the town museum. An SHF grant of $12,116 enabled the town and residents Lionel and Starr Oberlin to remove five layers of roofing material and restore the original shake shingles at the Hammar House.

CHRISTENSEN'S HOUSE / CASTLE ROCK CHAMBER
OF COMMERCE
420 Jerry St. LL
Built: 1889; Benjamin J. Hammar, builder

Fondly called "Victoria's House" by locals, this two-story residence featuring local Castle Rock rhyolite was home to Victoria Anderson Christensen for much of her life. When Victoria married banker Thorwald Christensen, they came to live in her childhood home and play an active role in the community. Their civic spirit lives on in the building, as it became home to the Castle Rock Chamber of Commerce in 1992. An $89,965 SHF grant enabled a major restoration, including exterior repainting, a new roof, chimney and masonry repair, and electrical upgrades. The original residence is separated by a skylighted link from a new frame addition to the south.

Cedaredge

C

BAR I SILOS
315 W. 3rd St. (H) [NR]
Built: 1916–1917; Robert P. James, builder

Three spectacular 35-foot-high silos of stacked lumber are the only relics of the Surface Creek Livestock Company. Brothers W. B. and A. W. Stockham and James Zaninetti hired a local builder to construct the first two 9-sided silos in 1916, and

the third one, an 11-sided structure, in 1917. Builder Robert Phelps James was a master carpenter noted for constructing the first bridge over Surface Creek, the Cedar Mesa School, and the Reed School.

In 1981, the Surface Creek Valley Historical Society acquired the silos as a centerpiece for their Pioneer Town, a large private museum of buildings and artifacts. The Society received $46,590 from the SHF and provided a matching grant of $2,600 to raise the silos and install concrete foundations, repair the roofs, clean and seal the lumber walls, and restore the wooden catwalks that connected the two 9-sided silos. These 200-ton silos tower over two dozen buildings moved to or erected on the site by the Society, including the Cedaredge Jail, Lizard Head Saloon, First State Bank of Cedaredge, Coalby Store, and the Surface Creek Creamery.

STOLTE APPLE PACKING SHED
1812 CO 65 [NR]
Built: 1909; Virgil Bouldin, mason

In 1991, when the Surface Creek Valley Historical Society decided to move the apple-packing shed from the Stolte family farm to Pioneer Town in Cedaredge, crews from the Delta Correctional Facility built interior walls to keep the roof

from collapsing. Then they cut the shed in half; each side weighed 45 tons. Moving day was a holiday for this small agricultural community. Spectators came from all over, teachers brought their students, and the Historical Society sold T-shirts with a picture of the shed and the words "I saw it move."

According to Lillian Minor, general contractor on this project, "Much of the appeal for preserving and restoring the packing shed was its unique construction." The two-story building's roof beams are 32 feet long, and a clerestory monitor along the peak provides light and ventilation. The walls are so thick and well insulated that they kept the interior cool on the hottest summer day. The SHF contributed $26,661 to rehabilitate the shed's first floor for community use. The shed is part of the Pioneer Town tour, which gives visitors a glimpse into the world that early farmers and apple growers found near "the edge of the cedars."

Central City

Organized preservation in Colorado began in Central City with Anne Evans and Ida Kruse McFarlane, who began restoration of the Central City Opera House in 1932. Preservation efforts have accelerated in Central City since 1991, when it became one of three gaming towns in Colorado. Central City has been reshaped by gambling, and many buildings have been restored with gaming revenues. The Central City–Black Hawk National Historic Landmark District encompasses commercial and residential structures in both towns.

Former mayor Donald Mattivi, Jr., a fifth-generation resident of Central City, appreciates the fact that his town is steeped in history. The famous "Cornish" rock retaining walls (which, according to the U.S. Manuscript Census, were also built by Irish, German, Swedish, and Italian immigrants) hold a special place in his heart. Mayor Mattivi reflected, in a 2003 Gold Coin Saloon interview:

> Central City has used SHF and city funds to restore a lot of things, including the town's ancient stone walls.... Before the SHF fix-up, we had lots of wall bulges and blowouts. Did you see those two-foot buckles in that 20-foot wall behind the County Courthouse that we just fixed? If a rock wall like that collapses, you can lose a building, a street—or a life. On Christmas Day, 1972, a big chunk of retaining wall almost killed Mrs. Glendinning while she was cooking her Christmas ham. Missed her by only two feet. History is in our blood here—and in those retaining walls.

Photo courtesy of Denver Metro CVB

CENTRAL CITY HIGH SCHOOL / GILPIN COUNTY HISTORICAL SOCIETY MUSEUM

228 E. High St. NHLD

Built: 1870; Newton D. Owen, builder

"This schoolhouse has been our main museum since 1971," reports Linda Jones, president of the Gilpin County Historical Society. "We had to have a dozen buckets at strategic places on the second floor when it rained or snowed." SHF matched the Historical Society's funds with $78,812 to restore the roof, using rubberized latex over polystyrene insulation. The grant also provided for new soffits and downspouts and for repairs to the Italianate roof brackets, the cupola bell tower, and the frieze. "Now our school looks smart again," Jones says proudly.

CENTRAL CITY OPERA HOUSE

124 Eureka St. NR NHLD

Built: 1878; Robert S. Roeschlaub, architect

Colorado's first nationally noted preservation story began in 1929, when Central City entrepreneur Peter McFarlane left his three children a dubious heirloom: a deteriorated, 60-year-old opera house. Used in Central City's early days for variety shows and supposedly even Buffalo Bill's Wild West Show, the opera house had declined over the decades, hosting only sporadic entertainment such as movies, boxing matches, and high school graduations. The young McFarlanes considered selling the Central City Opera House as a warehouse or auto garage, seemingly the only feasible options in hard economic times. But Peter's daughter-in-law, Ida Kruse McFarlane, instead persuaded the family in 1931 to donate the structure to the University of Denver, to be restored and reopened for summer performances. Ida enlisted the aid of Anne Evans, Colorado's leading cultural philanthropist and a tenacious fundraiser.

Through social and theatrical connections, the newly formed Central City Opera House Association secured the services of Denver's top artists and architects— Allen True, Paschal Quackenbush, Allen Fisher, and Burnham Hoyt—for the ongoing preservation efforts. In 1932, Broadway producer Robert Edmond Jones staged the premiere performance—*Camille*, starring Lillian Gish—in the reborn opera house. Nationwide media coverage of the festival brought increasing numbers of visitors to this once forgotten town. With the growing importance of tourism in Colorado, restoration of the Central City Opera House has served as an early model for the economic rewards of historic preservation.

Since 1932, the opera house has been used nearly every summer for an acclaimed national opera festival. This historic theater benefited from extensive restoration projects in 1995 and 1996, funded in part by $301,340 from SHF.

"We were able to restore the opera house inside and out—from a repaired granite façade to a rebuilt orchestra pit," says Central City Opera's general director Pelham G. Pearce. "It's probably in better shape now than at any time since it was built."

C

COEUR d'ALENE SHAFTHOUSE AND MINE
101 Academy St. (H) NHLD
Built: 1884

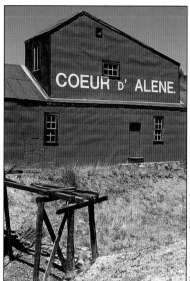

Central City's most prominently located mine, the Coeur d'Alene, produced gold, silver, lead, copper, and zinc until it closed in the 1930s. It was donated to the Central City Opera House Association, which turned it over to the Gilpin County Historical Society in 1987. "This shafthouse had been blown down flat when we took over," reports former president of the Gilpin County Historical Society, Chocolate Dan Monroe. With $50,000 from the SHF and Central City, the Society recon-structed and restored the old mine and its 700-foot-deep shaft. The shaft-house still has the original compressor, hoist, unusual double boilers, and signage. Monroe invites visitors to "come up, do a self-guided tour, and inspect the mining equipment on exhibit on the grounds."

Photo courtesy of Tom Noel

D'ALBE HALL (CAMPBELL HALL)
213 Eureka St. NHLD
Built: 1886

This two-story, clapboard Italianate house, once home to foundry worker Angus Campbell, was donated to the Central City Opera House Association in 1955 for cast housing. Like many homes built on the precarious, rubble-strewn hillsides of Central City, D'Albe Hall suffered from drainage and structural problems.

"SHF funds of $145,120 enabled us to restore this house," says Nancy Brittain, Central City Opera's director of development. Work included foundation stabiliza-tion, the restoration of the stone walls, installation of new sidewalks, and repair of the porch and windows. Inside, new kitchens and plumbing have made D'Albe Hall a favorite summer residence for Central City Opera artists, who prize its location just across the street from McFarlane Rehearsal Hall.

C

GILPIN COUNTY COURTHOUSE
203 Eureka St. **NHLD**
Built: 1900; Baerresen Brothers, architects

This two-story brick Italianate courthouse, with its distinctive symmetrical corner towers and entry arcade, enjoyed a $135,000 facelift with help from a $90,000 SHF grant and other funds from Gilpin County. "For starters," county service director Susie Allen explains, "we converted the 10 basement jail cells, in use until the new Gilpin County Justice Center was built in 1995, into records storage.

"We also removed an ugly rear addition, repointed our brick exterior, and removed the bars put on the windows to keep Black Hawk from stealing things," Allen notes. The hardwood floor was restored, and acoustic tile was removed to reveal the old 20-foot-high coved ceilings in the courtroom. The mineral display cabinets and a 38-star flag dating back to 1876—when Colorado became a state— were lovingly restored. "We even cleaned up Bob, the stuffed bobcat who keeps order in the court," Allen laughs.

MEDICAL BUILDING (HENDERSON BLOCK)
115–117 Pine St. **NHLD**
Built: 1863; David Henderson, builder

This two-story, red-brick building, with a flat roof and brick corbeling and cornice atop a stone foundation, originally housed the offices of two physicians. Acquired by the Central City Opera House Association, it now houses opera apprentices and staff. Restoration and stabilization were funded by the SHF's $152,630 grant and a Central City Opera House Association (CCOHA) match.

"Before this refurbishing, extreme water damage left the building in such great disrepair that the apprentice singers who stayed there jokingly called it 'Club Med,'" says Lew Cady, Central City historic preservation commissioner and editor of *The Little Kingdom Come.*

"We reframed the interior while preserving the building's exterior façade and roof structure," says the Association's Allan Fries. "To prevent the walls from collapsing, we had to follow a precise sequence of operations set out by a structural engineer. We'd remove a small area, install a new beam, rebuild that section of floor and wall, and move on to the next piece."

C

PENROSE COMPLEX
119 and 121 Eureka St. NHLD
Built: 1864–1866; William Roworth, builder

Julie Penrose, the Colorado Springs philanthropist who owned the Broadmoor Hotel, bought these two residences in 1944 and donated them to the Central City Opera House Association (CCOHA) to house cast members. The two front-gabled houses, with classically columned porches and front yards behind stone retaining walls, are clapboard and stone with rear additions for additional housing. As the closest residences to the opera house, these are favorites with the opera singers, including one who chirped, "The Penrose Complex and Central City are quaint, cute, and positive—and cooler than New York City, where I live."

"Our historic properties allow our artists to live and work together in Central City," says Central City Opera's general director, Pelham G. Pearce. "The logistics of our festival would become impossible without properties like these." These structures are among the finest of the cast residences that Penrose, along with other donors, purchased for the CCOHA. Architect Burnham Hoyt helped transform these two homes of middle-class merchants into apartments for world-class performers.

In 1994, the Penrose Complex received a much-needed interior rehabilitation funded by $75,000 from the SHF and a CCOHA match. The company's principal artists now enjoy comfortable summer accommodations in apartments named for famous guests like Helen Hayes and Mae West (who was even rumored to have had mirrors installed on the ceiling during her 1949 stay).

St. PAUL'S EPISCOPAL CHURCH
220 E. High St. NHLD
Built: 1873; Newton D. Owen and M. H. Root,
    builders

A $42,000 SHF grant garnered matches of $20,000 from Central City, $5,000 from Gilpin County, and $12,000 from the Episcopal Diocese of Colorado. St. Paul's bishop's warden-cum-architect and engineer Don Harvey reports, "Using our own church funds, we've restored the old wooden steeple and replaced the old two-by-four cross with a new, stainless-steel Celtic cross. Using SHF funds, we've redone the stone church walls and retaining walls, covered the stained-glass windows with Lexan, and added new steps, a new wrought-iron fence, and a wheelchair ramp. Now we're putting in a patio and benches and planting Harrison golden-yellow roses like those first brought to Central City back in the 1870s, when St. Paul's was built."

Photo courtesy of Tom Noel

THOMAS HOUSE MUSEUM
209 Eureka St. NHLD
Built: 1874; Benjamin Thomas, builder

This clapboard Greek Revival started out as a one-room cabin. The Benjamin Thomas family built the house and lived in it until 1897, when they sold it to

George N. Billings, whose family kept the place until 1987. It sports pedimented doorways and windows, a Tuscan-columned, full-length porch, corner pilasters, and a symmetrical design. The interior furnishings, virtually unchanged since 1917, inspired the Gilpin County Historical Society to open it as a house museum. Jim Prochaska, GCHS executive director, explains, "We used old photos and SHF support to guide the $38,767 restoration from the picket fence to the roof. We're hoping to reconstruct a long-lost bridge from the second-story bedroom to a three-hole outhouse on the hill in back."

Cheyenne Wells

MOUNTAIN STATES TELEPHONE BUILDING
15170 5th St. SR
Built: 1927

"The winged voice of radio and the electrical wizardry of telephony," as Pocky Marranzino rhapsodized in his August 21, 1946, *Rocky Mountain News* column, "were united in an auspicious ceremony in this little sun-baked ranch town with the world's first rural radio-telephone service."

When the Mountain States Telephone and Telegraph Company purchased the Cheyenne County Telephone Company in 1927, it built this small brick building and modernized Cheyenne Wells' and nearby Kit Carson's telephone systems. The facility opened with 161 telephones able to connect all the way to Europe. A 24-hour switchboard operator was available, and the number of Cheyenne Wells residents with telephones increased sharply. The building also housed living quarters for the company manager. In the 1960s, when telephones switched to the dial system, the telephone building found new life as the local public library. Its latest chapter started in 1996, when the Eastern Colorado Historical Society acquired the building. Betty Talbert, chair of the restoration committee, says, "We've used state energy-impact money and funds from the Cooper-Clark Foundation to help the Eastern Colorado Historical Society garner a 2003 SHF grant of $110,400." The money went toward restoration of the exterior and upgrading the building's mechanical, electrical, and plumbing systems. Restoration is ongoing, and the Society plans to turn the building into a museum focused on the history of telecommunications and featuring the original switchboard. The building will also serve as the Society's library and archives.

Clark

MOON HILL SCHOOLHOUSE
50710 CR 129 (3 miles south of Clark) [LL]
Built: 1913

The Moon Hill Schoolhouse and Community Center used $51,400 from the SHF to restore the exterior, including a new corrugated metal roof, and to rehabilitate the interior of this country school. The clapboard-sided edifice on a stone foundation sports a Tuscan-columned porch with benches. Under a plain, open bell tower, this simple, almost stark, one-room school retains its outdoor water pump and rural setting. "Such country schools were often the first rural community centers. Teaching took place during the day, and at night farm and ranch families came here for box socials, debates, and dances," explains Andrew Gulliford, former director of the Center for Southwest Studies at Fort Lewis College and author of *America's Country Schools*. Today, the building houses the nonprofit North Routt County Preschool.

Coalmont

COALMONT SCHOOL
1018 CR 26 (15 miles southwest of Walden) (SR)
Built: 1905, Hebron School; 1915, Coalmont School

Amid the vast flats of North Park, two clapboard, one-room schools snuggle together, a testament to the struggle to build schools and educate children in remote, sparsely settled places. The people of Jackson County used wagons and 12 horses to move the Hebron School building here in 1920. It was consolidated with the Coalmont School. Together, they reached an all-time-high enrollment of 60 pupils. The population dwindled as coal mining declined, however, and the school closed for lack of students in 1945.

A simple bronze plaque on the Coalmont School reads "Restored by Spicer Club with many thanks to friends, neighbors, and the Colorado Historical Society for their support, labor, and funding." This $80,650 community project, organized by a local civic club, was made possible by a $69,950 SHF grant and the volunteer labor and in-kind assistance of many locals, including Boy Scout Troop No. 146. The two historic schools have been re-sided, re-roofed, and given a fresh coat of white paint. In the tiny town of Coalmont, where the coal played out long ago, this landmark recalls the youthful, vibrant community of yore.

Cokedale

C

GOTTLIEB MERCANTILE BUILDING
C-1 Elm St., CO 12 (7 miles west of Trinidad) **H** NRD
Built: 1906; James Murdoch, architect

The Cokedale Historic District, between Church, Maple, Pine, Elm, and Spruce Streets, is an unusually well-preserved example of a company camp. The American

 Smelting and Refining Company owned and operated this camp from its construction in 1906–1907 until its closing in 1946. Heralded as a model company town, Cokedale offered housing, education, recreation, as well as this general store.

Gottlieb Mercantile served the community from 1909 to 1942. Vernon Williams of Abilene Christian University, who conducts a public-history summer field school in the museum, notes, "It stocked everything from baby clothes to caskets, from food to furniture. The post office was in there. It was the economic and social center of the town."

In 1988, the town purchased the Mercantile Building for $700 to house the Cokedale Mining Museum, a collaborative effort of the Town of Cokedale Mining Museum Committee, residents, and other interested parties. The SHF granted $132,750, which was matched by the committee. "The SHF's grant was extremely helpful," says Cokedale mayor Pat Huhn. "We are a very small town, and they provided the bulk of our funding to restore the exterior and interior of our general store. Their technical advisers came in on a regular basis and helped when we ran into difficulty." Cokedale's 120 residents are proud of the building, which recalls their town's booming mining days.

Collbran

STOCKMEN'S BANK / COLLBRAN BRANCH, MESA COUNTY PUBLIC LIBRARY
111 Main St. **SR**
Built: 1929; R. C. Skinner & Co. and A. D. Mitchell, builders

The present building replaced a bank built on the same site in 1908 and was constructed around the earlier building's vault. When the Collbran Branch of the Mesa County Public Library faced closure, the Plateau Valley Friends of the Library raised $65,000 in this tiny town to buy the bank building, which had been converted into offices. The organization received a $37,612 SHF grant to restore this elegant, one-story Romanesque Revival bank. The old bank vault has been converted into a children's play area. Librarian Sharon Jordan notes that "nearly 75 percent of the 3,000 residents in the Plateau Creek Valley have library cards, and they patronize this book bank heavily."

Colorado Springs

The second largest city in Colorado was founded in 1871 by General William Jackson Palmer, whose likeness, astride a horse, oversees the city at the intersection of Nevada and Platte Avenues. Palmer, president of the Denver & Rio Grande Railroad, planned his model town with wide, tree-lined streets and ample parks, and he envisioned Colorado Springs as the state's elite residential city. Smoke, sweat, and noise would be banished to Denver, the rail hub, and Pueblo, the manufacturing center. Palmer's chief construction engineer, William H. Greenwood, platted a city of 70 blocks, each 400 feet square, with broad avenues lined by irrigation ditches, planting strips, and parks. After Greeley, this was perhaps Colorado's best-planned city. The ideal of broad, tree-shaded avenues is perpetuated in the North End and North Weber Street–Wahsatch Avenue Historic Districts.

BEMIS HALL, COLORADO COLLEGE
920 N. Cascade Ave. [NR]
Built: 1908; Maurice Biscoe, architect

This Tudor Revival dormitory, built to house female students, features a "checker-board" slate roof, steeply pitched dormers and gables, and a medieval-style dining hall. SHF grants totaling $300,000 for exterior rehabilitation and restoration enabled Colorado College to address water damage that had resulted from problems with the slate roof. Inspired by this first step, the college is now assessing similar restorations of other aging landmarks on its campus.

C

CAR No. 59, COLORADO SPRINGS & INTERURBAN RAILWAY
2335 Steel St., in the Roswell Trolley Barn (SR)
Built: 1901; Laclede Car Company, St. Louis, Missouri, builder

Winfield Scott Stratton, who made his fortune in Cripple Creek gold, consolidated Colorado Springs trolley operations in 1900. To add polish to his new Colorado Springs & Interurban Railway, he ordered nine elegant, 40-passenger cars from

St. Louis. When the CS&I Railway closed in 1930, the roomy, 48-foot-long, 11-foot-high, and 8-foot-wide coaches were sold off to area residents who used them as summer cottages, chicken coops, and storage sheds. Car No. 59 became a garage addition. Now the only survivor, No. 59 forms the centerpiece of a fleet assembled by the Pikes Peak Historical Street Railway Foundation (PPHSRF) as part of its effort to return trolleys to the streets of Colorado Springs and Manitou Springs. SHF grants of $112,000 have enabled PPHSRF volunteers to begin a meticulous restoration of Car No. 59, starting with the stabilization of its frame. This state-of-the-art, double-truck passenger car once again boasts etched-glass transoms, quartersawn oak paneling, polished bronze hardware, bird's-eye maple veneer, and mother-of-pearl call buttons. As PPHSRF continues to work toward its goal of a fully operational railcar, visitors can view Car No. 59 and other historic trolley cars on Saturdays or by appointment.

CARNEGIE BUILDING, PENROSE PUBLIC LIBRARY
21 W. Kiowa St. (H) [NR]
Built: 1905; Calvin Kiessling, architect

The former Carnegie Public Library has witnessed the transformation of Colorado Springs from a vacation destination for the affluent and the ill to a military town with a modern Air Force Academy and high-tech businesses. This library, in what the architect called "Neo Grec" style, combines a pressed-brick edifice with Platte Valley granite and Pueblo sandstone trim. The band of large, upper-floor windows provide plenty of natural light and views of Pikes Peak.

With the 1967 addition of the modern Penrose Library, the Carnegie Building's ceilings were lowered and its windows painted over in

Photo courtesy Special Collections,
Pikes Peak Regional Library

the name of energy efficiency. Thirty years later, asbestos-abatement procedures left the deteriorating building looking even sadder. The library underwent a $3 million restoration starting in 1998, boosted by $794,699 in SHF support. Windows were restored where feasible and replicated as needed. The high, plaster ceilings were uncovered and restored, revealing elegant rosette designs, and the carpet was removed, uncovering a gorgeous terrazzo floor. During the entire restoration process, the library remained open. Appropriately, its most cherished treasure is a local history collection that has facilitated research on many other buildings in the Pikes Peak region.

CHAMBERS RANCH (ROCK LEDGE RANCH)
3202 Chambers Way NR
Built: 1875, Robert Chambers, builder; Orchard House, 1907,
   Thomas MacLaren, architect

Pennsylvanian Robert Chambers and his family moved west in the 1870s to seek the "climate cure" after his wife, Elsie, had contracted tuberculosis. They chose this site at Camp Creek Valley, just east of the Garden of the Gods. Chambers himself apparently designed the residence, using rough-cut sandstone blocks

quarried from the property. Originally called the Chambers House, the estate was later re-named the White House Ranch and, later still, Rock Ledge. It was altered many times—by the Chambers family to accommo-date boarders, and by subsequent owners, including General William Jackson Palmer, who purchased the property in 1900. In 1907, Palmer hired Thomas

Photo courtesy of Tom Noel

MacLaren to design the nearby Mission-style Orchard House on the property for Palmer's sister-in-law and her husband.

In 1968, the City of Colorado Springs acquired the ranch and in 1993 began restoration to make the property a living-history museum. SHF grants of $254,206 aided stabilization of the Chambers House, interior restoration, and removal of unoriginal stucco from the stone-and-mortar exterior. SHF also granted $35,000 toward the rehabilitation of Orchard House.

Pat Grove, a ranch staff member, notes that the restoration was "a long time coming" and enables visitors "to experience something that went on 100 to 130 years ago." Rock Ledge offers numerous outdoor education programs and events for schoolchildren and families. Ten-year-old Hunter Lang of Castle Rock found the Rock Ledge Historic Site to be "really neat." He enjoyed the menagerie of farm animals, the costumed staff, and the kitchen with its "funny smells."

C

CHEYENNE MOUNTAIN ZOO CAROUSEL
4250 Cheyenne Mountain Zoo Rd. **H** **SR**
Built: 1925; Allen Herschell Co., builder

Spencer Penrose, a prominent Colorado Springs booster and the founder of the Broadmoor Hotel, purchased the Herschell Carousel for the Cheyenne Mountain

Zoo. This fast-moving carousel was considered a thrill ride back in the 1920s and featured a band organ and horses partly fabricated from aluminum rather than the wood typically used at the time.

Decades of exposure to the elements and sparse maintenance, however, left the carousel in need of a facelift. With $93,411 from the SHF and $133,000 of its own funds, the zoo began the carousel's long-overdue restoration. The original band organ was entirely replicated by the Stinton Organ Company in Bellefontaine, Ohio. Will Morton restored each horse and the hub-and-spoke panel paintings, as well as the lighting and mechanical gears. In its new covered shelter in the zoo's Kid's Canyon, the carousel continues to entertain visitors of all ages.

COLORADO SCHOOL FOR THE DEAF AND THE BLIND
33 N. Institute St. **SR**
Built: 1906–1952; Thomas P. Barber, Edward L. Bunts, Thomas C.
    MacLaren, Charles E. Thomas, and Elmer E. Nieman, architects

Colorado's only school dedicated solely to the education of the deaf and the blind occupies a spacious 37-acre campus, expanded from the original 10-acre site donated by General William Jackson Palmer in 1876. Though they assume different architectural styles, many of the school's 18 buildings are constructed of Castle Rock rhyolite. More than 280 students attend classes here, and half of them live on campus during the school year. Over the years, historic doors were replaced with steel security doors. SHF grants of $254,480 enabled the Colorado Department of Education to undertake a campus-wide replacement of the prison-like doors with appropriate replicas and to study future restoration needs.

COLORADO SPRINGS CITY AUDITORIUM
231 E. Kiowa St. **NR**
Built: 1922; Thomas MacLaren, Charles E. Thomas, and
    Thomas D. Hetherington, architects

Three of the city's most prominent architects designed the last of the Neoclassical civic buildings built in the heart of Colorado Springs. The blond-brick structure with limestone trim features a grand portico supported by four two-story columns. Architecturally, the building departs from the Neoclassical mode in its rounded corners and lack of ornamentation. The lobby houses WPA murals from 1935 by artists Archie Musick and Tabor Utley. The building hosted a wide range of community events and fraternal organizations. In 1996 and 1997, the City of Colorado Springs Facilities Management Department matched $200,000 in SHF grants to replace the roof, repair the cornice and windows, and clean the exterior. Inside, the city also restored the stage and flooring, so that the auditorium can continue to host events, concerts, meetings, and trade shows.

COLORADO SPRINGS CITY HALL
107 N. Nevada Ave. [NR]
Built: 1904; Thomas P. Barber and Thomas MacLaren, architects

On land donated by Winfield S. Stratton, the city laid a cornerstone for this City Hall in April 1902. Local architects Barber and MacLaren used the Neoclassical Revival style, expressed in the Ionic columns, a grand portico, and an exquisite rotunda clad in dark green scagliola (a simulated stone painted to resemble marble).

This City Hall once housed various government functions, including administration and municipal courts, but found itself empty in 1998. During the 90 years of use, it had suffered numerous remodels, alterations, and reconfigurations resulting in the loss of significant architectural features. A $194,165 SHF grant helped to restore much of the building, including stained-glass windows and the City Council Chambers, while the city funded rehabilitation for modern use.

"I think this restoration is a reaffirmation of the pride of Colorado Springs in itself and in its future," observes Tim Scanlon, senior city planner. "This was a marvelous structure built in monumental style for a small town that was looking forward to continuing prosperity. The reestablishment of this building as the seat of government is a return to our roots, with a view to our future."

COLORADO SPRINGS DAY NURSERY
104 E. Rio Grande St. [NR]
Built: 1922; William White Stickney and John Gray,
    architects; murals by Allen Tupper True

Philanthropist Alice Bemis Taylor built this in nursery in memory of her mother, one of the original founders of the Day Nursery Association. The $275,000 home for children of working families, which also housed ill and orphaned youngsters, was modeled on Tudor castles Mrs. Taylor had admired in her travels to England. The interior of this unique building was scaled for children, and the playroom features Mother Goose murals painted by renowned Colorado artist Allen Tupper True. The Colorado Springs Child Nursery Center, Inc., matched $59,500 from the SHF to install a new roof, drainpipes, windows, and screens, and to hire Carmen Bria and his team of experts at the Western Center for the Conservation of Fine Arts to restore the True murals.

Photo courtesy of Tom Noel

COLORADO SPRINGS MUNICIPAL AIRPORT
Between Peterson Blvd., Ent Ave., and Suffolk St.,
    Peterson Air Force Base [NR]
Built: 1926

This Art Deco building of stucco-clad cement blocks is trimmed with glazed terracotta tiles and eagle motifs to symbolize flight. During the 1970s, the terminal

windows were sealed and covered with stucco. The building became part of the Peterson Air Force Base Historic District in 1991 and the Peterson Air and Space Museum in 1998. The museum foundation and the Air Force matched the SHF's $25,775 to remove the stucco covering the windows and transform the site into an airpark featuring such historic structures as the Broadmoor Hangar, City Hangar, the caretaker's house, and historic aircraft. Mary Elizabeth Ruwell, the museum director, says she hopes the new airpark will attract visitors, promote aerospace education, and preserve the aviation heritage of Colorado Springs.

CUTLER HALL, COLORADO COLLEGE
912 N. Cascade Ave. [NR]
Built: 1878; Peabody & Stearns, architects

Cutler Hall, the first building erected at Colorado College, was named for Henry Cutler, a major donor. Architectural plans came from the Boston firm of Peabody & Stearns, who also designed the original Antlers Hotel in downtown Colorado Springs. Cutler Hall is a striking Gothic Revival edifice of rough-cut Castle Rock rhyolite trimmed with Manitou sandstone. Using SHF grants totaling $399,844 and other funding, Colorado College has restored the weathered masonry, windows, porch, and distinctive bell tower that make Cutler Hall the symbol of Colorado's most prestigious private college.

EVERGREEN CHAPEL AT EVERGREEN CEMETERY
1005 S. Hancock Ave. NR
Built: Cemetery, 1871; chapel, 1906–1907, L. A. Pease, builder

C

Evergreen Cemetery's chapel was built following the burial of city founder General William Jackson Palmer. The chapel now provides for comfortable, all-weather services in a picturesque, 220-acre cemetery that is the final resting place of many Colorado Springs movers and shakers, including photographer Laura Gilpin, writer

Helen Hunt Jackson, and philanthropist and gold-mining tycoon Winfield Scott Stratton.

The Romanesque Revival chapel built of Turkey Creek sandstone is lit by sunlight streaming through the custom-made, stained-glass windows. The chapel also features a state-of-the-art casket lift and basement-level storage units that are designed to preserve bodies when the ground is frozen. City of Colorado Springs cemetery manager William "Will" DeBoer grew concerned about threats to the chapel from lack of maintenance, overgrown vegetation, and pests. He contacted the SHF, which matched cemetery funding with $134,975 to restore the roof, walls, and foundation of this exquisite chapel.

FIRST BAPTIST CHURCH / OLD COLORADO CITY
HISTORY CENTER
1 S. 24th St. SR
Built: 1890, Walter F. Douglas, architect

Colorado City pioneer Jane Root Quinby donated the land, and a local architect produced the plans for the First Baptist Church. A century later, the Old Colorado City Historical Society (OCCHS) converted the church into a local history center in the town's historic district. The OCCHS relied on $128,195 from the SHF and other contributors for an impressive restoration. Using old photographs, Chuck Murphy of Murphy Constructors and restoration architect Michael Collins worked to return the building to its original charm. "With a good roof and foundation," says Murphy, one "can fix anything in between!" Murphy Constructors installed a new roof, fixed the foundation, and rehabilitated the windows, trim, and stained glass. They also removed the false ceiling and restored the choir loft of this spacious history center and museum.

C

LOWELL ELEMENTARY SCHOOL
831 S. Nevada Ave. (SR)
Built: 1891, Theodore Boal and Charles H. Lee, architects;
  1902 addition

Named for poet James Russell Lowell, who died the year it was built, this Romanesque Revival school reflects the City of Colorado Springs' commitment to education and to stylish public buildings. The red-brick structure with red sandstone

Photo courtesy of Tom Noel

trim originally housed eight classrooms; a 1902 addition added eight more. After closing in 1982, the building succumbed to neglect, vandalism, water damage, and fire. Finally, $634,997 in grants from the SHF enabled the Colorado Springs Housing Authority to give the building a beautiful rehabilitation. Exterior work included restoration of the cornice, windows, and façade, including brick repairs. The roof was also repaired and the drainage system upgraded. Inside, plaster, fixtures, and wainscoting were restored and floors refinished. Following the successful restoration, the Housing Authority, along with several other organizations, moved its offices into the building.

PAULINE CHAPEL
2 Park Ave. [NR]
Built: 1919; Thomas MacLaren and Thompson D. Hetherington,
  architects

Prominent Colorado Springs benefactor Julie Penrose commissioned Thomas MacLaren to design a chapel as a "thanksgiving" for the safe release of her granddaughter Pauline, along with her daughter and son-in-law, from house arrest in Belgium during World War I. The chapel is a Mission Revival structure, featuring Spanish Baroque detailing and a large collection of 16th- and 17th-century religious artifacts. Consecrated in 1918, it was given parish status in 1925 when a similarly styled rectory and garage were added. Four years after Mrs. Penrose's death in 1955, a larger church was erected to serve the growing parish.

In 1999, St. Paul Catholic Parish formed a group to protect and restore the chapel. They matched SHF grants of $33,810 for interior and exterior restoration, including new lightning protection and removal of an unsuitable stucco sealant from the lower two feet of the building. Workers repaired the moisture-damaged stucco and refinished it with a breathable, mineral-based paint. Windows, main doors, and flooring were also repaired or replaced. One of Colorado's finest examples of the Mission Revival style, Pauline Chapel is open for Mass several days a week and by appointment for tours and special occasions.

SECOND (OLD) MIDLAND SCHOOL / OUR LADY OF THE ROCKIES SCHOOL
815 S. 25th St. [NR]
Built: 1902

C

This three-story building of red sandstone and brick reflects the height, massing, and Classical architecture typical of turn-of-the-century urban schools. Our Lady of the Rockies School received $28,387 in SHF grants to repair the structure for continued educational use. The historic metal roof received restoration and drainage improvements, while additional exterior repairs addressed basement-level windows and masonry.

TRIANON / THE COLORADO SPRINGS SCHOOL
21 Broadmoor Ave. [NR]
Built: 1906; Thomas MacLaren, architect

Charles and Virginia Baldwin came to Colorado Springs seeking the "climate cure" and commissioned this mansion, inspired by the Grand Trianon at Versailles. The Baldwins selected Stanford White of the celebrated New York firm of McKim, Mead & White to design the home, but White was murdered before construction could commence. The Baldwins then decided on MacLaren, a Colorado Springs architect, to finish the design. By 1907, the white-terracotta French Classical home embellished the affluent Broadmoor neighborhood. The Baldwins called it "Claremont" for its clear view of Pikes Peak, but others called it "Trianon" after its architectural ancestor.

Following Baldwin's death in 1949, his widow sold the home to Blevins Davis, who redecorated and restored the building. After a series of misadventures, including a plan to move it to Broomfield, the home became The Colorado Springs School in 1967. Using $213,875 in SHF grants, the school began a much-needed restoration in 2002, allowing it to continue bringing a taste of European elegance to the Rocky Mountain West.

Como

BOREAS PASS SECTION HOUSE
Summit of Boreas Pass Rd. [NR]
Built: 1882; Denver, South Park & Pacific Railroad, builder

Boreas, the frosty-bearded god of the north wind, blasted away just about anything erected atop this 11,482-foot-high pass. A stout, stone engine house with turntable inside, a post office, a two-room log telegraph office, a coal bin, and a 957-foot-long snowshed have all disappeared. Only the ruins of this five-room, two-story section house survived on this narrow-gauge railroad, which operated from 1882 until 1937. Park County, Summit County, the U.S. Forest Service, and the Park and Summit County Historical Societies received an $8,748 SHF grant to help restore this hewn-log building. It is now used as an overnight shelter for cross-country skiers and snowshoers in the winter and as an interpretive site during the rest of the year, complete with a boxcar and a kiosk made out of narrow-gauge rail equipment.

COMO ROUNDHOUSE
Off US 285 at Como [NR]
Built: 1881; Denver, South Park & Pacific Railroad, builder

Italian stonemasons working for the Denver, South Park & Pacific Railroad erected this six-stall, stone roundhouse. After the narrow-gauge line was scrapped

Photo courtesy of Tom Noel

in 1938, the roundhouse was used as a stable and for dredge-boat supply storage. The stone walls were fire-damaged and crumbling, with the chimneys falling through the roof, when Bill Kazel bought the roundhouse in 1984. Kazel matched $135,864 from the SHF to stabilize the fieldstone walls fronted with a tan sandstone also used for the buttresses, pilasters, and keystone arches. The windows and roof have been replaced to protect this much-loved relic, complete with a wrought-iron turntable. New owners Charles and Kathy Brantigan are working with Kazel to restore the roundhouse. "Our dream is to make it a museum," says Kathy. "In the meantime, new interpretive signs are up, and we hope people will enjoy this shrine to mountain railroading."

The nearby hotel (1896) is still open in the summertime, and the depot (1880s) also survives in the once-booming rail center, which immigrant railroad workers and miners named for the beautiful mountain resort town and lake located in the Italian Alps.

Conifer

PLEASANT PARK SCHOOL/GRANGE No. 156
22551 Pleasant Park Rd. (SR)
Built: 1894; Joe Huebner and Jess Ray, builders

C

In the 1860s, Harvey L. Corbin stopped in these foothills outside of Denver and supposedly commented, "This is a pleasant place to park," giving the place its name. Two decades later, settlers established the Pleasant Park Grange Hall and chose a woman, Clara M. Huebner, as their first grange master. The 56 charter members donated labor and helped raise the $750 needed to build this one-room schoolhouse and grange hall. After the elementary school moved to a new building in Aspen Park, the Grange purchased the building in 1956 for $10. In 1993, the Grangers launched a campaign to restore the schoolhouse by holding flea markets, pizza parties, chili dinners, and even a karaoke night. They raised $12,297 to add to the SHF's $35,703. Work included replacement of the roof and repairs to the foundation. Inside, floors, walls, and ceilings were restored, and the electrical system was brought up to code. The restored school, with its horse barn and two outdoor privies, now hosts barn dances, birthday parties, wedding receptions, and arts and humanities programs, making Pleasant Park pleasant again.

Craig

FIRST CHRISTIAN CHURCH / THE CENTER OF CRAIG
601 Yampa Ave. (SR)
Built: 1902

This church was born, as well as reborn, as a collaborative effort with land donated by Craig's first mayor and a bell contributed by a benefactor, after the community matched his funds. The original church, with its 12-by-6-inch sawn logs, is covered with clapboard siding, as are additions on the east and north. A quaint and solitary survivor of Craig's earliest years, this port for the town's first "sky pilot," as ministers were sometimes called on the frontier, has been reincarnated as a community and arts center. The SHF provided $145,789 to the City of Craig to restore the roof, walls, prominent dormers,

and distinctive shingled, octagonal bell tower. Northwest Community College, which is a major user of this city-owned center, along with the city and other interested parties, contributed an additional $345,000 to the restoration effort.

COLORADO STATE ARMORY / MUSEUM OF NORTHWEST COLORADO

C

590 Yampa Ave. NR
Built: 1921–1922; John J. Huddart, architect

After the armory moved to a new home in 1974, the old fortress was acquired by Moffat County, which owns and operates it as the Museum of Northwest Colorado.

The SHF contributed $54,500 in 1993 for a new roof, installation of heating and air conditioning, and gutter rehabilitation as part of a $124,000 restoration. Like most of Colorado's 19 other armories, Craig's is a variant of the standard armory plan created by Denver architect John J. Huddart. The two-story building, which sports twin towers with parapets, was constructed with wire-cut yellow brick and trimmed with red brick and terracotta. The main roof is vaulted with a bowstring truss. The largely intact interior now features a large exhibition space in the former drill hall overlooked by a balcony.

The museum houses a superb collection of firearms and ranching gear and an 11-by-16-foot painting of Craig in 1895.

Crawford

CRAWFORD SCHOOL / CRAWFORD TOWN HALL AND COMMUNITY CENTER

425 CO 92 (SR)
Built: 1913; E. C. Hill, builder

This imposing two-story, rough-cut sandstone building has a wooden three-story central bell tower over separate boys' and girls' entrances. The brown sandstone blocks were quarried locally from Smith Fork. As the only school in the area, it housed grades 1–12 until 1962 and grades 1–8 until 1981. The venerable building's location makes it the most prominent structure in Crawford, and since 1981 it has served as the town hall, community center, and library. The town provided a cash match to secure $50,675 in grants from the SHF for an exterior stabilization and restoration of the old school.

Drainage problems were addressed by grading the property so it sloped away from the building. Broken stonework was repaired, and repointing was done to spruce up this centerpiece of the community. Today, the town hall offices and children's library occupy the preserved school, and family trees of Crawford's longtime residents adorn the main hallway.

Photo courtesy of Tom Noel

Creede

RIO GRANDE DEPOT / CREEDE MUSEUM
201 Wall St. ⓈⓇ
Built: 1893; C. S. Thompson, architect

C

David Moffat, Jr., then president of the Denver & Rio Grande Railroad, claimed that this spur line to the silver bonanza city of Creede paid for itself within the first four months of operation. Built as a replacement for the town's original tent depot, this board-and-batten structure is a typical old-time depot with protruding telegrapher's bay. But one thing is not so typical about this building's design. What appears to be a second story, complete with gable roof and window, is actually just a decorative feature with no other practical use. There is no second floor at all.

The D&RG abandoned passenger service to Creede in 1932, but freight service continued until 1949. In 1961, ownership of the Creede depot was transferred to Mineral County for use as a local history museum. In 1984, the Creede Historical Society, Inc., took over the building. Fifteen years later, they received a grant from the SHF to assess its condition. The SHF has invested $136,544 in the restoration of this example of railroad corporate architecture. The original baggage room door has been restored, code-required emergency exiting has been added, site drainage has been improved, a new foundation and roof have been installed, chimneys have been reconstructed, and the depot has been painted using the D&RG's distinctive yellow and chocolate brown colors. Reconstruction of the trackside platforms, where many hellos and goodbyes were said, has helped inspire proposals that would revive rail service to Creede for tourism purposes. The depot continues to remind Creede's visitors of the glory days when silver was king and the railroad was the way to travel.

RIO GRANDE HOTEL
209 W. 2nd St. Ⓗ ⓈⓇ
Built: 1892

The discovery of silver in 1889 led to the founding of Creede. Just three years later, this two-story clapboard boarding house was built near the D&RG depot. One of the few wooden structures to survive Creede's devastating 1892 fire, it is notable for its spartan simplicity. Wooden buildings at high elevations suffer from the onslaught of harsh winters and exposure to intense ultraviolet light. As the exterior faded and crumbled, the decision was made to cover it completely with old lumber, probably salvaged from other deteriorating buildings. The once stylish Rio Grande looked more like a derelict

C

from an abandoned ghost town than the tidy hostelry it had been. The Creede Repertory Theatre, a well-respected local venue for the performing arts, used the building to house staff and workers. But it was hardly a source of pride. They appealed to the SHF for support in restoring and rehabilitating this aging landmark, to allow for its continued use as living and working space for visiting artists and theater company members, and as a venue for community meetings, lectures, and exhibits. The SHF provided $136,250 matched by the Repertory Theatre, building owner Mineral County, and other partners. A complete makeover inside and out included a new roof and foundation; substantial site work; removal of the inappropriate rough wood siding and installation of historically accurate siding; work on doors, windows, and chimneys; interior mechanical systems; restoration of wooden floors; and new paint and appropriate wallpaper. Reconstruction of the decorative veranda and second-story porch, which had been removed many years ago, provided a crowning touch.

Crested Butte

This once grimy coal-mining town has been reborn as one of Colorado's best-preserved and most fashionable resort towns. Founded in 1878, Crested Butte sits in a remote, magnificent mountain valley at 8,885 feet and is named for the most prominent of many nearby peaks. The Crested Butte National Historic District embraces most of the town, roughly bounded by Whiterock and Maroon Avenues between 1st and 8th Streets. New buildings within the district play on the traditional massing and materials of the historic structures. The town also established its own Board of Zoning and Architectural Review to preserve buildings and outbuildings. A preservation pacesetter, Crested Butte has restored its old Town Hall as an arts center and old stone school as the public library. The Town of Crested Butte was the recipient of the Colorado Historical Society's Stephen H. Hart Award in 2005 for its historic preservation activities over many years.

MIHELICH HARDWARE / CRESTED BUTTE MOUNTAIN HERITAGE MUSEUM
331 Elk Ave. NRD
Built: 1883; John McCooker, builder

This remnant of the old blue-collar coal town has a 1902 potbellied stove in a typical frame, false-fronted structure with a glass storefront that opened in 1883 as the town's first blacksmith shop. It became Crested Butte Hardware in 1911. Later, the town's first gas pumps were added to what became Tony Mihelich's Hardware and Conoco Service Station, which operated from 1940 to

1996. The Crested Butte Mountain Heritage Museum began rehabilitating the place with $200,445 from the SHF and $85,905 from the town, Gunnison County, and private donations. Crested Butte Museum director and curator Susan A. Medville notes, "We're establishing our local history museum and the Mountain Bike Hall of Fame. Like the hardware store and Tony's before us, we hope to become a town hub."

OLD ROCK SCHOOL / CRESTED BUTTE LIBRARY
507 Maroon Ave. NRD
Built: 1883

This two-story school composed of coursed, rough-faced stone has a square front bay centered between separate boys' and girls' entrances. The bay rises to a shingled mansard roof topped by an open bell tower with a weathervane. The schoolhouse is grouped on a cul-de-sac with the two-story, brick high school (1927) and the contemporary, frame middle school (1991). The Town of Crested Butte acquired the Old Rock School building from the school district in 1981 and was awarded an SHF grant of $33,600. An additional $272,848 was raised by the town, while the Colorado Department of Local Affairs, the Callaway Foundation, Gunnison County, the Crested Butte Rotary Club, the Crested Butte State Bank, and other sponsors also contributed to the school's rehabilitation as the town library.

SPRITZER RESIDENCE
200 Sopris Ave. NRD
Built: 1892

This wooden, one-story, false-front structure was originally a saloon that allegedly hosted the likes of Wyatt Earp, Butch Cassidy, and the Sundance Kid. It was converted into a private residence by Martin and Apolonia Spritzer in 1924. It became the home of the *Crested Butte Chronicle* in 1968, and Don and Linda Fletcher restored it as a bed-and-breakfast in 1992.

The Crested Butte Mountain Heritage Museum used a $100,000 SHF grant toward a $470,790 purchase price to acquire the house in 1995. Support also came from the Bacon, Boettcher, El Pomar, and Madigan Foundations, as well as contributions from the First National Summit Bank, Gunnison Bank of Crested Butte, Community Bank of Crested Butte, the Town of Crested Butte, and the Gunnison County Lodging Tax Panel. After restoration, the house was sold for use as a private residence, and the proceeds were used to purchase and renovate Tony Mihelich's Hardware for the new Crested Butte Mountain Heritage Museum.

UNION CONGREGATIONAL CHURCH
212 4th St. NRD
Built: 1882

Eastlake trim adorns this wood-frame Gothic Revival church. The square corner tower rises to an open cupola with a Gothic-arched cutout, elaborate brackets, and

Photo courtesy of Tom Noel

a balustrade. Horizontal clapboard siding contrasts with vertical trim boards punctuated by Gothic windows. Eaves have decorative molding and brackets, and the bargeboard on the front gable end has shamrock cutouts. The $65,830 exterior and structural restoration of the church was accomplished with the help of an SHF grant of $29,830 and private and church donations. One of Colorado's most handsome small-town churches, it still attracts an active congregation and hosts local meetings for Alcoholics Anonymous, Crested Butte Land Trust, Girl Scouts, Brownies, and the Wildflower Festival.

Crestone

CRESTONE SCHOOL/COMMUNITY BUILDING
242 N. Cottonwood St. NR
Built: 1880s

At its school and community meeting place, the Town of Crestone made do with an outhouse, but at the turn of the 21st century, the building finally received indoor plumbing as well as other updates. The new bathroom, housed in an old storage room off the kitchen, fits well in the floor plan, reports Crestone's former mayor Kizzen Laki. "We found $6,000 to fund the small stuff," Laki says. "But we sure needed the SHF expertise and their $7,838 grant for the major overhaul." This included stabilizing the foundation, installing a septic system and modern plumbing, and putting in ramps to provide access for the disabled. The town has also repainted the interior with original historic colors, repaired the windows, and added some landscaping. Although it has not been used as a school since 1949, the clapboard-over-board-and-batten structure hosts social events, wedding receptions, funerals, fire department fundraisers, and bazaars.

Cripple Creek_____

This National Historic Landmark District was once dubbed "The World's Greatest Gold Camp." The area produced more than $400 million after Bob Womack's 1890 discovery in Poverty Gulch. Millions more are still being mined every year at the Cripple Creek and Victor Gold Mining Company's Cresson Mine. Cripple Creek, one of Colorado's three designated gaming towns, also collects millions each year from those "donating" to local casinos.

The City of Cripple Creek's Historic Preservation Commission has awarded gaming tax grants to assist homeowners, businesses, and nonprofits in restoring their buildings. More than 60 residences and 10 commercial buildings have been thus funded, along with two churches, the Cripple Creek District Museum in the old Midland Railway station, and the Old Homestead, a once lavish bordello now reused as a museum. Along with preserving all the mining lore, Cripple Creek historian and preservation commissioner Jan MacKell notes, the commission has fought to preserve the brothel, which other towns might dismiss as unworthy, to commemorate the "brides of the multitude."

COLORADO TRADING AND TRANSFER BUILDING / CRIPPLE CREEK DISTRICT MUSEUM HERITAGE GALLERY
500–502 Bennett Ave. **NHLD**
Built: 1895; John H. Eisenhart, builder

The only downtown Cripple Creek frame building to survive the two great fires of 1896 was used by Albert E. Carlton as a transportation hub for his horse, mule, burro, and ox teams. Carlton dominated the hauling business, running wagons from the mines to the railroad depot next door. He used his profits to open the Golden Cycle Corporation and the Carlton Mill, the most active mine and mill, respectively, in the district from 1910 until the 1950s. With $50,000 from the SHF, the Trading and Transfer Building has been restored to house a photo gallery, gift shop, archives, and the offices of the Cripple Creek District Museum.

C

GOLD MINING STOCK EXCHANGE / ELKS LODGE No. 316
373–379 Bennett Ave. NHLD
Built: 1896; John J. Huddart and T. Robert Wieger, architects

Perhaps to reassure gold stock investors, this sturdy red-brick and sandstone Romanesque Revival exchange radiates wealth and stability. One of three Cripple Creek mining exchanges, it closed in 1903. In 1911, the Benevolent Protectorate

of the Elks Lodge No. 316 purchased it for $12,500. The Elks added dining rooms, bars, a ballroom, a third-story grand hall, and sleeping rooms. The Elks and the City of Cripple Creek matched the SHF's $145,775 to cover a total restoration bill of almost $250,000. Years of water draining against the alley wall slowly caused the foundation and brick wall to deteriorate. Shoring was put up to prevent a catastrophe and to allow for stabilization work to pro-

ceed. The brick exterior and its stone trim were repaired and repointed, a new roof installed, and windows repaired or replaced.

The boarded-up, long-neglected street-level storefronts were also restored and made functional and attractive to retailers. The interior work involved carefully removing the tin ceiling and numbering the pieces for exact replacement so that the beams and trusswork of the roof could be stabilized. Structural improvements to the front and rear façade and the storefronts were done with the goal of keeping the Elks in the building. Rehabilitation of the retail space, which quickly found tenants, provides income for the Elks' ongoing maintenance needs.

TELLER COUNTY COURTHOUSE
101–105 W. Bennett Ave. NHLD
Built: 1904; A. J. Smith, architect

Interior restoration has preserved the courthouse's hardwood floors, oak finishes, mahogany trim, marble counters, Venetian blinds, and gilt chandeliers. Fifty-three

windows were repaired, and new ramps and an elevator were added. Masonry was carefully restored around all of the windows, resulting in freshly pointed sills and brickwork. A $293,050 SHF investment, matched by $272,662 from the County, also covered roof replacement and exterior restoration to help keep this debonair courthouse the center of Teller County's political scene.

Photo courtesy of Tom Noel

Crowley

CROWLEY SCHOOL
301 Main St. (H) [NR]
Built: 1914

This red-brick school, designed in the Renaissance Revival vernacular style, features round-arched windows anchoring an ornate bell tower. Built for $8,000, it served children of many ethnicities, including Russian, German, Japanese, and Hispanic. Church services were held here from 1914 to 1918, and during the 1918 flu epidemic the building served as a makeshift hospital.

The school sat vacant for 15 years until a restoration was spearheaded by the Crowley County Heritage Society, which secured $113,018 in SHF grants, $10,690 from the State Lottery Conservation Trust Fund, $3,500 from the City of Crowley, and 5,000 hours of labor from Arkansas Valley Correctional Facility inmates. Exterior and interior restoration included ceiling, window, and door repairs; refurbishment of light fixtures; and woodwork restoration. Crowley's mayor, Norene Aydelotte, who attended school here, reports that the venerable school now serves as City Hall offices, a community center, and the Crowley historical museum.

Cumbres Pass

CUMBRES SECTION HOUSE
CO 17, 30 miles west of Antonito [NRD]
Built: 1881; Denver & Rio Grande Railroad, builder

The Cumbres Pass depot disappeared in the 1950s, but the section house survives. The structure, which housed work crews and tools in the old days, is now used to store tools and equipment and is also being rehabilitated as an interpretive center. The Cumbres & Toltec Scenic Railroad received a $30,075 SHF grant to repair the building's foundation, and Friends of the Cumbres & Toltec donated the labor to restore the clapboard section house as well as the nearby snowshed.

Del Norte

WINDSOR HOTEL
650 Columbia St. (SR)
Built: 1874; 1882 and 1888 additions

D

One of Colorado's oldest hotels, the 1874 Whitsitt House was consolidated with the adjacent 1882 Windsor Block and the 1888 Foote Block with a new stucco façade shared by all three structures. Combined SHF grants of $584,425 to the Windsor Restoration and Historical Association have brought back the exterior of this two-story complex, which showcases locally quarried rhyolite and one of the San Luis Valley's oldest examples of the Italianate style. The Windsor operated continuously from 1875 until the late 1970s, when it was abandoned. Deteriorated, left to suffer neglect and vandalism, the Windsor was scheduled for demolition in 1993. A last-minute purchase by a local benefactor (who later transferred ownership of the hotel to the Windsor Restoration and Historical Association) saved the building. An interior rehabilitation project of the original 1874 hotel's main floor will feature the historic wooden staircase and the original dining room and parlor. The project, with a total cost of more than $988,375, included a new roof and structural steel reinforcements of the 21,114-square-foot landmark, which will be protected by a perpetual façade easement. Once restoration of the public areas is complete, the Windsor Restoration group plans to house a living history museum in part of the building.

Delta

DELTA NATIONAL BANK/CITY HALL
360 Main St., northeast corner of 4th St. (SR)
Built: 1910; Merrill Hoyt, architect

This Beaux-Arts bank was the only one in Delta to survive the Great Depression of the 1930s. In 1962, the city acquired it and converted it into a jewel box of a City Hall. The Delta Historic Preservation Board garnered $85,065 from the SHF, and the City of Delta also contributed $29,428 to help restore the town's oldest bank building. The 1981 aluminum doors were replaced by a custom-made iron entrance. The beige brick, terracotta, and beige sandstone were all restored, along with the proud rooftop balustrade and flag. This project is one of several showcase restorations in downtown Delta, where the chamber of commerce also rehabilitated the seedy Last Chance Saloon (originally the Delta County Bank) in 1987 as an elegant visitor center.

EGYPTIAN THEATER
452 Main St. **H** **NR**
Built: 1928; Montana S. Fallis, architect

Colorado's only Egyptian Revival edifice is one of the few such theaters left in the country. Fascination with the 1920s excavation of King Tut's tomb inspired an architectural idiom that reached even small-town America. Fallis, the Denver architect who designed Denver's Mayan Theatre, gave Delta this specimen of Egyptomania. "Delta County Ranks First in Everything with the Most Modern Theater in the Best Town in Colorado," crowed the *Delta County Independent*, which described the Egyptian as "verily a treasure chest with jewel lights that gleam and glow all colors of the rainbow."

This theater is also famous for inaugurating Bank Night during the Great Depression. This was an effort to boost dwindling theater attendance by giving away cash prizes to audience members. Bank Night became a popular promotion nationwide after a very successful premier at the Egyptian Theater.

By the 1980s, the Egyptian was fading. The tattered curtains and organ had been removed, as had columns supporting the proscenium arch over the stage. The leather upholstery was cracked and frayed. The Egyptian murals with their hieroglyphics had grown dirty and scarred and been covered with paint and wallpaper. By the early 1990s, demolition seemed imminent, but then local leaders, theater buffs, and preservationists stepped in.

The City of Delta, property owner Barbara Jeanne Dewsnup, and other partners obtained an SHF grant of $165,698 toward a $220,000 restoration. Conservators painstakingly removed paint and wallpaper to restore the lost murals. They re-created 16 carved busts of pharaohs and lotus-flower columns, bringing the interior back to its opening-night glory. On the outside, the Egyptian was stabilized and then given a first-rate restoration. Using original drawings, artisans re-created the ornate Egyptian Deco façade, complete with its winged sun frieze.

FIRST METHODIST CHURCH OF DELTA
199 E. 5th St., northwest corner of Meeker St. [NR]
Built: 1910, Samuel A. Bullard, architect; J. A. Johnson, builder

Gothic arches and parapets prevail on this Tudor Revival, beige-brick church, with a foundation, capstone, lintel, and portal trim of Windgate sandstone from nearby Escalante Canyon. A pyramidal roof with parapeted gables rises into crenellated towers at the streetside corners. The 1891 cornerstone is from an earlier church on the site. The Springfield, Illinois, architect Samuel Bullard designed a square sanctuary that is an example of the Akron Plan, popular during this time. On November 6, 1993, a devastating fire gutted the church, destroying the Hinners 18-rank organ and the curved oak pews.

"Up from the Ashes" became the slogan of the restoration committee headed by Robert Floyd Harding. Although the city code in Delta states that if more than half a building is destroyed by fire, the remainder has to be razed, the community rallied to save this beloved religious icon. They used $175,100 from the SHF, a match from the congregation of $125,000, and a $400,000 endowment to restore the building inside and out. The stained glass from Midland Glass Company of Omaha, Nebraska and the Conrad Schmitt Studios was restored by Schmitt Studios, which also assisted in restoring the Egyptian Theater.

Denver _____

This boomtown, founded with an 1858 gold strike, built fast and recklessly. Jerome Smiley, in his 1901 History of Denver, *wrote that key downtown sites had been serially occupied by three or four different buildings. A single corner, within a short span of 43 years, might have originally housed a log cabin, replaced by a two-story residence, then*

by a three- to four-story commercial building, then by a six- to eight-story masonry edifice.

Among those distressed by the disappearance of frontier structures was Mrs. Margaret Tobin "Unsinkable Molly" Brown. She took action, becoming Colorado's first notable preservationist in 1927 by saving the cottage of poet-journalist Eugene Field from demolition. Molly led the crusade to move Field's clapboard home from 315 West Colfax Avenue to 715 South Franklin Street in Washington Park, where it was first made a branch of the Denver Public Library. It is now home to The Park People, a nonprofit organization dedicated to preserving and enhancing public parks.

During the 1960s and 1970s, much of the old core city was demolished by the Denver Urban Renewal Authority. Citizens alarmed by wholesale bulldozing of entire city blocks persuaded the mayor and city council to form the Denver Landmark Preservation Commission in 1967 to identify and recommend structures for landmark

Photo courtesy of Roger Whitacre

designation. More than 325 individual landmarks (LL) and 45 historic districts (LLD) have been set aside as historical and architectural treasures. Individual landmarks and any buildings within a historic district are eligible to apply for State Historical Fund grants, which have helped to restore more than 140 Denver sites.

Denver's use of SHF monies, as well as its tight ordinance against demolishing or desecrating landmarks, has made the Mile High City a national pacesetter for preservation. By landmarking much of the core city, Denver has curbed the typical American pattern of urban blight and suburban flight. Denver's rejuvenated downtown has helped make it one of the nation's few urban cores that is gaining population, jumping from 467,610 in 1990 to 554,636 in 2000.

D

Central Denver *(between 6th Ave., Lincoln St., 20th St., and the South Platte River)*

BARTH HOTEL
1514 17th St. [LL] [NR]
Built: 1882; Frederick Carl
Eberley, architect

The Barth Hotel, built as the Union Wholesale Liquor Warehouse, became the Union Hotel in 1890 and the Elk Hotel in 1906. In 1931, after the owner died, his son, M. Allen Barth, renamed it the Barth Hotel. Barth lost the property in the Great Depression, when this once stately edifice began a 50-year downward spiral.

In the early 1980s, Senior Housing Options, a nonprofit assisted-living organization, bought and rehabilitated the four-story hotel, ending its long decline. Senior Housing Options received $872,987 in SHF funds, as well as $200,000

from the City of Denver, to replace the roof, repair windows, remove lead-based paint, and repoint the exterior brickwork and stone trim. SHF grants also helped Senior Housing Options to comply with code-required upgrades costing more than $1.2 million. The hotel now provides 62 subsidized units for low-income people with disabilities and the elderly in what has become one of the city's wealthiest neighborhoods, typified by million-dollar lofts. Teri Whelan, Senior Housing Options' executive director, says the restoration will help care for people whose median income is $7,700 a year or lower. These residents now call this refreshed jewel of the LoDo Historic District their home.

THE BOSTON BUILDING / KISTLER BUILDING / BOSTON LOFTS
828 17th St. [LL] [NR]
Built: 1890; Andrews, Jacques & Rantoul, architects

D

Originally trimmed in much more elaborate Manitou red sandstone, the Boston Building was shaved of much of its ornament after chunks of the stone began bombarding pedestrians below. This distinctive Richardsonian Romanesque office building was designed by the same Boston architectural firm that created the Equitable Building a block up 17th Street. In 1916, the Boston Building got a new neighbor, the Kistler Building. This late Gothic Revival edifice housed Kistler Kwill, one of Colorado's leading stationery retailers, until 1966. The handiwork of Denver architect Harry W. J. Edbrooke, the Kistler Building was overshadowed by its taller, more elegant neighbor.

By the early 1990s, both buildings had become run-down and were mostly vacant. In 1996, Grandhaven LLC, owner of both properties, and the Denver Urban Renewal Authority (DURA) used a $100,000 SHF grant to spur a $17.8 million restoration of the two buildings as the Boston Lofts.

Grant funds went for restoration and replacement of windows, façade repairs, repair and refinishing of ornamental stairs and terrazzo floors, and restoration of the lobby and retail storefronts. DURA, which brokered the deal, is delighted, reports Marianne LeClair, who adds, "The developers beautifully renovated this vacant office space as 130 units of market and below-market housing."

BROWN PALACE HOTEL
17th St., Broadway, and Tremont Place [LL] [NR]
Built: 1889–1892; Frank E. Edbrooke, architect

Amazingly, the Brown Palace has been open every single day since its 1892 completion and has never been eclipsed as Denver's grand hotel. When built for $2 million, it was the most expensive, largest, and tallest building in town. *Scientific American* magazine featured the Brown as its cover story, celebrating it as one of America's first fireproof buildings. Designed by Denver's premier architect to suit an awkward triangular site, its rooms are wrapped around an enormous nine-story atrium, a prototype for 20th-century hotels such as John Portman's Hyatts. The Brown has hosted nearly every U.S. president since Theodore Roosevelt and showcases Eisenhower, Reagan, and Roosevelt Suites. The Ship Tavern, one of Denver's most notable saloons, features a "crow's nest" and other nautical fantasies that bring a cheery seaport to landlocked Colorado. The hotel matched a $5,000 SHF grant to repair the exterior Arizona red-sandstone façade and replace decaying window frames. Inspired and guided by SHF funding and expertise, the hotel has since continued restoration with its own funds.

BUERGER BROTHERS BUILDING AND DENVER FIRE CLAY BUILDING
1732–1740 and 1742 Champa St. **H** NR
Built: 1929; Montana S. Fallis, architect

Buerger Brothers Supply Company built this office and warehouse as the head-quarters of what would become the largest barbershop and beauty salon supplier in the Rocky Mountain region. In 1937, the company acquired the neighboring Denver Fire Clay Building and, in a major remodeling, connected the two buildings behind a new façade that matched the Art Deco front on its original building. In the 1990s, developer David Cohen converted the two buildings into 31 rental lofts, of which seven are reserved for low-income residents. Using $466,845 in matching funds, tax-exempt bonds issued by the City of Denver, a loan from Denver's Community Development Agency, and $196,760 from the SHF, Cohen restored these Art Deco dazzlers. Behind their sparkling white terracotta

façade, interior work included cross-bracing the front and rear masonry walls for stability and converting the basement into a parking garage.

Photo courtesy of Tom Noel

D

BYERS-EVANS HOUSE MUSEUM
1310 Bannock St. LL NR
Built: 1883, Halleck & Howard, contractors; 1902, 1905, 1909, and 1911 additions

William N. Byers, founder and publisher of the *Rocky Mountain News*, built this house for himself and his family. He sold it in 1889 to William G. Evans, son of his friend, territorial governor John Evans. Upon the death of William Evans' daughter Margaret Evans Davis in 1981, the family donated the house and grounds to the Colorado Historical Society for museum use.

This house celebrates early Colorado's great builder, John Evans, and great booster, William Byers, and also the often forgotten Byers-Evans women. Elizabeth Byers and Margaret Gray Evans devoted much of their time to establishing, running, and raising money for charities. While their husbands lured any and all to Colorado with golden promises, their wives worried about those who did not strike it rich, or even have enough to eat. They organized the first known charitable institution in Colorado, the Ladies' Relief Society, which was also Colorado's first women's organization. The Old Ladies Home, the Denver Children's Home, the Young Women's Christian Association, and the United Way are also part of these women's legacies.

Anne Evans, the youngest daughter of John and Margaret, never married but was wedded to advancing art, culture, and civic causes. She helped establish the Central City Opera House Association, the Denver Public Library, and the Denver Art Museum, now located just behind her house. Anne especially championed

Indians and Indian culture, establishing the Denver Art Museum's Native Arts Department, which claims to be the first such museum department in the country.

This charming two-story Italianate has been restored with the help of $92,340 in SHF funding and more than $26,000 in matching funds. Renovations included replacement, repair, and restoration work on the roof, masonry, and skylights; new paint; and upgrades to the fire, security, and lighting systems. "We've even restored our Victorian gardens," reports former museum administrator Vicki Morton. "We

are a wonderful place to discover Denver's colorful past. Thank goodness for the SHF, which enabled us to get back to our 1912–1924 appearance."

One of Colorado's most faithfully restored Victorian interiors contains much Evans family memorabilia. The small museum features a superb video overview, gift shop, and guided tours, as well as children's and special events year-round.

Photo courtesy of Tom Noel

DANIELS & FISHER TOWER
1101 16th St. at Arapahoe St. [LL] [NR]
Built: 1911; Frederick J. Sterner and George H. Williamson, architects

Downtown Denver's most distinctive landmark became the symbol for Colorado preservation during a long struggle to keep the Denver Urban Renewal Authority from tearing it down in the 1980s. The Colorado Historical Society went to court and narrowly saved the tower—but not the attached department store—from the wrecking ball.

The Mile High City's tallest edifice for decades, this 372-foot tower was the fantasy of William Cooke Daniels, the only son of a wealthy Denver storekeeper. Young Daniels, interested in history and art, traveled the world but seemed most fascinated with a bell tower in the Piazza San Marco in Venice.

Returning to Denver and the family business, William devoted himself to building a lavish new store, with a corner bell tower inspired by the campanile he saw adorning the Basilica in the Piazza San Marco. Until the 1960s eruption of taller highrises, the D&F Tower dominated downtown.

Residents and tourists alike took the elevator to the 20th-floor observation deck for a grand view of the Mile High City and its Rocky Mountain backdrop. The tower wore a gigantic American flag for July Fourth and a huge electric lightbulb Santa Claus every December. In 1928, Colorado's first airplane beacon—a $2,000 revolving lamp visible 75 miles away—was installed atop the tower. Couples were married on the tower observation deck. Less happily, the deck has also been used for suicide jumps.

The Daniels and Fisher Tower Preservation Foundation, Inc., oversaw the $2 million restoration with the help of $551,188 from the SHF and additional support from the Bonfils-Stanton and Taurus Foundations. Newly installed night lighting spotlights the tower, with its restored rooftop flag and observation deck. The terracotta entry façades include huge, replicated carriage lanterns framing bronze revolving doors salvaged from a Ford Motor Company administration building in Dearborn, Michigan, a reasonable facsimile of the lost original. The exquisitely restored lobby sparkles with refurbished Carrara marble wainscoting, stenciling, Neoclassical plaster trim, a coffered ceiling, and copies of the original architectural drawings. The project included restoration and electrification of the original Seth Thomas clock and bell, along with regilding the dome with gold leaf. The ultimate restoration surprise came while workers restoring one wall found an urn hidden in the tower. It contained the ashes of the romantic who turned a department store into a Venetian dream.

DENVER CHAMBER OF COMMERCE / CHAMBER LOFTS
1726–1742 Champa St. NR
Built: 1909–1910; Willis A. Marean and Albert J. Norton, architects

This terracotta tribute to Beaux-Arts Neoclassicism housed the Denver Chamber of Commerce from 1910 until 1950. Chamber members working within these walls helped make Denver the business hub of the Rocky Mountain states. The six-story, steel-frame building is faced with terracotta and granite illuminated by hundreds of lightbulbs that outline the ornate façade. It reflects Denver's City Beautiful and City of Lights era of the early 1900s, both championed by the Chamber to highlight downtown.

Even before the Chamber moved out in the 1950s, the structure had been damaged by water, neglect, and façade modernizations begun in the 1930s. A 1950s-era enameled steel panel façade was screwed into cladding after remodelers chiseled away projecting granite and terracotta elements to accommodate the flush panels. In order to restore the Chamber building to its former glory, developer David Cohen worked with Historic Denver, Inc., to replace damaged or missing items on the façade. With the help of the original architectural drawings and historical photographs, the terracotta tiles were remolded and replaced, including the destroyed entry crest of the Chamber of Commerce.

Kathleen Brooker, president of Historic Denver, Inc., says, "one of Denver's best-lit terracotta Art Deco gems is restored and back in the spotlight." Chamber Apartments, L.P., completed this $7.8 million project, with the SHF contributing

$285,000 toward the façade restoration. Inside, the building is now a 39-unit loft apartment complex, including 16 units of affordable housing. Residents relish the restoration of the historic domed metal roofs and skylights, and the return of the original lobby with its marble wainscoting and terrazzo floors.

DENVER DRY GOODS BUILDING
California St. from 16th St. to 15th St. **H** **NR**
Built: 1888 and 1898 addition, Frank E. Edbrooke, architect;
   1906 and 1924 additions

This three-story building once housed the McNamara Dry Goods Company, which reorganized in 1894 as the Denver Dry Goods Company. Between 1888 and 1924, the company expanded to fill the 1600 block of California Street, with Frank Edbrooke himself designing the 1898 addition. Open until the 1980s, the store offered a wide range of merchandise and a popular tearoom. In 1987, the May Company bought the building to demolish it.

The following year, the Denver Urban Renewal Authority (DURA) acquired the building in order to preserve it and convert it to mixed-use. In 1992, DURA obtained a $60,000 SHF grant to help with the $934,000 renovation. The remake stripped white paint from the façade and repointed the red-brick, stone trim, and roof parapets, and repainted the metal cornice. This reborn landmark now houses retail, offices, low- to moderate-income rental housing, and a deluxe loft in what was once the top-floor tearoom and terrace.

DENVER MUNICIPAL AUDITORIUM / QUIGG NEWTON DENVER MUNICIPAL AUDITORIUM
14th St. and Curtis St. **LL** **NR**
Built: 1908, Robert W. Willison, architect; 1934, 1940, 1956, 1970s,
   1994, and 2005 additions

As the culmination of his City Beautiful program to create public parks, parkways, and buildings, Mayor Robert W. Speer erected this $400,000 municipal auditorium. It attracted Denver's only national political convention to date, the 1908 Democratic Party gathering that nominated William Jennings Bryan for president. At the time of its completion, this Renaissance Revival–style buff-brick building was second in size only to New York City's Madison Square Garden. Pilasters rose from the dressed stone foundations and ran the full three stories of the building. The corners each featured a tower topped by a gilded cupola, with a fifth cupola in the middle of the roof. The main entrance boasted a pair of stone lions that held the corners of the entryway canopy in their teeth.

Inside the building, movable walls allowed the facility to be converted from a 12,000-seat convention hall into a 3,341-seat theater. A proscenium arch constructed in three pieces could be pulled up into a pocket in the ceiling. The building also had its own steam heating system and electrical generator, as well as connections to the public power company. This helped illuminate some 12,000 lightbulbs that outlined the entire edifice.

The first major renovation came in 1934 when the Civil Works Administration made $50,000 in improvements to the ventilation, electrical, and public-address systems. In 1940, another $150,000 added meeting rooms for conventions and updated seating. During the 1950s, Mayor Quigg Newton ordered the damaged cupolas removed. Exterior windows were also bricked up, and extensive additions carried the building to 13th Street. During the 1970s, the buildings comprising the Denver Performing Arts Complex were constructed on the city blocks to the west and north, expanding the complex to Arapahoe Street and Speer Boulevard. In 1994, the Temple Hoyne Buell Theater replaced what had been part of the 1950s arena addition.

In 2002, Denver voters approved $25 million toward a $100 million project to restore the auditorium to its former glory on the exterior but install a completely new, state-of-the-art Ellie Caulkins Opera House inside it. This $100 million deal was expedited by $716,712 from the SHF for the exterior restoration, $7 million from Ellie Caulkins, and $2 million from the Chambers Family Foundation for the 2,280-seat Ellie Caulkins Opera House. To honor the mayor, who had greatly expanded the building, it was renamed the Quigg Newton Denver Municipal Auditorium.

The SHF-assisted restoration, according to Chris Wineman, an architect for Semple Brown Design involved removing the 1950s-era entrance on 14th Street. The resulting hole was replaced in 2004 with new brick, mortar, and precast concrete plinths exactly matching the original in type, size, color, tooling, surface finish, and texture. All around the exterior, stone trim and the blond brickwork were repaired or replaced with matching materials. Restoration undid various alterations made since the auditorium's 1908 opening, replacing newer brass-framed windows and the 1991 galleria entrance with the original wooden frames and ornate, fanlighted door and windows. "Someday maybe we will also be able to reinstall the lost rooftop cupolas with their flags and electric lightbulbs," Denver Director of Theatres and Arenas Jack Finlaw muses. "Meanwhile we are grateful to the Colorado Historical Society's State Historical Fund for enabling us to restore the auditorium façade to its original beauty. This was the first municipal auditorium in the country and is something to celebrate and preserve."

Because of the widespread support and interest in this project, temporary viewing windows were placed along the Curtis Street wall in the galleria to accommodate sidewalk superintendents. The reborn auditorium includes a restored Pikes Peak granite cornerstone bearing the chiseled, gilded inscription "September 18, 1907—The People of Denver by Popular Vote Committed the Erection of this Building." A century later, equally proud Denverites can applaud their reborn auditorium. This grand old monument for public gatherings, conventions, rallies, music, dance, ballet, theater, opera, and children's programs is once again Denver's pride and joy.

D

DENVER PRESS CLUB
1330 Glenarm Pl. [LL]
Built: 1925; Merrill H. Hoyt and Burnham F. Hoyt, architects

Although the Denver Press Club was founded in 1884, this building was its first exclusive home. The red-brick clubhouse is trimmed in white terracotta, with quoins and window surrounds that hint at the Collegiate Gothic style. Ghosts of prominent journalists haunt the first-floor bar and dining room, basement pool hall, and second-story meeting room. Some of these hallowed writers were immortalized by Herndon Davis in his basement mural depicting a composite newsroom with twenty-two portraits of leading journalists, including Eugene Field, Eugene Fowler, Lee Casey, Jack Foster, and Damon Runyon.

Six decades of journalists had left a nicotine varnish that muted the mural, and water seepage had damaged the tile ceiling. Assistance came with $19,360 in grants from the SHF and a $4,646 Press Club match, with more funding from the *Denver Post* and *Rocky Mountain News*, to assess the building, restore the mural and the interior, and rehabilitate the roof and windows of a historic club, now open to the general public as a bar, restaurant, and shrine of memorable journalists.

DENVER TRAMWAY POWERHOUSE /
RECREATIONAL EQUIPMENT, INC.
1416 Platte St. [LL] [NR]
Built: 1901, Stearns Rogers Engineering; 1911 addition

The Denver Tramway Company Powerhouse, a Romanesque Revival landmark, was the sole source of electricity for the Denver Tramway Company (DTC) system. Its setting on the South Platte River provided water for cooling the turbines and a convenient place to dump ash from the boilers. The plant's generating capacity was increased in 1907, 1911, and

Photo courtesy of Tom Noel

1924, paralleling the growth of the DTC system, which expanded from 155 miles of track in 1903 to 253 miles of track by the 1940s, when Denver had the largest urban rail system between Chicago and California.

After Denver decided to discontinue the use of electric streetcars in 1950, the powerhouse became the Forney Transportation Museum, jammed with antique vehicles ranging from bicycles to a "Big Boy," the Union Pacific's largest steam locomotive. In 2000, the handsome red-brick powerhouse became

the flagship Colorado store of Recreational Equipment, Inc. (REI). Brickwork received extensive repointing and stabilization. Restoration included redoing or removing many detrimental, stopgap repairs and additions done over the years. The most visible part of the project involved restoring the large exterior windows that had been eliminated or modified. To restore the building's original sense of proportion and rhythm, windows were returned to their original size and placement. For the exterior restoration, SHF granted $412,400 to the Denver Urban Renewal Authority.

D

"Everybody had to have a lot of faith," says REI vice president Jerry Chevassus. "Instead of new plans, we started working with historical photos. If we had razed the building, we would have saved money, but we'd have lost 100 years of history and the story this structure tells." Now a showcase at the confluence of the South Platte River and Cherry Creek—the cradle of the city—this structure adjoins the South Platte River Greenway and Confluence Park. The restoration project won the National Trust for Historic Preservation's National Honor Award in 2001.

DENVER TRAMWAY COMPANY TOWER / HOTEL TEATRO
1100 14th St. at Arapahoe St. LL NR
Built: 1912; William E. Fisher and
    Arthur A. Fisher, architects

William G. Evans, son of territorial governor John Evans, built these corporate offices of the Denver Tramway Company on the site of his father's pioneer home. Fisher and Fisher designed this brick tower with Renaissance Revival–inspired terracotta trim, grand entry arches, brass entry lamps, and a rooftop frieze with the tramway's monogram. An equally elegant interior features pink Tennessee marble floors, a base of green Vermont marble, white Arizona marble wainscoting, and bronze fixtures.

In 1950, Denver abandoned its trolley system, and in 1957 the eight-story building became part of the University of Colorado's Denver campus. After CU Denver moved out, the building was purchased by a group of developers who undertook a $20 million rehabilitation. According to Jeff Selby, the managing member of Tramway Hotel, LLC, they replaced plumbing, mechanical, and electrical systems. On the outside, with the aid of $250,000 from the SHF, the restoration, designed by David Owen Tryba Architects, cleaned up the brick, frieze, and cornice, leaving the façade glistening like new. A discrete, set-back ninth floor was added to what is now one of Denver's finest small hotels.

FIRE STATION No. 1 / DENVER FIREFIGHTERS MUSEUM
1326 Tremont Pl. LL NR
Built: 1909; Glen W. Huntington & Co., architects

This two-story Renaissance Revival building originally housed the horses and fire wagons of Denver's Engine Company No. 1. It was then remodeled in 1934 to house fire trucks and remained in service until 1974, when it became the Denver Fire-fighters Museum. Visitors can inspect vintage fire trucks and other equipment, as well as the dormitories and fire pole. This museum has used $108,880 in SHF grants and over $25,000 in matching and in-kind funds to restore the exterior, improve lighting, repair leaks, install a new boiler and security system, and restore the second floor.

FIRST NATIONAL BANK / AMERICAN NATIONAL BANK / MAGNOLIA HOTEL
818 17th St. at Stout St. H LL NR
Built: 1911; Harry W. J. Edbrooke, architect

The First National Bank helped transform 17th Street into the "Wall Street of the Rockies." Its 13 floors made it Denver's first building with more than 10 stories. Occupied by the First National Bank from 1911 to 1958, the building was remodeled in 1960 and housed the American National Bank until 1981. In 1995, the Holtze brothers restored the exterior and converted the interior into a luxury hotel. They removed a "modernizing" cement screen on exterior elevations and repaired and restored the original façade, including its missing grand cornice, in a prize-winning project.

A $100,000 SHF grant helped pay for repairs to the building façades, replacement of the lost cornice and terracotta detail, re-creation of the historic windows, and repainting of the building in a historic color scheme selected by paint expert James Martin. According to James Stratis, SHF preservation projects manager, the restoration was "a terrific job, which has added greatly to Denver's principal commercial street."

GUARANTY BANK / BANK LOFTS
817 17th St. at Stout St. [LL] [NR]
Built: 1921; William E. Fisher and Arthur A. Fisher, architects

Denver entrepreneur John A. Ferguson constructed this nine-story edifice to replace the earlier three-story Century Building. The Chicago-style commercial building opened as the U.S. National Bank and later became the Guaranty Bank and Trust Company.

D

The Denver Urban Renewal Authority and owner National Properties, encouraged by a $100,000 SHF grant, spent $11.1 million to rehabilitate the bank and offices into 118 low- and moderate-income rental lofts. The street level hosts retail shops and a restaurant. Workers cleaned and repaired the exterior walls and storefront and restored and reconstructed the first-floor elevator lobby with its plaster groin-vaulted ceiling, pendant light fixtures, marble floor, pilasters, and cornices. In the banking hall, they restored the ornamental plaster, ceiling, ceramic tile, and marble mosaic floor, and reconstructed missing columns, a stair rail, and marble wainscoting.

THE HOUSE OF MIRRORS
1946 Market St. [LLD]
Built: 1889

Once the most glamorous sex palace of the Rockies, the House of Mirrors has returned to its original luster and reopened as a restaurant, bar, and shrine to shady ladies. Denver madam Jennie Rogers built this splendiferous bordello. The pedimented stone façade was capped by her bust, with other stone ornaments carved into phallic symbols, gargoyles, and likenesses of the men she supposedly black-mailed to pay for this bagnio. Architect William Quayle was in Denver at this time, but his biographer, Karna Webster, could not verify that he designed this house of shame.

Rival madam Mattie Silks bought the building in 1911 and installed her name in the tile entry. In 1919, it became the Tri-State Buddhist Church, serving Colorado, Wyoming, and Utah. When the Japanese community moved to their new Buddhist Temple at 1947 Lawrence Street in 1948, Royal Judd converted the building into a warehouse, replacing the elegant entry with a loading-dock door. The beautiful walnut banister staircase was ripped out and replaced by a conveyor belt. The stone façade was stripped away and stuccoed over, and the interior bird's-eye maple and mirrors were removed.

D

New owners spent more than $650,000 to bring the house back to its original glamour with the help of the SHF's $18,600 to reconstruct the missing façade and replicate the stone figures on the edifice. Once the stucco was removed, the original stone was found intact, minus its elaborate detailing. SHF funding helped restore the cornice and parapet. Photographs and detailed research enabled Denver mason Chris Wolfe to replicate the faces and the likeness of Jennie Rogers on one of LoDo's most fascinating and hospitable reborn landmarks.

HOVER BUILDING
1390 Lawrence St. LL NR
Built: 1901; Robert S. Roeschlaub, architect

Denver's first licensed architect created this building for the W. A. Hover whole-sale drug supply company. This edifice was one of Roeschlaub's last designs and is one of only two of his commercial buildings left in Denver. Conceived as a simple but elegant house of business, it exemplifies early 20th-century commercial architecture.

After the departure of the W. A. Hover Company, later owners remodeled it with drop ceilings, interior walls, and mezzanines; removed and boarded up the 14th Street storefront; painted the rear façade; and added a stair and elevator core with a modern vertical aluminum frame. From the 1960s to the 1980s, the building contained the bookstore, library, and School of Planning and Architecture for the University of Colorado at Denver.

After CU Denver's departure, the building stood vacant for eight years. Design Workshops and DHM, Inc., two of Denver's leading landscape-architecture firms, then purchased the building and obtained a $100,000 SHF grant. They used this money, along with $1,062,983 in matching funds and $9,920 in in-kind payments, to undo decades of "improvement," to restore the brick façade with its limestone trim and to replicate the windows, doors, and cornice. Inside, the rehabilitation exposed historic steel columns and wooden beams.

IDEAL BUILDING
821 17th St. LL NR
Built: 1907, Montana S. Fallis and John Stein, architects; 1927 addition, William E. Fisher and Arthur A. Fisher, architects

German-born Charles Boettcher, who founded the Ideal Cement Company, along with Great Western Sugar and many other businesses, constructed this as his own office and Ideal's national headquarters. Boettcher ballyhooed the eight-story building as Colorado's first reinforced-concrete, fireproof structure. To dramatize that point, he had the wooden forms burned off after the concrete set. Crowds gathered to watch the new building burn down—but it did not, a marvel duly celebrated in the local press. Henceforth, Boettcher suggested, builders would do well to use his fireproof Ideal Cement.

Some consider this building the most notable design of the Denver firm Fallis and Stein. In 1928, the building returned to the cutting edge when its new owner, Denver National Bank, commissioned brothers William E. and Arthur A. Fisher to further beautify the structure with sculpture reflecting Western themes. The remodeling added rich detailing and ornamentation to the exterior while completely changing the interior. The bank hired artists to decorate the public spaces with bronze, stone, terrazzo, murals, and friezes. A bronze entry and elevator features American Indian motifs. Two huge buffalo heads of travertine marble guard the main entry.

In 1997, Kesef, LLC, with support from Historic Denver, Inc., bought the building and used a $200,000 SHF grant and $254,000 of its own funds to restore many of these details. Once again this is an ideal building, with restored, decoratively painted ceilings, reopened original entrances, restored bronze doors, and Indian motifs. The travertine sheathing the concrete walls of the first two stories has been cleaned and repaired, as has the terracotta trim. In the basement restaurant, The Broker, the original bank vault is also restored and used as a small private dining room. In recent years the building made history again as the home of the Colorado Women's Bank, then as the Colorado Business Bank.

JOSLIN DRY GOODS / MARRIOTT HOTEL
934 16th St. NR
Built: 1887, Frank E. Edbrooke, architect; 1927 addition

This red-brick, stone-trimmed commercial block was constructed for one of Colorado's leading dry-goods dealers. Originally built with four floors, it received a fifth in 1927. A modern exterior was added during the 1960s.

In 1998, the owners of the building obtained a $35,500 SHF grant, along with $852,035 from the Denver Urban Renewal Authority and other sources, to revive the original edifice. This involved reconstructing the original cornice and 16th Street main-entrance canopy and pediment. The renovated building became the home of a Courtyard by Marriott Hotel and the Rialto Café.

A. T. LEWIS BUILDING / RIO GRANDE LOFTS
800–816 16th St. [LL] [NR]
Built: 1891, Robert S. Roeschlaub, architect; 1917 addition,
    Harry W. J. Edbrooke, architect

D

This structure for decades housed a succession of dry-goods and department stores between 1891 and 1970, including Salomon's Bazaar (1891–1895), A. T. Lewis and Son (1896–1936), and the W. T. Grant Company (1940–1970). By the 1990s, the building had become functionally obsolete, dilapidated, and 75 percent vacant. In 1995, it underwent a $4 million restoration and rehabilitation with the help of $299,500 from the SHF. Work included replacing a lost historic cornice, repairing masonry, and rejuvenating the original façade. Inside, the old store became 47 rental housing units, called the Rio Grande Lofts. According to Marianne LeClair of Denver Urban Renewal Authority, which sponsored the project, "The building was in pretty bad shape and had no future as offices but was ideal for moderate-income housing."

GOLDA MEIR HOUSE
1146 9th St., Ninth Street Historic Park [LL]
Built: 1911

Golda Meir (1898–1978), Israel's first female prime minister, lived in this single-story, flat-roofed duplex for several years while a student at North High School. Meir came to Denver to stay with her older sister in 1913 after running away from her family in Milwaukee to pursue her dream of becoming a teacher. While in Denver, Golda Meir came in contact with many young intellectuals and Zionists who gathered around her sister's kitchen table to discuss politics and philosophy.

Over the years the Meir House has been set on fire, defaced with graffiti, threatened by a tornado, and used as a cult meeting place. When Meir lived here, it stood at 1606–1608 Julian Street in the working-class neighborhood of Little Israel along West Colfax Avenue. To escape demolition, the building was relocated twice, finally in 1988 to the Ninth Street Historic Park. The SHF provided $100,410 to restore the interior of the house after supporters raised some $250,000. Work included fixing all electrical and mechanical systems and reconstructing floors, ceilings, walls, and finishes, as well as the bathroom and kitchen. The side of the duplex in which Meir lived has been restored to the 1913 era as a museum. The Auraria Higher Education Center also uses the house as a conference and teaching center.

MOREY MERCANTILE / MERCANTILE SQUARE
16th St. Mall between Wynkoop St. and Wazee St. LLD
Built: 1888, Henry Lee Building; 1896 building; 1902, Morey Mercantile
Building, Aaron Gove and Thomas Walsh, architects

These three warehouse buildings once owned by the Chester S. Morey Company
housed the largest wholesale mercantile supplier in the Rocky Mountain region.
Henry Lee, a Denver pioneer, agricultural entrepreneur, state legislator, and founder
of the Denver park system, built the first of the three. The building, which still
bears his name, served as a factory, producing and packaging goods. Morey later
acquired Lee's production plant and constructed the other two buildings in 1896
and 1902 as warehouse and display space.

In the mid-1990s, John Hickenlooper of the Wynkoop Brewing Company,
Joyce Meskis of the Tattered Cover Book Store, and other new owners decided to
restore the historic structures for retail, commercial, and residential uses. With the
help of Del Norte Neighborhood Development Corp., a nonprofit corporation
working in housing development, the owners used a $100,000 SHF grant and
$806,944 in matching funds to remove paint, soot, and other pollutants from the
brick buildings; replace damaged bricks; restore sills and other parts of historic windows; and revive historic storefronts and entrances. Recent users now include the
Tattered Cover Book Store, Dixon's Restaurant, low-income lofts, Historic Denver,
Inc., the alley-access Wines Off Wynkoop shop, offices of the Wynkoop Brewing
Company, and others. "We tried to keep this a gritty urban complex," says architect
David Owen Tryba, "with alley activity and antique metal, stone, brick, and wood."

NINTH STREET HISTORIC PARK
9th St. between Champa St. and Curtis St. LLD NRD
Built: 1870s–1905

A corner grocery store and 13 middle-class dwellings make Ninth Street Historic
Park one of Denver's most fascinating and nationally significant preservation stories:
a typical 1800s face block, successfully recycled and creatively reused. Originally a
project of Historic Denver, Inc., Denver's oldest restored residential block was turned
over to the Auraria Higher Education Center for educational uses. Originally, many
higher-education bureaucrats balked at the idea of saving the old-fashioned houses.
But Colorado's State Historic Preservation Office and other preservationists stood
firm, and Historic Denver, Inc., raised a million dollars to restore the block. Today
these "funny little houses" are some of the most coveted spaces on campus.

Dean Wolf, executive vice president of the Auraria Higher Education Center,
reported in 2005 that "thanks to the SHF grants of $386,113, we have been able to
begin a first-class restoration. We have provided a cash match of $351,430 and are
scrambling to find more matching funds in these budget-cutting times. This park is
our campus showplace and a center for the social events and relaxation of some
36,000 students on what has become the largest campus in Colorado. The SHF
grants have enabled us to establish a maintenance plan to keep the park and the old
houses, which contribute 35,660 square feet of office space, in good repair."

PRIDE OF THE ROCKIES FLOUR MILL / LONGMONT FARMERS MILL / FLOUR MILL LOFTS
2000 Little Raven St. [NR]
Built: 1906, J. R. McDonald and Burell Engineering and Construction Co., builder; 1920 addition, Nordyke & Marmon Co., builder

D

State-of-the-art when built, this mill boasted electricity and employed a gravity-based, Hungarian process used in high-altitude milling. Strategically located between the railroad tracks and the South Platte River, the site also proved popular with vagrants after the building had been vacated. Developer-preservationist Dana Crawford purchased the derelict eyesore and turned it and a new, matching companion building into 34 upscale lofts. The $456,166 façade renovation was assisted by the SHF's $100,000. Residents now occupy the grain silos, in which Crawford retained some of the stairwell graffiti from its days as a hobo hangout.

St. CAJETAN'S CATHOLIC CHURCH
W. 9th St. and Lawrence St. [LL]
Built: 1926; Robert W. Willison, architect

This stucco-and-red-tile, Spanish Colonial Revival–style church was the first built in northern Colorado for Spanish-speaking Catholics. John K. Mullen, a millionaire flour miller and philanthropist, donated the site (formerly occupied by his home) and $50,000 to construct the church with its distinctive curvilinear parapets, quatrefoil windows, and twin bell towers.

St. Cajetan's, with its now-gone school, health clinic, and credit union, served the emerging Hispanic community as a refuge and a support for upward mobility. When the neighborhood was cleared to create the Auraria Higher Education Center (AHEC) campus in the 1970s, the church was converted into an auditorium and remained a focal point for the campus. In 1994, AHEC used a $40,000 SHF grant and various matches to replace modern doors with historically accurate ones and replace missing stained-glass windows on one of Denver's finest architectural celebrations of Colorado's Hispanic heritage.

St. ELIZABETH OF HUNGARY CATHOLIC CHURCH
1062 11th St. [LL] [NR]
Built: 1898; Frederick W. Paroth, architect

Bishop Joseph P. Machebeuf established St. Elizabeth's parish in 1878 for Denver's German community, the largest single foreign-born group in Colorado from the 1858 gold rush until World War I. A small church was constructed on 11th Street, followed by a monastery and church school. The number of parishioners increased steadily over the years, and the current building was erected on the same site, pushed along by the efforts of Father Francis Koch and Brother Adrian. Their original plan was refined by architect Frederick W. Paroth. The Romanesque Revival structure utilized rough-cut Castle Rock rhyolite on the exterior, culminating in a corner spire soaring 162 feet. In 1936, Denver architect Jacques J. B. Benedict designed cloisters behind an arcade, a prayer garden, and a fountain. At the east end of this curving arcade, the old school was replaced in 1980 by the St. Francis Conference Center. Designed by architect Marvin Hatami, this modern glass-and-brick greenhouse mimics the massing of the church.

The SHF awarded $4,750 to the owners of the church, the Franciscan Order of Friars Minor of Province of Most Holy Name, to help preserve the doors of an active church. This architectural and cultural landmark now has bells ringing again. The bells were donated by the brewer Adolph Zang, supposedly with the proviso that they ring "Zang! Zang!" not "Clang! Clang!"

St. JOSEPH'S REDEMPTORIST CATHOLIC CHURCH
600 Galapago St. at W. 6th Ave. [NR]
Built: 1888–1889

"Preaching in both Spanish and English," says Father Kyle Fisher, C.S.R., the pastor since 1987, "I asked parishioners how they could let a church get so run-down. Everybody just got used to this being a dump. Every dime had gone into trying to keep the school open. Many people thought the church had been closed and abandoned. I finally started with the beautiful little cloistered courtyard designed by Jacques Benedict along 6th Avenue. Then people could see how beautiful the brickwork is and how exquisite the wood and stone trim are."

A $198,365 SHF grant gave the parish hope. They stripped off layers of red paint that had been used to hide decaying wood and neglected brick. "Ultimately," says Father Fisher, "we redid all the brickwork and replaced or repaired 600 stones." To continue what the SHF initiated, the church raised $250,000, thanks to a lot of angels, according to Father Fisher: "Our parishioners also grew prouder and more interested in the church. Our collections have climbed from about $1,000 to $3,000 per Sunday. We reopened the school for classes in English as a second language and converted the restrooms into showers and laundry facilities for the homeless. We also provide free hot meals and free barbering for the many poor and homeless people in this neighborhood."

Father Fisher himself pulled out all the pews to clean the terrazzo floors and strip the ornate pews of paint to restore their golden-oak glow. He stripped as many as 8 to 10 layers of paint off woodwork throughout the church to get to the wood, which he varnished himself. Outside, restoration uncovered the two brick towers, which had been covered with asphalt shingles to stop leaks and hide rotting wood. Tempered-glass protection was installed over all the stained glass. "Without the SHF," says Father Kyle, "this would have never happened." The 60,000 souls who drive by every day can't help but notice this miracle on 6th Avenue.

SUGAR BUILDING
1530 16th St. at Blake St. [NR]
Built: 1906, Aaron Gove and Thomas Walsh, architects;
   1912 and 1916 additions

D

A giant in Colorado's agricultural history, the Great Western Sugar Company expanded rapidly and enlarged its headquarters. Originally a four-story building, it received two upper stories in 1912 and a large rear addition in 1916. All three sections are of blond brick with terracotta trim based on geometric and stylized foliage forms. Inside lies the city's oldest, still functional Otis "bird cage" elevator. After the Great Western Sugar Company closed in the 1970s, the building stood vacant and deteriorating. In 1996, new owners obtained a $99,250 SHF grant with $99,250 in matching funds and a partnership with the Denver Urban Renewal Authority and Historic Denver, Inc., to restore the Sugar Building to prominence as a modern office complex.

Besides upgrading all of the mechanical and electrical systems, the restoration involved cleaning and repairing masonry, washing and repairing the structure's tin cornice, and restoring the windows and the storefront. The Sugar Building name was proudly restored over the entry, and new public art was installed by the City of Denver, just across the 16th Street Mall, featuring a life-size sugar beet, Colorado's most lucrative single crop during the first half of the 20th century.

SUNKEN GARDENS
W. 8th Ave. to W. 11th Ave. along Speer Blvd. [NR]
Built: 1907–1912; George Kessler and Saco R. DeBoer,
   landscape architects

Sunken Gardens, one of downtown Denver's most visible and historic parks, was created from a garbage dump. This showplace park boasted a pavilion and a large lake, both now gone. George Kessler, the nationally famous Kansas City landscape architect, designed the park. Denver planner and landscape architect Saco R. DeBoer helped develop the shallow lake, ideal for ice-skating. Piping water from Cherry Creek, DeBoer improvised a small creek that flowed over stones and into the pond. When West High School was built next to the park in 1926, DeBoer removed both pool and pavilion. By the 1980s, the park had become dilapidated, and the site of the pond was used as a soccer field. Denver Parks and Recreation Department, using $79,349 from the SHF for a cultural landscape assessment, is now considering restoration of the pavilion and water features.

TRINITY UNITED METHODIST CHURCH
1820 Broadway, northeast corner of E. 18th Ave. LL NR
Built: 1888; Robert S. Roeschlaub, architect

Trinity United Methodist Church, one of the few churches to survive amid down-town's office towers and parking lots, is the masterpiece of Colorado's first licensed architect, Robert S. Roeschlaub. Although this church located at a key city inter-section has aged very well, close inspection revealed persistent, damaging roof leaks.

The first 1995 SHF grant helped replace a decaying asbestos shingle roof with slate similar to the original. The new roof incorporates an electrical ice-melt system that keeps snow and ice from building up. Restorationists consulted Roeschlaub's original architectural drawings, housed at the Colorado Historical Society Stephen H. Hart Library, for guidance.

Subsequent grants have helped the church repair the rhyolite stone walls and Utah sandstone trim. Work included repointing mortar joints, damp-proofing, reinforcement of the structural ties, and creation of ducts to ventilate the foundation.

Inside, the church's original Roosevelt Organ, with its 4,202 pipes, was revived to once again fill the 1,200-seat interior with joyful music. The glorious sanctuary is popular for public musical performances, theater, lectures, and weddings. This still-

vibrant downtown church, which caters to the general public with its concerts as well as to the hungry and homeless with its social pro-grams, remained in full oper-ation throughout restoration. The Colorado Historical Society awarded Trinity the 2006 Governor's Award for Historic Preservation.

Lynn Willcockson of the church's restoration commit-tee remarks, "The SHF has helped us preserve a historical landmark to ensure that its activities will continue for the next century. Without the $841,000 from the SHF, matched by the church and Bonfils-Stanton Foundation, this $2.5 million restoration of a cornerstone of downtown Denver would never have happened. With the SHF we've been able to restore everything from the pipe organ to the steeple."

D

TWENTIETH STREET BATH HOUSE
1101 20th St. at Curtis St. [LL]
Built: 1908; Robert W. Willison, architect

In a Progressive Reform–era effort to encourage hygiene and physical fitness at a time when many homes lacked running water, Mayor Robert W. Speer built Denver's first public bathhouse and recreation center. SHF awarded $25,000 to help Denver Parks and Recreation reconstruct the long-gone metal cornice on this

Neoclassical public bathhouse, gymnasium, and recreation center serving Denver's downtown and Five Points neighborhoods. Freshly cleaned and repaired gray brick and mortar, as well as restored windows and entry, herald a health club open to all.

Photo courtesy of Tom Noel

UNION STATION
1701 Wynkoop St. at 17th St. [NR]
Built: 1881, William E. Taylor, architect; 1895 remodel, Van Brunt & Howe, architects; 1912 remodel, Aaron Gove and Thomas Walsh, architects

Union Station, the Beaux-Arts–Renaissance–style apparition at the lower end of 17th Street, opened in 1881 as Colorado's largest and finest edifice. This consolidated train station was a great improvement upon the four scattered depots that had served the passenger lines of the 1870s.

Union Station quickly emerged as the town hub. Once the station opened, 17th Street began attracting the city's tallest banks, hotels, and office buildings. Facing Union Station, a row of warehouses sprang up, which still stretch from Coors Field to Auraria as part of the LoDo Historic District. Paul Goldberger, America's premier architectural critic, has called Union Station and Warehouse Row Denver's greatest architectural gems.

Union Station's Great Hall still evokes the golden age of railroading. Rusticated pink-gray rhyolite from Castle Rock and white sandstone trim from Manitou Springs sheath the original Second Empire edifice, whose wings have survived fires and remodelings. The 1912 Neoclassical center-section expansion introduced grand round-arched windows that flood the hall with natural light.

The Denver Union Terminal Railway Co. sold the depot in 2003 to the Regional Transportation District. RTD has recruited Historic Denver, Inc., Lower Downtown Denver, Inc., the Rocky Mountain Masonry Institute, and other

Photo courtesy of Tom Noel

D

partners in a planned $1.1 million restoration of Union Station. The SHF started the ball rolling with a $100,000 match to restore altered walls.

Besides restoring the crown jewel of LoDo, this project is revitalizing Union Station as a transportation hub. Amtrak, the Winter Park Ski Train, and the Regional Transportation District now offer rail passenger service at this station. With the opening of RTD's light-rail line to Union Station in 2001 and additional rail planned for Denver International Airport, Boulder, Golden, and the Denver Tech Center, the station is to become a multimodal transportation center for not only expanding rail transportation but also motor vehicles, buses, bicycles, and pedestrians.

Barbara Gibson, former executive director of the LoDo District, Inc., says, "Union Station is the cornerstone of LoDo, Denver's core neighborhood—which used to be called the 'Union Station' district. The building is also symbolic of the railroads that made Denver the transportation hub of the Rockies."

Capitol Hill *(between Lincoln St., 20th Ave., Colorado Blvd., 1st Ave., and Speer Blvd.)*

AUSTIN BUILDING
2400–2418 E. Colfax Ave. LL NR
Built: 1904; A. W. Reynolds, architect

Frank Austin opened these luxury apartments to take advantage of a prime intersection along the streetcar lines. Street-level storefronts have included a classy pharmacy and one of Denver's first ski shops. By the 1990s, the roof and skylights had deteriorated, allowing rain and snow to damage the ceilings and walls. The Northeast Denver Housing Center received a $100,000 SHF grant to kick off what has become a $2.3 million restoration complete with a new roof and skylights, restored sheet-metal cornice, repaired brick masonry, lead paint removal, and replacement of the roof deck.

BLUEBIRD THEATER
3315–3317 E. Colfax Ave. LL SR
Built: 1914; Harry W. J. Edbrooke, architect

D

The Bluebird opened as the Thompson Theater in a blond-brick, Beaux-Arts–Mediterranean Revival structure with a prominent marquee, culminating in the neon silhouette of a bluebird. In 1922, movie mogul Harry Huffman acquired the building as the first in his large Denver theater chain and renamed it the Bluebird. By 1974, the out-of-date venue could no longer compete with modern

theater chains and began showing adult movies before closing in 1987. After six empty years, Christopher Swank, a Denver businessman, bought and restored the old movie palace. He spent $500,000 to reopen the Bluebird in 1994 as a cabaret offering live concerts and films. The bird is flying again and earned a $5,000 SHF award to revive its trademark bluebird neon marquee.

Photo courtesy of Tom Noel

BOETTCHER MANSION / GOVERNOR'S MANSION
400 E. 8th Ave. at Logan St. LL NR
Built: 1908; Willis A. Marean and Albert J. Norton, architects

Walter S. Cheesman, the utilities magnate instrumental in building Union Station and what is now the Denver Water Department, planned this Colonial Revival mansion but died before its completion. His widow and daughter moved in and later added a rear three-story carriage house in the same architectural style. Besides

automobiles and storage, the carriage house also provided living quarters for the mansion's caretaker.

John Evans, Jr., and his wife, Gladys—who was also Cheesman's daughter—subsequently lived in the house until 1926. At that time, Claude Boettcher, son of the founder of the Great Western Sugar Company, bought the property, where he and his wife, Edna,

Photo courtesy of Tom Noel

resided for decades. In 1959, the Boettcher Foundation gave the estate to the State of Colorado for use as a governor's mansion.

The complex received SHF grants of $706,591 and provided $530,000 in matching funds to rehabilitate the mansion, landscaping, and carriage house. A landscape restoration plan reintroduced several missing elements that existed historically, such as a lily pond and trellis. In the mansion, the Palm Room has been restored, including leaded-glass windows and skylights, while exterior woodwork was painted and repaired. One grant has gone into the rehabilitation of the carriage house for use as a visitor center and guest suite. Inside, workers removed asbestos from the basement furnace and lead-based paint from the walls, repaired the lath and plaster, and refinished floors. Outside, repairs were made on the perimeter brick wall and the foundation was stabilized.

BURR STUDIO / DENVER WOMAN'S PRESS CLUB
1325 Logan St. LL SR
Built: 1910; Ernest Phillip Varian, architect

George Elbert Burr, the premier etcher of Colorado nature scenes, used this English Craftsman–style cottage as his home and studio. In 1924, he donated it to the Denver Woman's Press Club for use as its headquarters. At that time, women were barred from membership in the Denver Press Club.

To further enhance this cozy home and studio, with its balcony and hearth, the women matched $114,690 in SHF grants to repair the plumbing and electrical systems, install French drains, and restore historic Craftsman elements, wall coverings, and a courtyard doorway. The club also rehabilitated the rear entry and south elevation, installed a new roof and copper gutters, repaired the wood trim, repainted inside and out, and restored the garden and grounds.

CAPITOL HEIGHTS PRESBYTERIAN CHURCH
1100 Fillmore St. SR
Built: 1911; Montana S. Fallis and Robert W. Willison, architects

Capitol Heights Presbyterian Church, begun as the York Street Presbyterian Church in 1896, built the current Gothic Revival–style structure in 1911 and later added an education wing. Since then, the oldest church in the neighborhood has overcome declining membership by opening its doors to other denominations. Restoring its building as well as its membership, this church matched a $7,784 SHF grant to fix its tower and 24 windows.

CATHEDRAL OF THE IMMACULATE CONCEPTION
1530 Logan St., northeast corner of E. Colfax Ave. [LL] [NR]
Built: 1902–1912; Leon Coquard, Aaron Gove, and Thomas Walsh, architects

D

The cathedral opened as the largest church building in Denver and the city's most notable example of the French Gothic Revival style. Faced with Bedford, Indiana, limestone, it features Carrara and Colorado Yule marble inside. Its twin 210-foot-tall spires tower above East Colfax, competing on the skyline with the nearby gold dome of the Colorado State Capitol.

By 1990, the limestone balustrades, which circled the building's roof to protect people below from falling snow, water, and other debris, had deteriorated. SHF grants totaling $209,317 made possible a $600,000 exterior restoration, as well as an organ restoration inside. Bishop José Gomez of the Cathedral reports that the seven musical angels in the giant choir-loft rose window now really have something to celebrate—the rebirth of a church. "Restoration of the cathedral," Bishop Gomez elaborates, "has also helped bolster our membership, which sunk to only about 300 families in the 1980s, but has now climbed back to almost 1,000 families."

CENTRAL PRESBYTERIAN CHURCH
1660 Sherman St., southeast corner of E. 17th Ave. [NR]
Built: 1892; Frank E. Edbrooke and Willis A. Marean, architects

Edbrooke, Denver's most prominent early architect, designed this Richardsonian Romanesque church the same year his Brown Palace Hotel was completed two blocks west. He used large blocks of Manitou red sandstone for the walls and trim. This soft stone had been eaten away by moisture and pollution, and the deteriorated slate roof and mortar joints further water-damaged the interior. Iron ties used to fasten together the bricks and concrete blocks had rusted, leaving the upper parts of the exterior walls in danger of collapse.

Central Presbyterian used an SHF grant of $105,000 towards a $145,000 stabilization of exterior stone, installation of flashing and 360 new steel masonry ties, replacement of deteriorated stone finials, and repointing of 9,715 linear feet of masonry joints. Central Presbyterian plans to perform additional stone restoration, but is now ready to face a second century of downtown ministry, reports assistant pastor Amy Miracle.

D

CHEESMAN PARK FOUNTAIN
1000 High St. in Cheesman Park NR
Built: 1910; Willis A. Marean and Albert J. Norton, architects

Initially, the Cheesman Memorial Pavilion featured a beautiful marble fountain with three basins. Ninety years later, the fountain had grown feeble. Pollutants stressed the pump, and the pools had deteriorated and sprung leaks. Denver Parks and Recreation completed a $149,907 restoration of the fountain with $112,430 from the SHF. Other funds came from The Park People and many other groups, including James A. and Hazel Gates Woodruff; the Gates Family; and the Helen K. and Arthur E. Johnson, Boettcher, Bonfils-Stanton, Adolph Coors, and Denver Foundations.

As part of the fountain's resurrection, bronze nozzles brought back the original water jets. The crumbling coping stones that edge the three basins, the foundation, and surrounding landscapes and walks have also been returned to their original condition. "Now," says Mark Upshaw, Denver Parks and Recreation planner, "we have something beautiful—and historically accurate."

CHEESMAN PARK MEMORIAL PAVILION
1000 High St. in Cheesman Park LL NR
Built: 1910; Willis A. Marean and Albert J. Norton, architects

In 1907, in response to a suggestion by New York engineer and city planner Charles Mulford Robinson, Mayor Robert W. Speer decided to transform the old city cemetery into a park. Naming rights would go to whomever made the largest contribution to the project. At about the same time, the widow of recently deceased real-estate and public-utilities magnate Walter S. Cheesman was striving to rehabilitate the reputation of the miserly tycoon, whom critics complained overcharged Denverites for their water. For her donation of $100,000 to construct a Neoclassical pavilion, fountains, pool, and surrounding park, Denver named the western half of Congress Park "Cheesman Park." The prominent architectural firm of Marean and Norton designed the park's mountain-viewing pavilion, with its double Doric columns, as the park centerpiece.

Thanks to SHF funds of $100,000 for cornice restoration, matched by contributions from the City of Denver and The Park People, the pavilion of Colorado Yule marble has been restored to its original radiance. Close inspection of the cornice reveals replaced dentils and marble blocks in the structure, a new pedestal, and a new "Mountain Panorama" viewing guide, which interprets the full sweep of the Front Range, from Pikes Peak to Longs Peak.

CHEESMAN PARK RUSTIC SHELTER
In Cheesman Park LL NR
Built: 1906; Reinhard Schuetze, landscape architect

D

To the north of the pavilion lies another reborn delight of Chessman Park—a Rustic-style shelter assembled in 1906. Denver's pioneer landscape architect and park planner Reinhard Schuetze personally designed what he called a "Japanese Tea House." This six-sided gazebo with a circular roof lost its log-and-stick railing; suffered from innumerable carved hearts, names, and obscenities; and took on a troublesome lean over the years. Denver Parks and Recreation projects manager Tom Hawkey undertook to save the structure before it collapsed. Using $50,000 from the SHF, he found matching funds, preservation architect Nan Anderson, and a skilled log construction worker, a team that restored this whimsical structure for its 100th birthday. Douglas Fowler, a carpenter with the White Construction Group, spent months meticulously restoring the log and stick work.

CITY PARK DeBOER'S WATERWAY, BOX CANYON, AND LILY POND
City Park, southwest side of Denver Museum of Nature and Science LLD
Built: 1953; Saco R. DeBoer, landscape architect

This landscaping masterpiece consists of a waterway flowing through a man-made box canyon, waterfall, and rock gardens to two lily ponds that once contained thousands of water lilies tended by Denver Botanic Gardens. After Denver Botanic Gardens moved to Cheesman Park, the waterway and lily ponds suffered. With the aid of volunteers from the Colorado Water Garden Society and the Colorado Federation of Garden Ponds, and $38,000 from the SHF, all three areas were restored for $75,000, beginning with the lily ponds in 1995. Volunteers planted lilies, rebuilt the rock gardens and box canyon, and reconstructed the waterfall. Once dry and nearly indiscernible, the reactivated waterway uses water from nearby Ferril Lake, which it aerates and recirculates back to the lake.

CITY PARK ELECTRIC FOUNTAIN
City Park, center of Ferril Lake LLD SR
Built: 1908; Frederick W. Darlington, landscape architect

On May 30, 1908, Mayor Robert W. Speer pulled the switch to activate water jets and 10 colors of light shining on the columns of water, all choreographed to band music playing in the nearby pavilion. Thousands thronged to these nocturnal galas, but few saw the fountain engineers row out to the concrete vault in the middle of Ferril Lake to manually operate the water valves and light switches. This vault had become unusable by the 1990s. The Park People, a volunteer organization dedicated to supporting Denver's park system, persuaded the Denver Parks and Recreation Department to undertake a $121,000 restoration by volunteering time, money, and expertise—and by raising $79,460 from the SHF. Mrs. Robert "Cappy" Shopneck, president of The Park People, observes, "This is a unique fountain. The only other such electric light fountain in the world—in Rochester, New York—is no longer working. But thanks to SHF, ours is spouting again."

CITY PARK PAVILION
City Park, west side of Ferril Lake [LLD] [NRD]
Built: 1896; John J. Humphreys and William E. Fisher, architects

D

This two-story, twin-towered pavilion in the Spanish Colonial Revival style contains a basement, kitchen, storeroom, toilets, refreshment parlor, and open-air veranda. During its early years, the pavilion saw use as a shelter for animals from the nearby zoo and a drunk tank for unruly *Homo sapiens.* It later became unused and was vandalized. In 1993, Denver Parks and Recreation used a $75,000 SHF grant and additional donations to begin restoration. K-M Concessions, which operates concession stands in the zoo and paddleboats on Ferril Lake, rented the second floor of the pavilion for its offices and helped restore and maintain the building. The building's exterior was restuccoed, and lockable gates were placed in the pavilion's arched entryways.

Photo courtesy of Tom Noel

On the inside of the pavilion, the north side was rehabilitated for use as a public meeting room. New restrooms were added and others restored. A later ceiling addition was removed to expose the beauty and strength of the original heavy timber-and-steel trusses. The elegant first floor is now available for public use.

COOPER BUILDING / ARNO APARTMENTS
325 E. 18th St. [NR]
Built: 1910; L. A. Des Jardins, architect

Once luxury apartments, this three-story Colonial Revival edifice had fallen on hard times by the 1980s. Homeless people moved in, sometimes setting fires inside the building to keep warm. This once-beautiful old building became a painful eyesore and a public danger.

In the mid-1990s, Capitol Hill United Neighborhoods (CHUN) decided to act before the building collapsed. The deteriorating roof had allowed water to penetrate the interior, causing significant damage. The windows, masonry, and brickwork had suffered extensive damage. Both the front and back doors needed repair, repainting, and hardware replacement. Parts of the exterior wood were missing entirely, and the balcony clung on precariously. Aided by a $100,000 SHF grant and $184,813 raised for a match, CHUN acquired the structure and set about restoring it, then added new mechanical and electric infrastructure for what is now affordable housing.

CORONA/DORA MOORE SCHOOL
846 Corona St., northeast corner of E. 8th Ave. [LL] [NR]
Built: 1889, Robert S. Roeschlaub, architect; 1909 addition,
  David Dryden, architect

Often the largest and most prominent buildings in residential neighborhoods, schools anchor the community. The Corona School (later renamed Dora Moore for a popular principal), with its building and playground occupying a full block, is a classic example of a school being the heart of a community. This celebration in brick and stone, with its soaring turrets with nipple finials, is one of the masterpieces of Colorado's first great school architect, Robert Roeschlaub. Reflecting its openness, it has entrances on each corner with long hallways that draw visitors to the center of the school and the stairs. In 1909, architect David Dryden designed an addition using darker bricks, including some with a greenish glaze.

The work of both architects was complemented by the 1992 gymnasium at the rear of Dryden's building with a glass atrium connecting the two buildings. A restoration project costing more than $2 million, aided by $209,512 in grants from the SHF and a citywide bond initiative, restored the exterior, including removal of green paint from the masonry and repair and replacement of brick and sandstone details. The project also included the repair of windows in the original 1889 building and 1909 addition, as well as reconstruction of lost stained-glass elements

—more than 270 window openings in all.

The project team found creative ways to carry out the work while school was in session without disrupting students and teachers, allowing them to learn about historic preservation firsthand. Denver Public Schools used the project to teach students about architectural styles, construction, and restoration techniques.

Students and alumni supported the effort to preserve the school, starting with their early 1970s role in keeping the old-timer from being replaced by a modern building. Student appeals proved irresistible to the Denver Landmark Preservation Commission and the Denver City Council, which designated this Denver's first landmark school in 1975. Denver Public Schools was awarded the Colorado Historical Society's Governor's Award for Historic Preservation in February 2004 for this exemplary project as well as for its district-wide program of designating historically significant school buildings and applying appropriate historic preservation treatments to their restoration.

DODGE AND GILLULY MANSIONS
1145–1173 Pennsylvania St., southwest corner of E. 12th Ave. LLD
Built: 1889 (North Building), 1890 (South Building), E. Gregory,
architect; c. 1936 (Central Building)

This three-building complex consists of two large old homes and a central structure linking them together. Colonel David C. Dodge, an executive of the Denver
& Rio Grande Railroad and the Mexican National Railway, commissioned the
north building as his private residence. John Gilluly, another D&RG executive
and close friend of Dodge, completed the south mansion a year later. Members of
the Dodge and Gilluly families occupied the houses until the late 1920s, sharing
the common yard and fountain.

After Nannie Dodge's death, Dr. John H. Tilden converted the complex into
a health institute, linking the two older homes with a central rear structure. Later
known as the Samaritan Nursing Home, it remained a care center until the 1970s,
when it was converted into 14 condominiums.

The SHF provided $189,625 toward the $300,000 restoration of stone foundations, stone lintels, chimneys, and parapets in danger of collapse. Restoration
workers stabilized the retaining wall with new steel supports and rebuilt the concrete
wall around it. They fixed the roof, replaced flashings, and repaired or replaced
gutters and the drainage system. They also reconstructed the chimneys and installed
new chimney ties, repaired and replaced broken lintels, removed white paint to
reveal the original red brick, repaired and repointed the masonry, and reconstructed parapets and cornices. Once ailing badly, this grand old landmark now
looks healthy again.

EAST HIGH SCHOOL
1545 Detroit St. and E. Colfax Ave. LL
Built: 1925; George H. Williamson, architect

East High's $312,600 restoration included the clock tower, main entrance, auditorium
seats, and landscaping. The SHF contributed $207,940, which East High alumni
and boosters matched with $207,940 to revitalize a fine English Jacobean design by
George Hebard Williamson, a Denver native and graduate of the original East High
at 19th and Stout Streets. Williamson distinguished himself as an innovative school
architect who incorporated modern efficiency while maintaining an aesthetically

pleasing design. Amid the surrounding City Park landscape,
East is one of the best-preserved
examples of the City Beautiful–
era practice of integrating
schools with parks. Inspired
by the restoration, East High
has long-range plans to further
enhance its landscaping and
restore the gardens on the south
side of the school.

Photo courtesy of Tom Noel

EL JEBEL TEMPLE / 1770 SHERMAN STREET EVENTS COMPLEX
1770 Sherman St. at E. 18th Ave. LL NR
Built: 1906; Baerresen Brothers, architects

D

This fanciful, five-story, red-brick Moorish Revival shrine has exotic onion domes, a roof balcony, and contrasting terracotta trim, most notably in the horseshoe-

shaped window arches. Sons of a noted Danish designer of ships and shipyards, Harold W., Viggio, Albert T., and William J. Baerresen designed this as a consistory for the Scottish Rite Masons. Of the Baerresens' many Denver works, this edifice is the most remarkable. It served as the headquarters for Colorado's Shriners, the 33rd Degree Masons who belong to the Ancient Arabic Order of the Mystic Shrine, until they moved to a new consistory at the southeast corner of East 13th Avenue and Logan Street and a new El Jebel Shrine next to the Willis Case Golf Course in northwest Denver.

Even more exotic than the exterior, the well-preserved interior boasts a Tudoresque dining room, a Japanese red room, and an Egyptianesque, lotus-motif columned audi-torium. The two-story ballroom, with a roof modeled after an Arabian tent, contains a small

east-wall inscription: "The Dream of the Architect—Baerresen Brothers."

The owners have received $188,788 from the SHF toward the purchase of the building, roof restoration, and feasibility and restoration planning. Now called the 1770 Sherman Street Events Complex, the building hosts public and private events, dances, theater productions, and Colorado Preservation, Inc.'s statewide Saving Places conference. The building's interior and exterior are protected by a preservation easement funded by SHF and held by Historic Denver, Inc.

Photo courtesy of Tom Noel

EMERSON SCHOOL / COMMUNITY CENTER
1420 Ogden St., northeast corner of E. 14th Ave. LL NR
Built: 1885, Robert S. Roeschlaub, architect; 1917, Emerson Cottage

The oldest surviving school by Roeschlaub, architect for the Denver School District from 1875 to 1895, is notable for its central court, allowing for easy inspection of the building's interior layout. Before restoration, the school's façade sundial was chipped and blackened by pollution. Next to the main building, the porch of the abandoned cottage school was boarded up. Capitol Hill Senior Resources, which owns and operates the site, matched $50,440 from the SHF to clean and repair the exterior brick, stone trim, sundial, chimney hoods, and ridge cresting.

The cottage school, now restored for use once again as a preschool, makes this rejuvenated structure a home for juniors as well as seniors. Capitol Hill Senior Resources rents office space in the old school to various senior, community and nonprofit groups ranging from the Alliance Française to the Grey Panthers.

D

FIRE STATION No. 15 / FAY RESIDENCE
1080 Clayton St, southeast corner of E. 11th Ave. LL
Built: 1903; John J. Huddart, architect

This Beaux-Arts, residential-scale building housed firefighters until 1985, when the Denver Fire Department moved Station No. 15 to a larger structure. Nathaniel and Kathleen Fay bought and restored it, with the help of architect Ron Abo, as a private residence with a king-sized garage. The interior conversion entailed the first use of the State Income Tax Credit, a 1991 Colorado provision that allows owners of designated landmarks to claim tax credits for a portion of restoration expenses. On the exterior, the Fays have restored the classic metal cornice, repointed the blond-brick walls, and made structural repairs with the help of a $10,000 SHF grant obtained through the nonprofit Congress Park Neighbors and $17,085 of their own money.

"We love living in this firehouse and keeping it a part of the neighborhood," reports Kathy Fay. "The SHF has enabled us to preserve and update this house as our family has grown. Our two kids love it, especially since we bought our bright red 1949 Ford-Pirsch fire truck. They can slide down the fire pole to breakfast and play in the truck. After the kids are grown we hope to open a bed-and-breakfast here—The Firehouse Inn."

FIRE STATION No. 18 / DENVER POLICE STATION
2205 Colorado Blvd. in City Park LL
Built: 1912; Edwin H. Moorman, architect

To complement the adjacent Park Hill neighborhood along the east edge of City Park, this firehouse was built in a bungalow style unique among fire stations in Colorado and perhaps the country. After No. 18 moved to bigger quarters in 1987, the Denver Police Department converted this into a police substation. To spruce up the aging landmark, the department used a $91,395 SHF grant and $214,165 in matching funds to restore the firehouse; update its heating, cooling, and electrical systems; renovate the interior; and install bulletproof windows. "By helping refurbish this landmark, the SHF has taken an important step toward maintaining the historic nature of City Park," says George Sparks, CEO of the Denver Museum of Nature and Science, the station's neighbor to the south.

FIRST CHURCH OF DIVINE SCIENCE
1400 Williams St., northeast corner of E. 14th Ave. (SR)
Built: 1922, Jules Jacques Benois Benedict, architect; 1950s addition,
William Muchow, architect

D

Along with her sisters, Nona Brooks, one of Denver's earliest female ministers, founded the Divine Science denomination in the 1890s. Three decades later, members commissioned this Classical Revival church as a serene gathering place. In the 1950s, the building received an addition, which harmonized with the original design. This work of Denver's great Beaux-Arts architect Jacques Benedict needed help by 1996, when its $119,800 restoration was facilitated by $54,350 from the SHF. This project included a new boiler; a new roof with ceiling insulation; and repair, cleaning, and painting of the exterior terracotta ornamentation and pebble-finished stucco. Although the congregation has dwindled, the church remains an important cultural center, providing plays, workshops, seminars, and lectures.

GERMAN HOUSE / DENVER TURNVEREIN
1570 Clarkson St., southeast corner of E. 16th Ave. [LL] (SR)
Built: 1921; George L. Boettcher, architect

"SHF helped restore the building and its facilities to their original beauty," says Hans Pott, a longtime Turnverein member. Formed in 1865, Denver's oldest ethnic

Photo courtesy of Tom Noel

club is the local branch of the international German cultural and physical-fitness society. Their Mediterranean-style Denver headquarters, built as the Coronado Club, has undertaken a $121,503 exterior restoration supported by the SHF's $88,503. This included reroofing, repairing the ballroom ceiling, repairing and repainting exterior stucco, and installing a new front door, steps, railings, and signage. Julie Fletcher, project manager for Denver Turnverein, notes, "Our active membership, which includes fencing, tango, and swing dance clubs, and men's and women's German choirs, has greatly appreciated this rejuvenation of our clubhouse, where we are also developing a German library and art archives."

GILPIN GRAMMAR SCHOOL
1300 Gilpin St., northeast corner of E. 13th Ave. [LLD]
Built: c. 1905

This large residence was converted into the Gilpin Grammar School after its acquisition by Warren Village, Inc. The Village assists homeless families by providing training, employment, and housing and made this house into a community and educational center. Among major restoration problems, the roof leaked and the entry porch needed to be stabilized.

Using two SHF grants totaling $117,235 and other donations, Warren Village enlisted more than 500 volunteers to help in the project. They scraped wallpaper, painted, did masonry work, washed windows, cleaned floors, and installed carpeting and furniture. Susan France, CEO of Warren Village, comments that "this restoration process created a family feeling for our volunteers and clients who worked together to make it happen."

THE GRAFTON
1001–1020 E. 17th Ave., northeast corner of Ogden St. [LL] [NR]
Built: 1890; James Murdoch, architect

Albert Brewster built these classy townhouses as The Aldine, renamed by subsequent owner Katherine Grafton Patterson, wife of Colorado U.S. senator Thomas Patterson, for her family. In 1916, building ownership passed to a daughter, Mrs. Richard Crawford Campbell. The family sold the building in 1971, and it passed through several hands until 1980 when it was bought and then remodeled into condominiums.

Photo courtesy of Roger Whitacre

Despite this remodeling, deterioration ate at the brick-and-sandstone façade and foundation. Concerned, the Grafton Home Owner's Association matched a $64,690 SHF grant with $125,576, as well as help from the Uptown Partnership and a bank loan, to restore the roof, masonry façade, windows, porches, foundation, interior hallways, and rooms. The association also regraded the soil to prevent water from seeping toward the foundation. Today, The Grafton is one of Capitol Hill's most architecturally distinguished multiple-family buildings, with its two-story, semicircular bays and two-tiered porches. "The rehab of The Grafton is a welcome and much-needed improvement to our neighborhood," says Tom J. Knorr, executive director of Capitol Hill United Neighbors.

D

D

GRANT-HUMPHREYS MANSION
770 Pennsylvania St. LL NR
Built: 1902; Theodore D. Boal and Frederick L. Harnois, architects

Denver's best-known Neoclassical residence has a monumental semicircular portico supported by four two-story, fluted Corinthian columns. Georgian balustrades for the first- and second-story porches and terraces are echoed by a rooftop balustrade. Built for James B. Grant, a smelter owner and Colorado governor, the peach-brick house employs lavish terracotta trim in window surrounds, balustrades, cornices, corner pilasters, and frieze. This early use of terracotta as a substitute for decorative stonework set an example widely copied by other Colorado architects and builders. Interiors are on a grand scale, featuring exotic woods, plaster trim, and a sunroom addition. Second owner Albert E. Humphreys, an oil tycoon who later became embroiled in the Teapot Dome scandal, added a two-story, 10-car garage, complete with a car wash and gas pump, for his fancy fleet of Rolls-Royces.

Humphreys' son Ira donated the house in 1976 to the Colorado Historical Society, which rents it out for special occasions, such as weddings. Splendidly sited on the southwest corner of Capitol Hill, it has an extensive lawn, which flows into Governor's Park to the west across a grassed-over block of Pennsylvania Street.

The terracotta that lended a lot of majesty to the building's design had deteriorated over the years. As cracks developed, water penetrated. On warm Colorado winter days, snowmelt found its way into balustrades and column bases. Freezing nighttime temperatures did the rest, and pieces of the rooftop ornamentation came crashing down. SHF grants in excess of $500,000 have contributed toward substantial repairs, not only to the terracotta but also to the structure and interior plaster surfaces damaged by leaking roofs. Much remains to be done, but the house is once again safe for public use and still remains one of Denver's finest mansions.

LeFEVRE HOUSE / 1311 CLUB
1311 York St., northwest corner of E. 13th Ave. NR
Built: 1891; Kirchner & Kirchner, architects

Owen E. LeFevre, a Denver district attorney, county judge, and district judge, built this mansion-sized residence for $45,000. His widow, Eva, lived here until her death in 1948, at which time the family transferred the home to Alcoholics Anonymous for use as its clubhouse. AA has soberly and skillfully restored the house and grounds with the help of $223,750 from the SHF. Club manager Jim Severson says, "The gaming fund fix-up has helped us to attract new members and also spruce up this Victorian mansion as a cornerstone of the Wyman Historic District."

MILHEIM HOUSE
1515 Race St. LL
Built: 1893; John J. Huddart, architect

John Milheim, a Swiss immigrant who owned the extant Colorado Bakery and Saloon Building at 1444 Market Street, built and lived in this large house, originally located at 1355 Pennsylvania Street. After Milheim's death, his wife, Mary, resided in the house until 1930. After that, the place became apartments and suffered from neglect. On the eve of scheduled demolition in 1989, Denverite Ralph Heronema stepped in, bought the structure, and transported it to its current location. The cost of transporting it, $500,000, set the Colorado record for the most expensive house move to date. Even before its widely publicized trip down East Colfax Avenue, the house's roof and chimneys were in poor shape. By the 1990s, the subroof was rotting and the interior ceiling was damaged. Heronema and Capitol Hill United Neighborhoods received a $42,144 SHF grant and raised the cash match of $14,048 to stabilize the roof; reroof the house; and repair the chimneys, gutters, and downspouts. "We're now a special-events venue," Heronema states proudly, "and Colorado's largest mobile home."

MOLLY BROWN HOUSE
1340 Pennsylvania St. LL NR
Built: 1889; William A. Lang, architect

Margaret Tobin Brown, a poor Irish girl whose husband struck it rich in Leadville mining, became a self-educated socialite and world traveler who played a heroic role in the *Titanic* disaster, after which she became known as "The Unsinkable Molly Brown" in a popular play and motion picture.

James J. and Margaret "Maggie" Tobin Brown bought this house and lived here some of the time until 1910, when J. J. died. When Maggie died in 1932, her former residence had already become a boarding house. By 1960, the city had leased it from owner Art Leisenring as a home for wayward girls. When a developer announced plans to demolish it in 1970, Leisenring and a group of grassroots preservationists rallied to form Historic Denver, Inc., which bought and began restoration of the house as a museum.

Since 1993, SHF grants of $497,390 have expedited a $665,526 restoration of the Molly Brown House Museum. This model exterior-interior restoration has included interpretive efforts such as a booklet, video, signage, and other outreach projects. The Molly Brown House has been showcased nationally on Home & Garden TV's *Restore America*, a series produced in partnership with the National Trust for Historic Preservation. With such publicity, it has become a popular tourist stop, attracting some 40,000 visitors per year.

Kerri Atter, director/curator of the Molly Brown House Museum, reports, "With SHF funds, we've restored the back family parlor and rear sun porch to their original finishes of the 1910 period. This involved removing a false ceiling in the parlor, where we found a long-hidden Arts and Crafts willow-patterned wallpaper frieze, of which we made a replica and reinstalled. We stripped about

D

25 layers of paint off the Cuban mahogany woodwork to revive its original, rich reddish brown luster. Underneath the linoleum, we found and redid the red oak and fir floors. SHF also expedited moving our offices to the second floor of the carriage house, opening up more of the main house for tours. We will use these newly rehabilitated back rooms to expand our interpretation, documenting Molly's social activism on behalf of women's rights and the labor movement."

OGDEN THEATRE
935 E. Colfax Ave. [LL] [NR]
Built: 1918; Harry W. J. Edbrooke, architect

Built as a vaudeville house and then later converted into a movie theater, this Mediterranean-style theater closed during the 1980s. Its future appeared to be in jeopardy following its closure, but in March 1993, Corn Dog, LLC, purchased the property to restore it for concerts, business seminars, live theater, weddings, and special events.

In 1993, the Ogden reopened its doors to the public, safe for public occupancy but still in need of cosmetic restoration, maintenance, and repair. The SHF granted $56,000 for a $713,091 restoration that replaced the original clay roof tiles, twin façade towers, marquee, doors, and windows, and fixed up the auditorium and stage.

PEARCE-McALLISTER COTTAGE / DENVER MUSEUM OF MINIATURES, DOLLS AND TOYS
1880 Gaylord St. [LL] [NR]
Built: 1899; Frederick J. Sterner, architect

Harold V. Pearce, a British investor in Colorado railroads, mining, and smelting, built this house as a wedding present for his wife. The newlyweds occupied the

two-and-a-half-story Dutch Colonial brick house until moving to England in 1907. The next occupant was Henry McAllister, general counsel for the Denver & Rio Grande Railroad. In 1971, the McAllister family donated it and all its 1920s-era furnishings to the Colorado Historical Society.

The CHS obtained a $133,000 SHF grant to replace the wood-shingle roof, paint the exterior, and restore the front porch and the gardens. Inside, security and fire alarms were upgraded, hand-painted wallpaper in the dining room was restored, and cracks in the decorative plaster ceilings were repaired. Since 1987, the CHS has leased Pearce-McAllister to the Denver Museum of Miniatures, Dolls and Toys, which welcomes visitors to a lilliputian world.

PERRENOUD BUILDING
836 E. 17th Ave. [LLD]
Built: 1901; Frank Snell, builder

Opened as Denver's "swellest yet" luxury apartments, the Perrenoud has reclaimed its swellness and is back again as one of Denver's most exclusive addresses. The Neoclassical four-story building contains 24 apartments (now converted into condominiums) arranged around four Tiffany-skylighted courts. The $218,000 exterior restoration was assisted by a $45,000 SHF grant and collaboration with Capitol Hill United Neighborhoods, Inc. Repairing, restoring, repainting, replacing, and cleaning enhanced the red-brick walls, stone trim, sheet-metal dentils, and cornice. Inside, the four stained-glass skylights, along with balconies, windows, and security grilles, were also restored. The marble-wainscoted lobby with French plate-glass mirrored walls, fireplace, and brass birdcage elevator also sparkle anew under the Tiffany skylights.

D

Photo courtesy of Tom Noel

RAYMOND HOUSE / CASTLE MARNE
1572 Race St., southeast corner of E. 16th Ave. [LL] [LLD] [NR]
Built: 1890; William Lang, architect

William Lang's flowery stone detailing is exemplified in this three-story, rusticated pink- and gray-rhyolite residence. The trim is Indiana limestone, which is much easier to carve than rhyolite. Exquisite stonework characterizes the fluted limestone chimney and balustrades crowning the porch and corner tower.

Real-estate developer Wilbur S. Raymond built this Richardsonian Romanesque edifice on three lots for $40,000. After a two-story addition in 1920, the house was converted into the Marne Apartments. James Peiker and his family bought it in 1988 for $184,000 and spent $300,000 lovingly restoring and refurnishing it as the Castle Marne bed-and-breakfast. This spectacular revival, which encompasses the matching carriage house, helped spark the renaissance of the once weedy Wyman Addition as a Denver Landmark District. The SHF, in partnership with Capitol Hill United Neighborhoods, helped with the showcase restoration, contributing $2,100 for replacing the original dining room, parlor ceiling, and frieze murals.

RICHARD CRAWFORD CAMPBELL HOUSE / DENVER BOTANIC GARDENS HOUSE
909 York St. LL NR
Built: 1926; Jules Jacques Benois Benedict, architect

D

Benedict, the genius behind many of Denver's most beautiful residences, labeled this house "Beaux-Arts." The 8,000-square-foot masterpiece boasts superb crafts-manship restored with the help of an $82,500 SHF grant. These funds allowed Denver Botanic Gardens, which added $78,900 to the preservation pot, to address long-standing problems, including cracks in the decorative plaster walls, outdated mechanical systems, and deteriorating finishes and fixtures. Foundation and drainage problems were corrected, and then the original frescoes, plaster, terrazzo floor, stone balustrades, and exterior masonry were repaired. The interior now sparkles with restored craftsmanship, showcased in radiators hidden under bay window seats and a built-in bookcase concealing a secret staircase to the master bedroom. High frescoed ceilings, large French windows, wall tapestries, and leaded glass provide a palatial atmosphere with a romantic addition in the north-side Juliet balcony. This exquisite, French-inspired landmark is open to the public, as are the adjacent Boettcher Conservatory and 23-acre gardens.

RUSSELL GATES MANSION ASSISTED LIVING RESIDENCES
1375 Josephine St., southwest corner of E. 14th Ave. LL NR
Built: 1892; H. Chatten, architect

Russell Gates, president of the Summit Fuel and Feed Company, built this Romanesque castle with its distinctive stone-arch openings, circular tower, half-timbering, and prominent porch of rusticated stone. One of Denver's most spectacular rhyolite residences subsequently became an apartment house, then an office building. The Del Norte Neighborhood Development Corporation sought to convert it into a group residence for persons living with HIV/AIDS. "There has been a need for this type of housing for a long time," says Marvin Kelly of Del Norte. "This dream came true thanks to a $100,000 SHF grant that expedited the $894,700 restoration." The interior and the rusticated rhyolite façade were brought back to fine form. Renamed the Russell Gates Mansion Assisted Living Residences, it is a home and hospice for 15 residents who have a comfortable, safe, handsome environment to live in, complete with restored original fireplaces and orchestra loft.

SAYRE'S ALHAMBRA / THE PROVIDENCE HOUSE
801 Logan St., northwest corner of E. 8th Ave. LL
Built: 1892

D

"Sayre's Alhambra" was the home of Hal Sayre, one of Colorado's first mining engineers. The inspiration for the house came from the Spanish Alhambra, which Sayre had seen on a trip to Europe. Upon his return to Denver he commissioned the house, reputedly designing or helping to design it himself. The 25-room residence is distinguished by ogee-arched transom cutouts inspired by the Spanish original. The Sayre family sold the house in 1939 after Hal Sayre's wife died. In the 1990s, Alhambra became The Providence House, a haven for the homeless. The Providence House used a $30,555 SHF grant and found matching funds of $47,937 to rehabilitate the exterior. The work included replacing shingles, damaged decking, structural support, damaged eaves, flashing, and fascia on the roof, and replacing and repainting all damaged wood, including the ogee-arch cutouts.

Photo courtesy of Tom Noel

SHERMAN SCHOOL / DENVER ART STUDENTS LEAGUE
200 Grant St. LL
Built: 1887 or 1893, Henry Dozier, architect; 1920, bungalow annex

This two-and-a-half-story, red-orange sandstone edifice sits on a rusticated stone foundation and sports a rusticated sandstone entry arch. The Romanesque-style school has horizontal window groupings and a kindergarten "cottage school" annex with two classrooms, each with a fireplace. The school closed in 1982 but reopened in 1987 as the home for the Denver Art Students League. The school has undergone $1 million in restoration work, using SHF grants of $586,076. All the original windows, some of which had been filled in, were restored, as was the exterior sandstone. The basement and the annex were rehabilitated to create new classrooms. Ceilings, which had been lowered, were opened up. In place of parking lot asphalt, there is now a sculpture and art garden. Students and staff aspire to bring back the original tower as the crowning achievement of a first-rate revival.

STATE CAPITOL
E. Colfax Ave. to E. 14th Ave. between
Lincoln St. and Grant St.   `LLD` `NR` `NRD`
Built: 1886–1908; Elijah E. Myers and Frank E. Edbrooke, architects

D

This brick building has Colorado gray granite facing and a cast-iron skin on the cylinder supporting the dome. Myers, the original architect, provided a Neoclassical

Photo courtesy of Tom Noel

Renaissance design. In 1889 the legislature dismissed him and hired local architect Frank Edbrooke, who completed the structure using Myers' design. At the urging of a penny-pinching legislature, Edbrooke cut out some of the frills, including the feminine form of Liberty with her lamp that was to have capped the gold dome. The legislature also eliminated three of the four proposed stairways to the upper stories and dome.

The one completed stairway and the others that were never built became an issue with the growing fire safety and homeland security concerns of recent years. A fifth of America's historic state capitols have been either destroyed or severely damaged by fire. To ensure that such a tragedy does not strike Colorado's statehouse, the SHF has awarded more than $24 million toward a $30 million project to help improve life safety at the Capitol.

"Structures like this domed Capitol were not built with fire safety in mind," explains James Stratis, preservation projects manager for the State Historical Fund. "If a fire were to start, the dome would create a chimneylike effect. And without a protected escape route, people would be left vulnerable to the dangers of smoke inhalation, which is the largest cause of fire-related deaths."

Scheduled for completion in 2008, the Capitol Life Safety and Preservation project being implemented by Fentress Bradburn Architects and contractor Gerald H. Phipps, Inc., updates the fire alarm and suppression systems and builds four enclosed, fireproof stair towers. The project will also create a comprehensive Historic Structure Assessment to help guide future preservation planning and maintenance.

In order to ensure that the highest standards are met, many unusual materials

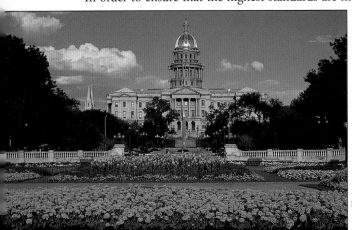

needed to be located. For example, Italian Verona red marble was obtained for the new stair towers to closely match the existing wainscot of Beulah red marble, which had been completely mined out of its Pueblo County quarry in the late 1800s.

Photo courtesy of Denver Metro CVB

"Integrating modern safety features into a historic building often happens in an ad hoc manner, which can damage its original character," explains Stratis. "With the right attention to detail, however, these needed upgrades can still be achieved while also maintaining the building's historic integrity."

Other SHF grants for the Capitol building have helped pay for a historic landscape master plan, Civil War cannon restorations, as well as dome observation-deck upgrades. Besides the governor, legislators, state officials, and lobbyists, the Capitol hosts over 250,000 visitors a year, according to Manager of Visitor Services Edna Pelzmann. All these folks, she adds, will enjoy a safer environment and, with other building upgrades, a newly expanded attic museum showcasing Capitol history.

St. JOHN'S EPISCOPAL CATHEDRAL
1313 Clarkson St. between E. 13th Ave. and 14th Ave. NR
Built: 1905–1911; Tracy and Swartwout, architects

Originally established in 1860 as St. John's Church in the Wilderness in the raw, two-year-old frontier crossroads of Denver, St. John's occupied two earlier churches before moving into this English Gothic Revival design executed in Indiana limestone and distinguished by two 100-foot bell towers. St. John's used SHF grants of $355,335 and raised $4.3 million for exterior repairs, replacing damaged roofing and repairing or replacing gutters, downspouts, and flashing. Craftsmen also tended to damaged stones, repointing and cleaning them, then refinished the original exterior, sanctuary doors, and pews. The basement has been converted into a choir rehearsal hall. Indiana limestone matching the original was used to restore the front porch and steps and to build a wheelchair ramp.

Photo courtesy of Tom Noel

St. PAUL'S ENGLISH EVANGELICAL LUTHERAN CHURCH
1600 Grant St., northeast corner of E. 16th Ave. NR
Built: 1926; Richter & Eiler, architects

St. Paul's was first built at 22nd and California Streets but outgrew that home by the early 1920s. The parish bought this prominent Capitol Hill site for $20,000 and engaged the Reading, Pennsylvania, architectural firm of Richter & Eiler, specialists in Lutheran churches. They planned the church with local supervision by architect Frank Redding. This Gothic Revival edifice, which cost $200,000 to construct, is rich in buttresses, pointed stained-glass windows, and vaulted ceilings. The red-brick skin is banded with cast-stone ornament, window tracery, parapet caps, and a distinctive square, crenellated bell tower.

The 500-seat sanctuary features pews fashioned out of white and plain oak and stained-glass windows crafted at the George Hardy Payne Studio in Paterson, New Jersey. The church raised $30,000 to match the SHF's $161,351 to restore the bell tower as the first step in an ongoing restoration program.

TEARS-McFARLANE HOUSE / CENTER FOR THE PEOPLE OF CAPITOL HILL

1290 Williams St., southeast corner of E. 13th Ave. LL NR
Built: 1898; Frederick Sterner, architect

D

One of Denver's better examples of the Georgian style, this residence was commissioned by Daniel W. Tears, a railroad attorney, and his wife, who became prominent socialites and lived in the house for almost 40 years. In 1937, Frederick and Ida Kruse McFarlane bought the house. The daughter of the mayor of Central City, Ida Kruse was a University of Denver English professor who helped restore the Central City Opera House and establish its still-thriving summer opera. After her death in 1950, Frederick married Lillian Cushing, a professional actress and dancer who gave dance lessons in the basement studio.

When the house changed hands in 1966, it served as both offices and residence for, among others, U.S. senator Gary Hart. In 1977, the City and County of Denver bought the house as a home for the Greater Capitol Hill Events Center, a nonprofit agency offering office rentals and meeting space for nonprofit and community organizations and their programs. The drainage system, masonry, and exterior elements are being repaired with the SHF's $127,299 and a $37,600 cash match.

TEMPLE EMANUEL SYNAGOGUE / TEMPLE EVENTS CENTER UPTOWN

1595 Pearl St., southwest corner of E. 16th Ave. LL
Built: 1899, John J. Humphreys, architect; 1924 addition, Thielman Robert Wieger, architect

Ogee arches, minarets, and copper domes adorn this beige-brick building whose design celebrates Judaism's Middle Eastern origins. The central and north towers

Photo courtesy of Tom Noel

are octagonal and taller than the south tower, which fronts the 1924 addition with its buttressed corners. This synagogue, which housed Colorado's largest Jewish congregation from 1889 to 1957, was owned from 1982 to 1987 by the City and County of Denver and used as an events center. Since 1987, it has been owned and operated by the Pearl Street Temple Emanuel Foundation. SHF funding has helped restore its brick walls and banding, stone trim, metal filigree, red-tile roof, and the floral and geometric motifs evident in the door panels and stained-glass windows. Temple Events Center Uptown executive director Roger D. Armstrong says, "The SHF's $245,091 has been essential in restoring this landmark as a home for arts and culture. Our rehabilitation has been a careful balance between aesthetics and critical structural and safety issues."

Northeast Denver *(between the South Platte River, 20th St., 20th Ave., E. 52nd Ave., and Colorado Blvd.)*

ANNUNCIATION CATHOLIC CHURCH
3601 Humboldt St., northwest corner of E. 36th Ave.
Built: 1907; Frederick W. Paroth, architect

This cornerstone of the Cole neighborhood boasts one of Denver's least-altered Romanesque Revival exteriors. Its traditional Gothic interior boasts 34 stained-glass windows by renowned Munich artists Franz Mayer and F. X. Zettler, a Kilgen pipe organ, and a 25-foot-high altar of Carrara marble adorned with 6-foot-tall angels.

The Capuchins (the Franciscan Order of Friars Minor) have worked with parish volunteers and the SHF to resurrect this church along with its K–8 school, convent, and rectory. Workers restored the exterior brick; improved the drainage; removed hazardous asbestos; replaced the roof, rusted pipes, rotten window frames, and front doors; and redid the electrical system.

Michelle Pearson, an Annunciation School seventh-grade history teacher, a White House Fellow in Preservation, and the parish preservation specialist, reports, "We hope to have the interior restored, God willing, by 2010. We just finished restoring Annunciation's stained-glass rose window. Philip Watkins, whose great-grandfather probably installed our windows, is redoing and putting protective shields on what he says are among the finest examples of Munich stained glass in North America. To match the SHF's $232,748, we have already raised a good chunk of our $130,000 with the help of guardian angels, wine and cheese tours, bake sales, and burrito sales in front of the church on Sundays."

AVERY APARTMENTS
2514 Champa St. [LLD] [NRD]
Built: 1904

"The pigeon building," as neighbors called this long-abandoned, graffiti-splattered eyesore, started out as two stories. It later received a third-floor addition, and then was carved into many small apartments. In the early 1990s, Hope Communities, a nonprofit agency that develops affordable housing, purchased the Avery. Using a $100,000 grant from the SHF, Hope installed a new roof, removed paint on the exterior brick and restored it, then rebuilt the recessed grand entrance leading to a foyer with 30-foot-high ceilings and hardwood floors. The SHF grant inspired a $1.3 million facelift. Ray Stranske, Hope's executive director, says "We have created residences for 23 low-income families and made the Avery once again a credit to the historic Curtis Park neighborhood."

BETHEL CHURCH OF GOD IN CHRIST
2455 Tremont Pl. (SR)
Built: 1920

This one-story brick building built by African-American parishioners is trimmed with quoins and crenellated parapets. The church used $61,624 in SHF grants to fix the masonry, stucco, windows, and front door. Rev. Frank Davis says that "the building's restoration adds to the beauty of the community and uplifts its spirit."

BURLINGTON HOTEL
2205 Larimer St. LL NR
Built: 1891; Frank E. Edbrooke & Co., architects

Once Denver's most notorious skid-row flophouse, it was nicknamed "The Slaughterhouse" for the many murders that occurred there. This stately three-story hotel nearly collapsed after being abandoned in the 1980s. Salvation arrived when the Burlington Hotel, LLC, partnered with Historic Denver, Inc., the Mayor's Office of Economic Development, and the North Larimer Merchants Association. An SHF grant of $103,500 kindled this resurrection and helped deteriorating upper Larimer Street make a comeback, culminating in designation of the surrounding Ball Park Historic District in 2002. NoDo, as this once dangerous edgy, and poor district was known, is joining in the urban renaissance of its more famous neighbor, LoDo.

Photos courtesy of Tom Noel

DOUGLASS UNDERTAKING PARLOR / LA PAZ POOL HALL
2745 Welton St. LL
Built: c. 1892; 1915 façade, Merrill Hoyt, architect

This small building has a big history. William Sprague, an African-American employee of the Stearns and Rogers Manufacturing Company, lived here in the 1890s. In 1915, the Douglass Undertaking Company, founded by a son of abolitionist Frederick Douglass, converted the house into a mortuary. This was just one of many African-American-owned businesses moving into the area during the early 20th century. Douglass added a new façade, designed by one of Denver's most prominent architects, to give the building a Greek Revival dignity.

After the Douglass Company left in 1943, many different businesses, including upholsterers, cleaners, and roofers, occupied the storefront. Later it served as a pool hall under many different names, including La Paz, which reflects current Hispanic migration into what had been an African-American neighborhood. In 1993, Two Hype, a clothing design company, bought the property. Their application for an SHF grant described the façade as "practically falling off the building." The floor was also filled with holes, the electrical wiring exposed, the exterior bricks decaying, and the roof collapsing. Two Hype attained a $100,000 SHF grant to rehabilitate the façade by offering $72,000 in matching funds to restore it as a retail outlet.

FERRIL HOUSE / COLORADO CENTER FOR THE BOOK
2123 Downing St. [LL] [NR]
Built: 1889, Franklin Goodnow, architect; Hughes & Lewellyn, builders

Will Ferril, a curator for the Colorado Historical Society, and his artist wife, Alice, raised their son, Thomas Hornsby Ferril, in this house. Tom grew up to become Colorado's poet laureate, achieving national prominence for his poetry. He lived to the end of his life in this house where he entertained such literati as John Ciardi, Robert Frost, Dorothy Parker, Carl Sandburg, and Thomas Wolfe.

After her father's death in 1988, Anne Ferril Folsom sold the house to Historic Denver, Inc., for a dollar. HDI restored the house, which has been used by the Colorado Center for the Book and the Colorado Endowment for the Humanities for community meetings, tours, book readings, book signings, after-school reading programs, and research in its resource library.

HDI and the Colorado Center for the Book used SHF grants of $156,651 for an exterior restoration and systems upgrade and to address public safety and accessibility for the disabled. Before restoration the building was in dreadful shape: "The walls were cracked so severely that it appeared as if the house would collapse in the next strong breeze," testified Kimberly Taylor of the Colorado Center for the Book. "A trip to the restroom was an adventure with plumbing so old that flushing the toilet was always dramatic." Now restored, the gracious residence showcases Thomas Hornsby Ferril memorabilia, houses the offices of the Colorado Center for the Book, and hosts poetry readings and writers' workshops.

Ferril, one of the founding members of the Denver Landmark Preservation Commission, immortalized this house with his poem, "House in Denver":

I can remember looking cross-lots from
This house over the evening thistle and
The bee flowers, watching people come home
From downtown. In the morning I could stand
A long time watching my father disappear
Beyond the sunflower which you noticed farther
In the morning. Now tall buildings interfere
In piles of shining masonry, but are there
Walls yet to come no more secure than these?
My city has not worn its shadows long
Enough to quiet even prairie bees.
I often hear a droning sunflower song
Dissolving the steel . . .

Photo courtesy of Tom Noel

D

MAYFAIR BUILDING
2543–2547 California St. [LL]
Built: 1889

This Curtis Park apartment house had been trashed by the time that Hope Communities bought it. Vacant for six years, it was little more than a shell. A nonprofit developer of multifamily dwellings, Hope Communities rehabilitated the structure and made it their headquarters. To achieve this goal, Hope got a $211,500 SHF grant with $908,000 in matching funds from other sources, including $250,000 from the City and County of Denver, for interior and exterior restoration.

MARGERY REED MAYO DAY NURSERY/DAY CARE
1128 W. 28th St. at Lawrence St. [LL]
Built: 1926; Harry J. Manning, architect

After the untimely death of young Margery Reed Mayo, she was memorialized by her mother, the philanthropist Mary Reed, with a beautiful, state-of-the-art new facility for Denver's oldest child daycare center and nursery, started in 1898 by Johanna Breusch. This haven, Reed decreed, would have everything designed especially for children by the society architect Harry James Manning, who had planned Reed's mansion at 475 Circle Drive. Manning scaled everything in the nursery for children. A bas-relief of zoo animals marches around the wall of the lunchroom, and a frieze of terracotta monkeys watches over the children.

In addition to its special design, the nursery was far ahead of its time in serving children of all races and religions, although staffed by the Catholic Sisters of Charity. Located in one of the poorest neighborhoods in Denver, it had served many working and single parents.

The Archdiocese of Denver closed the center in 1995 when it had fallen into dangerous disrepair. With a $100,098 SHF grant to assist with exterior and interior restoration, the archdiocese began replacing the front steps, broken windows, and shutters, and cleaning and restoring the exterior brick and the terracotta friezes. Once again, restored second-story wooden shutters are graced with animal-shaped cutouts and the frieze features the wise old owl and see-no-evil, hear-no-evil, speak-no-evil monkeys. This elegant refuge for some of Denver's youngest and poorest residents is again a haven in a neighborhood short on such amenities.

McPHEE & McGINNITY BUILDING
2301 Blake St., north corner of Broadway [LL] [NR]
Built: 1913, Fisher & Fisher, architects; 1919 addition

D

McPhee & McGinnity Company, Colorado's largest building materials supplier in the late 19th and early 20th centuries, erected this monumental, clock-towered building in the Renaissance Revival style as its offices, showroom, paint factory, and warehouse. Charles D. McPhee founded the firm in 1869 and took on John J. McGinnity as a partner in 1879. At the height of its success in the 1920s, the company operated lumberyards in 14 states.

David Cohen and Donald Silversmith, developers of the SHF-assisted restoration of the Chamber of Commerce and Buerger Block lofts in the 1700 block of Champa Street, took on this monumental reincarnation in partnership with Historic Denver, Inc. They purchased the building and converted it into loft apartments at a cost of $7 million. The SHF contributed $128,000 to help restore the four-story, red-brick and glazed white-terracotta exterior, which rises into a three-story clock tower. Cohen reports, "We've converted the clock tower building, as some call it, into 37 lofts—50 percent of them in the middle-income level—and found renters for every unit. We've restored and illuminated the giant tower clock, which fortunately had operating and repair instructions taped to it."

SACRED HEART CATHOLIC CHURCH
2760 Larimer St., south corner of 28th St. [LL]
Built: 1880; Emmett Anthony, architect

In 1879 and 1880, poor Irish and Italian immigrants constructed what is now Denver's oldest continuously operating church still in the original building. Lacking money for stone, the builders used wood for the trim and even for the altar, which they painted to look like marble. Always a poor parish, Sacred Heart eventually fell into disrepair. Its many problems included a steeple that had been shortened by six feet and covered with tin in an attempt to stop water damage. The exterior woodwork was decaying and the brick crumbling. The church undertook a $495,000 restoration, encouraged by SHF grants totaling $365,599. This funded removing the old paint, repointing bricks, and restoring the exterior woodwork.

In 1999, a 75-ton crane crowned the church with a new 25-foot-high, gilded aluminum steeple—a replica based on photographs of the long-gone, ornate original. Exterior restoration inspired the parish to begin restoring the interior, led by a pastor who happened to be a master woodworker. Father Marcus Medrano recruited workers from the church's soup kitchen to assist with needed carpentry and woodwork repair, even restoring the church murals and paintings. Thanks to the SHF and a lot of itinerant laborers, as well as a carpenter priest, Denver's oldest operating church is rejuvenated inside and out.

SAVAGE CANDY COMPANY
2158–2162 Lawrence St., south corner of 21st St. LL
Built: 1910

D

The Savage Candy Company, founded in Pueblo in 1888, built this Denver factory where some 65 employees made everything from children's penny treats to chocolate extravaganzas. This two-story, red-brick commercial building with storefronts has fancy brickwork, notable especially in the parapet, pediment, and angled corner entry. The Phoenix Concept, a social services provider addressing problems such as alcoholism, drug addiction, and homelessness, moved into the building in 1988, buying it in 1993. Phoenix Concept embarked upon a $650,000 restoration aided by $91,161 from the SHF. Following asbestos removal, restorationists focused on the roof, brick walls, foundation, basement floor, wood framing, and ornate brick trim. "We house as many as 30 residents," says Tom Schulte at the front desk, "and help them rehabilitate themselves in this rehabilitated building."

SCOTT METHODIST CHURCH / SANCTUARY LOFTS
2201 Ogden St. at E. 22nd Ave. LL NR
Built: 1889; John J. Humphreys and Frank E. Kidder, architects

Built as Christ Methodist Episcopal Church, this structure was renamed for a pioneer Black Methodist bishop, Isaiah B. Scott, after an African-American congregation bought the church in 1927. Gothic arches prevail on a structure whose massing and rusticated stone skin are otherwise more Romanesque. Gray-rhyolite walls are trimmed in red sandstone on an elaborate exterior, where the pressed-metal crockets and finials have been painted red to match the sandstone. The interior meeting hall has little ornament other than the colored-glass windows in floral and geometric patterns and the cast-iron support columns. The 190-foot-tall wooden steeple, the tallest in town when erected, was removed from the stone corner bell tower after 1976 wind damage. Historic Denver, Inc., administered the $113,708 SHF grant and other funding to restore the exterior of this landmark recycled as the Sanctuary Lofts.

SHORTER AMERICAN METHODIST EPISCOPAL CHURCH / CLEO PARKER ROBINSON DANCE STUDIO
119 W. Park Ave. LL
Built: 1925

In 1865, Mary Smith and Mary Randolph founded the African Methodist Episcopal Church at 19th and Market Streets. Later, the congregation built a church at 19th and Stout in honor of Bishop James A. Shorter. After a 1924 arson fire, allegedly started by the Ku Klux Klan, gutted the church, the congregation began work on this new church, encompassing not only a large sanctuary but a multipurpose hall, nursery room, kitchen, and pastor's study. After the congregation moved to an even larger church in the 1990s, the Cleo Parker Robinson Dance Studio occupied the building. Cleo Parker Robinson, a Denver native educated at Colorado Women's College, founded a nationally prominent, multiracial dance troupe.

Her troupe used a $100,241 SHF grant and matching funds to restore the exterior of an African-American historic landmark that is now the dance group's home, studio, and performance hall.

St. IGNATIUS LOYOLA CATHOLIC CHURCH
E. 23rd Ave., northwest corner of York St. NR
Built: 1924; Frank Frewen and Frederick Mountjoy, architects

This Gothic landmark on the west side of City Park received $293,254 in SHF grants after raising almost $600,000 with second collections at each Mass, fund-raising dinners, bequests, auctions, and donations. This helped install a new roof and repair deteriorated front steps, and allowed for repointing of the exterior brick and cast-stone trim, including the twin towers. Inspired by the fresh exterior, the church restored the interior Carrara marble, white-oak pews, and murals by the Austrian artist Antoine Shwerzler.

Tom Crane, a retired Air Force lieutenant colonel who oversees preservation for the Archdiocese of Denver, reports, "The SHF has made the restoration of many other inner-city churches possible. It has been tricky, because we cannot use state funds for religious artifacts. So we have to restore anything with a religious theme, from stained-glass windows to the crosses, with private or church monies. In every inner-city church restored with SHF funds, we have seen parishioners increase their donations. Although poor parishes, they have responded to this miraculous outside help."

Father C. Thomas Jost, S.J., pastor of St. Ignatius, says that his poor parish could not even have dreamed of this million-dollar rejuvenation without SHF advice and up-front money. Asbestos removal alone cost $44,000, the new steps $60,000. "Our friends at the State Historical Fund should be canonized," Father Jost adds, "St. Mark. St. James. St. Lyle. St. Rachel. St. Estella." Sprucing up the church has brought new pride and new parishioners to this reborn church.

H. H. THOMAS / L. C. McCLURE HOUSE
2104 Glenarm Pl. at 21st St. LLD NR NRD
Built: 1883; William Quayle, architect

William Quayle designed this house for Hugh H. Thomas, co-owner of the Gano & Thomas Furniture Store. Later, Louis C. McClure, a renowned Denver photographer, lived here for many years before his death in 1957. The house is the cornerstone of the Clements Historic Residential District, which is also known as the Enterprise Hill or Centennial Hill Historic District.

This Italianate-style, two-story residence boasts fine detailing in the elaborate brick chimneys, sandstone belt coursing, wooden porch columns, and carved stone lintels. The rejuvenation of this highly visible house on a prominent corner near downtown helped transform a blighted neighborhood into an attractive one. Historic Denver, Inc., which holds a façade easement, obtained $20,950 from the SHF to restore sandstone banding, sills, lintels, and brick chimneys.

WYATT-EDISON SCHOOL
3620 Franklin St., northeast corner of E. 36th Ave. Ⓗ 🔲
Built: 1887; Robert S. Roeschlaub, architect

One of the oldest surviving Denver public schools, Wyatt started out as Hyde Park Elementary. In 1932, DPS officials renamed it after George W. Wyatt, a longtime principal. Architecturally, it is one of the most celebrated of Roeschlaub's distinctive Romanesque Revival designs. Closed in 1982 due to insufficient enrollment, it stood empty until purchased by businessman Chuck Phillips in 1994. By that time, windows were broken and boarded up, the interior stairs had suffered fire damage, and pigeon guano frosted the inside of the structure. But Phillips had a

Photo courtesy of Tom Noel

vision of what this neighborhood landmark could become. From his office across the street, he imagined the old school brought back to life. Constructed to serve the community's children, the building was destined to return to service. Phillips leased the building to the Edison Foundation for a token amount and with them began raising the funds necessary to accomplish this enormous project. With the assistance of the New Cole Economic Development Corporation, Edison and Phillips obtained $400,000 in SHF grants and completed an $803,500 restoration, repairing windows and stairs, removing the guano, and restoring the structure for a

1998 reopening as a charter school. Contributors were invited to a grand reopening ceremony, where singing children lined the ornate central stairway and expressed their appreciation for this reborn landmark. Wyatt's halls once again ring with the sound of children laughing, learning, and experiencing the wonder that great architecture can play in their lives.

D

ZION BAPTIST CHURCH
933 E. 24th Ave., northwest corner of Ogden St. LL
Built: 1893; Frank H. Jackson and George F. Rivinius, architects

Colorado's oldest African-American congregation, formed by former slaves in 1865, bought this structure, the former Calvary Baptist Church, in 1911. A rusticated rhyolite edifice that is trimmed in the same gray stone, the church exemplifies the Richardsonian Romanesque style. Inside, distinctive stained-glass windows brighten an interior dominated by dark ceiling beams and woodwork.

With $423,599 in SHF funds the church has installed a new roof and restored its exterior. This was the first step in a $790,000 rehabilitation that included the installation of wheelchair ramps, as well as repairing windows, replacing sidewalks, and adding landscaping. SHF funds have gone to repoint mortar joints and install protective covers for the stained-glass windows. Rev. Wendell T. Liggins, pastor from 1941 until his death in 1991, was a famed orator and civic activist who made this a popular and influential church. Noted for services so lively that parishioners fainted with excitement, Rev. Liggins kept a nurse on hand on Sundays, when he would energetically exhort the congregation to praise the Lord and share their blessings.

Photo courtesy of Tom Noel

East Denver *(from Colorado Blvd. east)*

D

FAIRMOUNT CEMETERY LITTLE IVY CHAPEL
400 S. Quebec St. at E. Alameda Ave. ⬜LL⬜
Built: 1890; Harry T. E. Wendell, architect

With SHF grants of $68,267, the Fairmount Heritage Foundation began exterior restoration of the Ivy Chapel, a Denver landmark seen and used almost every day by hundreds of people. As a community service, Fairmount allows free access to what is perhaps Colorado's finest example of High French Gothic Revival architecture. Concerned about early stages of decay, Fairmount removed the Boston ivy from the chapel's light gray sandstone walls in 1995 and added a protective coating. Alas, the stone has remained "diseased." In a state-of-the-art program, Fairmount enlisted $77,517 in SHF help, which the cemetery matched, to thoroughly study the problem and develop plans to restore the sandstone to good health. The Foundation held a workshop and brought out renowned conservator Norman Weiss from New York to study the stone. This pioneering work has been very valuable to other preservation projects statewide coping with restoration of deteriorated stone.

FOUR MILE HOUSE
5000 E. Exposition Ave. at S. Forest St. ⬜LL⬜ ⬜NR⬜
Built: 1859, many additions

Denver's oldest structure survives from the city's gold-rush origins when it was a way station on the Smoky Hill–Cherry Creek Trail four miles southeast of Denver. Originally a hewn-log cabin of ponderosa pine resting on a cottonwood foundation, it has been modified many times, including clapboarding over the logs, a frame wing addition, and a two-story, red-brick addition. The house was restored in the

1970s, at which time a vanished bee house was re-created for educational purposes at this historical park and living-history museum. A stallion barn, blacksmith shop, family (three-hole) outhouse, and carriage barn have also been added.

Four Mile House's $1.8 million expansion, completed in 2002, was supported by $109,953 from the SHF for preservation planning and interior and exterior rehabilitation. Four Mile director Barbara Gibson says, "Ours is an example of how SHF grants preserve an important resource and use it to educate people, especially young people, about the past. The SHF grant enabled us to create a strategic plan and expand Four Mile with outbuildings, a new educational center, and better use of our 12-acre outdoor site. Many Coloradans —especially children— know little about Colorado's golden past."

LOWRY BRICK BARRACKS/BASE HEADQUARTERS / GRAND LOWRY LOFTS
200 N. Rampart Way [LLD] [NR]
Built: 1940

The Spanish Baroque Revival grand entry of these blond-brick barracks fronts an I-shaped four-story edifice with a red-tile roof. Note the second-story balconies flanked by bas-relief stone emblems of the Air Corps Technical School, its motto *Sustineo Alas* ("I Sustain the Wings," or, more popularly, "Keep Them Flying"), and twin stone eagles perched on the entry cornice.

On October 16, 1940, troops moved from Lowry's initial tent city into this building designed for 850 men. By 1943, as many as 3,600 men lived here in cramped dorms jammed with bunkbeds. Besides dorms, the Brick Barracks contained at various times a dining hall, bakery, pastry shop, laundry, dry cleaner, post exchange, bowling alley, recreation rooms, barbershops, a post office, the Lowry Federal Credit Union, the finance office, and the traffic management office. This structure became base head-quarters in 1961 and remained so until Lowry Air Force Base closed in 1994.

With Lowry's reincarnation as a residential community, the Brick Barracks have been restored outside and rehabilitated inside as loft resi-dences. There are 261 one- and two-bedroom lofts with 11- to 14-foot-high ceilings that include amenities such as a swimming pool, spa, volleyball court, and heated underground parking. The elegant exterior revival was assisted by the SHF's $96,600.

LOWRY HANGAR No. 1 / WINGS OVER THE ROCKIES MUSEUM

7711 E. Academy Blvd. [LLD]
Built: 1940

D

Located on the former Lowry Air Force Base, this industrial wonder may have been designed by the great modern architect Louis Kahn, who did similar work for the army elsewhere. It began life as Hangar No. 1, with 163,000 square feet framed by steel girder trusses and twelve bays, all sheathed in corrugated steel. The hangar is 38 feet high with 250-foot-wide doorways, consisting of 12 six-ton rolling door panels mounted on rails. It housed aircraft maintenance, shops, classes, and—briefly—soldiers, before Lowry's Brick Barracks were built. Classes in aircraft maintenance, munitions, fighter systems, and bomb loading met here. In 1994, it became the Wings Over the Rockies Museum.

Besides the B-52 at the front door, the hangar features over two dozen military and civilian aircraft. One room honors President Dwight Eisenhower's "Summer White House" at Lowry from 1953 to 1955. Another offers photos and memorabilia of the Air Force Academy's beginnings at Lowry in 1955. The museum received a $15,750 SHF grant for $21,000 in roof repairs to keep visitors and exhibits dry at this museum and events center and $34,813 to develop plans to restore the roof to its original appearance.

LOWRY SENIOR OFFICERS' GARAGE / STANLEY BRITISH PRIMARY SCHOOL

350 Quebec St. [LL]
Built: 1939

Lowry trained 1.2 million men and women from all branches of the armed forces from 1938 until 1994. Presidents Franklin D. Roosevelt and Dwight D. Eisenhower

visited the base, and Eisenhower used it as his "Summer White House" from 1953 to 1955. It was also the first home of the Air Force Academy. After the base closed in 1994, the Lowry Redevelopment Authority aimed to preserve some of the structures to commemorate the base's past. Among those that were preserved were 10 buildings sold for $1 to the Stanley British Primary School (BPS), a private K–8 academy.

The new BPS campus even includes two vintage five-car garages that were built in the Mediterranean style with red-tile roofs, limestone detailing, and embellished entrances. With the help of SHF grants of $72,020, the garages were rehabilitated as multiuse classroom space with new plumbing, electrical, and fire-alarm systems, as well as brick repairs and new glazing.

RICHTHOFEN MOLKERY
6280 E. 12th Ave. in Montclair Park Ⓗ ⃞LL⃞ ⃞LLD⃞ ⃞NR⃞
Built: 1888, Alexander Cazin, architect; 1908 remodel, Frederick W. Ameter, architectural engineer

When Baron Walter von Richthofen founded the east Denver suburban town of Montclair in 1885, he hoped to make it Colorado's most fashionable health spa. To attract the tuberculosis patients then flocking to Colorado for the climate cure, he built this picturesque Molkery. Modeled after German and Swiss health spas, the Molkery offered fresh air, mountain views, and open-air sun porches. Patients drank milk fresh from the Jersey cows stabled below and breathed the supposedly healthy barnyard effluvium rising through special grates built into the floor. Apparently this sure cure failed, because shortly thereafter the Molkery

was converted to a mental hospital.

In 1908, Denver acquired the building and remodeled it as the city's first community center. During the 1990s, the city allowed it to deteriorate and it was boarded up. The Molkery suffered from a fire, vagrants sleeping inside it, and teenagers partying there. For a long-postponed $850,000 restoration of the Molkery, Denver Parks and Recreation received $450,000 from a 1989 Denver bond issue and $177,000 from the SHF. The Historic Montclair Community Association, Inc., the city, and SlaterPaull Architects achieved a historically correct restoration, bringing back the maple floors, oak staircase, canvas wall covering, and other interior features, even restoring the radiators to retain the building's historic character. On the exterior, the rhyolite stone and brick were cleaned and repaired, the porches restored to their original open-air design, and the cupola and chimneys—which had been lost in a 1920s windstorm—reconstructed. The Denver Parks and Recreation "Hands On" staff, who coordinate volunteers in the parks, occupy the second story of this reborn landmark. The first floor once again houses community events. This spectacular restoration shines day and night thanks to new exterior lighting that spotlights the structure and its cupola.

St. THOMAS EPISCOPAL CHURCH
2201 Dexter St., northwest corner of E. 22nd Ave. LL
Built: 1908; Harry J. Manning, architect

D

Manning made this one of Denver's best examples of the Spanish Colonial Revival style with a fabulous Churrigueresque entry surround of cast stone. A triple-arch bell tower, stucco walls, and red-tile roof distinguish this church, which, with its auxiliary buildings and cloister, frames a landscaped courtyard. The Mission-style

interior features a wood-beamed, open-truss nave. Social activism and outstanding architecture have distinguished it as one of Denver's first racially integrated churches, which was also one of the first to welcome African-Americans and to include female acolytes and clerics, among them a female bishop. Parishioner-architect Patric Dawe designed the expansion, complete with solar energy. SHF funding of $59,477 helped replace gutters and downspouts and repair the roof.

TREAT HALL
1800 Pontiac St. LL NR
Built: 1909; Frank H. Jackson and Betts, architects

Colorado Women's College was established in 1888 on a campus that was bounded by Quebec and Oneida Streets and East 18th Avenue and Montview Boulevard. The silver crash of 1893 delayed construction. Finally, Treat Hall, a three-story Romanesque structure with rough-faced walls of Castle Rock rhyolite and red-sandstone trim, opened as the first campus building. Named after Jay Porter Treat, the school's first president, it was for years the only building on campus. A 1913–1916 addition to Treat Hall used brick and terracotta instead of rhyolite and sandstone. Between the 1920s and the 1960s, other distinctive buildings were added to the campus.

In 1982, Colorado Women's College closed and became the University of Denver's Park Hill Campus. In 2000, DU sold the campus to Johnson & Wales, a culinary and hospitality university based in Providence, Rhode Island, with five U.S. campuses. Started by Miss Gertrude Johnson and Miss Mary Wales in 1914, J&W now claims to be the world's premier culinary-arts college. J&W has matched SHF grants of $226,126 to replace the roof and conduct hazardous-material abatement. J&W plans a $15 million restoration of Treat Hall, which it hopes to convert into a boutique hotel and restaurant showcasing the hospitality skills of its students.

Northwest Denver *(between the South Platte River, W. 52nd Ave., Sheridan Blvd., and W. 6th Ave.)*

ALL SAINTS EPISCOPAL CHURCH / CHAPEL OF OUR MERCIFUL SAVIOR

D

2224 W. 32nd Ave. [LL] [NR]
Built: 1890; James Murdoch, architect

To restore the church and repair its historic pipe organ, the Episcopal Diocese of Colorado used more than $200,000 in SHF grants and their own matching funds. Restoration included replacing the worn-out leather bellows in the 1891 Farrand & Votey pipe organ. A soaring steeple on a corner bell tower distinguishes this refurbished red-brick Gothic Revival chapel. Built as All Saints Episcopal Church, it was renamed Chapel of Our Merciful Savior after the original congregation moved to a larger church in 1961. Rusticated rhyolite trims the entrance beneath a rose window. Inside, the original carved wooden statues, pulpit, baptismal font, and pews survive under hammered ceiling beams set in a herringbone pattern. The marble angel that holds a scalloped holy water basin was sculpted by Elsie Ward Hering, a Denverite who studied under and worked with Augustus Saint-Gaudens.

Pastor Christopher A. Johnson reports, "We're also using SHF funds and our match to put up vented protective glass over our stained-glass windows. When we cleaned out the steeple, we found pigeon remains eight inches deep on the steeple floor. On a hot summer day, you could smell this church a block away." Redoing the gutters, downspouts, and masonry, and installing new roof shingles as well as door repair and replacement, inspired the church and the community also to transform the weedy vacant lot next door into a pocket park.

BERKELEY SCHOOL

5025–5055 Lowell Blvd. [LL] [NR]
Built: 1906, David W. Dryden, architect; 1923 addition, Glen W. Huntington, architect

John Brisben Walker, one of Colorado's most prominent developers and promoters, donated part of his alfalfa farm as a site for Regis University and this elementary school. Initially a one-story, two-room schoolhouse, it was replaced in 1906 with this imposing three-story building. After Denver Public Schools vacated the building in 1976, it stood abandoned for almost 20 years.

In 1996, Cornwell Construction bought the building, and with the help of a $100,000 SHF grant and $893,000 in matching funds, the company partnered with the Potter Highlands Preservation Association to restore the school and convert it into loft-style apartments. The process included replacing 118 contemporary windows with historic replica ones; repairing and repointing the brick; repairing and restoring the original exterior doors, trim, and drainage; and removing a 1980s-era bubble skylight.

CRESCENT HAND LAUNDRY BUILDING
2323–2329 W. 30th Ave. [LL]
Built: c. 1891; James A. Hamman, builder

Originally occupied by William W. Bewley's coal, hay, and feed store, this structure housed the Crescent Hand Laundry from 1902 to 1916. Later occupants included a restaurant and other businesses. Renovations failed to halt the decline of the building, which had become dilapidated and run-down by 1995, when Carey Bringle and Susan Proctor bought it. With the aid of the nonprofit Potter Highlands Preservation Association, the owners obtained a $16,875 SHF grant towards a $92,015 restoration. Repointing, cleaning, stone repair, and paint removal have returned the antique façade to its original design and retrofitted the interior with four loft apartments.

ELITCH GARDENS THEATRE
W. 38th Ave. and Tennyson St. [LL] [NR]
Built: 1890–1891; Charles Herbert Lee and Rudolph Liden, builders

On May 1, 1890, Elitch Gardens opened as an amusement park, botanical gardens, and zoo. Despite a torrential downpour, many Denverites put on their finery for the festivities and a vaudeville show. The latter was so well received that park owners John and Mary Elitch decided to open a summer theater the following year. John made the theater his main concern but died suddenly in 1891 in San Francisco. Mary Elitch remarried and ran the theater and gardens until her own death in 1936.

The theater was left behind when Elitch Gardens, Denver's oldest, largest, and best-known amusement park, moved to the Central Platte Valley in 1995. This unusual frame playhouse, which claimed to be America's oldest continuously operating summer-stock theater, had hundreds of nationally prominent actors grace its stage until it closed in 1987. A rare example of frame construction combining Stick-and-Shingle style elements, it evolved over the years from the original circular frame building into an octagon two stories high with a tent-shaped roof crowned by a flagpole. Wood drop siding covers each 43-foot-wide exterior side. A two-story addition (c. 1900) forms a vestibule with two enclosed stairways to the balcony.

In 1995, Denver's Office of Planning and Community Development used a $30,000 SHF grant for a feasibility study to restore the theater and adjacent carousel house and flower warehouses. Developer Perry Rose, LLC, who designed and built the surrounding New Urbanist residential neighborhood on the old amusement-park site, has restored the carousel building for public use. They teamed up with Denver Botanic Gardens to restore some of the famous gardens that distinguished the original Elitch's Gardens. With city help and the SHF's $35,532, Chuck Perry and Jonathan Rose are restoring the now decrepit theater as a mixed-use performance and event center, scheduled to open in 2010 after a $14.2 million restoration.

HANIGAN-CANINO TERRACE APARTMENTS
1421–1435 W. 35th Ave., northeast corner of Navajo St. NR
Built: 1890

Irish immigrant Frank Hanigan constructed these modest apartments to house his compatriots. Later, other working-class groups moved in, notably Italians, who transformed this neighborhood into north Denver's "Little Italy". The building's

second owner, Joseph Canino, represented this 1880s–1920s wave of Italian immigrants. In 1935, he remodeled the corner unit for use as his meat market and family home.

By the 1990s, the terrace no longer met federal and city standards for occupancy. The Del Norte Neighborhood Develop-ment Corporation undertook a $150,000 restoration of the interior, exterior, and landscaping with support from the SHF's $50,000. These funds paid for repairing the roof, masonry, chimney, and walls; replacing nonhistoric windows and exterior doors; and upgrading the electrical and security systems.

SEVENTH AVENUE CHURCH
666 King St. and W. Seventh Ave. LL
Built: 1913; William N. Bowman, architect

The Villa Park Congregational Church, formed in 1871, built this west Denver landmark when its congregation grew too large for its old church. The Villa Park congregation may have been Denver's first to have a woman in the pulpit, as the wife of Rev. E. R. Drake often filled in for her sickly husband. It is the oldest surviving church in Denver's Barnum neighborhood. Architect W. N. Bowman created an American Gothic design with a variation on the Akron Plan used in many Protestant churches at the time. The church is notable for the wooden gables of its sanctuary and the 1890 cornerstone of the earlier church, which the congregation built into the new church. By the 1990s, the building had become dilapidated before obtaining SHF grants of $104,646 to repair the roof, gutters, brickwork, and masonry.

St. DOMINIC'S CATHOLIC CHURCH
3005 W. 29th Ave. at Federal Blvd. NR
Built: 1926; Robert W. Willison, architect

On a sunny, snow-frosted Sunday, February 14, 1926, white-robed Dominican priests, brothers, and sisters gathered to help the bishop of Denver consecrate this home base for Rocky Mountain Dominicans. Their English Gothic–style church glories in a nave of Caen stone rising to groined arches 80 feet overhead. The parish of many blue-collar immigrants never could afford to install stained-glass windows but did open the first parish credit union in Colorado to help members get through the Great Depression. Long-postponed reroofing was made possible by an SHF grant of $182,850.

St. ELIZABETH'S RETREAT CHAPEL
2825 W. 32nd Ave. LL NR
Built: 1897; Frederick J. Sterner, architect

In 1894, Rev. Frederick W. Oakes, an Episcopalian, erected a sanitarium for victims of tuberculosis, then the most common cause of death worldwide. This sanitarium, one of Colorado's first and largest, contained 25 buildings, clustered around what is now St. Elizabeth's Retreat Chapel.

By the 1930s, newly discovered drugs and antibiotics reduced the need for sanitariums like Oakes'. In 1941, the Sisters of St. Francis bought the ailing sanitarium, which they converted into their mother house, a retreat, and a healthcare center. In 1974, after inspectors pronounced the buildings unsafe, the Sisters demolished everything but the chapel. They replaced the handsome old buildings with modern, three-story residential units and a 14-story highrise for seniors.

In 1998, the Sisters combined $156,948 in SHF grants with $71,299 in matching funds to restore this Neoclassical apparition reminiscent of Christopher Wren's London chapels. One of the most exquisite works of master architect F. J. Sterner, this brick beauty culminates in a lovely bell tower with nine Meneeley bells and an original 1903 Austin organ, two rare antiques that have also been restored.

ROBERT W. STEELE GYMNASIUM / BOYS AND GIRLS CLUB OF METRO DENVER
3914 King St. (SR)
Built: 1914–1915; Robert W. Willison, architect

D

This gymnasium stands as a legacy to the Progressive Era sentiment that govern-ment should take an active role in bettering the lives of all its citizens. Robert W. Steele, a chief justice of the Colorado Supreme Court who had taken an interest in reforming juvenile offenders, died at the time of the building's construction. In his memory, his family launched a fund drive to construct this recreational and social center for underprivileged children. Various businesses, philanthropists, tradesmen, and neighborhood residents contributed to the construction. Many of the same constituencies also contributed to the restoration of this structure, which continues its recreational and educational activities for children. The Mission-style structure is constructed of light tan brick with buttresses and a curvilinear roof parapet over an arched main entrance. The Boys and Girls Club of Metro Denver, the current owner of the building, obtained a $31,416 SHF grant with $10,525 in matching funds to maintain the building. Although it was in generally good shape, some of the exterior bricks had deteriorated. The Club used SHF funds to pay for selective repointing of damaged bricks and for the application of graffiti guard to make the exterior easier to clean.

WESTSIDE COURTHOUSE / BERNIE VALDEZ HISPANIC HERITAGE CENTER
924 W. Colfax Ave. at Speer Blvd. LL NR
Built: 1921–1922; Edwin H. Moorman and James B. Hyder, architects

Before the city courts relocated to the City and County Building in 1952, they occupied this three-story, red-brick edifice. Although a setting for many famous trials, the Westside Courthouse deteriorated during the 13 years when it mostly sat vacant after the departure of the district attorney's offices in 1986. Its old-fashioned courtroom was used for a time as a setting for the long-running *Perry Mason* televi-sion series.

The Bernie Valdez Hispanic Heritage Center, LLC, partnered with the SHF (which awarded $250,000 to the $375,000 restoration), the Coors Foundation, and others to restore the exterior and rehabilitate the interior. The large arched windows were repaired or replaced and the central staircase was restored. The courthouse's masonry exterior was repaired and cleaned, and now the building is alive with activity once again.

The Valdez Center commemorates a Denver activist who fought to improve the lives of migrant farmworkers and became a Denver Housing Authority official, manager of the Denver Welfare Department, and a member and president of the Denver Board of Education. Located in the heart of Denver's largely Hispanic Westside neighborhood, the center provides offices, training, and conference facilities for Denver's Hispanic community and other tenants such as Habitat for Humanity.

South Denver *(south of W. 6th Ave., Speer Blvd., E. 1st Ave., and Cherry Creek)*

D

WILLIAM N. BYERS JUNIOR HIGH / DENVER SCHOOL OF THE ARTS
150 S. Pearl St. 🔲
Built: 1921–1922; Harry J. Manning and
   William N. Bowman, architects

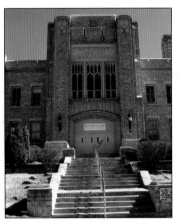

Byers Junior High School was built on the site of the last earthly home of William Newton Byers, founding editor of the *Rocky Mountain News*. This imposing, two-and-a-half-story Collegiate Gothic design in buff brick with terracotta trim used an "E" plan that lets natural light into every classroom. Sunrooms on the south served as lunchrooms until they were enclosed to form more classrooms. Byers Junior High became an alternative learning center in the 1980s and then the Denver School of the Arts during the 1990s. Denver Public Schools matched SHF funding of $9,667 with $54,082 to assess the building and restore or replace the transoms and main entry with historically correct replicas.

FLEMING MANSION / PLATT PARK SENIOR RECREATION CENTER
1510 S. Grant St., southeast corner of E. Florida Ave. 🔲
Built: 1882

James A. Fleming, a mining and real-estate man, constructed his mansion in South Denver, once an independent municipality that elected him its first mayor. Fleming turned the block surrounding his house into a public park, known as Fleming's Grove. He later sold the house and the park to the Town of South Denver for use as a town hall and public park. Following South Denver's annexation by Denver, the park was renamed for Sarah Platt Decker, a leading clubwoman and civic activist for whom the branch library in the park is also named. In 1957, Denver converted the Fleming house into a neighborhood senior recreation center. Denver Parks and Recreation used a $100,000 SHF grant and its own cash match of $70,000 to repair the masonry, restore woodwork on the veranda and the main entry door, repaint the exterior wood trim, and replace weather stripping. To correct a drainage problem and protect the foundation, workers removed the sunken perimeter concrete walk and regraded to allow water to flow away from the building through an underground drainage system. The retaining wall was rebuilt to match the building's stonework, and landscaping has added a final flourish.

FORT LOGAN FIELD OFFICERS' QUARTERS
3742 W. Princeton Cir. **H** LL
Built: 1889; Frank Grodavent, architect

In 1887, Congress authorized the construction of Fort Logan on a site chosen by Lieutenant General Phil Sheridan. Named for Union general John A. Logan, the fort was architecturally distinguished by its handsome field officers' quarters

D

designed in a modified Queen Anne style. After the post closed in 1946, Governor Stephen McNichols acquired a portion of it in 1960 for the Fort Logan State Mental Health Center. Other organizations, including Fort Logan National Cemetery, also occupy parts of the 980-acre site.

Since 1994, the nonprofit Friends of Historic Fort Logan have raised more than $140,000 in funds, grants, and volunteer service to match $160,222 in SHF grants to renovate the field officers' quarters and convert it into a museum. The Friends stabilized and restored the exterior and restored the first floor for exhibits. "Fort Logan is a special part of Colorado's heritage," says Earl McCoy of the Friends of Historic Fort Logan. "We are delighted to have the field offi-cers' quarters restored and open to the public. We now hope to pursue designation of the parade grounds and surrounding original buildings as a National Register Historic District."

SOUTH HIGH SCHOOL
1700 E. Louisiana Ave. between S. Franklin St. and S. Race St. LL
Built: 1924, William E. Fisher and Arthur A. Fisher, architects;
   1964 southwest wing addition, Charles Gordon Lee, architect;
   1989 gym, MCB Architects

South High Alumni and Friends, Inc., raised more than $12,000 and were granted SHF funding of $34,511 to restore the clock tower on one of Denver's most dis-tinctive schools. Elaborate brickwork, extensive terracotta friezes, and ornate trim distinguish this Romanesque structure featuring a prominent clock tower, copied from the Santa Maria in Cosmedin in Rome, Italy, complete with zodiac figures replacing numbers on the clock face.

Grant funds were used to replace the clock tower's roof deck, install new wrought-iron and pigeon-repelling mesh, update the electrical system, and paint and seal the room housing the antique E. Howard and Son clockworks. Funds also went toward the cleaning and restoration of the distinctive Allen Tupper True murals in the main entry hall and the bas-reliefs of Robert Garrison, a well-known Denver sculptor responsible for perhaps the most memorable of this school's many notable features. Perched Above the main west entrance, Garrison's three-and-a-half-foot gargoyle welcomes all visitors to the school. Also, on either side of the main entrance are carved figures of teachers with raised creatures in their hands. These creatures represent exams, and they are busy trying

Photo courtesy of Tom Noel

to devour students, whose weary heads lie on piles of books. The door contains two friezes, *Faculty Row* and *Animal Spirits*: the former resembles a frieze of the Last Supper, with the principal occupying the central space, while the latter depicts studentlike creatures making mischief.

St. PETER & St. MARY EPISCOPAL CHURCH
126 W. 2nd Ave.
Built: 1891; Theodore Boal and Charles H. Lee, architects

This exquisite stone structure has rough gray-rhyolite walls under the sloping eaves of steep-pitched roofs. Inside, the nave's open trusses, exposed rafters, and beaded roof decking suggest a beautifully crafted boat. The parish matched $10,000 from the SHF for interior and exterior restoration of one of the cornerstone landmarks of the Baker Historic District. The masonry was repointed, new gutters were installed, and old Plexiglas was replaced with laminated safety glass in order to better protect the stained-glass windows.

WASHINGTON PARK BATHHOUSE
Washington Park, northwest shore of Smith Lake LL NR
Built: 1912

This bathhouse dates from Washington Park's days as one of Denver's favorite swimming holes, when a sandy beach stretched from this bathhouse to Smith Lake. Designed to promote public cleanliness and order as well as recreation, the beach also helped keep youth out of trouble by providing them with healthy exercise. The bathhouse fell into disuse after swimming was prohibited in 1957 because of a polio scare. Not until 1995 did Volunteers for Outdoor Colorado (VOC) spend $600,000, including $100,000 from the SHF, to rehabilitate the building inside and out as offices, meeting rooms, a reading room, and headquarters for the VOC, which promotes, builds, and supports public parks statewide.

Dillon

DILLON SCHOOL HOUSE MUSEUM
403 La Bonte St. [LL]
Built: 1883

D

Dillon's first school—whose first class, taught by Mrs. R. N. DeBecque, included seven girls and six boys—escaped a watery grave in the old town, which today sits at the bottom of Dillon Reservoir.
Locals moved the cherished landmark to high ground where an $18,000 SHF grant enabled the Summit Historical Society to stabilize the foundation and install a new wood-shingle roof. The SHF grant also provided for the installation of new wood-shingle roofs on the adjacent Myers Ranch House as well as the Honeymoon Cottage, which along

with the school form a history park. This one-room, white clapboard schoolhouse, according to Rebecca Waugh, the former administrator of the Summit County Historical Society, "is a great little museum, complete with vintage classroom."

RICE BARN
375 Cove Blvd. [LL]
Built: 1918–1920; Benjamin Rice, builder

In her book *Roadside Summit: The Human Landscape*, Sandra S. Pritchett notes that ranchers used a haystacker and then a wooden apparatus to push cut hay up the incline and into this barn through an opening at the roof peak. Rebecca Waugh, former administrator of the Summit County Historical Society, reports that "the most fascinating aspect of this property is the trapdoor that unfolds on the side of the roof. This was used to bring hay into the loft." The restoration has made this old hay-loading system functional again.

    This relic of Summit County's cattle-and-sheep raising days now houses antique ranching equipment and is the centerpiece of a historic mini-park, together with the ranching artifacts in the surrounding field, adjoining the Soda Creek Apartments. A $27,004 SHF grant has enabled the Summit County Historical Society to stabilize the structure under a gambrel roof covered with corrugated metal, regrade the site, and rechink and redaub the logs.

Dolores

ANASAZI HERITAGE CENTER SITES
27501 CO 184 LL
1060–1280; Ancestral Puebloan Peoples

D

On June 9, 2000, a presidential proclamation set aside 164,000 acres of rugged desert canyons and high mesas for preservation as Canyons of the Ancients National Monument. The Anasazi Heritage Center is the gateway to this significant archaeological landscape, and was completed in 1984 as part of the Dolores Archaeological Program. Nearly 1,600 archaeological sites—hunting camps, granaries, households, villages, etc.—have yielded artifacts, some of which are on display at the museum. Owned and operated by the Bureau of Land Management, the Anasazi Heritage Center also provides information on a number of sites that have benefited from SHF grants. Nearly $1.5 million has been awarded for approximately 24 projects to various nonprofit organizations to conduct research, stabilization, and interpretation involving archaeological resources in the Canyons of the Ancients. The goal of the Heritage Center is to increase public awareness of archaeology and cultural resources, as well as the Ancestral Puebloan (Anasazi) and other peoples of the Four Corners region.

The BLM has often partnered with Crow Canyon Archaeological Center in its study of ancient sites such as Lowry Pueblo, Painted Hand Pueblo, Castle Rock Pueblo, and Sand Canyon Pueblo. Located at 23390 County Road K, west of Cortez, Crow Canyon has collaborated with the BLM and other partners to expand public knowledge and interest with its education programs, digs, exhibits, and site reports. Its computerized site reports include maps, photographs, interpretive text, and databases to address topics in architecture, artifacts, and archaeological method and theory. SHF-funded educational materials help guide current and future generations in learning about the history, and prehistory, of this area. According to Mark Varien, director at Crow Canyon, "Approximately 50,000 students of all ages and from all walks of life have worked with Crow Canyon archaeologists to excavate these sites and conduct laboratory analysis of archaeological materials."

An important aspect of these sites is their connection to contemporary Native Americans. Twenty-four tribes trace their ancestors to the land in Canyons of the Ancients. Visitors to these sacred sites would do well to heed the words of Hopi tribal member Harlan Mahle: "When you are at these places, you should leave a prayer to the Ancient Ones and the spirits."

CASTLE ROCK PUEBLO
Access information available at:
Anasazi Heritage Center
27501 CO 184 (SR)
c. 1250–1290; Ancestral Puebloan Peoples

Located in McElmo Canyon on the northern side of Sleeping Ute Mountain, Castle Rock Pueblo was built at the base of Castle Rock Butte and inhabited by

D

an estimated 75 to 100 people who lived in some 40 to 60 rooms. This pueblo was first documented by the official U.S. Army survey of Colorado conducted by Ferdinand Vandiveer Hayden. Led by Captain John Moss, the Hayden team explored the area and heard a story from a Hopi elder that the location had once been the scene of a great battle between the Puebloan people and enemies from the north. William Henry Jackson photographed the site and called it Fortified Rock on the McElmo. The SHF granted Crow Canyon Archaeological Center $87,358 for research and preservation of this site. This research has been incorporated into Crow Canyon's first electronic site report, *The Archaeology of Castle Rock Pueblo: A Thirteenth Century Village in Southwestern Colorado.* This comprehensive report is fully integrated with an electronic database and is designed to reach archaeological professionals as well as the general public.

ESCALANTE RUIN
Access information available at:
Anasazi Heritage Center
27501 CO 184 NR SR
c. 1129 (initial development); c. 1150–1200, Ancestral Puebloan Peoples

Escalante Pueblo was named for Father Silvestre Veléz de Escalante, who, along with Father Francisco Atanasio Domínguez, documented their explorations near present-day Dolores, Colorado. They were camped along the edge of El Rio de Nuestra Señora de Los Dolores ("Our Lady of Sorrows") when they first documented an Ancestral Puebloan site in present-day Colorado. In his 1776 diary Father Escalante wrote, "Upon an elevation on the river's south side, there was in ancient times a small settlement of the same type as the Indians of New Mexico, as the ruins we purposely inspected show."

Escalante Pueblo is one of the northernmost Chacoan outlier communities, showing strong Chaco influence. Reminiscent of New Mexico's Chaco Canyon, the architecture at Escalante Pueblo includes a large rectangular room enclosing a kiva in the center, surrounded by some 28 rooms and living quarters. The masonry is also Chacoan in style—stones similar in size and shape alternating with bands of smaller stones, called "chinking," a form common in structures throughout southwestern Colorado. The SHF's $98,525 grant to the University of Colorado facilitated using advanced technologies, including photogrammetry, to map the ruins site and create drawings for research and public education. The SHF also granted $40,100 to the Public Lands Interpretive Association for educational curriculum development. When the roof of the kiva at Escalante collapsed under heavy snows in 1997, the photogrammetric maps enabled the archaeologists at Escalante to restore and stabilize the kiva. A short interpretive trail, which provides access to the disabled, leads from the Anasazi Heritage Center to Escalante Ruin, from which visitors can take in panoramic views of McPhee Reservoir and the entire Four Corners area.

LOWRY RUIN
Access information available at:
Anasazi Heritage Center
27501 CO 184 NR SR
c. 1060–1280; Ancestral Puebloan Peoples

D

Named after homesteader George Lowry and located in Canyons of the Ancients National Monument, the Lowry Ruin site boasts one of the largest kivas in southwestern Colorado. Approximately 100 people lived here on the mesa between the north and south forks of Crow Canyon, where they hunted, painted elaborate designs on pottery, and wove cotton obtained through trade. As with many archaeological sites in southwestern Colorado, Lowry shows more than one period of habitation, ranging from around 1060 to approximately 1280. The architectural style of the early Chacoan culture was followed by later influences of the Mesa Verdean people. This awe-inspiring location offers beautiful views of Sleeping Ute Mountain.

With the data collected from Lowry Ruin, an interactive CD-ROM titled *People in the Past* was developed using funds from the SHF, Bureau of Land Management, and Southwest Natural and Cultural Heritage Association. This award-winning introduction to archaeology uses photographs, interviews with modern Puebloan people, and computer-generated imagery to guide viewers through the Lowry Ruin and interpret the daily life of the Ancestral Puebloan

farmer. Perspectives of both scientists and Native Americans are presented to achieve the balance necessary in educating the public about this historic area. Not only can CD-ROM users participate in virtual archaeological "digs," they will also develop a greater appreciation for the Pueblo culture and the need to preserve these archaeological sites for future generations.

The Lowry Ruin site is the only location within Canyons of the Ancients that has been developed as a recreation site, with picnic areas that provide access to the disabled, a parking lot, restrooms, and an interpretive trail. The SHF gave $173,120 to the Public Lands Interpretive Association for a protective roof structure, regrading, signage, site interpretation, and exhibits.

PAINTED HAND PUEBLO
Access information available at:
Anasazi Heritage Center
27501 CO 184 (SR)
c. 1200S; Ancestral Puebloan Peoples

Painted Hand Pueblo was a small village with about 20 rooms that contains rock paintings and petroglyphs. A SHF grant to Crow Canyon provided funding to document the site and bring Puebloan elders from Acoma, Laguna, and Hopi to help interpret the rock art and architectural layout. The SHF grant also helped produce a brochure that explains many of the Puebloan terms for the site and its features, such as *kaach-ta kaact*, which is Acoma for a "wide area of dwellings"; *kiikiqo*, which is Hopi for "footprints"; and *Ship'aap*, which is Laguna for "the place of emergence".

SAND CANYON PUEBLO
Access information available at:
Anasazi Heritage Center
27501 CO 184 (SR)
c. 1225–1280; Ancestral Puebloan Peoples

Sand Canyon is one of the area's largest single villages, with 450 surface rooms, 90 to 100 kivas, 14 towers, and a Great Kiva. Its D-shaped layout is also seen at several other large village sites in the area. Today the site resembles a large mound of rubble, with few of the walls exposed. Intensive architectural research and dendrochronology (tree-ring dating), as well as the initial plan and subsequent expansion of the site, special-use buildings, and public spaces, indicate that Sand Canyon Pueblo may have served both as a large-scale village and as an integrative center for outlying communities. A SHF grant of $41,120 facilitated survey and designation of this prehistoric city, which is now protected as part of Canyons of the Ancients National Monument. Additional SHF grants funded further study and interpretive signs and trails.

RIO GRANDE & SOUTHERN MOTORCAR No. 5 / GALLOPING GOOSE
421 Railroad Ave. (SR)
Built: 1933; Jack Odenbaugh and Forest White, builders

D

"All aboard!" That famous conductor call was heard once again in Dolores as the Galloping Goose Historical Society and rail fans from far away boarded Galloping Goose No. 5 in Dolores for her 1998 revival, after a 50-year hiatus. A narrow-gauge

locomotive that was created by the Rio Grande & Southern Railroad, the Galloping Goose used a gas-powered automobile motor instead of a locomotive. To cool its engine when over-heated, side panels could be opened, giving the appearance of wings. As the locomotive honked and waddled down the tracks, its distinctive name was born. Seven geese were built in all, and Motorcar No. 5 and another one at the Colorado Railroad Museum in Golden are back in operating condition.

In the 1940s, Jack Odenbaugh and Forest White had rebuilt the Goose to keep it, and the Rio Grande & Southern Railroad, in business. But by 1987 the roof was caving in and the wood-framed freight box was rotting. With $28,213 from the SHF, over 40 local businesses and townspeople contributed labor, monies, and volunteer hours during the 11-year restoration project. Restoring the Goose to her grandeur was no small feat. Tin sheets on the sides of the Goose were removed, repaired, and reinstalled, with new nails driven into the original nail holes. The boards for the freight car were cut using machinery similar to that used in the 1930s. One volunteer who saw the engine replacement said it looked "like a heart transplant."

After restoration, the Goose took its first trip on the Cumbres & Toltec Scenic Railroad. Restorationist Wayne Brown notes, "Among old friends—snow removers, steam locomotives, and old boxcars—the Goose felt happy!" Today, the Galloping Goose No. 5 is an important cultural and educational asset to Dolores and a shining example of community spirit and hard work.

Dumont

Photo courtesy of Tom Noel

DUMONT SCHOOL
150 CR 261 [NR]
Built: 1909; George Keys, builder

This small Romanesque Revival school received a $2,212 SHF grant, aided by $1,123 from the Mill Creek Valley Historical Society. Volunteers restored the interior wainscoting and exterior porch. Joan Drury, president of the Mill Creek Valley Historical Society, says the one-room school closed in 1959 when area schools consolidated. It was restored as a community center and a place for kids to experience old-fashioned education—including blackboards that are actually black. A large bell tower sits atop this lovely building, with matching beige-brick outhouse, set in a park with antique slides and swings.

Durango

Denver & Rio Grande Railroad vice president William A. Bell laid Durango out in 1880 as a planned community with parks and other public spaces. He platted Durango with a county courthouse site, church sites, and the 3rd Avenue Parkway residential district on the bluff east of town. Coal-rich Durango boomed as the smelter city of the San Juans. Since the smelter closed for the last time in 1963, Durango has concentrated on tourism and education. Fort Lewis College, established in 1933, is the town's single largest employer, followed by the Durango & Silverton Narrow Gauge Railroad. The railroad, which draws some 200,000 passengers a year, has kept Main Avenue the center of activity in Durango, eclipsing even the new, dun-colored Durango Mall south of town. Both Main Avenue and the 3rd Avenue Parkway have been set aside as National Register Historic Districts and Durango also has an energetic landmarks board designating local landmarks and districts.

D

ANIMAS CITY SCHOOL / ANIMAS MUSEUM
3065 W. 2nd Ave. ⬚LL⬚
Built: 1904, Joseph Mentzel, architect; Don J. McGillis, builder

The Cummins family, who were leading local masons, provided sandstone quarried from the bluff just behind the site to clad this three-story brick school with rough-cut, quarry-face stone in warm, tawny tones. Time took its toll on the building, especially a 1919 fire that destroyed the third story and bell tower. "Gaming funds have given the county's oldest school a second chance," says Durango historian and La Plata County Historical Society board member Duane A. Smith. "Our Society has restored this school as a museum thanks to $447,667 from the SHF, which we matched. Now we've restored the doorways and windows as well as the stonework with the help of architect Jim Sims and hope to bring back the hipped and gabled roof and bell tower." Since 1980, the La Plata County Historical Society Museum has occupied this edifice on spacious, landscaped grounds, which include an 1877 log cabin. The 2,500 square feet of exhibit space showcase local history and Southwest Indian arts and crafts. One schoolroom inside has been restored as a 1908 setting in which to teach local history to time-tripping youngsters.

CENTRAL HOTEL
975 Main Ave. NRD
Built: c. 1892; M. P. Blum, builder

D

One of the most striking structures on Durango's Main Avenue, this narrow, three-story Italianate hotel has a mansard roof with prominent dormers and a red-brick skin trimmed with white stone in hand-carved floral patterns. On the first floor is

El Rancho Bar, where a 20-year-old Jack Dempsey, the future heavyweight world champion, supposedly knocked out Andy Malloy in the 10th round. A mural on the side of the building commemorates that bout, while a large mural over the pool tables inside celebrates more recent exploits of regulars. Restored but not gentrified, this remains a blue-collar bar.

The huge plate-glass storefront has been restored, along with the arched and keystoned windows and antique neon sign. In 2001, artists Tom Murray and James McCliment restored the Dempsey mural. The $136,000 exterior restoration, facilitated by $100,000 from the SHF, resurrects a first-class building, which remains a working-class hotel and tavern.

Photo courtesy of Tom Noel

D&RG LOCOMOTIVE No. 315 AT DURANGO DEPOT
479 Main Ave.
Built: 1895; Baldwin Locomotive Works, builder

The Denver & Rio Grande's distinctive yellow and brown colors shine on the debonair Durango depot, a clapboard affair with a second-story central pavilion and cross-gable roof, designed by English mining engineer J. H. Ernest Waters in 1882. Charles Walker supervised its construction. The well-maintained depot and gift shop serve the tourist armies boarding America's most celebrated narrow-gauge steam excursion train.

The Durango & Silverton Narrow Gauge Railroad has been in use since 1882 when D&RG construction engineer Thomas Wigglesworth oversaw construction of the 45 miles of rail from Durango up the Animas River Canyon to Silverton. Despite the tortuous mountain terrain, Wigglesworth achieved a maximum grade of 2.5 percent. He also used all-steel track instead of the iron track previously used by the D&RG. Narrow shelves were cut into rock cliffs as high as 400 feet above the Animas River gorge for this cliff-hanging railroad. After abandoning the San Juan Extension from Alamosa to Durango in 1968, the D&RG continued service between Durango and Silverton until 1981, when Charles E. Bradshaw, Jr., bought the line and upgraded it. The line has been designated both a National Historic Landmark and a National Historic Civil Engineering Landmark.

Locomotive No. 315 was built in 1895 by Baldwin Locomotive Works in Philadelphia for the Florence & Cripple Creek Railroad, and purchased by the Denver & Rio Grande Western Railroad in 1917. This durable engine is being restored to its 1940 appearance with the help of $131,279 in SHF grants to the Durango Railroad Historical Society (DRHS). SHF grant funds have helped provide for an evaluation of the locomotive's boiler and is assisting in the full restoration of the locomotive. DRHS continues to restore the locomotive, removing movie props added in the 1940s and 1950s for the movies *Colorado Territory* and *Around the World in 80 Days*, and returning the engine to working order.

D

DURANGO HIGH SCHOOL / DURANGO SCHOOL DISTRICT 9-R ADMINISTRATION BUILDING
201 E. 12th St. [LL] [NR]
Built: 1916, Thomas MacLaren and Charles Thomas, architects; M. J. Kenney, builder; 1927 swimming pool and locker room addition, Eugene Groves, architect

The SHF granted $491,627 to the Durango School District toward roof repairs, restoration of windows, and development of a master plan for this beige, black-speckled brick, three-story structure. The Beaux-Arts–Neoclassical Revival school sports a terracotta entry with a curvilinear, scrolled parapet and lamp of learning. The intricate brickwork includes a bas-relief "DHS" monogram, ornate round arches, and protruding diamonds. The Four Corners Rose Society maintains the garden in front. Durango architect R. Michael Bell rehabilitated the

interior to house the Durango School District administrative offices after a new, larger high school opened in 1976. Although the old swimming pool is now storage, several rooms are still adorned with the original slate chalkboards. The old auditorium has also been restored for public meetings.

Restoration of the windows in a sensitive and appropriate manner was key to maintaining the historic appearance of the building. For this work, the school district hired Charles and John Shaw as the window contractors. The brothers also restored all 275 windows in the Smiley Junior High building across the street from Durango High School. These sensitive projects provide a model for successful preservation and adaptive reuse of historic school buildings.

FLORIDA RIVER RAILROAD BRIDGE
Rancho Florida Rd. (CR 240), 7 miles southeast of Durango (SR)
Built: 1887; Denver & Rio Grande Railroad, builder

Historic iron and steel truss bridges, such as this well-preserved example on the abandoned San Juan line of the D&RG, are disappearing rapidly. In Colorado, for example, the National Register of Historic Places listed 27 vehicular through-truss bridges in 1985; only 10 remained in 2002. The local El Rancho Florida

Photo courtesy of Tom Noel

Metropolitan District used $60,340 from the SHF for an $80,455 restoration of this Pratt through-truss bridge, which included stabilizing the abutments and replacing the 82-foot-long wooden decking and handrail for what is now a bridge for automobiles.

GEER HOUSE
943 E. 5th Ave. [LL]
Built: 1898; J. C. Taplin, builder

Jon and Linda Geer used a $2,500 SHF grant for exterior restoration of this modest Queen Anne cottage, representative of middle-class housing of the era. A simple, small, one-story blond-brick structure, it has some distinctive Carpenter Gothic trim, most notably on the arch over the front porch. Little altered since 1915, it also has a carriage house with the original hardware and doors.

HOCKER MOTORS BUILDING / DURANGO ARTS CENTER
802 E. 2nd Ave. [LL]
Built: 1927

Opened as Benjamin Hocker's showroom for Jeffrey and Saxon automobile sales, the building most recently housed Pat Murphy Motors, a General Motors dealership. The parapet, course work, and intricate inset designs were all done in the same beige brick, making this an understated Deco delight whose elevations must be studied to be appreciated. Local bridge builder Al Metz constructed the intricate original wooden trusses, similar to early bridge truss systems, for the domed roof over what is now a roomy children's museum.

D

Almost doomed to demolition in 1996 for use as a parking lot, this building was saved thanks to the Durango Arts Center, which persuaded the city to partner in purchasing and restoring it as a regional arts center serving 26 organizations. Supported by a $112,916 SHF grant, the DAC and the city brought back this brick beauty and rehabilitated the inside to create a gallery and performance space. Work included structural reinforcement of the trusses and roof rafters, repair of the roof and masonry, restoration of the windows, and addition of a sprinkler system to keep visitors safe. Rehabilitation of the space provided for a 250-seat performance venue in the former repair garage, offices, a conference room, and a dance studio and art gallery. Durango preservation architects R. Michael Bell and C. Richard Feeney, project coordinator J. William Vega, and engineer Don Johnson collaborated on this reincarnation of a once-again showy automobile showroom.

LA PLATA CARNEGIE LIBRARY
1188 E. 2nd Ave. LL NRD
Built: 1907, Charles E. Thomas, architect; 1967 addition,
    George King, architect

Durango's public library used a $14,000 SHF grant for the restoration of the stone foundation, brick first floor, and stucco second floor, and to provide access to the disabled. This two-story, Beaux-Arts–Renaissance Revival brick landmark has fine landscaping and architectural details, including a low-pitched tile roof and broad eaves reminiscent of the Craftsman style, with exposed tongue-and-groove wood soffits, extended roof beams, and elaborate brackets.

EMORY E. SMILEY JUNIOR HIGH / SMILEY SCHOOL STUDIOS
1309 E. 3rd Ave. LL
Built: 1937; Charles E. Thomas, architect

D

Durango's only junior high until 1961, this three-story, WPA-era school sports Mission Revival elements such as curvilinear parapets, buttresses, protruding brick arches, and round windows. Designed by a prominent architect and former mayor of Colorado Springs, the blond-brick edifice closed as a junior high in 1994. In 1997, a new use was proposed by brothers Charles and John Shaw and Charles's wife, Lisa Bodwalk. They wanted to turn the old junior high into a community arts and crafts center with studios, workshop spaces, and educational and community meeting spaces. The school, however, was in sorry shape after years of water damage, deferred maintenance, and vandalism. Fortunately, the Shaws' experience in the building trades equipped them for the thousands of hours they spent transforming Smiley into a community arts and education center. They also enlisted volunteers who donated hundreds of hours cleaning, scraping, and painting the dingy school walls.

Smiley Studios, a nonprofit started by the Shaws and Bodwalk, received a $129,889 SHF grant to restore all of the school's wood double-hung and steel casement windows, as well as the third-floor greenhouse. The Shaws set up a window restoration shop in the school that allowed the entire project to take place on-site. Another $395,919 in SHF grants facilitated repair and cleaning of the school's

distinctive blond-brick exterior. The Shaws made this an exemplary project by transforming the old-fashioned building into one that is energy-efficient. They use a solar thermal collection system for much of the heating, a solar energy system that provides 40 percent of the building's electricity, water-efficient plumbing, a water heater exchange system, and high-efficiency boilers. Their efforts made Smiley a model project for others hoping to preserve historic school buildings in an energy-efficient manner.

Eaton

EATON HIGH SCHOOL
114 Park Ave. (SR)
Built: 1929; Robert Kenneth Fuller, architect

Restoration of this Collegiate Gothic style high school was accomplished during the summer breaks with the help of $296,991 from the SHF. The $492,000 interior and exterior restoration focused on the brick masonry, terracotta trim, windows, skylights, and doors.

Photo courtesy of Tom Noel

Richard Urano, a math teacher at the school since 1966, says, "To see the school returned to the showplace it used to be was heartwarming. All the doors and windows were stripped and natural wood surfaces restored, so all of those names carved in the woodwork over the years show up again. We restored the terracotta book over the entry and also replaced new metal doors with reproduction wood ones. The bronze plaques of Lincoln's Gettysburg Address and the Eaton High School creed shine again in the lobby. The auditorium was restored, but with a widening of the rows. Now if only they could restore some of us teachers!"

Elbert

St. MARK UNITED PRESBYTERIAN CHURCH / ELBERT PRESBYTERIAN CHURCH
225 Main St. [NR]
Built: 1889; Taylor Green, architect

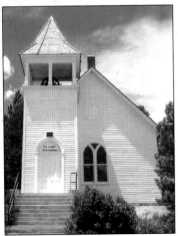

The SHF's $222,147 is enabling a major restoration of this white frame church, including repair of the roof and the square-corner tower housing the original bell, as well as replacement of damaged siding, electrical updates, drainage improvements, restoration of the stained-glass windows and their Gothic-arched moldings, and reconstruction of the entry stairs and doors.

"Unless we take these steps, the church will disappear," says Barbara Sjaastad, church elder and project chairman. As a focal point of the town for 120 years, the church formerly known as the St. Mark United Presbyterian Church will continue to serve as a church and a community center, hosting spaghetti dinners, ice cream socials, and weddings.

Elizabeth

ELIZABETH TOWN HALL
321 S. Banner St. ⃞LL
Built: 1905

Before being carved up into offices, this once roomy edifice hosted public gatherings, meetings, plays, and even roller-skating. To return the hall to its visitor-friendly past, the Town of Elizabeth raised matching funds and SHF funds totaling $234,216 to restore the building's exterior, remove asbestos siding, repoint the foundation and

E

chimneys, repaint with historically appropriate colors, and reinstall or re-create all of the historic doors and windows. The second step was interior removal of the offices and restoration of the original maple floors and ceiling crown molding.

The 16-foot ceiling height allowed addition of second-story office space at the north end without changing the exterior façade. The Restore Elizabeth Historic Advisory Board raised money and donated volunteer labor to reopen the assembly hall.

HUBER SALOON / CARLSON BUILDING
239 Main St. ⃞LL Ⓢ🅡
Built: 1890; Francis Joseph Huber, builder

This typical small-town storefront has been restored by the Town of Elizabeth with the assistance of a $52,400 SHF grant, which helped repair and upgrade the second-floor hall, restore exterior doors and windows, and install a new roof. This two-story frame structure anchored Main Street, first as Huber's Saloon, later as a survey office, and most recently as an artist's studio. "The Carlson Building is a beacon of hope for what can be done with other sites within Elizabeth," says Dorothy Stone, chairperson of Elizabeth's historic preservation board. "It has inspired the purchase, restoration, and opening of some other historic Main Street structures."

Empire

EMPIRE TOWN HALL
30 E. Park Ave. (US 40) (SR)
Built: 1898

Since its completion in 1898, the Empire Town Hall has been the seat of local government but has also served as a social, religious, and commercial center. Various retail establishments have occupied the first-floor storefronts, including

the Hard Rock Café founded in 1932, long before a global chain of rock music–themed restaurant/nightclubs opened with the same name. The Empire Town Hall has long occupied the second story of this shiplap-sided building. The large flag flown from the roof for decades has been restored and is now exhibited in the Town Hall. The town matched SHF grants that totaled $115,524 to replace the roof, restore the cupola and the flagpole, and reconstruct the transomed storefronts. The project took an unexpected turn when what could have been a disastrous fire started on November 7, 2000. It gutted the first floor and also caused serious smoke damage to second-floor offices. Undaunted, the town continued on with the restoration project, and the building now stands proud for the estimated five million travelers who pass through town on US 40 every year. Lori Short, mayor of Empire, says, "The November 2000 fire enabled our town to combine insurance money with SHF funds to do the restoration, repair the foundation and drainage, and spread the word about SHF assistance to other business and property owners interested in preserving Empire's rich heritage."

MINT SALOON
13 E. Park Ave. (US 40) [NR]
Built: c. 1885

This tiny, 15-foot-wide, one-story frame building has been a tavern or liquor store for much of its life. The Town of Empire and owner Fran Richardson received SHF funds of $20,250 to install a new roof and restore the exterior, including the old storefront.

PECK HOUSE
83 Sunny Ave. [NR]
Built: 1862, James Peck, builder; 1863 two-story addition;
1880 addition and veranda; 1955 west addition

The oldest hotel and tavern in Colorado still in operation on the original site in the original building is being restored by the town and the owners, Gary and Sarah St. Clair, with the help of $21,356 from SHF and a local match of $22,228. This two-story clapboard hotel, with its full-length veranda overlooking the town, was

once the social center of Clear Creek County, with such registered dignitaries as Phineas T. Barnum and General William Tecumseh Sherman.

Photo courtesy of Tom Noel

    Restoration architects Kathy Hoeft and Gary Long oversaw rebuilding of the front porch and missing veranda railing, repairing the original front door, and the installation of a lobby exhibit addressing the history and preservation of this historic country inn. The St. Clairs, Peck House proprietors since the 1970s, report that such preservation projects "turn owners into historians."

Englewood

ARAPAHOE ACRES
Between E. Bates Ave. and E. Dartmouth Ave. and S. Marion St. and S. Franklin St. [NRD]
Built: 1949–1957; Edward Hawkins, architect

Along the border between Englewood and Denver amid typical 1950s-era suburban construction is an enclave of Modernism so unique that it earned a niche on the National Register of Historic Places. Arapahoe Acres is the result of Denver architect Edward Hawkins' desire to design an entire neighborhood in which the homes would fit the terrain, rather than altering the terrain to fit the homes. Sensing a close affinity between Modern and Japanese design concepts, Hawkins brought in a Japanese landscape architect whose influence is still evident today.

    Born in Denver and educated at Colorado State University, Hawkins lived in Chicago, where he was influenced by Frank Lloyd Wright. He used Wright's Usonian style in Arapahoe Acres, with low overhanging rooflines, clerestory windows, and layouts that make each house an individual work of art in harmony with its surroundings. Hawkins and his family personally lived in and worked on a dozen different houses here, trying to set a design pace for neighbors.

    Arapahoe Acres homeowner and architectural historian Diane Wray has spearheaded efforts to preserve the neighborhood. According to Wray, SHF grants of $58,500 enabled residents to get together in workshops to produce design guidelines and pursue appropriate repairs and reproduction of lost design elements. SHF funds matched by homeowners helped rehabilitate roofs and masonry and remove updates inconsistent with Hawkins's original concept for Arapahoe Acres. "One of the ways the state funds were used was to restore the uniquely styled street signs and house numbers," says Wray, who adds that 80 of the 124 households participated in the program.

E

THOMAS SKERRITT HOUSE
3560 S. Bannock St. (H) (LL)
Built: 1864

In 1860, Thomas Skerritt and his wife, Mary, obtained 640 acres in what is now Englewood between Quincy and Yale Avenues and South Santa Fe Drive and

Clarkson Street. The area's first white settlers, they built this house, which they called Shadyside. This pioneer residence in what became the town of Englewood originated as a small cabin, to which the Skerritts made subsequent additions. The original cabin is now the living room of a much larger dwelling.

The City of Englewood purchased the house in 1999 and came to within a cat's whisker of tearing it down, but citizen protest and fast action by the SHF saved the house from demolition. Preservation supporters pointed out that Skerritt was the father of Englewood and the man who first plowed out the dirt lane now known as South Broadway, Englewood's main street. The City of Englewood had a change of heart and used the SHF's $16,900 for hazardous-material removal. The SHF granted another $63,100 to transfer the site to Colorado Preservation, Inc. (CPI). CPI used an additional SHF grant of $197,330 to remove inappropriate additions and restore the core house. Restoration architect Gary Petri of SlaterPaull Architects left one of the cabin's original clapboard walls exposed as a historical exhibit in the main hallway.

CPI executive director Mark Rodman, who oversaw the project, put the house on the market after arranging for a façade easement with Historic Denver, Inc. Rodman reports that a buyer soon emerged—a chiropractor appreciative of a fixed-up landmark where he can fix up people's aches and pains.

Erie

WISE HOMESTEAD
11497 Jasper Rd. [LL]
Built: 1872; Oliver E. Wise, builder

Prime farmland out West and his bad case of asthma back in the Midwest led
Oliver E. Wise to bring his family from Wisconsin by covered wagon in 1868.
Their homestead became a hot property after they noticed prairie dogs excavating
black dirt—a sure sign of coal. Besides a profitable coal mine, the Wises operated
a large mill, grain-storage elevator, blacksmith shop, and the Canfield General Store.
Thanks to a balanced combination of coal and agriculture, Canfield, which the
Wises platted on their homestead, grew into a town of approximately 500.

In recent decades, much of what was once Canfield has been annexed by
fast-growing Erie, a larger coal-mining town two miles east in Weld County. By
the 1990s, Erie had become a bedroom community for neighboring Boulder
County, with commercial development along I-25. Canfield, meanwhile, became
a ghost town.

One of the few remaining residents is the great-granddaughter of Oliver,
Dr. Sarah Wise, who returned to the old family farm after a teaching career. Dr.
Wise tends the family farm and looks after a few decaying landmarks. "I don't
know why I work so hard to keep up this place and to preserve what's left," she
said in a 1998 interview. "I guess because no one else will do it. So many new-
comers—and their kids—don't know anything about our past. So I'm donating
the 1872 Wise Family Homestead as a museum." To facilitate this dream, the
SHF granted $105,000 to the Erie Historical Society to rehabilitate the interior
and stabilize the exterior.

Estes Park

FALL RIVER HYDROELECTRIC PLANT MUSEUM
CO 34 and David Dr., 3 miles north of Estes Park [NR]
Built: 1909; Vail Walbran and Read, architects

This 23-acre site contains the original one-room power plant and a
clapboard cottage for the caretaker.
Begun as the Estes Park Power and
Light Company with a waterwheel
generator that supplied power to the
town as well as to the Stanley Hotel,
the plant was acquired by the Public
Service Company of Colorado in
1928. That Denver-based utility
installed a six-cylinder, 300-horse-
power Fairbanks Morse diesel and a

Photo courtesy Fall River Hydroelectric Plant Museum

200-kilowatt generator. In 1945, the Town of Estes Park bought the plant, and it retains ownership to this day. The 1982 failure of the Lawn Lake Dam and subsequent flood down the Fall River into Estes Park badly damaged the buildings, but the thick concrete floor under the heavy equipment survived and guided a reconstruction expedited by

Photo courtesy of Tom Noel

$400,000 in SHF grants. In ceremonies on July 15, 2002—exactly 20 years after the flood—the Fall River Hydroelectric Plant reopened as a municipal museum with four reborn clapboard buildings and a new interpretive kiosk.

HALLETT HOUSE
1861 Mary's Lake Rd. [NR]
Built: c. 1881

An $8,000 SHF grant and a Town of Estes Park match for roof repair helped owner Eugene E. Oja restore one of the oldest homes in Estes Park. William L. Hallett of Springfield, Massachusetts, built this clapboard summer home after acquiring the three-acre site, which he called Edgemont. Hallett, who also had cattle ranches in Colorado Springs and Loveland, used Estes Park for summer grazing. He helped form the first climbing association in Colorado, The Rocky Mountain Club, in which he served as the vice president and as chairman of explorations. In Rocky Mountain National Park, Hallett Peak above Bear Lake and Hallett Creek, which flows into Grand Lake, are both named for him. In his honor, Dr. Oja and his wife oversaw this restoration of the roof with wood shingles, the original material chosen by Hallett.

MacGREGOR RANCH
180 MacGregor Ave. **(H)** [NR]
Built: c. 1873, Alexander Q. MacGregor, builder

The 2,931-acre spread settled by Muriel MacGregor's grandfather, Alexander Q. MacGregor, in 1873 is set in a ponderosa pine–fringed meadow snuggled up against Rocky Mountain National Park. The splendid site overlooks Longs Peak and the famous Twin Owls rock formation. In the years before her death in 1970, Muriel MacGregor refused to sell out to developers swooping down on one of Colorado's most scenic and historic ranches. She made clear her wishes that the ranch stay intact and retain the MacGregor name as a working cattle ranch and education center for children who may have never seen a working ranch or a cow.

She left the property to what became the Muriel L. MacGregor Charitable Trust. The trust sold a conservation easement, preventing development, to Rocky Mountain National Park for $4 million. The trust paid out more than $300,000 and turned over half the original ranch to placate a swarm of relatives

Photo courtesy of Tom Noel

E

and lawyers who saw the ranch as their windfall, then used the remainder to set up an endowment.

The still-working ranch used the SHF for technical advice and $252,721 in grants to help restore 11 of the 28 ranch buildings for what is now a living-history museum of ranching life. Today, more than 5,000 schoolchildren and other visi-

tors tour it annually to learn firsthand about farming and ranching. Hay and horse-power run the original equipment and artifacts, even the now-restored, spring-fed, gravity-flow water system which provided Estes Park with its first indoor plumbing. MacGregor Ranch's 100-head cow operation even helps support itself by selling all-natural beef to the public.

Ranch buildings have been restored from the foundations to the roofs, according to MacGregor Ranch executive director Eric D. Adams. Without SHF funding, Adams says, this would have been impossible. "We could restore everything faithfully, because Muriel kept a diary from the time she was nine detailing all the ranch chores and operations. She also kept at least 800 old photos showing how the ranch looked over

the years. Now we can make her dream come true by showing kids where their milk and eggs and meat come from, at a time when most Coloradans are four to five generations removed from the land."

McGRAW RANCH
Cow Creek Trailhead, Rocky Mountain National Park,
5 miles north of Estes Park **H** NR
Built: 1884

E

John and Irene McGraw bought this ranch from Henry Farrar in 1908. They transformed it into a dude ranch that attracted such notables as Republican presidential candidate Alf Landon of Kansas, who supposedly worked on his 1936 campaign at the ranch. The McGraws operated the ranch until 1988, when Rocky Mountain National Park bought the site, initially planning to demolish the buildings for a

700-acre elk habitat. After preservationists pointed out that these Rustic structures should be spared the fate of so many other historic ranches, the Park Service changed its mind. They worked with the National Trust for Historic Preservation and area universities to save the ranch as the Continental Divide Research Center. The National Trust helped raise $800,000 toward rehabilitation, including donations from the Log Cabin Syrup Company,

plus $382,108 from the SHF, and a commitment of some $600,000 from the National Park Service completed this $2 million rehabilitation of 14 ranch buildings.

The 1884 main house has become a lodge, with cooking, dining, and meeting rooms; the bunkhouse, a library and computer room; and a laundry, a natural-resource laboratory.

Former park superintendent A. Durand "Randy" Jones notes the turnaround in Park Service attitudes toward preservation and concludes, "Not only will this rehabilitation protect significant historic structures—the only surviving intact dude ranch left in the park—it is also a central element in the park's expanding science and research program." Mrs. McGraw, who lives nearby, says she is delighted to see the old Cow Creek spread reborn. She figured it was a "goner." Instead, researchers now stay at the ranch, which conducts natural-resource studies and training sessions for preservationists and craftspeople.

STANLEY HOTEL
333 Wonderview Ave. [NR] [NRD]
Built: 1906–1909; T. Robert Wieger, architect

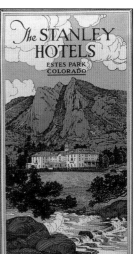

Freelan O. Stanley and his twin brother, Francis, developed a photographic process, which they sold to George Eastman, founder of Kodak. The Stanleys also invented the steam-powered automobile named for them. After contracting tuberculosis, Freelan moved to Colorado in 1903 for the climate cure. He bought 1,400 acres from Lord Dunraven to build his summer home and this $500,000 hotel complex, one of the finest examples of Georgian Revival architecture in the Rockies.

Freelan, who fancied himself an architect, helped T. Robert Wieger design the 150-room complex. Twelve clapboard buildings are arranged in a row facing south across a meadow with unobstructed views of the surrounding mountains. From a rough-cut sandstone foundation the main hotel rises to fourth-floor dormers and an octagonal cupola. Inside, the Dunraven Tavern, MacGregor Dining Room, music room, billiard room, and lounges generally echo the Georgian Revival theme. Stanley himself designed the kitchen, one of the first all-electric kitchens in the country. The spacious, sunny lobby is laced with arches, columns, and a grand staircase.

After Stanley sold the hotel in 1926, it weathered hard financial times when its frame construction made it hard to keep up and insure. Closed during World War II, it afterward opened intermittently during the summers. Following a 1980s renovation, it is now open year-round and enjoying a renaissance. Stephen King's horror novel *The Shining*, which was made into a very popular 1980 movie, was inspired by and partly written at the Stanley. A 1997 TV adaptation of the novel was also filmed here. With the help of $80,878 from the SHF, including $6,878 for the carriage house, the Stanley has installed a new roof, opened a mini-museum, and carried out long-postponed restoration of one of the best-known and most fabled of Colorado's historic mountain hotels.

WILLIAM ALLEN WHITE CABIN
Moraine Park Visitor Center, Moraine Park Rd.
in Rocky Mountain National Park [NR]
Built: 1912

Photo courtesy of Tom Noel

William Allen White, the nationally prominent editor of the Kansas *Emporia Gazette*, purchased the second-largest unit of a five-cabin complex, where he and friends summered. The cabins exemplify the Rustic style in their use of native stone, log and slab-log construction, and expansive front porches. The National Park Service bought the cabins in 1973 and then converted them into artist-in-residence quarters. The Moraine Park Museum occupies the main cabin.

Rocky Mountain National Park Associates received $134,204 from two SHF grants. The first grant addressed drainage and foundation problems, repaired the stonework, reconstructed and stabilized the front porch and stairs, and repaired and painted windows and frames. The subsequent grant went toward stabilization and preventive measures for four outbuildings—a privy and three sleeping cabins. Roof work, foundation repair, stabilization, and window and door repair were components of this project. Now safe for visitor use, the complex provides artists, writers, and photographers with a secluded place to perfect their crafts—or just to gaze out the windows at the incredible view.

E

Evergreen

CHALMERS HOUSE, EVERGREEN CONFERENCE CENTER
27618 Fireweed Dr. at CO 74 NRD
Built: c. 1923; John "Jock" Spence, builder

Evergreen's notable master carpenter, Jock Spence, built this summer residence for Robert S. Chalmers, dean of Evergreen's Episcopal Church. The house is now part of the Evergreen Conference Center, and is a summer retreat and education center. By 1994, the house was so badly deteriorated that demolition seemed inevitable. The roof leaked in spite of five layers of shingles and intermittent modernization attempts had destroyed its historical integrity. Raccoons and other critters were its only residents.

E

To revive the Chalmers House, the Evergreen Elks Club and Rotary Club donated volunteer labor and matched $73,690 from the SHF. Thanks to the restoration, visitors can now tour Chalmers House and other buildings of the conference center, remarkable for its Rustic-style architecture as well as its history. Inspired by this project, the center is now working with the SHF on future restoration of the 22 Rustic structures within the Evergreen Episcopal Conference Historic District.

DODGE RANCH
201 Evans Ranch Rd., about 10 miles west of Evergreen SR
Built: 1903–1911; John "Jock" Spence, builder

John Newman originally homesteaded what he called the Haystack Ranch around 1890. Clarence Phelps Dodge, Sr., owner of the *Colorado Springs Gazette*, and his wife, Regina, purchased it as a summer home in 1903. They hired craftsman Jock Spence to construct a two-story, five-bedroom ranch house, based on a design provided by Regina. Clarence, Jr., and his wife later turned the weekend retreat into a working guest ranch.

The Dodges sold the ranch to Jefferson County Public Schools in 1961 for use as an Outdoor Education Lab School to teach history and natural history. Besides the main lodge, the ranch consists of three guest cabins, nine outbuildings, and structures added by Jefferson County Public Schools. The historic buildings exemplify Rustic architecture, with elements such as board-and-batten siding and stone foundations and chimneys.

Jefferson County Public Schools has used SHF grants totaling $312,750 for a $465,800 restoration of the main lodge and other buildings. Inside the lodge, non-historic lighting was replaced with fixtures more sympathetic to the design. Exterior wood fascias and exposed rafters were repaired, stone steps reconstructed, and the historic windows repaired. Roofs and wooden siding were also repaired on the hay shed and barn, as were the exterior, interior, and fireplace in the guesthouse.

Approximately 3,600 sixth graders from Jefferson County attend the Outdoor Lab School here every year. Their one-week stay in such an attractively rehabilitated historic setting offers them a unique experience and memories that last a lifetime.

HIWAN HOMESTEAD MUSEUM
4208 S. Timbervale Dr. NR
Built: 1887–1896, John "Jock" Spence, builder; many additions

E

Over a 10-year period, John Spence built this 17-room, peeled-log lodge with two octagonal towers for Mary Neosho Williams. She called it Camp Neosho and left it to her daughter, Dr. Josepha Williams, who married Episcopal clergyman Charles Winfred Douglas in 1896. The west tower in the upper floor housed Douglas' private chapel, with hand-hewn logs and a vaulted and beamed ceiling. Upon this property's purchase by Darst E. Buchanan in 1938 it became known as Hiwan Homestead.

To protect the house and its surrounding grounds from development, Jefferson County Open Space purchased the site in 1975 for use as a museum, archives, and open space operated by the Jefferson County Historical Society and Evergreen Garden Club.

Hiwan administrator John F. Steinle states, "We've used Jefferson County Open Space funds to match $75,422 from the SHF to install new roofs and new storm windows, rebuild the historic wooden footbridge, and get behind the interior siding to look for the Indian art that Eric Douglas painted on the walls of the main house. Thanks to the SHF, we are retaining the exterior logs, repairing the stone chimneys, and replacing rotting logs."

ERIC'S HOUSE AT HIWAN HOMESTEAD MUSEUM
4208 S. Timbervale Dr. at Meadow Dr. NR
Built: 1896; John "Jock" Spence, builder

Eric's House, another of Jock Spence's creations on the Hiwan Homestead, originated as a "baby house" when Eric Douglas was born and later served as his summer quarters. Today, Eric's House serves as staff offices and as a resource center, with thousands of historic photos, documents, and books that were in serious danger because of the leaky roof. Thanks to $7,652 from the SHF and a county match, open-space crews have removed five layers of shingles from the old roof, installed a new roof, and repaired the chimney.

STONE HOUSE AT HIWAN HOMESTEAD MUSEUM
4208 S. Timbervale Dr. NR
Built: 1931; John "Jock" Spence, builder

A photograph of the Stone House at the Hiwan Homestead is inscribed by Spence, the master carpenter and stonemason, "This is my masterpiece." Built from local granite and gneiss as a playhouse for Eric Douglas' three children, Eve, Polly, and David, it has Spence's trademark slanted rock slabs and stair-step pattern. The wooden eaves are trimmed with an Indian symbol for mountains. Thanks to the SHF providing $6,000, Stone House now has a new slate roof protecting inside exhibits on Eric Douglas and his passion for the Native American arts. With his friend Anne Evans, he helped establish the Native Arts Department of the Denver Art Museum, whose research library is named for him.

E

HUMPHREY MEMORIAL PARK AND MUSEUM
620 S. Soda Creek Rd. NR
Built: 1878, John J. Clark, builder; many additions

John J. Clark, a businessman elected to the state legislature in 1888, constructed the original log cabin here in 1878. He and his wife, Sarah, called this summer home Kinnikinnik Ranch. In 1912, a portion of the original 160-acre homestead became Filius Park, a Denver mountain park. Lucius Edwin Humphrey purchased the remaining property in 1920. With his wife, Hazel, a wealthy Chicagoan, and their daughter, Hazel Lou (who would live in the house until her death in 1995), he traveled worldwide to furnish this summer place. Hazel Lou's room, showcasing her collection of feline figurines, looks exactly as it did on the day she died. According to museum director Peggy Shaw, "The most interesting thing about this museum is that this is the way they lived, and we have everything that they owned—even their toothbrushes. Hazel Lou set up a trust to make the house a museum."

Photo courtesy of Tom Noel

The original ranch house has been stabilized, along with its three-seat outhouse. The extraordinary gardens, including a formal walled croquet field, rustic statuary, and birdbaths, make this one of Colorado's funkiest mountain homes. SHF funds totaling almost $100,000, plus $71,000 raised by the museum, have enabled a restoration of this ornate log home inside and out, not including the Model A Ford in the garage. With SHF help, the museum has regraded the grounds, torn down the dilapidated 1970s-era porch, and bolstered the foundations. Today, Hazel Lou's dream of a cultural facility is coming to fruition, as the museum has hosted writers' workshops, the Moscow String Quartet, a bluegrass festival, and many school and college groups.

MEDLEN SCHOOL AND OUTHOUSES
8569 S. Turkey Creek Rd. (SR)
Built: 1886

"We wanted to save one of the oldest schoolhouses in Jefferson County," recalls JoAnn Dunn of the Jefferson County Historical Society, "for educational programs and as a tribute to pioneer schoolmarms and the community barn raisers who built it." To accurately restore the structure and bring it up to code, the Society matched $30,000 from the SHF to jack up the structure, install a concrete foundation with crawl space for utilities, a new entry, and heating. With no other restrooms, the two outhouses were restored as functional privies (after an archaeological investigation). The Medlen School program, which caters to first- through sixth-graders, gives students a realistic one-room schoolhouse experience, complete with optional visits to one of Colorado's most endangered building types—functional outdoor bathrooms.

STEWART HOTEL CONFERENCE CENTER
27649 CO 74 near Meadow Dr. (NR)
Built: c. 1860s–1870; 1897 remodel, John "Jock" Spence, builder

Robert H. Stewart homesteaded on Upper Bear Creek in 1868, milled lumber, and built a small bunkhouse. During the 1870s, Stewart sheathed his bunkhouse of large hewn logs with clapboard, added dormers and two wings, and opened it as a hotel. By 1893, Stewart's summer resort included eight guest cottages, a milk house, and an icehouse. After Stewart's death in 1897, Episcopalians, who had long held meetings in Stewart's hotel, bought it and changed it to the Mission of the Transfiguration. Noted carpenter Jock Spence sheathed each building with vertical slab siding and installed an inlaid cross in the chapel. The conference center is now used by Evergreen's Episcopal Church of the Transfiguration, the Evergreen Players theater, the Attachment Center, the Evergreen Elks Club, and others.

The Church of the Transfiguration took on restoration of its old hotel home with the help of $381,700 from the SHF. That process brought many surprises: phone books held up one corner of the hotel while rotting floors and ceilings had become dens for raccoons. Due to the haphazard way in which the building had been assembled, several wall sections rested directly against the adjoining hillside. Drainage, water infiltration, and deterioration of the Spence-installed siding was a problem. Regrading the hillside directed water away and deteriorated siding was repaired or new material was carefully inserted where needed. Nonhistoric windows were replaced with replicas more compatible to the building's age and construction. Inside, years of remodeling schemes were reworked into a more cohesive plan.

Many parish volunteers helped by donating labor, organizing material removal, conducting yard sales, and setting up displays to promote the restoration fund to resurrect this multifunctional community landmark. New posts have been replaced on the front porch, which is ready to greet visitors for another hundred years.

Once again, Evergreeners of every faith—and of no faith—hear the church bells toll for fires, funerals, and Sunday morning services. The sanctuary retains its clear-glass view of a grove of evergreen trees. The rehabilitated church also houses Evergreen Christian Outreach, the church's ministry to the poor.

Fairplay

FAIRPLAY SCHOOL / EDITH TETER SCHOOL
639 Hathway St. LL SR
Built: 1880, Wright & Ingalls, builders; c. 1940 addition, Frank
   Frewen, architect; 1947 addition, Carl Bueler, architect

This Italianate edifice, now renamed the Edith Teter Elementary School, is made
of local red sandstone with ornate stone lintels and quoins. It received a variety of
additions over the years. The SHF contributed $113,600 to Park County School

District RE-2 to repair the
walls and windows, recon-
struct the chimney, replace
the roof, and restore the
prominent open bell tower.
This old-timer is now the
centerpiece of a kinder-
garten-through-high-school
campus that adjoins the
dramatic Gothic Revival–
style Sheldon Jackson
Memorial Chapel (1874).

PARK COUNTY COURTHOUSE / PARK COUNTY LIBRARY
418 Main St. LL NR
Built: 1874, George W. Nyce, architect; Robert Frazier and
   Lewis W. Lewis, builders

Judge Kitty, the presiding dignitary here, is a chatty Siamese, a stray male adopted,
named, and pampered by librarian Michelle Kingsford. Judge Kitty oversaw the
reroofing of Colorado's oldest still-used courthouse, a two-story, Italianate-style
antique made of local red sandstone. The county matched $68,640 in SHF funds
to replace the roof, and it hopes to reconstruct all six chimneys. A fine spiral staircase leads to the second-floor courtroom, where sessions are held at least once a year
in "the court that never adjourns." This reference to vigilante justice dates to 1880

when "Judge Lynch" hanged John J.
Hoover from the second-floor window and left him dangling as a
warning that law and order had
come to town. Hoover had accepted
a plea bargain and was sentenced to
eight years in jail. A mob, angered
by that deal, broke into the jail and
hanged him.

Photo courtesy of Tom Noel

The upstairs courtroom is now home to the Park County Historic Preservation Advisory Commission, while the public library is downstairs. Courthouse grounds are shared by an old jail (now book storage) with 18-inch-thick sandstone walls and steel door- and window-guards. Judge Kitty and the preservation team have also fixed up the grounds, which contain a monument to the burro Shorty and his canine companion, Bum.

SUMMER SALOON
3rd and Front St., South Park City LL NR
Built: 1879

Along Front Street in the town of Fairplay is the South Park City Museum, a pioneer town consisting of some existing structures and many buildings that were moved here from mining camps and towns around the South Park area. The museum is one of Colorado's best collections of early mining camp architecture. One of these buildings is the Summer Saloon, still sitting at its original location. Built in 1879 by Leonard Summer adjacent to his brewery, the one-story building is of red sandstone quarried near Red Hill Pass. On its façade, the stone rises high above the flat roof to an Italianate cornice, resulting in the "false front" appearance typical of old frame commercial buildings.

The South Park Historical Foundation used a $75,000 SHF grant to assist in the restoration of the saloon and to rehabilitate its interior. The wood box cornice was in danger of falling onto the wooden sidewalk below. Guided by SHF advice and funding, the museum stabilized and repointed the stone walls, which had suffered water damage. Steel bracing and a gutter system were installed on the rear of the building. Inside, nonhistoric walls were removed and mechanical upgrades made so that the front section can be used for museum exhibition space, with room in the back for offices and a maintenance shop.

Flagler

HOTEL FLAGLER / FLAGLER TOWN HALL
311 Main Ave. [NR]
Built: 1909; William H. Lavington and W. L. Price, builders

This two-story, red-brick box, now stuccoed, has a front porch with a balustraded second-story balcony supported by square fluted columns. Converted into a hospital in 1937 by Dr. W. L. McBride, it became the Flagler Town Hall in 1967. Two years later, the library moved in with its Hal Borland Room, commemorating the writer, novelist, poet, and naturalist who grew up in Flagler. Borland worked with his father on the town newspaper, and wound up with the *New York Times*. The collection includes all 44 of Borland's books and numerous articles and artifacts donated by his widow after his death in 1978. One of Borland's accounts of life on the high plains, *Country Editor's Boy* (1970), describes Flagler, which his father promoted as the "Best Little City in Eastern Colorado, a community of tree-shaded streets and municipal power and water." More realistically, the younger Borland recalled, "Waves of homesteaders had lonelied out or discouraged out or dried out." The Town of Flagler and the Flagler Historical Society matched $16,600 from the SHF to restore the exterior and rehabilitate the interior. With this handsome Town Hall restored, Flagler can once again claim to the title of "Best Little City in Eastern Colorado."

SECOND CENTRAL SCHOOL
404 4th St. (SR)
Built: 1915

This two-room clapboard schoolhouse with a shingled, hipped roof closed in 1950. The old school was eventually donated to the Flagler Historical Society, which raised $7,258 to capture an SHF grant of $17,275. The funds have enabled exterior repairs, repainting, roof replacement, and reinstallation of the original interior trim, which had been in storage. Today the old school is a museum.

Florissant

FLORISSANT SCHOOL
2009 CO 31 NR
Built: 1887, Elias Ashby, builder; 1889 addition, W. P. Allen, builder

The Florissant Heritage Foundation, Pikes Peak Historical Society, and Ute Pass Historical Society partnered with the SHF to restore this clapboard school. Preservationists also rehabilitated the teacher's cottage and a small, gable-roofed building that is now the town library. After the school closed in 1960, the building became the Florissant Grange Hall. It still serves as Grange Hall No. 420, as well

as the Florissant Heritage Museum. "We used the SHF grant as seed money," says project coordinator Celinda Kaelin, "allowing us to leverage the $22,507 from the SHF into $160,000 worth of work, including new heating and electrical systems, a kitchen, and even a modern bathroom as a backup for the restored outhouses."

Photo courtesy of Tom Noel

FOUR MILE COMMUNITY BUILDING
High Park Rd. (Teller CR 11) SR
Built: 1911

The Four Mile Dance Hall, as locals call it, was built as a center for the tiny, informal community west of Cripple Creek known as Four Mile. Dances are still held at the community's annual fair but were particularly lively during the 1920s when bootleg whiskey was plentiful, according to John Tremayne, whose family homesteaded at Four Mile. "All the drinking was done outside," he recalls, "and the fighting also." Since 1923 it has housed the annual 4-Mile Fair, which includes a barbecue, baked goods, crafts, crops, and 4-H contests.

The community provided matching cash and volunteer labor to capture $34,517 in SHF funds to reroof their simple frame structure and repair its rubble stone foundation. They also restored the porch, front steps, and windows and rehabilitated the interior for boot-stomping dances that still bring lively times to this rural area.

Fort Collins

Fast-growing Fort Collins, whose population jumped from 87,491 to 118,652 during the 1990s, is now Colorado's fifth largest city. Despite tremendous growth, Fort Collins has used local preservation ordinances and planning to create many local landmarks and districts as well as National Register designations. Fort Collins preservationists have captured national attention with the highly successful Old Town Historic District, a reincarnated municipal railway, and even a Spanish Mission–style house that was converted into an award-winning Taco Bell franchise.

The city's renaissance was sparked by the 1978 National Register landmark designation of the Old Town Fort Collins Historic District, part of the original town grid paralleling the Cache la Poudre River. Bounded on the west by College Avenue, on the south by Mountain Avenue, and on the north and east roughly by the railroad tracks, Old Town stayed old while newer additions emerged around it.

Old Town Fort Collins has grown to include 51 contributing historic buildings. The quick and contagious success of this once seedy triangle has led to restoration of many nearby buildings and ongoing rejuvenation of the core city. Old Town offers a maze of vintage buildings with new uses, as well as new masonry structures designed to complement the historic ones. Splashing fountains, flower planters, benches, and a pedestrian orientation make Old Town an antidote to the usual auto-oriented big-box stores, strip malls, and shopping centers.

"Old Town is thriving and growing," reports Fort Collins preservation planner Carol Tunner. "More commercial properties are being added, and we hope to celebrate the site of the original Fort Collins on Linden Avenue along the Cache la Poudre River. We're starting off with archaeological research to find out what's there and hope to resurrect the old fort as an interpretive and recreational amenity."

Fort Collins has also restored the Mountain Avenue line of its Municipal Railway, which had been abandoned in 1961. This streetcar ride to yesterday offers a three-mile round-trip from City Park to Old Town along the grassy median of Mountain Avenue. Reactivated in 1985, it is one of the few restored city streetcar operations in the western United States. With city support, volunteers run the trolley on weekends and holidays.

ARMSTRONG HOTEL
259 S. College Ave., northwest corner of Olive St. NR
Built: 1923, Arthur E. Pringle, architect; Ora E. Long, builder

In the heart of downtown Fort Collins, Charles Mantz constructed this three-story polychrome brick hotel with a distinctive parapeted façade. He named it for his wife's father, Fort Collins business pioneer Andrew Armstrong. As the city's first motor tourism hotel, the Armstrong celebrated the automobile age. During the late 1900s, the hotel's name was changed to the Empire Motor Hotel, and then to the Mountain Empire Hotel.

In 2003, the Levinger family purchased the hotel and undertook a $2 million restoration, assisted by an SHF grant of $197,500. The Levingers rehabilitated all elevations of the three-story E-shaped structure. That configuration provides every room with outside windows. Interior restoration included bringing back the original sweeping staircase with its Art Deco iron railing, glass-brick transoms, the antique O'Keefe elevator, and the lobby's pressed-tin ceiling and terrazzo floor. Upstairs doorways and transoms were returned to their 1923 appearance for 38 rooms and suites containing both modern and vintage furnishings.

Exterior reconstruction of the storefronts from historic photos was an amazing feat of structural engineering and ingenuity by the preservation architectural engineer and contractor, according to Fort Collins planner Carol Tunner. She notes that the Armstrong is protected in perpetuity by a Colorado Historical Foundation preservation easement. When given the 2005 Colorado Preservation, Inc., State Honor Award for reincarnating the Armstrong, the Levingers remarked, "We're proud that after a fascinating journey, we've brought back to its original condition and use what had been a dead corner of downtown."

COLORADO & SOUTHERN FREIGHT DEPOT
136 LaPorte Ave. LL
Built: 1906; Colorado & Southern Railroad, builder

A handsome brick depot has been restored as the Fort Collins Transit Center for TRANSFORT (the municipal bus company), TNMO Greyhound, and other bus

services. A new park setting has bike lockers, bus boarding sheds, bike racks, and vanpool facilities. A 1996 SHF grant of $97,000 to Fort Collins, matched by city funds of $1,623,000, paid for interior and exterior restoration, as well as cleaning, repairing, and repointing 150,000 bricks from the Fort Collins Pressed Brick Company. Next to the Colorado & Southern Freight Depot, a track-side tombstone commemorates Annie, known to old-timers in Fort Collins as "the railroad dog."

Photo courtesy of Tom Noel

Back in 1934, C&S crew members discovered a sick, pregnant, mixed-breed mutt in the blacksmith shop. They nursed her back to health, and Annie delivered eight puppies. For years she greeted trains arriving at the freight depot and the adjacent passenger station. When she died in 1948 the railroaders laid her to rest under a tombstone reading, "From C&S men to Annie, our dog, 1934–1948."

COLORADO STATE UNIVERSITY CAMPUS
College Ave. to Shields St. between Lake St. and Laurel St.
Built: 1878, numerous additions

Chartered in 1870 and opened in 1879 as Colorado Agricultural College, Colorado State University has gone through several name changes over the decades. Campus architect James White notes that CSU is proud of its history as an institution. "We value our historic buildings as integral components of our legacy, and we are grateful that the State of Colorado also recognizes its rich historical legacy and has identified historical preservation as a priority by supporting the Colorado Historical Society as a catalyst for preservation." The university has, over the years, aggressively pursued grants from SHF, the City of Fort Collins, and other preservation partners to preserve its architectural resources, which are concentrated around the Oval, the historic centerpiece of today's greatly expanded modern campus.

F

CSU AMMONS HALL
711 Oval Dr. [NR]
Built: 1922; Eugene Groves, architect

Built as a women's gymnasium and social center, this beige-brick structure with Italian Renaissance Revival elements departs markedly from the Romanesque Revival style of many earlier campus structures. Ammons Hall was not named for CSU's

first woman professor, Theodosia G. Ammons, but for her brother, Colorado governor Elias M. Ammons. The building originally held a swimming pool, gymnasium, auditorium, and offices. Although the swimming pool has been filled in, the skylighted atrium remains an elegant reception hall. A $99,506 SHF grant, matched by CSU's $113,645, provided for

restoration of the masonry as well as repainting of the spectacular stenciled butterflies, pinecones, and dragonflies under the wide second-story eaves. Restorationists also addressed the windows, doors, and damaged clay tiles on the roof to reincarnate this campus showcase, which now houses the career center offices and also hosts special events.

F

CSU BOTANICAL AND HORTICULTURAL LABORATORY / ROUTT HALL
151 W. Laurel St. NR
Built: 1890; Otto Bulow, architect

One of the earliest surviving buildings on the old Colorado Agricultural College campus, this stone-and-brick structure is a landmark for both the college and the

town. The building was first called the Botanical and Horticultural Laboratory, and also housed the first Domestic Economy department in the state. It later became Alexander Emslie's Conservatory of Music, the Veterinary Science Annex, and the Technical Journalism Department. The building was renamed in 1999 in honor of Eliza Pickerell Routt, the wife of Colorado governor John Routt and the first woman to sit on the State Board of Agriculture, which oversaw the former Colorado Agricultural College. The Office of Admissions now occupies Routt Hall.

A $167,000 SHF grant and CSU's $344,765 made possible interior and exterior rehabilitation and restoration. Work consisted of repair and replacement of sandstone foundation and trim, and cleaning and repointing the masonry on this one-and-a-half-story building. A new roof and local flagstone sidewalk shine, and the original arched stained-glass window accents have been cleaned and repaired to further showcase this fine example of Victorian vernacular design.

CSU MECHANIC SHOP / INDUSTRIAL SCIENCES BUILDING
251 W. Laurel St. SR
Built: 1883; 1892 addition, Harlan Thomas, architect;
1896, 1899, and 1925 additions

The oldest section of this two-story, red-brick and sandstone structure received a two-story Richardsonian Romanesque addition in 1892. It was designed by Harlan

Thomas, a 21-year-old student who would later become dean of the University of Washington's School of Architecture. To tie the design of the two structures together, Thomas added a new Romanesque-style entry to the east façade of the original Mechanic Shop. A replica of the 1892 addition was added in 1896 that doubled the length of the structure's Laurel Street façade. Over the years called Mechanical Engineering, Arts, and finally Industrial Sciences, the building originally held a "forge room," "molding room," and "modern machines room." Wall cases in the first-floor halls hold an interesting display of antique tools. Industrial Sciences now houses shops, offices, and workrooms for the school's Construction Management Department, which offers a master of science degree with a historic preservation emphasis.

CSU provided $336,900 and the SHF $100,000 for this reincarnation. Work included cleaning and repointing stone and brick masonry, as well as restoration of the ornate wood doors, reroofing, and replacement of wood windows. Construction Management Department classes in historic preservation now use the building as a teaching tool, requiring students to use the clues provided in the building's materials and design to determine the chronology of its complex construction history.

F

CSU OLD LIBRARY / LAUREL HALL
700 Oval Dr. at Old Main Dr. (SR)
Built: 1884; 1915 addition

Originally used as a barn, this structure was changed a year later to the chemistry laboratory. Subsequently, it became the business school, the library, chemistry and

veterinary science lab space, Student Health Services, and the printing and publications department. It's now the home of the university's international programs. CSU put up $1,331,080 and obtained an $88,920 SHF grant for exterior work. That money repaired and restored masonry, doors, windows, skylights, and paint.

CSU POTTING SHED
191 W. Laurel St. (SR)
Built: 1891

The Agricultural Forcing House, as the Potting Shed was more formally named, was built of brick salvaged from the original 1874 shed with which the campus originated. An SHF grant of $29,200 matched by CSU's $49,300 for interior and exterior restoration allowed repair of the local red sandstone used for the foundation, lintels, and trim. The red brick was cleaned and repointed, the fish-scale gable restored, and a new roof installed. This humble but handsome building is now used for storage. Many still remember it as the longtime office, laboratory, and skull storage of the late CSU professor of forensic anthropology, Michael Charney. Nationally noted for his uncanny ability to recreate a face from the

slenderest of skeletal remains, he crammed this shed with reconstructed human skulls, giving rise to no end of spooky stories.

COY/HOFFMAN BARN
1103 E. Lincoln Ave. (SR)
Built: 1862; John G. Coy, builder

In 1862, John and Emily Coy were on their way to California when they wintered in Fort Collins. By spring they had decided they liked the area and made a homestead claim. Their descendants, the Hoffmans, operated the old Coy farm until the 1980s when the land around the barn was turned into a golf course. An SHF grant for $51,736 to the Fort Collins Historical Society helped restore this rare Colorado example of a stone and wood-frame barn. The Hoffman family and other community members raised thousands of dollars in cash and in-kind contributions to match the SHF grant. The funds helped replace the roof and repair the structural framing, stone walls, exterior siding, windows, and hayloft door. A golf tournament was held as a fund-raiser to provide for replacement of the severely deteriorated second floor. This project also served as a workshop to demonstrate timber-framing techniques. Peter Haney of Single Tree Woodworking and Rocky Mountain Workshops brought in some of the country's finest timber-framing consultants to educate interested parties with this model stabilization, disassembly, cataloging, and preservation case study.

Today, the Coy/Hoffman Barn is one of the oldest and most distinctive barns in Colorado, featuring stone-and-grout construction with timber framing and mortis-and-tenon joinery. "This barn was on the verge of collapse," says Fort Collins preservation planner Carol Tunner. "Without the SHF, it would be history."

FIRST BAPTIST CHURCH / NORTH POINTE
   COMMUNITY CHURCH
328 Remington St. LL NR
Built: 1904; Robert K. Fuller, architect

After its congregation moved to a new church in the 1960s, First Baptist housed a variety of tenants, most recently a dance and film school. Now, in partnership with the SHF and the Downtown Development Authority (DDA) of Fort Collins, the North Pointe Community Church is once again using this Gothic Revival structure as a house of worship. SHF grants totaling $229,830 enabled the church to repair the roof, stabilize the masonry, and make electrical, plumbing, and Americans with Disabilities Act (ADA) upgrades. The DDA assisted with major items such as conservation of the historic art-glass windows, including what may be the only rose window in Fort Collins.

FORT COLLINS MUNICIPAL POWER PLANT
430 N. College Ave. [LL]
Built: 1936; Burns and McDonell Engineering, builders

This Streamline Moderne industrial edifice includes a cooling pond disguised as a large water garden. A 1938 WPA fountain fronts this building used as a laboratory for CSU's mechanical engineering department. The SHF gave CSU $75,000, matching CSU and City of Fort Collins funding, to reconstruct the front steps and ornamental

Photo courtesy of Tom Noel

F

stonework, repoint and repair the ornamental terracotta trim, and replace or repair windows and their frames. Possible plans are to integrate the old water gardens, which served to cool water from the plant, and other once splendid landscape elements with the Cache la Poudre Riverwalk, extending along the north boundary of the reborn power plant.

FORT COLLINS MUNICIPAL RAILWAY STREETCAR BARN
350 N. Howes St. [LL]
Built: 1907

The City of Fort Collins matched the SHF's $103,800 for exterior restoration of this structure's façade, which is distinguished by large, wooden, double-leaf doors on five bays. Funds also provided for a new roof and repair of the brick walls and stone trim. The streetcar barn now houses Fort Collins Museum artifacts and vehicles impounded by the police. Local historian Wayne Sundberg says that Fort Collins hopes to convert this into a transportation and firefighters museum. As the hub for a once extensive city mass-transit system, this barn, like the restored line of the Municipal Railway from City Park to Old Town, is a picturesque reminder of a once thriving streetcar system.

FORT COLLINS MUSEUM, ANTOINE JANIS CABIN
Fort Collins Museum Heritage Courtyard, 200 Matthews St. [LL]
Built: 1859; Antoine Janis, builder

Antoine Janis came from a family of St. Louis trappers who gave the Cache la Poudre River its name by hiding their gunpowder in the canyon through which it runs. Janis married an Oglala Sioux woman and took an Indian name meaning "Yellow hair all messed up." Janis worked as a Sioux interpreter at Fort Laramie and guided General Albert S. Johnston's U.S. Army expedition against the Mormons in 1857. In 1858, he led a trading party to supply the new settlements known as Auraria City and Denver City at the junction of Cherry Creek and the South Platte River. He also worked at Camp Collins. To restore and reroof the cabin of this pioneering settler, the Fort Collins Museum matched a $5,000 SHF grant. Today, the cabins are used for children's summer programs and year-round interpretive activities.

FORT COLLINS MUSEUM, AUNTIE STONE CABIN
Fort Collins Museum Heritage Courtyard, 200 Matthews St. [LL]
Built: 1864; Henry Clay Peterson, builder

The Fort Collins Museum got a SHF grant of $4,999 to stabilize and restore the cabin of Colorado's best-known female town founder. Like other frontier forts, Fort Collins attracted civilians, including Elizabeth Hickok Robbins Stone. Born in 1801 in Hartford, Connecticut, she had moved out West, settling into this two-story log cabin in 1864. She opened a mess hall that later was a boarding house for officers, then Fort Collins' first private residence, hotel, school, and dance hall.

In 1894, a year after Coloradans approved women's suffrage, Stone voted in her first election, exclaiming that she had "waited a lifetime for this privilege." When she died a year later, the town closed for the funeral of "the founding mother of Fort Collins." Auntie Stone's town, now a fast-growing city, remembers her through this restored cabin celebrating the woman who first nourished Fort Collins.

FORT COLLINS MUSEUM, FRANK MILLER STAGECOACH
Fort Collins Museum Heritage Courtyard, 200 Matthews St. [LL]
Built: 1874; Abbott-Downing Co., builder

Frank C. Miller, a Fort Collins sharpshooter and showman, purchased this nine-passenger stage in the early 1900s for his shows, which featured his marksmanship from a moving stage. This vehicle had been used by Buffalo Bill Cody in his Wild West Show, where Miller had been a performer. Miller donated the stage to the City of Fort Collins in 1948.

Inmates at the state prison in Ordway restored this stage for the Fort Collins Museum, which matched a $4,880 SHF grant. The Colorado Historical Society (CHS) established the Colorado Artifact Conservation Center with the Colorado Department of Corrections, says CHS president Georgianna Contiguglia, "to restore lives and self-esteem as well as artifacts. Those guys especially love working on stagecoaches." Although the Conservation Center is now closed, its good work is exemplified by this restored and operational stage.

FORT COLLINS MUSEUM, FRANZ-SMITH CABIN
Fort Collins Museum Heritage Courtyard, 200 Matthews St. LL
Built: 1882

Displaced from its South Shields Street location by a subdivision, this homestead cabin found a home in the Heritage Courtyard of the Fort Collins Museum. A major restoration project, funded in part by an $82,907 SHF grant, stabilized or replaced damaged logs, reconstructed the roof, and restored the exterior, including the chimney, windows, and doors. To complement the frontier-era structures in the courtyard, the cabin has been restored to its 1920s appearance.

F

"We liked the idea of interpreting a rich agricultural history that spans into the 20th century," says Cheryl Donaldson, the museum's director. "Selecting this time period also allows us to tap into technology, including electrification and 'modern' appliances."

Funding from the Gates Family Foundation, Wilkins Trust, Overland Trail Questers, and private donations aided this effort, which is part of a larger three-year rehabilitation of the museum building and its Heritage Courtyard.

FORT COLLINS WATERWORKS
2005 Overland Trail LL SR
**Built: 1882, H. F. Handy, engineer; E. S. Alexander
and John Russell, builders**

Poudre Landmarks Foundation, Inc., (PLF) used SHF grants totaling $155,592 to carry out archaeological studies of this site and perform stabilization of walls and a waterway drop structure. Preservation partners include the PLF's Friends of the Waterworks, who helped with matching funds and support. Supervising archaeologist Richard Carrillo reports, "We've been excavating and leaving the stonework exposed so engineers can stabilize the foundation. We've found artifacts that tell us about the workmen here and about vagrants who lived here after this waterworks was replaced in 1903 by a new waterworks in Cache la Poudre Canyon at its confluence with the North Fork. We've unearthed bottles, a crucifix, and suspender clips. Probably from the period when this was abandoned and people squatted here, we've found women's shoes, jewelry, and a garter clip, along with beer bottles and old issues of the *Fort Collins Express* used for insulating the walls. We've also found pieces of the original roof. We've reconstructed the original water flow from a canal of the Cache la Poudre, which provided Fort Collins drinking and fire protection water."

Carrillo's work guides restoration of this handsome brick building, generously trimmed with local buff sandstone. Two later additions matched the original brick and fine rusticated stone trim. The waterworks will become the showplace and interpretive center of a 26-acre, city-owned site sheltered by giant old cotton-woods. SHF-supported interpretive efforts include local historian Wayne Sundberg's 2004 book, *Fort Collins' First Waterworks*. Sundberg details the history, including current restoration efforts, of "a small-scale, publicly constructed water delivery system that improved everyday life."

LINDEN HOTEL
201 Linden St. Ⓗ LL LLD NRD
Built: 1883; William Quayle, architect

William Quayle, a prominent Denver architect, designed this elegant three-story cornerstone of the Old Town Historic District. It opened as the Loomis Block, housing a Masonic lodge on the third floor and the Poudre Valley National Bank on the first. Quayle used local sandstone trim and ornamental brick pilasters beneath an elaborate pressed-metal cornice. It became the Linden Hotel in 1904 when the matching wings were added. The City of Fort Collins received a $100,000 grant from the SHF in 1994 for structural stabilization and façade restoration with the aim of rejuvenating this gem for first-floor retail and upper-story offices. Hotel owner Veldman Morgan Commercial put up a match of $1,904,100 to make this a signature restoration of the Old Town Historic District. SHF money helped to remove a pink stucco façade, after which the underlying brick with its stone trim was repaired. The project also added a new roof, repaired the cornice and windows, stabilized the distinctive double-oriel corner window, and restored the first-floor storefronts. The interior was rehabilitated as commercial space.

"During the restoration project the entire west wing of the building was almost lost," says City of Fort Collins preservation planner Carol Tunner. "If not for the temporary structural system that had been put up to add strength to the façade during restoration, when the alley wall collapsed due to a construction accident, it might have taken the entire west wing with it." Now the building is sound and once again an anchoring landmark in Fort Collins' Old Town.

MOSMAN HOUSE
324 E. Oak St. LL NR
Built: 1891; Montezuma Fuller, architect

Eastlake elements such as the porch spool work and cutout skirt enhance this one-and-a-half-story, brick-and-frame residence. The home was originally built for the prosperous Fort Collins merchant William O. Mosman and may have been designed

by Fort Collins' first architect, Montezuma Fuller. With the help of $63,000 from the SHF, matched by CSU's $28,140, it has been restored inside and out. New or restored roof, gutters, wood trim, windows, screens, railings, blue stone walkway, and interpretive plaques grace the property. Inside, the five first-floor rooms have refinished floors, woodwork, lighting, paint, and wallpaper as well as interpretive signage. The house is now used by Colorado State University for seminars, meetings, classes, and housing for a history graduate student in the upstairs apartment.

NELSON MILK HOUSE
1035 Swallow Rd. LL
Built: c. 1880; John W. Nelson, Sr., builder

This is the last relic of the 240-acre farm of John Nelson, Sr., which has now become a residential subdivision. Nelson erected this rough-cut Stout sandstone edifice for his dairy farm. The one-story gabled structure had a raised cellar to store milk from

his Jersey cows. The City of Fort Collins used an SHF grant of $10,000 for exterior restoration, including a new wood-shingle roof, stone and brick repair, and repair and repainting of the eaves and fascia. Frugal use of this grant left funds to do additional reconstruction of the windows and door. Exhibits inside include dairy farming equipment and displays.
Located at a busy intersection, this restoration, as architect Richard Hill says, is "a surprise, a gem amid the new development—the old, honey-warm stone barn where Nelson kept his milk cool for the market." The Fort Collins Parks and Recreation Department maintains this site, which is popular with school tours studying the city's agricultural roots.

NORTHERN HOTEL
172 N. College Ave. LL NRD
Built: 1887; 1905 addition

The 1873 Agricultural Hotel on this site was replaced in 1887 by the three-story, red-brick Commercial Hotel. That Victorian structure was given a fourth story, an Art Deco façade and lobby remodel, and a new name—Northern—in 1936. During its heyday, the Northern hosted such famous visitors as Franklin D. Roosevelt, John Wayne, Olivia de Havilland, Arthur Godfrey, and Vincent Price. The hotel's fortunes waned after World War II, and a fire in 1975 severely damaged the third and fourth floors, leaving them uninhabitable. Although the Northern Hotel always housed restaurants and anchored the north end of Fort Collins' downtown, its deteriorating appearance and insensitive remodels made it stick out among so many other beautifully restored buildings.

Funding Partners for Housing Solutions, a Fort Collins nonprofit, purchased the hotel for $1.5 million and then rehabilitated, updated, and restored the building. Vaught Frye Architects of Fort Collins oversaw the design to keep the hotel a sympathetic corner-stone of the Old Town Historic District. Funding Partners did find partners, including the City of Fort Collins and another nonprofit afford-able housing organization. The SHF's $450,000 also helped to bankroll an $11,756,000 rehabilitation of this landmark as affordable housing for low-income senior citizens, with commercial space on the ground floor. The SHF grant covered restoration of the façade and lobby—not to their original Victorian-era appearance but back to their 1930s Art Deco glory.

Today, the façade is resplendent again with blue and white, floral and geometric terracotta ornamentation and black glass adorned with brass medallions on the storefronts. Inside, restored stained-glass skylights and Art Deco lights illuminate the marble reception counter and terrazzo floor in the lobby. During rehabilitation, the 1970s-designed vertical sign was removed from the building. Inside the project team discovered the 1930s-era sign encased within and restored it.

"Beautiful—beautiful!" exclaims John, a resident of the Northern Hotel. "I can remember when the Northern burned so bad they talked about taking her down." John proudly shows off his fourth-floor apartment, including a dishwasher, quietly confiding, "I never use it, but it's nice to have. I couldn't be in a better place."

OLD POST OFFICE / FORT COLLINS MUSEUM
OF CONTEMPORARY ART
201 S. College Ave. LL NR
Built: 1912; James Knox Taylor, supervising federal architect

SHF funds of $110,700 and city funds of $60,000 helped restore the Pikes Peak granite base and Bedford, Indiana, limestone walls of this High Italian Renaissance–style palace, complete with bas-relief rosettes on the broad eaves of the red-tile roof. Trees in front have been replaced by modern scrap-iron sculpture representing the contemporary art museum, now housed in the building. The restoration has revived the splendid details carved into the limestone: egg-and-dart trim, dentils, and window spandrels with bas-relief cornucopias teeming with grapes, corn, fruit, and garlands.

PRESTON FARM
4605 S. Ziegler Rd. NR
Built: 1906; numerous additions

Agricultural sites and cultural landscapes within Fort Collins' city limits are vanishing fast. One of the few survivors, the Preston Farm, has been rehabilitated with the help of the SHF and the efforts of the Historic Fort Collins Development Corporation. A vestige of what used to be the town's economic bedrock, Preston Farm contains not only the original farmhouse but a chicken house, cistern, coal house, milk barn, grain elevator, hog house, icehouse, blacksmith/machine shop, pump house, smokehouse, spring house, and turkey house. SHF funds of $262,500 aided restoration of the house and grain elevator.

Preston Farm attracted Mary Humstone, who founded the National Trust for Historic Preservation's Barn Again! program in 1987. Humstone subsequently became a founder and president of Historic Fort Collins Development Corp., which was established in 1993. Humstone reports that "the two-acre remnant of the Preston Farm at the corner of Harmony and Ziegler Roads was once part of the little farming community known as Harmony. Harmony has become unraveled with development in recent years. We've at least saved the Preston Farm buildings, Harmony School, and Harmony House."

ROMERO HOUSE
425 10th St. [LL]
Built: 1927, John Romero, builder; numerous additions

Located in the Hispanic neighborhood of Andersonville, this dwelling housed the family of John Romero, who worked at the once immense Fort Collins plant of the Great Western Sugar Beet Company. This humble cottage of adobe brick typifies New Mexican folk architecture. The Romeros, who raised seven children here, occupied the house until 2001, when the City of Fort Collins acquired it. The City and the Poudre Landmarks Foundation, thanks to SHF support of $201,396, have restored this one-story corner residence as the Museo de las Tres Colonias. The city has created the pocket Romero Park on the lot next door. The SHF funds helped remove additions and restore the Romero House to its original four-room configuration. Marion Jones, project director for the Poudre Landmarks Foundation, says, "The focus of the Museo is to recognize and honor the contributions of local Hispanic pioneers to the sugar beet industry in Fort Collins."

SILVER GRILL CAFE
210–218 Walnut St. [NRD]
Built: c. 1902

The Uneeda-Lunch Café was renamed the Silver Grill in 1933 by a hungry sign painter with an oversupply of silver paint. He was paid off in steak breakfasts and pork-chop lunches, still specialties of this breakfast-and-lunch landmark noted for its monster cinnamon rolls, milkshakes, and jalapeño-jack burgers. This popular eating place has expanded into five adjacent one-story, corniceless, red-brick storefronts. The beauty is inside—not only in the good food, but in the $140,000 SHF-assisted restoration of skylights, antique fixtures, pressed-metal ceiling, and plate-glass storefronts shedding sunlight on the refurbished hardwood floor and historic photographs of Fort Collins that adorn the walls.

"The SHF grant enabled us to do a first-class job on this restoration," say owners John F. and Lois Arnolfo. "Our building was falling down, and about all we could afford to do was basic maintenance. We kept our place open for business all during the restoration. The historical preservation research, believe it or not, explained our ghost and why we hear jingling, clanking chains at night. It turns out that prisoners were brought here from the old Town Hall and city jail next door for their meals. Some of them apparently escaped and still frequent this place, especially late at night."

TRIMBLE AND BARKLEY BLOCKS
132–144 College Ave. [LL] [NRD]
Built: c.1890, Trimble Block; 1903 addition, Montezuma Fuller, architect;
1906, Barkley Block

With $150,000 in grants, including $9,500 from the SHF, and low-interest loans, the City of Fort Collins helped the owners restore these elegant, two-story brick commercial buildings distinguished by elaborate stone lintels and trim. The late Michael Thomas McCormick, proprietor of the Trimble Block used the first-floor storefront for his Cache la Poudre Rifle Works, which specializes in antique weapons.

"The SHF," said Michael McCormick, "did a great job here—everything that they promised, bless their hearts. They helped us tear off the 1950s façade—sheets of fake pink Miami stone. You can still see the scars where it was attached to the old brick." The cornices on both buildings were also restored, and the lowered tile ceilings inside were removed to expose the pressed-metal originals. Next door, the Rolling Thunder Ranch store sells authentic western-themed apparel. "We not only restored the Barkley and Trimble Blocks," McCormick said, "but we restore people's historical fantasies."

WINDSOR HOTEL / CHILDREN'S MERCANTILE CO.
111 N. College Ave. [LL]
Built: 1881, John F. Colpitts, architect

Restoration transformed this former hotel into an extraordinary children's store, with large glass display windows shedding light on wooden floors and antique wooden display cabinets inside. Modest Art Deco trim, cornice corbelling, and keystone round-arch lintels distinguish the restored historic façade, part of the rejuvenated Opera House Block. A $5,000 SHF grant enabled necessary roof repairs as part of the larger project, which was funded by the Fort Collins Downtown Development Authority and the building owner.

Fort Garland

FORT GARLAND
CO 159, 1 mile south of US 160 [NR]
Built: 1858; Charles Autobees, builder

Fort Garland's low-slung, one-story adobe structures are wrapped around a court-yard shaded by a few cottonwood trees. The fort, whose larger original grounds have been bisected by CO 159, was named for Brigadier General John Garland, military commander of the Department of the Army of New Mexico. The Colorado Historical Society acquired the site in 1945 and has converted five of the original structures, including the wood-floored officers' quarters and the barracks, into a regional museum.

The exhibits showcase the history of the San Luis Valley and this fort, which was once occupied by the 9th U.S. Cavalry African-American Buffalo Soldiers. The commandant's quarters have been restored to the 1866–1867 period, when Col. Kit Carson commanded the garrison. The CHS has received close to $260,500 in SHF grants since 1995 for land acquisition, sod-roof repair, replastering the adobe, and educational projects. "We've restored the commandant's quarters, the cavalry barracks, fixed the flagpole, and installed new bathrooms," says museum director Rick Manzanares. "We've also used SHF to help fund an interpretive program, 'Old Stories, New Voices' for schoolchildren. Come on down to see our newly landscaped adobe plaza and interpretive signage. Preserving and interpreting this old adobe fort is essential to understanding the role of the Indians, Hispanos, and Anglos who all called *El Valle* their home." The "Old Stories, New Voices" program was awarded the 2005 Presidential Coming Up Taller Award and is being replicated in Texas, New Mexico, and Pennsylvania.

FORT GARLAND'S BARLOW & SANDERSON STAGECOACH
Fort Garland Museum, CO 159, 1 mile south of US 160 (SR)
Built: 1871; Abbott-Downing Co., builder

During the 1870s and 1880s, Barlow & Sanderson's Southern Overland Mail & Express Company stagecoaches hauled passengers and freight through the San Luis

Valley between Colorado and New Mexico. This stagecoach has been repainted to its original colors and restored its straight body lines as opposed to the curved lines that were typical of a Concord stagecoach. The inside sat four, with a driver and "shotgun" guard outside up front. The Colorado Historical Society matched $32,500 from the SHF to restore this stagecoach with the help of inmates at the Arkansas Valley Correctional Facility.

F

Fort Lupton

DONELSON HOMESTEAD HOUSE
1875 Factory Dr. [LL]
Built: c. 1870; Thomas Donelson, builder

To save one of Adams County's oldest homesteads from demolition when it lay in the path of a new subdivision, the South Platte Valley Historical Society (SPVHS) undertook to move this house to its historical park in Fort Lupton. This $11,000 move received police escorts and lots of volunteer help, reports Esther McCrumb, executive director of the SPVHS. "But we could not get Qwest to answer the phone-—until I left a message asking how far their wires would stretch. I explained that we were moving a two-story house under their lines. That got their attention, and they sent someone right out."

After the house was moved and locally designated at its new site, the SHF contributed $65,930 toward the $90,000 restoration. Many volunteers, from old-timers to teenage Future Farmers of America, contributed much of the labor. The Donelson family donated the house and many family artifacts to furnish it. Freshly reroofed, repaired, resheathed, and repainted, this clapboard gem now sits on the SPVHS's 100-acre history park along the banks of the South Platte River.

FORT LUPTON PUBLIC LIBRARY/MUSEUM
453 1st St. LL
Built: 1929; John J. Huddart, architect

SHF granted $21,000 to the City of Fort Lupton to restore its old Carnegie Library, which became the Fort Lupton Museum in 1993. A miniature Renaissance Revival villa, this gem has a beige, wire-cut brick exterior with red-brick banding and bright blue terracotta accents, as well as fanlight windows, a metal cornice, and the roof parapet. Ladies of Fort Lupton raised $8,000 during the 1920s to build this new home for the town library, formerly housed in the dentist office of Dr. Walter W. Lee.

"We've put that gambling money to work," says museum curator Nancy Penfold. "It repaired the cracks in the foundation, steam-cleaned the building, and remortared the brick. We have taken the rags and patches out of the broken windows to repair them and fixed the cornice and the chimney, whose bricks had been falling off. Our rotating exhibits are donated by community people. For example, one of Colorado's best arrowhead collections, over 500 points, was found and donated by our old rural mail carrier, Ralph Haynes."

Both photos courtesy of Tom Noel

INDEPENDENCE SCHOOL
1875 Factory Dr. LL
Built: 1875

Photo courtesy of Tom Noel

SHF granted $29,998 to the South Platte Valley Historical Society to restore this school inside and out. Originally named Acorn Academy, it was moved from its original site in town to the Fort Lupton Historical Park. This one-room, clapboard school topped by a tiny bell tower was closed in 1956. Recycled as an outbuilding on the Watada Farm, it housed migrant laborers. SPVHS executive director Esther McCrumb says the community fund donated $2,000, and dozens of volunteers, including Future Farmers of America, donated $22,838 in labor and other in-kind help, while the SPVHS raised $3,200 in cash.

The restored school now has replicas of old-time desks, an old-fashioned black-board, a 38-star U.S. flag (celebrating the 1876 admission of Colorado as the 38th state), McGuffey's Readers, a washstand, and portraits of Presidents Washington and Lincoln. Students tour the building for summer sessions and field trips into the knuckle-rapping past. They then capture the experience in letters sent back to the old school. "I didn't like the stick hitting my hands," wrote student Calvin Garcia, "but thanks for helping us learn how interesting school was back in the 1900s. Writing with slates and chalk was awesome."

Fort Morgan

FARMER'S STATE BANK
300 Main St. NR
Built: 1930; Eugene G. Groves, architect

In this bank built for brothers John, Howard, Alvin, Charles, and Walter Bloedorn, noted Denver architect Eugene G. Groves combined vertical Art Deco and horizontal Moderne elements in this single-story, Indiana limestone building. Inside, marble accents, wrought-iron grilles, detached teller stations, and a classic stenciled ceiling with a green leaf motif impressed bank customers. By 1966, the bank outgrew its quarters and relocated. In 1970, the owners donated the building to Morgan Community College for its administration facility.

With $235,950 from the SHF, along with other funds, the college recaptured the bank's grandeur, restoring the interior to its original design, repairing the ceiling art, and reglazing the windows. Today, this jewel serves various community organizations, including the Chamber of Commerce and the Colorado Small Business Development Center, as well as college programs.

RAINBOW ARCH BRIDGE
CO 52 over the South Platte River, 0.5 mile north of I-76, Exit 80 **H** [NR]
Built: 1923, Marsh Engineering Co. and Charles Sheely's Colorado
Bridge and Construction Co., builders

Fort Morgan boasts the world's longest rainbow arch bridge, with 11 pairs of curves each spanning 90 feet. Retired by the Colorado Highway Department in 1963 with the opening of an adjacent, wider bridge for increased motor traffic, it spans the South Platte River by Fort Morgan's Riverside Park. Designed by James B. Marsh, this Marsh Arch bridge has curved arches constructed of concrete and steel. Sand and gravel from the river below were used to make the graceful concrete arches and railings, all with steel frames. This bridge, a designated Colorado Civil Engineering

Landmark, survived the South Platte River floods of 1935, 1965, and 1995. Yet, it was almost destroyed by neglect.

"A miracle of timing," as Fort Morgan preservationist Lyn Deal puts it, brought a combination of city funds, Colorado Department of Transportation support, federal Intermodal Surface Transportation Efficiency Act funds, and a $100,000 SHF grant to finance a structural analysis and restoration. The manufacturer of the original cast-iron and globe lamps that accented the bridge—gone since the 1950s—recast new replica lamps for what is now a popular pedestrian and bicycle bridge.

Franktown

CASTLEWOOD DAM
3 miles south of Franktown on CO 83 in
Castlewood Canyon State Park [NR]
Built: 1890; A. M. Wells, builder

SHF funds helped publish a booklet, *Where Were You When the Dam Broke?* that collects a flood of memories dating to August 3, 1933. That night Elsie Henderson's urgent voice raced down the Sullivan Telephone Exchange's wires, outpacing Cherry Creek's floodwaters. Notified by a Douglas County sheriff that Castlewood Dam had burst and that everything along the stream's path from Franktown to Denver was in danger, the operator told farmers and ranchers to gather their families and head for higher ground. She worked through the night and into the following afternoon, saving lives, livestock, and property. Five thousand fled the lowlands and only two people died in one of the worst floods in Colorado history.

In 1997, Castlewood Canyon State Park staff members assembled these memories into another book, called *The Night the Dam Gave Way: A Diary of Personal Accounts*. Funded in part by a $3,750 SHF grant, the book helps Coloradans understand the relationship between Castlewood Dam and the people and environment its failure affected. This Castlewood diary tells how developers built the dam thirty miles south of Denver in 1890, hoping to facilitate agricultural development in Douglas County.

Documented memories may be just as important to a historic site's preservation as bricks and mortar. Although the Army Corps of Engineers considered rebuilding Castlewood Dam as part of a Cherry Creek flood-control project as late as the 1970s, citizens opposed the idea, arguing that the new Cherry Creek Dam, built in 1946, was sufficient. So visitors to Castlewood Canyon State Park see only the old dam's ruins, a reminder of a battle that nature won.

F

PIKES PEAK GRANGE HALL No. 163
3093 N. CO 83 (Parker Rd.), 1 mile north of Franktown LL NR
Built: 1909; Grange volunteers, builders

Colorado once boasted 500 Grange halls, of which this modest, one-story clapboard building is one of the 88 Granges still active. Members raised $9,200 to match an $18,964 SHF grant to repair and restore the building's four chimneys and roof, repair and refinish floors, and reinforce the rhyolite foundation. In 2002, the Colorado Historical Society installed an interpretive sign discussing Franktown area history. The following year, Douglas County acquired 720 surrounding acres to insulate this landmark with open space.

From its founding in 1867 as the Patrons of Husbandry, the Grange organized rural men and women for political, economic, and social reasons, including the formation of cooperatives and the Montgomery Ward mail-order

house. The national Grange, whose membership peaked at almost two million in the 1870s, appealed to Coloradans engaged in agriculture. This hall, typical of pioneer vernacular construction, is a simple, front-gabled clapboard structure. A dining-room wing was added in 1916, and a shed addition and modern coal furnace in 1938. Grange meetings, Saturday night stomps, and potluck suppers in this hall, including a traditional December oyster dinner, perpetuate a long tradition of social and political solidarity among farmers and ranchers.

PRAIRIE CANYON RANCH
4620 CO 83, 6.5 miles south of Franktown [LL]
Built: 1870s clapboard house, 1878 barn, Frederick Bartruff, builder

Frederick Bartruff, a German immigrant, and his wife homesteaded here in 1868, initially living in the large cave on the site, which had been occupied by Native Americans since at least 800 BC. After diphtheria killed Bartruff and his two daughters, his widow buried them in the lonely cemetery that still haunts the hillside here. Then she married John Bihlmeyer. They increased the ranch to some 2,000 acres, including the canyons where East Cherry and West Cherry Creeks meet to form Cherry Creek. As a ranch, Prairie Canyon gained national notice for its show horses and breeding of bison, Red Angus, and Texas longhorns.

Photo courtesy of Tom Noel

Douglas County used its one percent sales tax for Open Space to acquire 978 acres of the ranch and its historic structures for $3.75 million. Douglas County Open Space matched SHF grants of $59,961 to reroof the main barn and to restore the Happy Days Saloon and the cave's stonework, door, and windows. The antique buildings, picturesque grounds overlooking Pikes Peak, and working ranch are maintained by Douglas County Open Space. The ranch is also a wildlife haven featuring pronghorn, badgers, bobcats, coyotes, elk, great blue herons, mountain lions, rattlesnakes, and other creatures large and small. Tours are given by reservation.

ROCK RIDGE RANCH BARN
7054 S. CO 83, 10 miles south of Franktown [LL] (SR)
Built: 1875; Peter Dumont, builder

Peter Dumont built the Rock Ridge Barn in an era before the mass production of nails, using post-and-beam construction with wooden pegs. The foundation of the barn consists of a mixture of heavy wooden beams and rhyolite stones, while

the siding and roof are rough-sawn pine planks from the Russellville Sawmill. The barn is Saxon style in its long sloping eaves and low sidewalls reminiscent of the north German province. The Dumonts raised cows, horses, and potatoes before switching to dairy shorthorns and hay. In 1899, Dumont sold out to Asher Hilyen, who gradually increased the farm to about 1,000 acres. The Hilyen family sold the place to Charles and Janet Herman in 1975. The Hermans worked with the Douglas County Historic Preservation Board to match the $9,540 SHF grant to replace the roof and put a protective stain on the frame exterior of their sheep and llama barn.

Photo courtesy of Tom Noel

Frederick

FREDERICK TOWN HALL
139 5th St. [LL]
Built: 1907

The Frederick Town Hall project began with a simple phone call to the SHF staff requesting that someone come to Frederick to give the town some advice. The town had moved its tiny, shiplap-sided, false-fronted frame building to the city park after it was replaced by a new structure in 1974. There it had become the town's storage closet, overflowing with Christmas decorations and fertilizer. The staff visit was productive, but SHF involvement would require that the building be designated, and designation of moved buildings can be problematic. Within just a few months, the town created a new historic preservation ordinance, designated the old Town Hall as its first local landmark, and completed a historic structure assessment. A few months later, the SHF awarded $101,103, matched by $33,702 in contributions from local businesses, residents, and the town itself, as well as in-kind contributions and volunteer labor from the community.

Preservation architect Gerhard J. Petri of SlaterPaull Architects oversaw the project, which included a new foundation and plumbing and electrical service. In a complete exterior restoration, the roof was replaced, siding repaired or replaced, a double-hung wood window restored, and doors replaced. Inside, the wood floor was restored; the wainscoting, walls, and ceiling repaired and the old stove and chimney fixed up. The reborn Town Hall, wearing a new coat of bright white paint, is now a community museum and, once again, Frederick's pride and joy.

Photo courtesy of Tom Noel

Fruita

FRUITA ELEMENTARY SCHOOL / CIVIC CENTER
325 E. Aspen St. (SR)
Built: 1912; 1936 addition, Works Progress Administration, builder

Abandoned as a school in the early 1980s, this two-story Neoclassical edifice was converted in 1994 into Fruita's Civic Center, housing government offices, a history room, and the public library. The City of Fruita matched SHF grants of $127,738

to restore the school inside and out, a $1 million effort including window restoration and replacement. Once a vacant eyesore, this now proud and highly visible and viable government and community center adorns a half-block site. Inside, the Community Development Office has a free walking tour brochure and information on more than 25 landmarks designated by the Fruita Preservation Board. A 30-foot-long dinosaur statue is pastured in the nearby town park, and a new slogan on the façade of the Civic Center reads, "Honor the Past—Envision the Future."

FRUITA MUSEUM / CHAMBER OF COMMERCE
432 E. Aspen St. [NR]
Built: 1938; Works Progress Administration, builder

Built as a museum to showcase geological displays, this miniature stone cottage with a stone chimney looks like the setting for a fairy tale. After some scary episodes, the tale has ended happily. When the museum failed, the cottage briefly housed the *Fruita Times* before becoming the town library in 1948. Inside, the fireplace has

a mantel of smooth scoria and incorporates pink agatized snail shells, opals, and gastroliths (dinosaur gizzard stones). Large, polished stone slabs form the floor, while sandstone walls contain the footprints of prehistoric animals. Perhaps it was these dragons that doomed the building until the SHF came to the rescue with $5,000 that helped the city restore this enchanted cottage. Known locally as the "Rock-A-Day Building" because of its slow construction, this geological and artistic masterpiece now houses the Fruita Area Chamber of Commerce. The Chamber welcomes visitors and offers free materials on Fruita's history and the prehistoric monsters showcased in the town's large Dinosaur Journey museum.

PHILLIPS HOUSE / STONEHAVEN BED AND BREAKFAST
798 N. Mesa St. [NR]
Built: 1908; A. B. Mahany and Harry Alvah Phillips, builders

This two-and-a-half-story, Queen Anne–style house was constructed of concrete blocks by builder A. B. Mahany and first owner and occupant, Harry Alvah Phillips. Phillips also used the rock-faced ornamental concrete block to build a generator house (now the bed-and-breakfast office) that gave him Fruita's first electric lights. Amy Kadramas began to restore this elegant ranch house as a bed-and-breakfast in 1994 and in 1999 obtained SHF funding for further restoration. The City of Fruita matched an $82,935 SHF grant to rehabilitate the exterior and replace the roof. Part of the 160-acre ranch has been sold for a residential subdivision, but the surviving hilltop site, surrounded by mature cottonwood trees, is still bordered on the east by agricultural operations and on the west by the old Elmwood Cemetery.

Photo courtesy of Tom Noel

Georgetown

Georgetown's pacesetting role in historic preservation began with town founder George Griffith, who brought his wife and family to "George's Town." Griffith encouraged other families to settle by offering free town lots to respectable women. The ladies fancied and encouraged painted houses, gardens, churches, schools, an opera house, and other refinements. Georgetowners also established four fire-hose companies to protect their genteel town.

Whereas some early towns regarded parks as wasted, non-income-producing land, Georgetown set aside a full block for a city park, between Taos, Rose, 10th, and Park Streets. This city park has a bandstand, playground, and wrought-iron entry arches. Tree-lined streets and gardens mixing wild and cultivated plants also enhance the community to this day.

From a peak population of some 3,300 in the 1880s, Georgetown dwindled to an all-time low of 301 in 1950. A private preservation group formed in 1970, Historic Georgetown, Inc. (HGI), worked with the town to enact one of Colorado's first and toughest local preservation ordinances. To keep development from creeping up the surrounding mountainsides, the town in the 1980s bought out a condominium developer preparing to build on the south side of town. Since 1970, Georgetown has lost few of its 211 19th-century structures in the downtown historic district and matched more than $1.5 million in SHF funding to remain Colorado's preservation queen.

ALPINE HOSE No. 2
507 5th St. LL NR NRD
Built: 1875; 1880, bell tower addition

Georgetown restored one of its oldest and most prominent landmarks with the help of a $121,500 grant from the SHF. Alpine Hose No. 2 was one of four

volunteer fire companies that prevented Georgetown from ever suffering a major blaze, leaving it among Colorado's best surviving examples of a predominantly frame 1800s town. Preservationists first stabilized the hose house and its 60-foot bell tower, which were in danger of collapsing. Next they installed a state-of-the-art "drench" sprinkler system to protect what the town hopes to make into a firefighting museum. "That bell tower," says preservation architect Gary Long, "is one of the most beautiful and well designed in Colorado. I suspect that Robert Roeschlaub, who also worked on the nearby Hamill House, designed it."

CHURCH/ECKLUND HOUSE
927 Rose St. LL   NRD
Built: 1876; John Adams Church and William Conant Church, builders

This clapboard house with a two-story bay window backs onto Clear Creek, whose frequent flooding is a threat. A duplex built as a home for the Church brothers, it was the Ecklund family house from 1900 to the 1980s. Wilma Ecklund, the last Ecklund owner, spent rainy seasons sandbagging Clear Creek in her backyard. To fight water and other damage, Historic Georgetown, Inc., was awarded $40,000 from the SHF, which helped undo a 1950s-era modernization and lift the house above the floodwaters and the eroding creek bank. New wood siding, stairs, kitchen, and bathrooms were installed, along with insulation, new electrical wiring, and a new roof. The chief of Georgetown's volunteer fire department, Kelly Babeon, notes that this rehabilitation project to create rental residences will lessen flood damage when the creek rises and save the fire department time, trouble, and sandbagging.

G

FIRST PRESBYTERIAN CHURCH OF GEORGETOWN MANSE
924 Taos St. LL   NRD
Built: 1882

Formerly known as the Samuel P. Allen House, this Greek Revival, one-and-a-half-story dwelling is being restored by the First Presbyterian Church of Georgetown using $44,912 in SHF grants and $8,000 in matching funds. Asbestos siding was replaced with a historically appropriate material. Restoration architect Kathy Hoeft reports that "with additional SHF funding we've completed the historical assessment on the 1874 church next door as well. It too needs attention."

GRACE EPISCOPAL CHURCH
408 Taos St. NR
Built: 1869–1870

Georgetown's oldest church has been reborn with a $51,725 SHF grant and a $16,675 match from the parish. This funding repaired the front porch and stairway, replaced siding and wooden beams in the bell tower, painted and repaired windows and doors, and repointed stonework on the second oldest continually used Episcopal church in Colorado. "Sinners repaint!" became the fund-raising slogan for the most recent restoration of this tiny congregation. Repainting included the steeple, which now sits beside the church rather than on top after Georgetown's notorious winds blew it off.

HAMILL HOUSE MUSEUM, CARRIAGE HOUSE, AND OFFICE BUILDING

305 Argentine St. NR
Built: 1867, Joseph Watson, builder; 1879 addition,
    Robert S. Roeschlaub, architect

William A. Hamill, a silver mining tycoon and state legislator, purchased this Gothic Revival–style, two-and-a-half-story frame house from brother-in-law Joseph W. Watson in 1874. This stylish estate was reworked and expanded in 1879 by Colorado's first licensed architect, Robert S. Roeschlaub, who designed Hamill's office to look like a miniature French chateau. Historic Georgetown, Inc., used a total of $330,435 in SHF grants to restore Georgetown's pride and joy. Matching funds were raised by HGI and local businesses whose annual Christmas Market has brought in $400,000 to preserve the Hamill House complex.

Restoration in the 1970s focused on the fine interior elements; later efforts have addressed the house exterior and outbuildings, including the famous six-seater outhouse. The office building in back of the house received a new roof thanks to SHF funds, which also provided for restoration of the first floor and its walnut woodwork, the rooftop wrought-iron cresting, and partial rehabilitation of the second floor. SHF funds also helped make the house accessible for the disabled. The carriage house, also designed by Roeschlaub, is being restored, as are the walkways, fountain, and landscaping. Although earlier archaeological investigations had gotten to the bottom of the privy, the SHF supported further digging in the gardens for insights to guide an accurate restoration of the landscaping.

HOTEL de PARIS
409 6th St. [NR]
Built: 1875–1890

Locally famous as "a little bit of France in the Rockies," this two-story hotel stands very much today as it did when Louis Dupuy constructed it. Dupuy, formerly Adolphe François Gerard, was born in Alençon, France. He came to Georgetown in the 1870s as a miner, but following a serious mining accident he opened the Delmonico Bakery, which he expanded into a restaurant and hotel. The two-story structure, inspired by buildings of Dupuy's youth in France, was constructed over the course of 15 years with wood, brick, and stone. In 1893, Dupuy stuccoed the entire building and painted it to mimic stone blocks. He offered fine food, drink, and sleeping quarters to guests who relished Dupuy's steam heat, hot and cold running water, 3,000-volume library, handsome furnishings, and "millionaire's dinners." Dupuy died in 1900, and the hotel slid into decline before closing in 1940.

The National Society of Colonial Dames of America acquired the building in 1954, began a restoration, and reopened the inn as a museum. The Colorado Branch of the Dames has used SHF grants totaling $525,361 to restore the hotel. They repaired the roof joists and electrical wiring in the attic and completed full interior and exterior restoration, enhancing the site's educational and hospitality potential. Better lighting and access for the disabled have made it more visitor-friendly. The Colonial Dames have raised cash matches totaling $438,881 to update the inventory of the historic furnishings; restore the basement; make alterations to the outbuilding; conduct an archaeological study of the west courtyard; restore the east courtyard, dining room, and kitchen; and install a security system. According to architect Kathy Hoeft, preservationists have made terrific headway and have been heartened by the National Trust for Historic Preservation agreeing to adopt the Hotel de Paris as its first Rocky Mountain region property.

KNEISEL HOUSE
910 Biddle St. (SR)
Built: 1875

In 1882, Henry Kneisel bought this one-story clapboard building that has stayed in his family, as has the still-operating grocery at 511 6th Street. The SHF granted $93,455 to Historic Georgetown Inc. (HGI), after it raised a cash match of $31,155 to purchase the house with a long-term plan to restore it as a museum. Many of the original furnishings are in the house, which had not been occupied since 1937. HGI stabilized the exterior. The structure, while awaiting full restoration, is being leased for use as a Montessori School. Prominently sited high on a hill behind a dry-stack stone retaining wall and picket fence, this tiny white cottage looks like a doll house.

MAHANY HOUSE
614 Taos St. Ⓗ ⦿LL⦿ ⦿NHLD⦿
Built: 1870

In 1974, a fire almost destroyed the Mahany House. Volunteer firefighters, handicapped by extreme cold, battled the blaze for over two hours. Despite their best efforts, authorities pronounced it a "total loss," and the building remained a vacant eyesore for 26 years. Locals dubbed it "BOB" (burned-out building) and urged demolition. Historic Georgetown Inc. (HGI), disagreed, pointing out that the two-story structure, with its ornate double-roof brackets and pedimented window tops, is one of the five oldest buildings in Georgetown. HGI acquired the building in 1999, and aided by $195,000 in SHF funds, began stabilizing it and restoring its interior and exterior. The Xcel Energy Foundation, the Town of Georgetown, Clear Creek County, the Clear Creek Economic Development Corporation, the Colorado Division of Housing, Clear Creek National Bank, and HGI members provided matching funds. As the first affordable-housing project in Clear Creek County, it now contains two two-bedroom apartments above the Idylls & Odysseys bookshop.

OHIO BAKERY / GEORGETOWN COMMUNITY AND VISITOR INFORMATION CENTER
613 6th St. ⦿LL⦿ ⦿NHLD⦿
Built: 1868; Cassius Clay and John Fillius, builders

This false-fronted, two-story clapboard store opened as a bakery owned by John Fillius and John F. Mahany. In 1874, it became the county courthouse and remained so until 1976 when a modern courthouse was built across Argentine Street. Saved from demolition and moved to its current site in that year, it has been converted into the Georgetown Community and Visitor Information Center. With $65,500

from the SHF, the center's restored and weatherized the structure, reinforced the second floor, and installed a new metal roof. Along with new lighting and access for the disabled, the building features interpretive exhibits, including photo panels of the preservation process.

PELICAN DIVES MINE OFFICE AND POWDER HOUSE
507 and 509 Taos St. LL NHLD
Built: 1865; A. R. Forbes, builder

Longtime Georgetown druggist Albert R. Forbes built one of the town's remaining wood-frame commercial structures. Later it became the offices of one of Georgetown's largest and longest-lived silver-mining companies, named the Pelican Dives. Historic Georgetown Inc., and a private owner used a $235,613 SHF grant with matching funds of $350,419 to restore and rehabilitate these two historic, fire-damaged buildings for reuse as apartments and retail space.

G

SNETZER BUILDING / GRACE HALL
414 Taos St. H LL NHLD
Built: 1869; John H. McMurdy, builder

Grace Episcopal Church matched the SHF's $74,940 to remove the stucco skin and restore the wood siding, false front, and glass storefront underneath, even recovering the old sign, "J. Snetzer Merchant, Tailor." Snetzer resided in this building from 1876 to 1913, followed by a family who stored and sold antiques.

Architect Kathy Hoeft recalls, "You never know what you'll find when you start a project. In Snetzer we found a box with old photos of Georgetown, including the Hotel de Paris and the Grace Episcopal Church, that will help guide their restorations." The building now houses two apartments upstairs and a first-floor parish and community hall. Hoeft and fellow architect Gary Long, shown here, note that Grace Hall, unlike the church, has indoor plumbing, which has facilitated longer and livelier church socials.

Photo courtesy of Tom Noel

Glade Park

COATES CREEK SCHOOLHOUSE
DS Rd., 16 miles west of Glade Park NR
Built: 1919; Elwood Brouse, builder

Photo courtesy of Tom Noel

The Coates Creek School Restoration and Preservation Society received a $4,875 SHF grant to stabilize the foundation and restore the windows of the sole surviving Mesa County log schoolhouse. In a remote farming and ranching area near the state line, this school attracted a few children from Utah. The one-room structure served as a school until 1971, when it became a community center. "His" and "Hers" outhouses still serve this rustic log structure restored for ongoing use as a community hall in a picturesque valley.

G

Glenwood Springs

EARNEST RANCH / FOUR MILE CREEK BED AND BREAKFAST
6471 CR 117, 7 miles south of Glenwood Springs NR
Built: 1919 barn; 1926 house, Hugh Earnest family and Peter Kirchen, builders

Locals once drove past the barn on Four Mile Road "just to see if it had collapsed," says owner Jim Hawkins, who with his wife purchased the Earnest Ranch for a bed-

and-breakfast operation. Considering the balloon-frame barn "an integral part of the ranch flavor of the property," the Hawkinses obtained a $34,815 SHF grant to replace and repair its cedar roof and to pour a new concrete foundation. Now stabilized, the big red barn with the "Circle 4M" brand greets guests of the Four Mile Creek Bed and Breakfast. This beautifully maintained complex in a rural setting on Four Mile Creek consists not only of the barn but also of a main house, two cabins, and a bunkhouse.

Photo courtesy of Tom Noel

GLENWOOD LIGHT & WATER COMPANY HYDROELECTRIC PLANT / GLENWOOD SPRINGS CENTER FOR THE ARTS
601 E. 6th St. [NR]
Built: 1888; Theodore von Rosenberg, architect

Since 1988, this decommissioned hydroelectric plant, set on the north bank of the Colorado River between the Hot Springs Pool and the Vapor Caves, has powered imaginations as a city arts center. But until recently, severe drainage problems threatened its future.

"We used to joke that a river ran through it," says Gayle Mortell, executive director of the center. "The plant suffered when the surrounding land was regraded for highway construction. Rainwater has drained into this building ever since."

The City of Glenwood Springs and the Glenwood Springs Arts Council used the SHF's $166,265 as the cornerstone for a $380,000 restoration completed in 2004. The first step was to redirect the water through a new drainage system and

reconstruct the parking lot. After addressing that basic problem, restorationists painted the stucco walls, door, brick and windows. The Arts Council has set out to raise the remaining funds through the HEART (Hydro Electric Plant for ART) capital campaign so the reborn power plant can continue to offer diverse arts programs, from dance and pottery classes to Japanese animation projects for teens to watercolor painting for adults and seniors. All can fit into this roomy, two-story space.

Photo courtesy of Tom Noel

Golden

Golden has revived its 9th Street, 12th Street, and East Street as historic districts. The Golden Historic Preservation Board, created by an ordinance in 1983, has also designated more than 36 individual landmarks (LL) in this well-preserved little town that once served as the territorial capital and aspired to replace Denver as Colorado's urban hub.

Photo courtesy of Tom Noel

Richard J. Gardner, president of the Golden Landmarks Association, noted in 2006, "We've done pacesetting preservation for a conservative suburban town. We've restored much of Washington Avenue—our main street—with its many antique storefronts and 1863 territorial capitol building. An 11-year-old girl, Rose Kalasz, successfully applied for State Register listing for our 1949 Main Street arch, Howdy Folks! WELCOME TO GOLDEN WHERE THE WEST LIVES!'"

ASTOR HOUSE MUSEUM
822 12th St., northeast corner of Arapahoe St. LL NR
Built: 1867; Seth Lake, builder

One of the oldest hotels in Colorado is made of sandstone cut from the Charles R. Foreman Quarry at the west end of 12th Street. Builder Seth Lake was a prominent

Photo courtesy of Tom Noel

hotelkeeper in Jefferson County, having run the Green Mountain Ranch and a hotel at what is now the Jefferson County ghost town of Apex. His Astor House suffered four fires and received attic and rear additions. In 1972, the Golden Landmarks Association tried to keep it from becoming a parking lot, a fate avoided by a citywide vote authorizing the city to purchase and save it. With $215,561 in SHF grants, more than $10,000 from the city, and $5,000 in community contributions, the Golden Landmarks Association has stabilized and restored it as a museum. Among other things, SHF funding helped repair plaster and wallpaper and install heating and air-conditioning.

Shannon Voirol, executive director of the Astor House Museum and Clear Creek History Park, reported in 2003, "We added steel beams between the first and second floors to correct Astor House's tilt. We conducted a paint analysis to restore the exterior to white—the first color the stone was painted. We also repaired the stone and brick walls and removed an added sleeping porch. Next door we also have a marvelous matching stone public bathroom. We call it the Taj Ma Stall. It is next to our free parking lot."

BOOTLEGGER CABIN
3873 CO 46 in Golden Gate Canyon State Park, 0.25-mile walk from trailhead at Bootleg Bottom on Mountain Base Rd. (SR)
Built: 1920s

At the edge of the forest at the foot of Tremont Mountain, a crumbling log cabin lies near a small tributary of Ralston Creek, whose waters were turned into firewater. In the creek lies the rusty hulk of an old bakery truck that Porky Edwards had used to deliver bootleg whiskey he claimed was "strong enough to turn your hair red." Near the delivery truck, the creek is littered with rotting barrel staves, rusting iron barrel-hoops, and copper piping. This rare relic, a reminder that Colorado once had hundreds of moonshiners, is being saved as the state's only commemoration of what became a major industry for remote, impoverished mining towns during Colorado's 1916–1933 dry spell. After a $3,500 SHF 1996 assessment grant, Golden Gate Canyon State Park plans to put the cabin's roof back on, repair the round-log walls, put in a floor, and repair the rubblestone foundation.

G

DENVER & RIO GRANDE LOCOMOTIVE No. 346
Colorado Railroad Museum, 17155 W. 44th Ave. (SR)
Built: 1881; Baldwin Locomotive Works

Photo courtesy of Tom Noel

The SHF contributed $99,106 to the Colorado Railroad Museum (CRM) toward a $190,000 restoration of this grand steam locomotive. For 66 years, Locomotive No. 346 hauled passengers and freight on the Denver & Rio Grande, the Colorado & Southern, and the Montezuma Lumber Co. Railroads before becoming one of the first exhibits of the Colorado Railroad Museum upon its opening in 1958. More than 65,000 visitors tour the CRM each year and relish seeing, or riding, working rolling stock such as No. 346. The CRM's staff and large team of volunteers keep the museum, library, and rolling stock in top condition. Future CRM projects include restoring three Galloping Goose railcars and a diesel locomotive.

FIRST PRESBYTERIAN CHURCH / FOOTHILLS ART CENTER
809 15th St., southwest corner of Washington Ave. [LL] [NR]
Built: 1872 church; 1899 manse, Perre O. Unger, builder

The Foothills Art Center consists of three historic structures: the First Presbyterian Church, its manse, and the Unger-Rubey House next door to the south. The Presbyterian Church was built on land donated by William A. H. Loveland. Its congregation had been established two years before by circuit-riding minister Sheldon Jackson. The Gothic Revival church was joined 20 years later by a Queen Anne–style manse. In 1898, local architect James H. Gow renovated the church with additions including a bell tower. In 1899, Golden builder Perre O. Unger designed and built a residence to the south of the church, an Edwardian-style speculative house with a distinctive corner tower. Unger sold it to Ella M. Rubey, matriarch of the Rubey family, prominent in Golden banking and clay mining. Additions built in 1892, 1898, 1920 and 1947 connected the church and manse. After First Presbyterian moved out in 1958, an arts group rallied to save the historic church and moved in. Today the place is famous as the Foothills Arts Center, which purchased the adjacent Unger-Rubey home and restored it as a gift shop with the help of SHF's $3,300.

GOLDEN HIGH SCHOOL / AMERICAN MOUNTAINEERING CENTER
710 10th St., northeast corner of Washington Ave. [LL] [NR]
Built: 1924, Eugene G. Groves, architect; numerous additions

For this $1.5 million reincarnation, the SHF contributed $383,054 and the rest was raised by the American Alpine Club and Colorado Mountain Club. This Beaux-Arts–Neoclassical edifice of beige brick served as a high school until 1956, then as a junior high until 1988. Alumni, the Golden Civic Association, the Golden

Landmarks Association, and others fought demolition until this gem was rescued by the American Alpine and Colorado Mountain Clubs. The building provided the expanded space and educational facilities needed by both of the organizations.

According to Charley Shimanski, the executive director of the American Alpine Club, "The entire building, including electrical, mechanical, and plumbing, had to be restored. The structure was in good shape, but the guts were not. We had some surprises, including a pleasant one. Removal of the lowered false ceiling tiles revealed the beautiful 1924 ceiling." The exterior terracotta-tile ornamentation, including sky-blue bas-relief columbines, was restored. The exterior masonry was repointed and windows and doors repainted. The entry mural, *Dawn of the West* by artist Gerald Cassidy, is now cleaned to greet mountaineers as it once greeted students. The reincarnated school has photo galleries, a rock-climbing wall, and America's largest mountaineering library. Recycled to educate mountain lovers, the classrooms and auditorium remain in a school that Golden resident Jane Sutton says "is sacred to us gray-haired locals who are tickled pink to see something so basic to our generation left in Golden."

LOVELAND, COORS, AND SCHULTZ BUILDINGS
1118–1122 Washington St. [LL] [NR]
Built: 1863, Loveland Building, Duncan E. Harrison, builder; 1900, Schultz Building, Julius Schultz, builder; 1906, Coors Building, Baernesen Brothers, architects, and Perre O. Unger, builder

These three adjoining structures represent much of importance in Colorado history, starting with the 1863 Loveland Block, perhaps the state's oldest brick commercial structure. The rear addition was made to accommodate the territorial legislature in 1866. William A. H. Loveland hired early contractor and Jefferson County commissioner Duncan E. Harrison to erect this first-floor mercantile and upper-floor Masonic hall. After the legislature left for Denver in 1867, this building was put to other prominent uses, including as headquarters of the Jefferson County government and the Colorado Central Railroad, as well as the Colorado School of Mines. During the 1980s, the Loveland Building became a restaurant.

G

Photo courtesy of Tom Noel

Next door, the mansard-roofed Coors Building, built by Adolph Coors to house a bottling plant in the basement and a street-level saloon, is one of many similarly styled Coors structures throughout Colorado. On the north side of the Coors Building, the Schultz Building was built by a German immigrant and was for many years a grocery, then the Foss Appliance Shop, and a Christian Science Reading Room before common ownership with the other two buildings led to its reuse as a restaurant.

The city matched $25,000 from the SHF to rehabilitate the interiors and exteriors of these three Golden nuggets. Golden historian and preservationist Rick Gardner of the Golden Landmarks Association notes that these SHF-aided projects involved removing the 1950s façades from all three buildings to restore their street fronts. At the Loveland Building, paint was removed from the eroding brick façade, which was then sealed to prevent any further deterioration. The building was also structurally reinforced and its arched windows restored, returning it back to its 1922 appearance. The two other, somewhat younger, structures, were restored to approximately original appearances.

TALLMAN RANCH
3873 CO 46 in Golden Gate Canyon State Park, moderate 2.5-mile
   walk along Buffalo Trail from trailhead on Gap Rd. (SR)
Built: 1876–1881; Anders Tallman, builder

In 1870, Anders Tallman emigrated from Sweden and homesteaded at this site, where he found a now-gone log cabin. He married Christina Bengson at Golden's

Swedish Lutheran Church, Colorado's first Swedish house of worship, and the Tallmans settled down on this ranch on Nott Creek, a tributary of Ralston Creek. In 1882, he constructed a frame ranch house by adding on to an old schoolhouse moved to the site. Additions to the main house and outbuildings were constructed over the years. Tallman's children and grandchildren married other local Swedes. His granddaughter-in-law, Ruth,

married John Wickstrom, who ran this place until his death in 1951. Subsequent absentee owners mostly neglected this remote, old-fashioned place in aptly named Forgotten Valley. The Kriley family owned 198 acres, which they sold to the state in the 1960s; Golden Gate Canyon State Park finally bought the spread in 1970.

This 400-acre farm and dairy is picturesquely sited in a meadow edging a large

pond. Beside the main house lie a log-walled workshop, a barn, a milk house, stables, and a chicken house. Malcolm Stevenson, park historian, says that $111,936 from the SHF enabled the park to begin preserving all five buildings and conduct interpretive programs. These celebrate three generations of a family who raised milk cows, grew vegetables, and marketed their dairy products and produce in the booming mining towns of Central City and Black Hawk.

Both photos courtesy
of Tom Noel

Goldfield

CITY HALL / FIRE STATION
Victor Ave. and 9th St. NR
Built: 1899

The SHF contributed $10,500 for the Goldfield Restoration Association's stabilization and preservation of this two-story frame city hall. It is the most prominent surviving structure in the town of Goldfield, which has shrunk from a 1900 population of 2,191 to a virtual ghost town. This structure, used as a fire station and Town Hall until 1940, remains the centerpiece of what was downtown Goldfield. In 1976, the Cripple Creek District Museum acquired and began restoration of the building, then turned it over to the Goldfield Historical Society, which is going to finish the preservation project.

Both photos courtesy of Tom Noel

G

Granada

AMACHE RELOCATION CENTER
1 mile southwest of Granada on 23 Rd. off US 50 NHL
Built: 1942; U.S. War Relocation Authority, builder

One of 10 relocation camps built in the United States during World War II, Amache today consists of little but the cement slabs left from the barracks of what once comprised Colorado's 10th largest city: 7,318 people of Japanese ancestry from the West Coast—the majority of whom were U.S. citizens—were imprisoned here. Internees included 90-year-old grandmothers and infants, seen as security threats in the panic that followed the Japanese bombing of Pearl Harbor. The Town of Granada, whose students and teachers have taken a special interest in the project, obtained a $4,900 SHF grant to complete a National Register of Historic Places nomination. Another $72,851 from the SHF supported an archaeological assessment of one of Colorado's most significant—and tragic—sites.

John Hopper, a Granada High School teacher working on the project with his history students since the 1980s, reports, "The Town of Granada has donated its old Town Hall as the Amache/Granada Trails Museum. Neighboring ranchers, who recycled the Amache barracks as outbuildings, have offered to donate them back to the site. With the help of these locals, our students, the National Park Service, and the SHF, we have assisted in the 2006 designation of Amache as a National Historic Landmark with appropriate interpretive facilities. We have already begun restoring the Japanese goldfish ponds."

Grand Junction

G

AVALON THEATRE
645 Main St., southwest corner of 7th St. Ⓗ 🆛
Built: 1923; Mountjoy and Frewen, architects

The SHF contributed $265,000 to a partnership headed by the City of Grand Junction to restore downtown's grand old theater as a community events center. Exterior rehabilitation, lobby restoration, stage improvements, and roof replacement revived the Beaux-Arts–Renaissance Revival, three-story brick theater, which had featured silent movies and doubled as a civic auditorium. Mary Pickford, Ethel Barrymore, Al Jolson, John Philip Sousa's band, and poet Carl Sandburg were among those to perform here. The fine façade was bricked in by a 1947 modernization that converted it into the Cooper Theatre. The restoration replaced the missing terracotta ornamentation with replica precast-concrete trim, including bas-relief features. Restoration brought back the three fan-lighted second-story windows above the entry. The Avalon is now a 1,200-seat performing-arts hall that serves as a venue for local and traveling entertainment, including cinema, plays, musicals, ballets, orchestras, and bands, as well as public meetings on downtown's Main Street Mall.

GRAND JUNCTION COUNTRY CLUB / REDLANDS COMMUNITY CENTER
2463 Broadway Ⓢ🆁
Built: 1920; Nunzio Grasso, builder

With its spacious hilltop site as part of a private country club, this was a haven for early Grand Junction grandees who teed off at Mesa County's first golf course. Purchased in 1935 by the Redlands Women's Club, this Mission Revival edifice became the Redlands Community Center (RCC) in 1950, hosting meetings, events, and weddings. The RCC

Photo courtesy of Tom Noel

received $61,046 in SHF funds to restore the old stone-and-stucco, Mission-style clubhouse, including the roof, oak flooring, windows, and doors.

HANDY CHAPEL
200 White Ave., northeast corner of 2nd St. NR
Built: 1892; Hunt McDonald & Co., builders

As Grand Junction's first African-American church, the Handy Chapel has been a physical as well as spiritual haven for residents and visitors. First known as the Wright Chapel after its original pastor, Silas Wright, the chapel was later sold to African-Americans. Some not only worshiped but boarded and ate here, at times in exchange for working on the building and grounds. In the late 1970s, the Rocky Mountain Conference of the American Methodist Episcopal Church sold the Handy Chapel to a group of Grand Junction investors planning to demolish it. The congregation subsequently filed suit, and in 1981 the court overturned the sale and ruled that a trust committee of local African-American citizens be named to administer the chapel for charitable and religious uses. The still-active congregation used the SHF's $5,000 to repair the roof, bell tower, and water damage to this humble, one-story stone structure with its mini-buttresses and bell tower.

Photo courtesy of Tom Noel

MESA COUNTY COURTHOUSE
544 Rood Ave., northwest corner of 6th St. LL
Built: 1922–1924, Eugene G. Groves, architect; 1974 addition,
Vanderwood & Henry, architects

The county used $52,765 in SHF grants to replace the roof as the final step in the restoration of this Classical Revival limestone structure. A parade of second-story, fanlighted windows separated by Ionic columns distinguishes one of the few buildings downtown that retains its original grandeur.

Photo courtesy of Tom Noel

RABER COW CAMP
Land's End Rd., east of Grand Junction (SR)
Built: 1930s; Ralph Foster, Frank Lucas, and Bill Raber, builders

The SHF awarded $5,000 to the Grand Mesa National Scenic and Historic Byway Association to restore and interpret this rare surviving camp used by high-country

cattlemen. The Raber family of Kannah Creek built these two log cabins with steeply pitched, side-gabled roofs that provide attic space above a single first-level room with tongue-and-groove flooring. The logs were hauled from the nearby forest, then hand-hewed, notched, and fitted together. The original corral and cattle-loading chute also survive as relics of the days when cattlemen drove their livestock up to the high country for summer grazing. Once, a dozen cow camps lined the west end of Grand Mesa where this is now the sole survivor.

St. REGIS HOTEL
359 Colorado Ave. [NR]
Built: 1892

The City of Grand Junction matched $100,000 from the SHF to restore this structure, originally opened as the Grand Hotel. It boasted a large cocktail lounge,

a ballroom for dances, and the Flemish Dining Room, known for its excellent cuisine. A third story was added in 1904 and a two-story west wing in 1906, when the cupola was installed atop the entry corner and the U-shaped brick hostelry became the St. Regis. KFXJ, Grand Junction's first radio station, broadcast from its ballroom in the 1930s when the Oriental Room and the Cocktail Lounge were local hot spots. By the 1970s, the St. Regis had become a pigeon-infested flophouse whose decadence suggested demolition. The SHF grant helped replace the roof, stabilize the east wing, replace windows and doors, and provide new heating, mechanical, and electrical systems. The handsome beige-brick hotel now houses offices and condos above a first-floor restaurant and bar.

VORBECK BUILDING
510 Main St., northeast corner of 5th St. ⬜LL⬜
Built: 1890

The SHF awarded a $10,000 grant to help restore this one-story plate-glass storefront with a new roof, awning, signage, and façade face-lift. On a typical 25-by-125-foot downtown lot, the Vorbeck is representative of simple 1890s brick structures. This pilot project is an example for other Main Street property owners considering restoration on Grand Junction's Main Street Mall, the 1962 project that became Colorado's first successful rebirth of a once struggling downtown retail district as a pedestrian friendly mall.

WHITMAN ELEMENTARY SCHOOL / MUSEUM OF WESTERN COLORADO
248 S. 4th St., northeast corner of Ute Ave. **H** ⬜LL⬜
Built: 1926; Eugene C. Groves, architect

G

The City of Grand Junction matched the SHF's $135,980 to restore the bricked-in façade, window openings, and interior of this two-story school. It housed grades one through four until declining enrollment led to its closure in 1962. Reopened as the Museum of Western Colorado (MWC) in 1966, this golden-brick structure serves as a regional history museum and library. The MWC also boasts two branches, the Dinosaur Journey Museum and the Cross Orchards Living History Museum.

"Restoration of the Whitman School and the expansion of our museum have been pivotal, along with the restoration of Main Street landmarks, in the redevelopment of downtown Grand Junction," says Michael Perry, executive director of the Museum of Western Colorado.

Grand Lake

Founded in 1879 as a mining settlement on Colorado's largest natural lake, the town of Grand Lake today is a peaceful, end-of-the-road community bypassed by US 34. Grand Lake retains rustic public buildings and private cabins, most of which were constructed before 1929 using the straight, skinny lodgepole pines that still envelop this sleepy summer resort. The town matched $17,400 in SHF funding to install interpretive signs and publish a walking tour booklet for this village of about 450 year-round residents. With its rough-hewn, log-and-slab structures and wooden sidewalks, Grand Lake seems frozen in an earlier time.

G

HOLZWARTH TROUT LODGE / NEVER SUMMER RANCH
Rocky Mountain National Park, 8 miles north of Grand Lake on Trail Ridge Rd. (US 34) NRD
Built: 1917, John Holzwarth, Sr., builder; numerous additions

German immigrant John Holzwarth, a Denver saloonkeeper forced out of business by statewide Prohibition in 1916, built the Holzwarth Ranch. Along with the usual hay and horses of ranch life, Holzwarth trapped, hauled freight, and began taking in dudes during the 1920s for $2 per day, or $11 per week. As he shifted increasingly to tourists, he renamed his place the Holzwarth Trout Lodge. The

complex grew to include the "Mama Cabin" where Mrs. Holzwarth served her famous German-style meals and fresh trout, as well as an icehouse, woodshed, taxidermy shop, and guest and tent cabins. As the business thrived, the family added an adjacent property, the Never Summer Ranch. John, Jr., ran both of the ranches until 1973. Refusing several lucrative offers, he instead transferred this picturesque spread along the headwaters of the Colorado River to The Nature Conservancy. They conveyed it to the National Park Service for use as an interpretive site.

Photo courtesy of Tom Noel

The Rocky Mountain National Park (RMNP) Associates, a private fund-raising group dedicated to improving the park, received a $62,970 SHF grant for stabilization and restoration of the Holzwarth Trout Lodge. Work included reconstructing the front porch, rechinking the Mama Cabin, replacing logs in the Twin Cabins, and restoring the taxidermy shop. The ranch is not only a popular interpretive site with living-history programs, but also houses offices of the park's volunteer program. "The SHF made this restoration possible," says Curt Buchholtz of RMNP Associates, adding, "and we encourage everyone to help the SHF by gambling at Black Hawk, Central City, and Cripple Creek."

KAUFFMAN HOUSE MUSEUM
407 Pitkin St. [NR]
Built: 1892; Ezra Kauffman, builder

Ezra Kauffman, a hunter, trapper, and guide, constructed this two-story log cabin. He sawed and hewed the logs, leaving a round, bark-covered exterior, with interior

walls smooth enough to be wallpapered after he had reinforced the chinking with flattened tin cans and muslin. Kauffman died in 1920, and his family continued to run their home as a hotel for summer visitors until 1946. In 1973, the Grand Lake Historical Society (GLHS) bought the cabin for use as its office and a museum featuring tourism, sailing, and skiing artifacts. The GLHS matched $29,150 in SHF funds to restore the exterior of this unusually well-crafted, all-log building. With the help of SHF funds, the Society did interior restoration, replaced the roof and electrical system, and rehabilitated the expansive, friendly front porch with its marvelous view of Grand Lake.

Greeley

Founded in 1870 by Nathan C. Meeker, agricultural editor of the New York Tribune, *Greeley is the second most successful Rocky Mountain agricultural colony after Salt Lake City. Meeker, with the aid and encouragement of* New York Tribune *editor Horace "Go West" Greeley, recruited colonists of good character able to buy $155 memberships for a "Union Colony that will be for the benefit of all the people, not for schemers and speculators." Each family would own a "comfortable, if not elegant home, surrounded by orchards and ornamental grounds."*

Greeley attracted some 1,500 settlers its first year and has grown to become Colorado's 11th largest city. Pioneers laid out 100-foot-wide streets, blocks 400 feet square, and generous public spaces. Today, the city preserves its past with a collection of restored buildings in its Centennial Village Museum at 1475 A Street and more than 50 buildings listed on the Greeley Historic Register. With SHF grants, the city has conducted architectural and historic resource surveys and installed interpretive signs throughout the historic downtown.

GREELEY UNION PACIFIC RAILROAD DEPOT / GREELEY/WELD CHAMBER OF COMMERCE AND CONVENTION AND VISITORS BUREAU

902 7th Ave. [LL] [NR]
Built: 1929; Gilbert Stanley Underwood, architect

One of Colorado's most exquisite depots has been beautifully restored, showcasing a Beaux-Arts–Neoclassical exterior and a stunning Mission-style interior. Underwood, the building's original architect, was known for his Rustic-style buildings for the Union Pacific as well as his grand resort lodges at Bryce Canyon, Grand Canyon, Yosemite, and Zion National Parks. This treasure, built for only $88,000, is his only Colorado work.

G

City, county, and Chamber of Commerce funds, along with the SHF's $62,890, went into this $1.5 million rebirth. Work included cleaning the polychromatic,

intriguingly patterned exterior brick, restoring the wooden windows and the doors, replacing the roof shingles, and landscaping the three-acre site. The interior is also impressive, with the original dark wood and open-beamed ceiling, as well as the stenciled birds, animals, and mythical beasts that adorn the Great Hall of the passenger waiting room. Interpretive signage, encouraged and overseen by the SHF staff and the City of Greeley Museums, provides insight into not only this marvelous depot but also Greeley's unusual town history.

MEEKER HOME

1324 9th Ave., southwest corner of 13th St. [LL] [NR]
Built: 1870; Nathan C. Meeker, builder

Nathan C. Meeker, the father of Greeley, built and lived in a two-story adobe house. As the agricultural editor for the *New York Tribune*, Meeker came out west to implement his dreams of a "utopian agricultural community." Meeker promoted his town with his *Greeley Tribune*, which remains the town's newspaper to this day. To show his confidence in Greeley's growth, Meeker built his home out in what was then the country. He used adobe bricks, claiming they were sturdier and had better insulation than wood. The town acquired the house in 1927 and converted it into a museum.

Neglect and misguided efforts to repair the adobe with cement and chicken wire were the targets of the 1995 restoration. With the SHF's $31,999 and $13,000 raised by the City of Greeley Museums, the city removed the cement and chicken wire and cleaned, repaired, or replaced the adobe bricks. After a new cement foundation was installed, the old hardwood floor and linoleum on top of it were scrapped and replaced by a replica hardwood. Interpretive markers were also installed to give visitors information during the off-season, as the museum is open only from mid-April to mid-October.

NORCROSS HOUSE
1403 2nd St. LL
Built: 1883; J. A. Barrett, builder

Photo courtesy of Tom Noel

This imposing, two-and-a-half-story Italianate house, with Eastlake trim and an inviting porch, was collapsing before the Greeley Urban Renewal Authority restored it as office space for community nonprofit organizations. William B. and Mary Ellen Norcross and their family lived here for 55 years, operating the amusement park on the western part of the block. Originally called Sall's Gardens, then Warnaco, it featured a swimming pool, an outdoor arena, big-band dancing, and a skating rink. The rink and the dance hall both survive, although they are abandoned and deteriorating. Fortunately the house, now elegantly restored and landscaped with the help of the SHF's $45,455, points to renewal both in the built environment and through social services offered by the nonprofits working out of Norcross House to rehabilitate this transitional neighborhood.

PLUMB FARM MUSEUM AND LEARNING CENTER
4001 W. 10th St., northwest corner of 39th Ave. LL SR
Built: 1904; Bessie Smith, architect

Designed by one of Colorado's first and most notable female architects, this story-and-a-half clapboard farmhouse exhibits Colonial Revival and Queen Anne elements. SHF gave the City of Greeley $97,628 to help with the restoration of the interior and exterior and installation of access for the disabled. Peggy Ford, research coordinator for the City of Greeley Museums, says, "The farmhouse and 5-acre farm have been restored as an outdoor classroom. Kids love to come here to see the animals and explore the fields. We have them help tend the kitchen and the gardens. They relive every aspect of farm life, including picking and preparing fresh vegetables, setting the table, and washing dishes. It is truly amazing how few kids nowadays have ever formally set a dinner table! We also give the kids cardboard and saws and let them build their own Union Colony box town."

Surrounded by 21st-century development, this rural enclave retains its headgate and working ditch, and remnants of a tree farm, chicken house, potato cellar, and descendants of plants brought here from Elmira, New York, by the Plumb family a century ago. The Plumb family also innovated irrigation practices that helped make Greeley, in "the Great American Desert," bloom as an agricultural center.

G

WELD COUNTY COURTHOUSE
9th St. and 9th Ave. [LL] [NR]
Built: 1915–1917; William Norman Bowman, architect

White Colorado marble columns, wainscoting, and floors, illuminated by fine stained-glass windows, sparkle anew inside this four-story courthouse of Indiana limestone. Detailed ironwork staircase rails and elaborate relief ceilings amplify the impressive Beaux-Arts–Neoclassical design. Repairing nine ornate stained-glass windows, restoring the pneumatic clocks, and installing interpretive signs were among the projects partially funded by the SHF. Of the stained-glass windows, Shairan Whitman, project coordinator, comments, "Below the years of grime on the windows we found the bright colors that the people of Greeley would have seen when the building first opened on July 4 of 1917."

Photo courtesy of Tom Noel

One of only a few operational pneumatic clock systems in America, the master clock operates eight "slave" clocks throughout the courthouse. The master clock forces air pressure to each slave clock, which drives the internal components. After not working properly for nearly 30 years, the clocks now function again.

People are "wondering how air could run so many clocks all at once," notes Whitman. She adds, "Almost daily, residents of Greeley and along the Front Range express their appreciation of the efforts we make to preserve the court house for future generations. It could not have happened without the $55,000 from the SHF." This proud old building is now again the rightful centerpiece of Greeley.

Photo courtesy of Tom Noel

G

Grover

GROVER DEPOT / GRASSLAND NATURE CENTER AND HERITAGE HOUSE
600 Chatoga Ave. (SR)
Built: 1887; Chicago, Burlington & Quincy Railroad, builder

When the CB&Q Railroad arrived in Grover, the small farming community blossomed, even building an extant opera house. This leg of the railroad's vast network transported passengers and freight between Cheyenne and Sterling via Grover. To accommodate the station agent, passengers, and freight, the railroad built a two-story, side-gabled, red wooden depot. Located above the first-floor ticket office and freight storage section were the station agent's four-room living quarters. When the railroad abandoned the line in 1973, the station agent decided to dismantle the depot and salvage the lumber.

In the nick of time, a preservation-minded angel heard of the salvage project and purchased the

depot. A group of Grover-area women voluntarily cared for the orphaned depot, which served as the community's Halloween haunted house. "Historically it is the oldest building in the area," claims Louanne Timm, president of the Pawnee Historical Society (PHS). "It's also one of the few remaining two-story wooden depots in Colorado and may be the only surviving first-generation depot of its type in Colorado."

With $12,572 from the SHF, the PHS, which owns the building and site, stabilized the foundation, painted the shiplap frame exterior, repaired the roof and brick chimney, and produced interpretive signage and brochures. The PHS was delighted to find that the brick foundation is four feet deep, providing very solid support. Now recycled as the Grassland Nature Center and Heritage House, the Grover Depot is open by appointment.

Guffey

31 MILE RANCH
*931 Badger Lane, via CR 88 off CO 9, 3 miles
    northwest of Guffey Junction* [LL]
Built: 1880–1920s

Eastern socialite Barbara Grace Monel purchased this ranch in 1925 to raise her show horses. She converted the 1880s homestead cabin into a bunkhouse and constructed an enormous and elaborate gambrel-roofed barn. The Park County Historical Society used a $20,180 SHF grant matched by the current property owner, Curley Reynolds, to repair the ranch house, barn, and windmill. "At age 85, Curley had personally done much of the restoration work," reported Park County Historic Preservation Advisory Committee coordinator Kathie Moore.

G

Gunnison

GUNNISON HARDWARE BUILDING / GUNNISON ARTS COUNCIL
102 S. Main St. (SR)
Built: 1882; Frederick Zugelder and Thomas D. Russell, builders

This two-story, Italianate-style sandstone building with a distinctive pair of Gothic-arched pediments on the west elevation became the Gunnison Arts Council in

Photo courtesy of Tom Noel

1993. The structure originally housed the Denver & Rio Grande Express Office and the U.S. Land Office. The Master stonemason, Frederick Zugelder, later served as the quarry master for the granite used in building the Colorado State Capitol which came from Gunnison County.

The Arts Council used $94,500 from the SHF to leverage matching funds from the Boettcher, Bonfils-Stanton, El Pomar, and Gates Foundations, as well as Gunnison City and Gunnison County, to restore this stone edifice and the adjacent clapboard building, including reconstruction of the historic pediments and the filling-in of nonhistoric openings. "Our two beautifully restored buildings," says Arts Council director Ashley King, "help capture audiences. We've reinstalled the windows and replaced deteriorated stone with matching sandstone from Gunnison's demolished La Veta Hotel. Our center operates a theater, dance studios, art galleries, music rooms, a poetry room, and, since 1977, a poetry review, the *Gunnison Valley Journal*."

MUNICIPAL BUILDING
201 W. Virginia Ave., southwest corner of N. Wisconcin St. (SR)
Built: 1931; Mountjoy & Frewan, architects

Decorative iron fixtures hold spotlights that illuminate
this public building's Art Deco vertical piers and floral
motifs. Before restoration, these light fixtures had been
converted to flower planters. Inside, ceilings had been
lowered and aluminum air-lock doors installed on the
two-story, concrete town hall. City planner Colleen
Hannon says, "Thanks to $71,237 from the SHF, com-
bined with city funds, we rewired and weatherproofed the
'planters,' where we install red and green lights at Christmas
time. The south end of the building, originally a fire station, is now our planning department. With city funds,
we also redid the interior and removed false ceilings to find floral motifs inside that
match the ones restored outside." SHF funds supported exterior work including
repainting, replacing nonhistoric windows and doors, repointing masonry, restoring
terracotta, and other items to bring back the appearance and architectural integrity
of this stylish public building.

TENDERFOOT/MOUNTAINEER ARCHAEOLOGICAL SITES
Access information available at:
Western State College
US 50 near CO 135 (SR)
7650–3000 BC; Early Archaic People

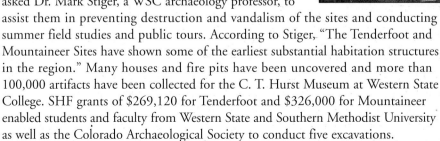

Tenderfoot is the mountain south of Gunnison with a
large white "W" painted by Western State College (WSC)
students. Two Tenderfoot Mountain archaeological sites
are major Paleo-Indian and Archaic culture sites, where
prehistoric hunters may have spent warmer months and
perhaps winters in rock dwellings and hunting blinds.

The City Council in Gunnison, which owns the land,
asked Dr. Mark Stiger, a WSC archaeology professor, to
assist them in preventing destruction and vandalism of the sites and conducting
summer field studies and public tours. According to Stiger, "The Tenderfoot and
Mountaineer Sites have shown some of the earliest substantial habitation structures
in the region." Many houses and fire pits have been uncovered and more than
100,000 artifacts have been collected for the C. T. Hurst Museum at Western State
College. SHF grants of $269,120 for Tenderfoot and $326,000 for Mountaineer
enabled students and faculty from Western State and Southern Methodist University
as well as the Colorado Archaeological Society to conduct five excavations.

Stiger's book, *Hunter-Gatherer Archaeology of the Colorado High Country*, includes
flaking tools, projectile points, knives, bone awls, scrapers, and choppers excavated
here. Fire pits suggest these sites were camps for prehistoric hunter-gatherers thousands of years ago. Stiger leads tours of the Tenderfoot Site for the public.

WESTERN STATE COLLEGE, LESLIE J. SAVAGE LIBRARY
600 N. Adams St. **H** **NR**
Built: 1939; Temple Hoyne Buell, architect

"After the restoration began," confides librarian Nancy Gauss, "excited workers took us to see where they had poked through the acoustical-tile ceiling to reveal a perfectly intact, high barrel vault with elaborate beaver-board trim and hand-carved ceiling beams."

Architect Buell supposedly took a fancy to the 1930s head librarian, Gauss confides further. That would help to explain why this library is one of his most elaborate structures, with a grandiose entry and large arched windows that flood the reading room with light. This Spanish Colonial Revival beauty has a dazzling Churrigueresque, terra-cotta entry-surround adorned with the college seal. Buell also designed the library's sturdy, oak reading tables and armchairs with their distinctive crests, echoing the entry and wall crests that give this immense space the flair of a medieval great hall.

Photo courtesy of Tom Noel

Western State College raised more than $500,000, matched by $273,131 from the SHF, for a restoration celebrated on the cover of *Choice*, the leading library journal for higher education. The Temple Hoyne Buell Foundation, established by the architect, donated the initial and final grants, totaling $100,000, with the Gates Foundation's $100,000 and substantial contributions from the Boettcher and Helen K. and Arthur E. Johnson Foundations. The main-entry foyer chronicles the library's history with photos, many architectural and restoration awards, and the Works Progress Administration's 1939 Franklin D. Roosevelt bronze plaque.

The restoration revived the exterior and windows as well as the great reading room. "Students normally aren't quiet in the library," librarian Gauss points out,

"but this restored reading room awes them. They actually tell us librarians to be quiet! The beauty of this restoration is that it not only rescues the historic integrity of Buell's original design, but brings back the grandeur of his Great Room, integrates state-of-the-art computer technology, and gives our campus showplace space."

Gypsum

FIRST EVANGELICAL LUTHERAN CHURCH
400 2nd St., northwest corner of Eagle St. [NR]
Built: 1890; S. Broughton, builder

"We have so many new people moving to Gypsum from other places that we need to show them our history," says Pastor Jeff Hanson. "First Lutheran is the second oldest building in town, and it provides our community with a sense of its history." Boosted by a $24,740 SHF grant, the congregation raised funds for the restoration with a "Steeple Chase" footrace at the annual Gypsum Days festival. This paid for removing 10 lancet windows and sending them to Denver Art Glass, where artisans carefully replaced poorly matched replacement pieces with glass made using 19th-century techniques. Cedar shingles on the steeple were replaced and the repaired windows returned to their settings. "With SHF resources and know-how," says Rev. Hanson, "the church handed down to this generation has been preserved for future generations."

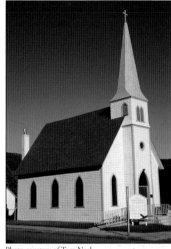

Photo courtesy of Tom Noel

Hartman

HARTMAN GYMNASIUM
School Ave. and 1st St. (SR)
Built: 1938; Works Progress Administration, builder

Made of locally quarried Fort Hays limestone from the Niobrara Formation underlying the community, this structure features a balcony stretching the length of the gymnasium. In 1959, the building was vacated when the Hartman and Holly School Districts were consolidated. Since 1998, the Town of Hartman has received SHF grants totaling $313,867 for interior and exterior restoration. The restoration team replaced the roof, restored the exterior masonry, retiled the ceiling, and repaired the plaster, stairs, and HVAC and electrical systems. Town clerk Linda Wilger, who wrote the grant proposals, says, "Our tiny community, which raised matching funds with bake sales,

chili cook-offs, and dances, now has a hall for family reunions, wedding receptions, and anniversary celebrations. We are looking forward to completing the interior so once again the walls will echo with the sound of locals cheering for the home team."

Hartsel

BUCKLEY RANCH
CR 59, 3 miles east of Hartsel [LL] [NR]
Built: 1880s–1940s; Putnam and Buckley families, builders

James B. Putnam homesteaded the original 160 acres of this ranch in 1881. By 1908, when the Buckley family inherited it, the ranch consisted of more than 2,500 acres, which they operated until 1949. In 1986, the Colorado Division of Wildlife (DOW) bought the ranch, which straddles one of its fishing-access trails

Photo courtesy of Tom Noel

to Spinney Reservoir State Wildlife Area. DOW and Park County utilized a $7,050 SHF grant to help stabilize the buildings and the fences on the 6.4-acre ranch complex, set amid meadows stretching for miles and miles to South Park's forested mountain rim. Besides the frame ranch house, this relic ranch includes round-and hewn-log outbuildings, board-and-batten and shiplap structures, and corrals and livestock loading ramps. Once near collapse, it is now a picturesque interpretive site on the banks of Spinney Reservoir.

SALT WORKS RANCH
3858 US 285, 13 miles west of Hartsel [LL] [NR]
Built: 1862–1870s; Charles L. Hall, builder

The Colorado Salt Works Ranch is a 128-acre spread homesteaded in 1862. Besides ranching, the Hall family developed the property's salt springs, which long ago inspired French mountain men to give South Park its earlier name, Bayou Salado. This salt attracted wild game, hunters, and the Halls. Their old frame barn and ruins of a two-story salt kettle house survive, although the huge smokestack has collapsed. Other nearby ranch buildings survive, most notably the Halls' elegant, Second Empire–style home. The SHF gave $31,535 to the Park County Historical Society for planned stabilization of some structures on the Salt Works Ranch. The only surviving U.S. kettle-and-pan salt plant, this pioneer Colorado industry produced more than a million pounds of salt.

Haxtun

FIRST NATIONAL BANK / HAXTUN CITY HALL
145 S. Colorado Ave. [NR]
Built: 1919; John J. Huddart, architect

Haxtun matched the SHF's $21,500 with $2,000 in city funds to restore the interior and exterior of this one-story Neoclassical Revival gem. The bank closed in 1932 during the Great Depression; the city bought it for $100 in 1939 for use as the Haxtun City Hall. The most stylish structure in Haxtun's three-block commercial district has blond bricks adorned with black speckling. The white terracotta trim shines in the distinctive pilasters, while a prominent corner clock reminds customers that time is money. Inside, the tile floors, marble baseboards, hardwood counters, leaded- and etched-glass windows, room dividers, and open-beamed ceiling all sparkle anew. Town clerk Karie Wilson comments, "This is a beautiful piece of Haxtun's history. People love to come in. They are in awe of the Art Deco stained glass, oak wood, 17-foot-high ceilings, and old photos of Haxtun we display on our walls."

Hayden

CARPENTER RANCH
13250 US 40, 3 miles east of Hayden [NR]
Built: 1887–1904; Abraham and Charles Fiske and John B. Dawson, builders

Long noted for its hay and Herefords, Carpenter Ranch is now noted as a pioneering conservation research and interpretive center. The ranch first began with Abraham Fiske's 1887 homestead, which grew over the years into a 2,000-acre ranch. John Barkley Dawson, who purchased the property in 1902, had blazed cattle trails north from Texas to Colorado along with Charles Goodnight during the 1860s. Dawson hired Abraham and Charles Fiske to build the 1904 barn, the oldest surviving structure on the spread.

   The ranch is nationally significant because of its association with Farrington "Ferry" Reed Carpenter. A local who graduated from Princeton and then Harvard Law School, he returned to become the town's leading attorney as well as its best-known rancher after buying this ranch in 1926. When the Taylor Grazing Act in 1934 brought an end to the era of free, open-range grazing in the West, Carpenter was instrumental in laying the foundation for public land management. President Franklin D. Roosevelt appointed him as the first director of the Federal Grazing

H

Service. In that capacity, Carpenter pioneered many of the practices associated with the modern livestock industry, including policies regarding ranchers' leasing of grazing land from the federal government. An innovator in the care and breeding

of Herefords, Carpenter was honored by the American Hereford Association in 1980, the year he passed away at 94.

Carpenter's multifaceted career is covered in his autobiography, *Confessions of a Maverick*. At its height, his ranch encompassed some 22,000 acres. His children tried to operate the spread after his death, then worked with The Nature Conservancy and the SHF to preserve one of Colorado's most historically significant ranches. For a project that will cost more than $1 million, the SHF contributed $205,000 to help with property acquisition and restoration. Starting with the oldest structure, the Carpenter clan restored the old cottonwood flooring in the barn. Other structural work on the barn reinforced the foundation and added new gussets and ties on the rafters.

The two-story frame ranch house and Bungalow-style bunkhouse have also been restored with new doors and windows, plumbing and heating replacement, and new siding, plaster, paint, and roofs. The new education center within the main house uses the old kitchen space, so a new kitchen was installed. The Conservancy now operates more than 900 acres as a working ranch and another 580 acres as a nature preserve, with a hiking trail and interpretive signage. Mark Burget of The Nature Conservancy says that "the Carpenter Ranch represents a new model for cooperation between agriculture and conservation interests."

HAYDEN DEPOT / HAYDEN HERITAGE CENTER
300 W. Pearl St. [LL] [NR]
Built: 1918; Frank E. Edbrooke, architect

The Denver, Salt Lake & Pacific Railroad (Moffat Road) constructed this two-story, Prairie-style passenger depot with a one-story attached freight depot. It retains its wide, overhanging eaves and telegrapher's bay window. The Denver & Rio Grande Railroad, which acquired the Moffat Road in 1947, abandoned the depot in 1969. It was acquired by the Town of Hayden, which reopened it as the Hayden Heritage Center. The Town of Hayden matched an SHF grant of $26,248 to install a new

roof and restore the exterior of this handsome, glazed red-brick station with its ornate, red Spanish tile roofing. The second-story stationmaster's apartments and downstairs waiting room and telegraphic office are fairly intact.

Holly

HOLLY DEPOT
302 S. Main St. [NR]
Built: 1912; Atchison, Topeka & Santa Fe Railway, builder

This Mission-style depot handled this agricultural community's passengers and freight. A $100,000 SHF grant matched by $124,000 from the City of Holly and private donations have allowed for interior rehabilitation, exterior restoration, and landscaping that have returned this brick depot to its dignified stature as a community hub. While trains no longer stop at Holly, the depot now houses city offices, the library, and public meeting rooms. City administrator Marsha Willhite says, "We have a lot of people who come off the highway and into Holly just to tour this building."

Hot Sulphur Springs

GRAND COUNTY JAIL
119 E. Byers Ave. [LL]
Built: 1897; S. M. Snider, builder

The Grand County Historical Association received a total of $14,650 from the SHF to stabilize and restore the exterior and conserve the interior of what was the county jail from 1897 to 1938. This structure replaced the original hole dug into a mountainside with bars over it. This jail was moved in 1976 to the Grand County Historical Society's museum grounds, which include two 1920s schoolhouses, the old brick county courthouse, and a sod-roofed blacksmith shop. Two iron cells and iron bunks remain in the 18-by-18-foot log jail, which was stuccoed outside and inside, providing a convenient surface for the cell-block graffiti, which has also been preserved.

Howardsville

OLD HUNDRED MINE BOARDING HOUSE, MULE BARN, AND TRAMHOUSE

721 CR 4A, Howardsville vicinity (SR)
Built: 1904

Perched precariously on a ridge high above the Old Hundred Mine, this cliff-hanging group of structures has been too remote to attract vandals. It is one of the few remaining historic mining resources of its type left in the San Juan Mountains. During an extraordinary preservation effort, materials were airlifted to the 12,000-foot-high site by helicopter. Local contractors using $86,000 in SHF grants tied the building to the cliffside and re-established the structural connections and rigidity. The Colorado Division of Minerals and Geology, San Juan County Historical Society, the U.S. Bureau of Land Management, the U.S. Forest Service Division of Wildlife, mining associations, private citizens, as well as the Colorado

Scenic and Historic Byway Commission all helped save this endangered boarding house, adjacent tramhouse, and mule barn. In the valley below, the Old Hundred Gold Mine is still operating as a tourist attraction that transports sightseers 1,600 feet underground in an electric tram.

Hugo

DICKINSON HOUSE
306 3rd St. [LL]
Built: 1880; Thomas McNeil, builder

One of the earliest and finest homes in this small high plains hamlet was built on a T-shaped plan. This two-story, clapboard frame house features hints of the popular Greek Revival style. Original owner/builder Thomas McNeil was an engineer on the Union Pacific Railroad, whose tracks ran just a block away. Later, the politician and businessman John P. Dickinson, who represented Lincoln County in the Colorado State Legislature and served multiple terms as Hugo's mayor, lived in the house for many decades. Subsequent owners changed and remodeled the structure over the years. To expedite restoration, the Town of Hugo designated Dickinson House as its first local landmark.

The nonprofit Prairie Development Corporation, which works to provide low- to moderate-income housing in several eastern Colorado communities, acquired the house to save it from demolition and restore it to its 1880s appearance.

With $129,300 from the SHF, Prairie Development removed several nonhistoric modifications, reconstructed the original porch, and installed replica windows. During the project, they met some tough challenges, such as finding a rotting wooden foundation under the bucking cement foundation, and having an over-zealous contractor replace the original crumbling brick chimney with a faux chimney constructed of wood. Additional time, expense, and work resolved these surprises and, with a preservation easement in place, the house is now ready to serve again as a family home.

HUGO UNION PACIFIC RAILROAD ROUNDHOUSE
3rd St. and 3rd Ave. (SR)
Built: 1909; Union Pacific Railroad, builder

This semicircular, eight-stall brick structure is one of only a few surviving UP round-houses. Once a busy maintenance facility, it was sold in 1953 to a farm implement dealer who covered the bay doors with plywood and glass to create a storefront. The building was later used for storage and then left empty.

Concerned about its future, Colorado Preservation, Inc., listed it in 2002 as one of Colorado's Most Endangered Places. To save it, Lincoln County bought the structure and surrounding property, using $122,297 in SHF grants. The county has now begun important structural stabilization. "This depot has had a hard life," says Colorado railroad historian Doris Osterwald. "All of its doors are gone, and only one engine pit is left. It now needs new windows, floors, masonry repairs, and much other attention. Part of the roof has fallen in and it will take at least a million to complete all the needed work." Using an additional $191,042 in SHF grants, the county plans to begin restoring the building as a railroad museum and county offices.

WALKS CAMP PARK COMMUNITY BUILDING
63551 CR 27 (SR)
Built: 1935; Civilian Conservation Corps, builder

Originally part of a community hall for Hugo's CCC camp, this structure was moved to the park in 1944 and re-enclosed with a new wall. Electrified and heated in the 1950s, the building has since served as a year-round facility for community groups like 4-H and the Colorado Trappers Association, and for events such as weddings and reunions. A $7,466 SHF grant helped restore the hall's roof and windows.

Idaho Springs

George A. Jackson's 1859 discovery of gold in Chicago Creek near its confluence with Clear Creek gave birth to this mining town. In 1863, Dr. E. E. Cummings opened a commercial hot springs, which is today the Indian Springs Resort. Stretched along Clear Creek Canyon, the town retains a well-preserved commercial main street (Miner Street), which anchors a National Register downtown commercial district. The Phoenix, Edgar, and Argo Mines, as well as the Argo Mill and Argo Tunnel, are open for tourists, who will find this one of Colorado's best-preserved and most accessible mining towns.

CARNEGIE LIBRARY
219 14th Ave. [LL] [NRD]
Built: 1904, Frederick J. Sterner, architect; Sidney Varney
and Silas Knowles, builders

Thanks to $10,000 from steel magnate Andrew Carnegie, this library opened as one of the most elegant, up-to-date buildings in town. City offices coveted the space and began moving in downstairs where the sheriff even added a two-cell jail. The jail did not move out until 1986. "We wanted to reach out to the community and especially the senior center just across the street," explains librarian Patricia Stelter. "Our $19,030 SHF grants enabled us to build a wheelchair ramp and improve our stairs, as well as to begin stabilizing and restoring our library." Now the building has returned to its original purpose. "We've returned that basement space to library use, including the children's section," Stelter adds. "We've replaced corroding metal pipes but kept the original golden-oak bookcases, armchairs, glass-top display tables, big transom windows, gilded radiators, the stately exterior and interior columns, and even cleaned up the portrait of Andrew Carnegie."

COLORADO & SOUTHERN NARROW-GAUGE LOCOMOTIVE No. 60 AND PASSENGER COACH No. 70

17th St. between Miner Ave. and Idaho St. LL NRD
Built: 1886, Rhode Island Locomotive Works;
   1896, St. Charles Car Co., builders

The Colorado Central steamed through Idaho Springs in 1877 on its way to Georgetown and its famous loop. Locomotive No. 60, one of the Colorado Central's original narrow-gauge engines, was built by the Rhode Island Locomotive Works. It served the Colorado Central and its successors for 64 years before operations ceased in 1941. Passenger Coach No. 70, built in 1896 by the St. Charles Car Co., was used until passenger service was discontinued on this line in 1927.

   "Our historical society raised $3,800, including $2,000 from Clear Creek County, to capture a $10,100 SHF grant," says Robert Bowland, the trustee in charge of railroading for the Historical Society of Idaho Springs. "This enabled us to restore the exteriors on the very rare 2-8-0 consolidation-type steam locomotive and equally rare 48-passenger coach."

   "Before we restored this train," Bowland recalls, "kids used to ambush it with rocks. Now they help us keep it spiffy. We've restored all seven kinds of wood in the coach, including red oak, poplar, and alder. We also plan to renovate the seats, original kerosene lamps, clerestory windows, and old coal stoves in the coach." After restoration to working order, this train is now being considered for employment on the Georgetown Loop railroad a few miles farther up the valley.

METHODIST EPISCOPAL CHURCH

1414 Colorado Blvd., northwest corner of 15th Ave. LL NR NRD
Built: 1880, Henry A. Choate, architect; 1905 addition

"My grandparents, parents, children, and I have all been members here," recalls Marjorie "Chee Chee" Bell, who is also a founding member, former president, and current trustee of the Historical Society of Idaho Springs. "The steeple and bell weren't added until 1905, because a neighbor who liked to carouse on Saturday night and sleep in Sunday morning gave the church money not to install the bell tower!"

   Well aware of such carousing, Rev. John L. Dyer, the "snowshoe itinerant" who brought religion to many Colorado mining camps, helped organize this congregation in 1868 above the Bucket of Blood Saloon on Miner Street. That tiny congregation raised $4,000 to build the church, which was dedicated by Methodist bishop Henry W. Warren in 1880.

   The church's now-consolidated, ecumenical congregation raised $30,000, solicited $25,000 from the Gates Foundation, and was granted $99,035 from the SHF to rehabilitate this Gothic Revival edifice from its stone foundation to its bell tower, repointing the red brick, replacing broken colored-glass windows, and restoring the curved pews. A new roof, new wiring, and new furnace have also helped return this 200-seat church and community center to its former glory.

SQUAW MOUNTAIN FIRE LOOKOUT
5 miles southeast of Idaho Springs, off CO 103; take Squaw Mountain
 Fire Lookout road 1 mile to a gate; from there, walk 0.8 mile (SR)
Built: 1940; Civilian Conservation Corps, builder

At 11,486 feet, this is one of the highest lookout towers in the United States. Boys aged 17 to 25 enrolled in the Civilian Conservation Corps constructed the square-buttressed base of native stone and topped it with a frame walkway and small wooden enclosure. Perched atop a talus pile on a southwestern shoulder of Squaw Mountain, this medieval-looking tower is now guarded by four lightning rods and features a restored interior, thanks to a $1,688 SHF grant. Like the nearby 240-acre Squaw Pass Ski Area, which operated from 1963 to 1974, the lookout is now closed but makes a scenic and historic hiking destination.

UNDERHILL MUSEUM
1416 Miner St., northeast corner of 14th Ave. [LL] [NRD]
Built: 1912; Bert Wright and Sidney Varney, builders

James Underhill, a Harvard-educated mineral engineer who earned his doctorate at the University of Colorado, taught engineering at the Colorado School of Mines (CSM). From his home office in this structure, he worked on surveys and legal affairs. An Idaho Springs town alderman, Underhill also assisted in the conversion of the Edgar Mine into the experimental mine still used by the CSM.

After the professor died, his wife lived here until 1963. She donated the house to the public library as a museum. "Lucy Stoller Underhill had seen building after building next to her house become a saloon," recalls museum curator Marjorie Bell, "so she insisted in her will that alcohol never be allowed there and that it should always be a museum. With $96,297 from the SHF and $35,000 from the Historical Society of Idaho Springs and city support, we've replaced the leaky roof and sealed the foundation, rewired and replumbed, restored the fancy agate and frosty glass skylights, put in insulation, and turned this into a year-round museum."

"Thanks to the SHF and locals who provided matching funds," Mayor Dennis Lunberg said in 2002, "Idaho Springs has been able to stabilize and restore the Underhill House as a museum, put together a walking tour and booklet, and install bronze interpretive markers on our locally designated landmarks. With our new historical attractions and the heritage and visitor center, we now can court those tourists whizzing by us on I-70."

Julesburg

HIPPODROME THEATER/ARTS CENTER
215 Cedar St. (SR)
Built: 1919; A. E. Lanning, builder

The volunteer help here is paid in pop and popcorn. They love working at the Hippodrome Theater, which was renamed the Chaka in 1973 for owners Charles and Kate DeCastro. This one-story brick edifice cost $10,000 to build and much more to restore, with $192,618 from the SHF and a cash match of $34,950 from concerned citizens. The Fort Sedgwick Historical Society and Sedgwick County also contributed to the restoration. The redone exterior features the original façade of terracotta blocks and movie-poster display windows under a curvilinear parapet outlined in lightbulbs. Inside, the domed, pressed-metal ceiling is covered with Celotex to aid acoustics. The theater retains its original projection room and 257 metal seats with triple-ribbed Art Deco speed lines. Several community groups, including the Ernest and Lillian E. Campbell Foundation of Julesburg, helped with the revitalization.

The family owner-operators reluctantly sold the theater in 1996 for use as a mattress warehouse. At that point, more than 100 volunteers organized the restoration effort and have since volunteered to operate the old Chaka as the nonprofit Hippodrome Arts Center. "We could not let the Hippodrome die," says volunteer Anna Scott. "Ask any person from Julesburg what they remember, and they will say cruising Main Street, cheering for the Julesburg Lions, and going to movies at the Hippodrome." With the acquisition of two adjacent storefronts converted to dressing rooms and other facilities, the old movie house is also preparing to stage live performances.

As the first building on the State Register of Historic Properties and the first SHF-funded restoration in Sedgwick County, the Hippodrome's rebirth inspired designation and restoration of the nearby Union Pacific Depot/Museum as well as the Revere High School, a Temple Buell design in Ovid, a tiny town five miles west of Julesberg.

Kiowa

ELBERT COUNTY COURTHOUSE
215 Comanche St. [LL]
Built: 1912; John J. Huddart, architect

Elbert County had one of the fastest-growing populations in the United States during the 1990s, when Denver and Colorado Springs suburbanization flooded the rural county. Yet, with a small commercial tax base, the county faced a difficult challenge in maintaining its historic courthouse. SHF grants of $217,500 enabled

the county to repair the courthouse brick walls and restore the historic sheet-metal sign above the entry door. The next step planned will be to restore the original wood floors, repair plaster, and apply historically appropriate finishes, including light fixtures, and signage. "The courthouse is a living reminder of our past, a place to go and recognize where we have been and where we are now," says county commissioner John Metli. "We need such historical anchors amid rapid growth."

K

Kit Carson

KIT CARSON POOL HALL
2nd and Main St. (SR)
Built: 1915; Roy H. Collins and Eivind Nilsen, builders

The one-story brick building known by locals as the Old Pool Hall typifies early 1900s commercial design. While housing various businesses over the years, including the Silver Spur Saloon and a liquor store, it has doubled as an informal community center for meetings, rollerskating, school performances, and movie shows.

The Chamber of Commerce, which bought the building in 1992, matched the $29,983 SHF grant with its own funds and volunteer labor. The restoration included reconstruction of a collapsed rear addition that now houses a kitchen and restrooms. Besides façade restoration, volunteers replaced the worn-out floor with the maple hardwood gym floor taken from the nearby, closed Arapahoe School. The full concrete basement, which housed the pool tables and a barbershop until the 1970s, has also been restored. Here, the annual Kit Carson Day Melodrama, a Labor Day tradition since the 1960s found a permanent theater. The Chamber of Commerce also leases this community center for private events.

KIT CARSON UNION PACIFIC RAILROAD DEPOT / KIT CARSON MUSEUM
Park St. and US 287 (SR)
Built: 1904; Union Pacific Railroad, builder

The Kit Carson Historical Society received $174,980 in SHF grants to restore this small depot, which has been operating as the Kit Carson Museum since 1969. The frame building is a well-preserved example of a Union Pacific standard-plan combination depot. In addition to handling passengers and freight, this depot served as the station agent's residence. With minor exceptions, the interior retains its original layout and materials. Preservation of the exterior involved replication of the original UP paint colors, the application of a fieldstone veneer resembling the original stone foundation, restoration of the windows, and reconstruction of the freight platform. Threatened with demolition in 1969, the building was moved from its original trackside location by the Kit Carson Historical Society for use as a museum. It remains architecturally important as the most intact example of this depot type in Colorado. Also on the site are a signal maintainer's cottage and UP Caboose No. 25400.

Kremmling

McELROY BARN, LIVERY & FEED
204 4th St. (SR)
Built: 1903; Henry McElroy, builder

This two-story, gable-roofed log barn wears a freshly repainted "Livery and Feed" sign on the roof and west gable end, signaling its recent restoration. First a stage stop and barn on the stage route to Steamboat Springs, it became a popular livery after the Moffat Railroad arrived in 1904 and Kremmling boomed. The Grand County Historical Association (GCHA) acquired the barn in 1993 and converted it into a museum. The SHF provided $57,547 toward a total budget of more than $200,000 to acquire, stabilize, and restore one of the county's best surviving round-log barns. It is the centerpiece of the GCHA Heritage Park, prominently sited next to the Kremmling Town Park.

"We had to lift her up and put a solid foundation under her," says Keith Nunn, Kremmling curator and past board member of the GCHA. "She had been sitting on a few stones and had rotted in the bottom one or two logs. We put on a new wood-shingle roof and remortared the eight-inch logs with a special horsehair mortar. It's amazing that she was still standing, but thanks to a great bunch of people at SHF, she's all fixed up for her 100th birthday and should last to 3003."

K

*La Junta*_____

KOSHARE KIVA MUSEUM
115 W. 18th St. (SR)
Built: 1949; Damon O. Runyon, architect

This stuccoed cinder-block museum complex on the Otero Junior College campus was built by Explorer Boy Scouts under the direction of James F. "Buck" Burshears (1909–1987). Buck and his Boy Scouts began studying and performing traditional Indian dances in 1933. The structure encompasses a 60-foot-wide kiva with a roof formed by 637 layered logs, all at least 26 feet long. Runyon, a Nebraska architect, supposedly studied Indian kiva roofs and designed the span using toothpicks and a teacup.

A SHF grant of $63,118, with matching donations totaling $24,500, stabilized and preserved this unique structure for future generations. The viga-studded museum houses a good collection of Native American artifacts and Southwestern art purchased by the Scouts with proceeds from their performances. Executive director Linda Powers notes, "The Koshare Kiva Museum is a wonderful asset for our community and brings in tourist dollars. The tribal dances performed by Boy Scout troops give us a unique attraction that helps bring in such diverse events as conventions, conferences, funerals, and weddings."

SCIUMBATO HOME AND GROCERY STORE
706 2nd St. [NR]
Built: 1908

One of six historic buildings of the Otero Museum Complex, this adobe grocery had a one-and-a-half-story brick home attached to it in 1908 when the Sciumbato family took up residence in the back and operated a grocery store in the front. Italian immigrant Daniel Sciumbato had worked for the Atchison, Topeka & Santa Fe Railway until he had saved enough money to start the store. His wife baked bread daily behind the store in a horno oven. The family added a false storefront in 1916 and operated the venerable grocery until 1976.

In 1999, volunteers raised a cash match of $2,486 to earn a $7,456 SHF grant to perform an interior and exterior restoration. "The SHF sent a technical adviser down three times to assist us and supervise the restoration," notes Otero Museum Association president Don Lowman. "They were courteous and professional, and we would gladly work with SHF in the future."

VOGEL CANYON ARCHAEOLOGICAL AREA
15 miles south of La Junta on CR 802 (SR)
5000 BC to AD 1500

Tucked away in the canyons of the Comanche National Grasslands are some of Colorado's premier petroglyphs. Visitors can hike to them on interpretive trails and view protected and interpreted Native American rock art thanks, in part, to an SHF grant of $75,000.

Vogel Canyon, according to U.S. Forest Service archaeologist Al Kane, "records so many diverse peoples, from recent Plains Indians back to the Archaic Era, including Spanish explorers and Mexican sheepherders, Santa Fe Trail traders, and, most recently, Whitlock Westbrook, who homesteaded here." Protection and interpretation was a team effort of the SHF, the Vogel Canyon Archaeological Volunteers, the Palmer Foundation, and the Pikes Peak Chapter of the Colorado Archaeological Society. Among those building the trail, installing interpretive work, and cleaning graffiti from the rock art were Comanche National Grasslands staff, Colorado Boys Ranch, Koshare Indian Dancers, La Junta Boy Scouts, La Junta High Schoolers, Otero County, Otero Junior College students, and the Timpas Grazing Association. Trail highlights include the Dragonfly Shelters, which ancient Coloradans decorated with depictions of dragonflies; petroglyphs of humanoids using the atlatl; and the likenesses of large mammals pecked into the rock.

L La Veta

FORT FRANCISCO PLAZA
312 S. Main St. [NR]
Built: 1862; John M. Francisco and Henry Daigre, builders

Colonel John M. Francisco first settled in the verdant Upper Cucharas River Valley in 1862. For protection and to attract commerce, Francisco built an adobe fort with 18- to 25-inch-thick walls. The fort's dirt-floored rooms open inward on the plaza, with no windows or doors in the outward-facing walls. The original flat roof has been replaced by a metal gable roof, and porches have been added over the years. After the Denver & Rio Grande Railroad reached La Veta in 1876, the fort's rooms were converted into other uses such as a hotel, telegraph office, post office, and railroad depot.

The Town of La Veta, which had grown up around the fort, bought it in 1957 and turned its operations over to the Huerfano County Historical Society. The museum grounds now include the one-room log Ritter School (1876), a clapboard Presbyterian church (1893) used since 1973 for the summer theatricals of the Spoon River players, and a tiny stone building that once was the town hall (1912). Other buildings that have been moved to the museum complex include a saloon (1888) and the Hiram Vasquez Blacksmith Shop (1863).

SHF grants totaling $204,071 stabilized the deteriorating adobe, where cracks were so large that chipmunks invaded the fort. The SHF grants helped the museum raise a cash match of $11,900 from volunteer contributions and $12,000 from the Town of La Veta and the Huerfano County Historical Society. Another $80,000 came from Jerry and Peggy Davis, who own and operate an inn occupying several rooms of the fort's west wing. Fort Francisco has now been "refortified" as the county's major historical, educational, and tourist resource.

Lafayette

CONGREGATIONAL CHURCH / MARY MILLER THEATER
300 E. Simpson St. [NR]
Built: 1892

Lafayette founder Mary Miller built this church, which served as a hospital during the 1918 flu epidemic. The building became the town library in 1964 and, most recently, a theater. The City of Lafayette, which provided a cash match of $13,083, restored much of its exterior with the help of $10,000 from the SHF. The converted church now has two dressing rooms and two restrooms accessible for the

disabled. Plans include reconstruction of the steeple, lost in 1901, and removal of a 1970s addition. Today this theater, according to Susan Koster of the City of Lafayette, "is working out beautifully; the acoustics are perfect for theatrical and musical performances, as well as meetings."

LEWIS HOUSE / LAFAYETTE MINERS MUSEUM
108 E. Simpson St. [NR]
Built: c. 1897; Oscar Padfield, Sr., builder

Oscar Padfield, owner of the Gladstone Mine, built this modest home for his family near his coal mine. His son, Oscar Padfield, Jr., moved the home into Lafayette around 1910 and sold it to the local union representative, William E. Lewis. Lewis, a miner, moved his family in and also used it as a union meeting hall. Strikebreakers and anti-union "law and order" ruffians attacked union members seeking refuge here in 1913 and 1914 and damaged the house. William Lewis died in 1914, but his family stayed on until his wife, Hannah, died in the home in 1975. The City of Lafayette purchased the home in 1976 to convert it into a miners' museum. The Lafayette Historical Society matched the SHF's $7,159 to replace the roof in 2003 and embark upon further preservation.

Photo courtesy of Tom Noel

Lake City————————————————

HINSDALE COUNTY COURTHOUSE
317 Henson St. [NRD]
Built: 1877

Hinsdale County matched $41,800 from the SHF to restore this two-story, lap-sided building. Although its old golden oak furniture and six-over-six wavy-glass windows remain, the structure had sagged on the southwest corner, cracking the plaster wall and buckling the floors. The county jacked up the building, put in a cement foundation, and repaired and replastered the damaged walls. Interpretive exhibits in the courthouse remind visitors that it was in this very building that Susan B. Anthony lectured for women's suffrage, and Alfred Packer, the cannibal, was sentenced to hang.

Photo courtesy of Tom Noel

KENNEDY BUILDING / JOHN WAGNER PUBLIC LIBRARY
221 Silver St. [NRD]
Built: 1876

Constructed as Peter Kennedy's Shoe Shop, this structure spent many years as a saloon before its rehabilitation. The Hinsdale County Library District used a $4,065 grant from the SHF to repair the roof and façade. Librarian Elaine Gray reports that her library is heavily used for its Internet connections, videos, children's section, and 6,000 books. Restoration brought back the fancy Italianate false front, which hides the adobe sidewalls, and a new public bench has been installed on the front walk. The library was named for John Wagner, a local carpenter who loved to read and talk philosophy, and who donated time, work, and books to the library.

Photo courtesy of Tom Noel

LAKE CITY OPERA HOUSE / ARMORY
230 Bluff St. [NRD]
Built: 1883

This former opera house was converted into an armory, then into a community center. The Town of Lake City received $42,594 in grants from the SHF to rehabilitate the brick exterior. "As the largest meeting space in town, with room for 250," says Grant Houston, editor of the *Lake City Silver World*, "this has been our most used building, but it was in dangerously poor shape. Now that it's fixed up we are using it more than ever for town meetings, shows, dances, roller skating, a teen club, potluck community dinners, basketball, concerts, and even a new climbing wall."

L

Lakewood

HILDEBRAND FARM / DENVER BOTANIC GARDENS AT CHATFIELD
Chatfield Reservoir, 8500 Deer Creek Canyon Rd.
Built: 1866; Frank Hildebrand, builder

Frank and Elizabeth Hildebrand settled here in 1866. Their descendants stayed until the federal government bought the 150-acre spread as part of the Chatfield Reservoir construction project after the disastrous 1965 South Platte River flood. Denver Botanic Gardens, which is landlocked on its current Denver site, purchased the spacious site and opened their arboretum here in 1989. In this model project, various stages of the ranch's evolution have been preserved. The main house, for instance, retains the original log-cabin center section, two 1880s additions, an 1890s kitchen, and early 20th-century porch. Recycled as a living-history farm complete with a stable, woodshed, bunkhouse, granary, blacksmith shop, icehouse, chicken house, and milking barn, the farm has interpretive signage as well as living-history interpreters to introduce moderns to blacksmithing and other farming and ranching chores.

SHF contributed more than $147,000 to Denver Botanic Gardens to restore the interior and exterior of the homestead house as a showpiece of what has become a 700-acre open space and arboretum. Other preservation partners were involved landowners: the Army Corps of Engineers, Jefferson County Open Space, and Chatfield State Park. The farm site also houses the relocated and restored Deer Creek School, a one-room 1885 schoolhouse used as the visitor center for some 71,000 people a year coming here for education, recreation, nature walks, concerts, and the autumn pumpkin festival.

Photo courtesy of Tom Noel

LAKEWOOD HERITAGE CENTER
797 S. Wadsworth Blvd. LL
Built: 1976

In 1976, the citizens of Lakewood passed a bond proposal to purchase the former May Bonfils estate, Belmar. The Historic Belmar Village project was begun shortly after through the involvement of the Lakewood Bicentennial Committee. It was originally administered by the Lakewood Historical Society until the city took over management in 1979. Renamed the Lakewood Heritage Center (LHC), this history park occupies 18 acres devoted to exhibiting 20th-century buildings and history. Lakewood Heritage Center matched $16,000 from the SHF to establish a walking tour and create a brochure celebrating the site. According to LHC administrator Kris Anderson, "SHF helped us to refine and specialize our niche mission and produce signs, brochures, and a walking tour for our 100,000 annual visitors." LHC has grown to include some original structures and many relocated structures such as a 1922 working windmill, the 1935 Wide Acres Denver, Lakewood & Golden Railroad shelter stop, the interior of an old West Colfax Avenue beer joint (Lane's Tavern), Gil and Ethel's Barbershop and Beauty Salon, the Ralston School, and the Valentine Diner.

GIL AND ETHEL'S BARBER SHOP AND BEAUTY SALON
Lakewood Heritage Center, 797 S. Wadsworth Blvd. LL
Built: 1948

Hairstylist Ethel Gomez treats her customers like family. Her salon opened in the back half of this Streamline Moderne-style building, originally located at 3043 W. Alameda Avenue. Some women recall getting their hair done while Ethel's husband, Gil, gave their husbands haircuts in his barbershop in the front half. This little one-story landmark, with its distinctive glass-block rounded corners, sleek aluminum window surrounds, and big cornice-mounted clock, served as a neighborhood gathering and gossiping place for nearly 40 years.

When Gil passed away in 1996, over 1,000 friends and relatives attended his funeral. But barely a week after Gil died, the City of Denver informed Ethel that she would have to vacate her building to allow for street-widening. Already mourning her husband, Ethel tried to cope with the impending loss of her shop, too. For two years, her story circulated among preservationists. In the end, Historic Denver, Inc. and the Lakewood Heritage Center (LHC), along with the Colorado Department of

Photo courtesy of Tom Noel

Transportation, and the Colorado Historical Society staff teamed up to find a way to preserve this modest structure.

In 1998, the City of Lakewood acquired Gil and Ethel's and moved it to the LHC, aided by $50,000 from the City of Denver. At the LHC, Lakewood came up with $255,000 to match a $95,000 SHF grant to restore the original terrazzo floor, replace the roof, stabilize the structure, fix or replace the curved glass-block walls, replace the stolen clock, fix exterior neon, and replace missing exterior ceramic tiles. Ethel donated photographs, furniture, and fixtures for the interior, and now visitors to the salon find three original styling stations and a manicure table. Prohibited from retirement by client demand, Ethel still styles hair in her new beauty salon in Lakewood on Wadsworth Boulevard, indulging those who want to talk about her old place, its restoration, and the days of $1.50 haircuts.

RALSTON SCHOOL
Lakewood Heritage Center, 797 S. Wadsworth Blvd. [LL]
Built: 1868

This much remodeled and moved school began its life on Ralston Creek as a Methodist church in the 1860s. In 1882, Ralston School District No. 12 purchased the church and hired contractor George H. Kimball to convert it into a school. After school-district consolidation, the building was abandoned. In 1956, the Ryberg Construction Company moved it seven miles down CO 72 to West 25th Avenue and Miller Street to serve as a temporary classroom building for the overcrowded Vivian Elementary School. In 1986, the Ralston School was moved again to the Lakewood Heritage Center and restored with the help of a $67,805 SHF grant, so today's schoolchildren can see what the good ol' days were really like.

WASHINGTON HEIGHTS SCHOOL
6375 W. 1st Ave. (SR)
Built: 1898

This Lakewood schoolhouse, closed in 1968, has been saved from demolition by the Foothills Recreation District. Pat Benton of the District says, "Our goal was to get the building back and serviceable. So we matched $200,000 from the SHF." After installation of heating and air-conditioning systems, restoration of the original brick, removal of the asbestos, and finishing of the hardwood floors, the schoolhouse is now a community cultural center owned and operated by the City of Lakewood.

Lamar

PROWERS COUNTY COURTHOUSE
301 Main St. [NR]
Built: 1929; Robert K. Fuller, architect

The three-story courthouse of Indiana limestone sitting on a granite-walled basement combines Neo-Renaissance and Neoclassical elements with Moderne massing.
The inside features brass chandeliers, ceiling stenciling, and local cattle brands
etched into the main corridor frieze. The elaborate third-floor courtroom has its
original dark walnut furnishings and a stenciled, barrel-vaulted ceiling. With a cash

match of $94,525 from Prowers
County and other sources, the county
secured SHF grants of $273,402 for
cleaning the limestone and repointing
the mortar joints, restoring the steel-
frame windows, reroofing, and also
restoring the parapet walls. In addition, the county restored three sets of
bronze exterior doors and lanterns.
Proudly, the county completed the
exterior restoration under-budget and returned some funds to the SHF. Eventually,
the county hopes to restore the building's interior finishes as well. "Everybody feels
they own part of the courthouse," observes county administrator Judy Ray. "Doing
the restoration made them feel good about their government."

L

Las Animas

BENT COUNTY COURTHOUSE
725 Carson Ave. [NR]
Built: 1887; Holmberg Bros., architects

One of Colorado's oldest active courthouses enjoys a spacious, full-block site. The
two-story, red-brick building features sandstone trim, recessed bays, and a roofline
of hipped and mansard elements, missing its original iron cresting. Between 1995
and 1997, the SHF contributed $449,599 toward a $567,701 exterior restoration,

including repointing, repairing
brick and stone, and refinishing
the woodwork. Now the distinctive round arches, dentiled
cornice, lintels, entry pediment,
and corner mansard towers look
fresh. Bent County Development
Foundation director Kathryn
S. Finau states, "Our courthouse
was renovated with the SHF
grant and with the match that

Photo courtesy of Tom Noel

was provided by Bent County. Today and for the future we finally have a beautiful, fully functioning courthouse and county administrative offices." In 2005, the SHF awarded additional funding to Bent County to develop plans to remove an elevator tower addition on the façade. County commissioners plan to relocate the elevator tower inside the building and restore and rehabilitate interior spaces.

BOGGSVILLE SITE
1.75 miles south of Las Animas on CO 101 NR
Built: c. 1862–1890s; Thomas Boggs, builder

Thomas Oliver Boggs, son of a Missouri governor and great-grandson of Daniel Boone, worked at Bent's Fort and married Rumalda Luna Bent. This alliance with the Bents helped Boggs establish his ranch and trading post along the Mountain Branch of the Santa Fe Trail, on the banks of the Purgatoire River near its confluence with the Arkansas River. The oldest surviving nonfortified settlement in southeastern Colorado, Boggsville served as a trading post and post office. Boasting the county's first public school and its first county seat, the town reached its peak from 1863 to 1873 and declined thereafter, when the Atchison, Topeka & Santa Fe Railway laid its tracks two miles north through Las Animas.

Abandoned in the mid-1890s, the 110-acre Boggsville town site has been undergoing restoration since 1985 as a historical park operated by the Pioneer Historical Society of Bent County. Historical research conducted in consultation with Long-Hoeft Architects has been used to restore the Boggs House (1866) and a wing of the Prowers House (1867), the only survivors of the original 22-building complex. Plans call for archaeological excavation of Kit Carson's last house, the school, sheep quarters, a general store, and other now-gone structures of this pioneer outpost.

In 1996, the SHF awarded an $87,101 grant toward the total cost of $115,750 for the Boggsville Archaeology, Planning, and Interpretive Project. Overseen by Historic Boggsville Education and special projects director and archaeologist Richard Carrillo, student volunteers from the University of Colorado at Colorado Springs, Otero Junior College, and Las Animas High School excavated four sites and developed an interpretive plan and displays. Carrillo notes, "The grants from SHF have allowed us, and continue to allow us, the opportunity to restore Boggsville. Initially, there was some resistance from the local populace about the restoration project, but most individuals have come along, since they see ongoing progress."

BOGGS HOUSE
CO 101, 1.75 miles southeast of Las Animas   NR
Built: 1866; Thomas Boggs, builder

Thomas Boggs and his wife, Rumalda Bent, settled in 1862 on her claim of a 2,000-acre Mexican land grant dating back to 1843. In 1866, Boggs built the L-shaped, seven-room house with 18-inch-thick adobe

Photo courtesy of Tom Noel

walls. The west wing was added in 1868, lending the complex a Spanish Colonial courtyard feel. Also added were stately columns and a formal entrance typical of Greek Revival architecture.

The Boggsville Revitalization Committee began restoration of this Territorial-style adobe house in 1985 and later was aided by $236,399 in 1993 from the SHF. A concrete foundation, brick chimneys, and a new roof were added to the U-plan house, and the old adobe was stabilized and covered with a lime plaster. Sections of the interior have been unaltered to show the original stone foundation, pine roof, and thick adobe walls.

ODD FELLOWS HALL / BENT COUNTY
HISTORICAL MUSEUM

L

560 Bent Ave. SR
Built: 1898

Built of local sandstone, this two-story commercial building features storefront windows and recessed entries with double doors. The structure's upper story was used principally for the Odd Fellows lodge and occasionally served as an opera house, hosting dances, movies, and stage shows. The ground floor was leased for retail and office space, with a saddle shop, barbershop, paint store, candy store, and dentist and optometrist offices. The storefront housed the U.S. Post Office from 1898 to 1937.

The Pioneer Historical Society of Bent County (PHSBC) purchased the structure with the help of $75,775 from the SHF in 1994. The PHSBC, in partnership with the Bent County Development Foundation, in 2001 began a program to secure funds for exterior restoration and rehabilitation for use as the Bent County Historical Museum. To repair and restore the windows, storefronts, sandstone masonry, and roof, the SHF provided $396,295. The Colorado Department of Transportation contributed $90,000, with the remainder coming from local contributions. "The SHF grant helped us raise enough matching funds to help bring back this abandoned, dilapidated building on Las Animas' major thoroughfare," notes Bent County Development Foundation executive director Kathryn S. Finau. "We will transform it into a historical museum to showcase Bent County's history."

PROWERS HOUSE
CO 101, 1.75 miles southeast of Las Animas NR
Built: 1867; John W. Prowers, builder

John Prowers came to Colorado in 1857 as assistant to the Indian agent at Bent's new fort near Big Timbers. There in 1861 he met and married Amache, the daughter of a Cheyenne subchief who was later killed at the Sand Creek Massacre in 1864. In 1867, the U.S. government gave 640 acres along the Arkansas River to each of the surviving members of the victims' families as compensation. Amache, her two daughters, and her mother each received land allotments, which all became part of John Prowers' land. Prowers brought purebred Hereford cattle to Colorado and eventually built up what was the largest cattle ranch in the Arkansas River Valley,

stretching over much of Bent County and eastward into what is now Prowers County. The cattle king built a 24-room, two-story, U-shaped adobe ranch house. Prowers' house also served as a stage stop, a hotel, and the first county courthouse.

Early in the 20th century, the main house and the north wing collapsed. The remaining third of the building—the south wing—was occupied until the early 1950s. The Boggsville Revitalization Committee stabilized and restored the venerable structure with SHF grants of $130,370 toward the total $184,327 cost. Under the direction of the Long-Hoeft architectural firm, construction supervisor Wayne Banta worked with structural engineer Jim Harris, archaeologist Richard Carrillo, and many volunteers to reconstruct Prowers House.

Lasauses

La CAPILLA de SAN ANTONIO de PADUA
7 miles southeast of Alamosa on Conejos CR 28 (SR)
Built: 1928

This stuccoed adobe church, adorned with stained-glass windows and an open bell tower, is a rich reflection of the southern Colorado Hispanic culture and communities. Graves of parishioners lie around and under the church. To match the SHF's $39,207, descendants of the first settlers and current residents of Lasauses held some fundraising fiestas. St. Joseph's Church in Capulin, the mother church for this remote mission chapel, administered the grant for

Photo courtesy of Kathleen Allen

interior and exterior restoration. Volunteers also helped out with the adobe repair of mission walls, which included the old east wall of the original 1880 chapel. The 1928 replacement now has a renewed bell tower, windows, and tiny choir loft.

L

Leadville

The City of Leadville has received more than $2 million from the SHF for stabilization and restoration projects in its downtown, a National Historic Landmark District from 2nd to 10th Streets between Hazel and James Streets. Once the richest silver city in the Rockies, Leadville has been in decline since the silver crash of 1893. Poverty, however, has led to the recycling of old buildings and very little new construction during the past century. Not only the aged buildings but also the denuded hillsides and many scars of mines, mine dumps, and smelters make Leadville Colorado's most vivid reminder of mining realities. At 10,152 feet, Leadville is the highest incorporated city in the United States and is haunted not only by its past but also by chilly weather that has brought it snow every month of the year. Despite the wintry climate and the long economic bust, the town has clung to, and restored, many of its grand old landmarks. "The SHF has been a boon to Leadville," Mayor Chet Gaede reflected in 2002, "restoring 14 of our historic buildings. This is essential to our City in the Clouds, whose economy hinges on heritage tourism."

213 HARRISON
213 Harrison Ave. **NHLD**
Built: c.1899

Edward C. Babcock's haberdashery first occupied this site but was demolished to construct this gray-brick building, which over the years hosted a saloon, restaurant, grocery store, shoe shop, and, during Prohibition, a soda shop that fronted for a local speakeasy specializing in Leadville moonshine. During World War II, a dry cleaners here did a booming business with nearby Camp Hale, cleaning uniforms for that army post. A later owner lowered the ceiling and added a rear mezzanine as office space above an automobile showroom. When the dealership closed, the building was "on its way to being condemned and demolished," according to co-owners Merilee O'Neal and Ken Chlouber. O'Neal found that treading on the floor was like "walking on a trampoline." The front of the building was near total collapse, with the decorative brick parapet sinking into the center of the storefront, taking both brick sidewalls along for the ride.

O'Neal and Chlouber developed a partnership with the Leadville Coalition, an economic development organization made up of taxing entities throughout Lake County. After completion of a thorough Historic Structure Assessment, the Coalition applied for and obtained SHF grants totaling $254,955. After stabilizing and repairing the second floor to create a mezzanine, the owners restored the exterior. They removed stucco from the brick on the sides of the building, revealing a painted sign for Model Cleaners and Dyers. Windows that had been filled in with brick were restored and returned to use. The brick storefront was disassembled to relay the bricks in their original pattern. This reborn storefront, returned to retail use, is one of the few surviving buildings on the block. O'Neal is "delighted with the SHF and its support of a project to give back to future generations a piece of Leadville's history."

AMERICAN NATIONAL BANK AND ANNEX
460 Harrison Ave., southeast corner of 5th St. NHLD
Built: 1891; Jeremiah Irwin, builder

The American National Bank first occupied this three-story, red-brick Romanesque Revival–style building distinguished by a corner tower with a bell-shaped copper dome and red-sandstone trim. The bank closed in the 1930s, and for many years, according to Linda Hollenback, director of administrative services for the City of Leadville, "the building deteriorated, with no heat except a woodstove." In 1999, Heavy Metal Investments purchased the structure to return it to its original grandeur. The City of Leadville received SHF grants of $269,000 to assist the owner, Tom Sprung of Sprung Construction, in the $754,560 restoration.

Major interior and exterior work included replacing the roof, repairing masonry, reglazing windows, re-creating the original entrance and storefronts, and restoring interior moldings, paneling, wainscoting, mantels, and floors. Of the end result Hollenback notes, "We are very proud of how this spruced-up building has uplifted the city of Leadville—which is already two miles high!"

CARNEGIE LIBRARY / HERITAGE MUSEUM
102 E. 9th St., northeast corner of Harrison Ave. NHLD
Built: 1904; Herbert C. Dimick, architect

This two-story brick building is distinguished by gray-sandstone trim, round-arched windows, and a rough sandstone foundation. When a new library opened in 1971, the Lake County Civic Center Association (LCCCA) formed to buy the building and convert it into the Heritage Museum and Gallery. By 1993 the building was "pretty well run-down," according to LCCCA president Ray Stamps. The LCCCA used $68,000 in SHF grants with a local match of approximately $20,000 for roof

replacement and restoration of the interior, in which much of the original woodwork is still intact. When walls began cracking and floors began rotting, the LCCCA used an additional $37,750 SHF grant to stabilize the walls, replace the rotted floor, repair the rear retaining wall, and build proper drainage to help protect the museum's displays from Leadville's silver age.

DEXTER CABIN
912 Harrison Ave. **NHLD** **NR**
Built: 1879; James Viola Dexter, builder

When Dexter, a wealthy mining man and banker, built his two-room, hewn-log cabin at 110 West 3rd Street, it looked like any typical Leadville miner's cabin—from the outside. However, the inside revealed an extravagantly furnished Victorian home with alternating black-walnut and white-oak floor planks and one of the Silver City's first bathtubs, with the unheard-of luxury of hot running water. Lincrusta-Walton wall covering above the wainscoting further enhances the deluxe cabin that was Dexter's Leadville summer residence.

In 1948, the Colorado Historical Society acquired the cabin and moved it next to the Healy House to serve as a house museum. The Colorado Historical Society matched SHF grants totaling $7,000 for a new electrical system and insulation, rechinking and replacement of logs, and repair of the roof and boardwalk. Larry Frank, then the museum director, noted that the Dexter Cabin is now in the "best shape it's been in many, many years." Moya Hansen, CHS curator of decorative and fine arts, adds, "The logs were rotting, endangering this gem with its elegant furnishings that contrast dramatically with the rough-hewn exterior."

GUGGENHEIM HOME
134 W. 6th St. **NHLD**
Built: 1880

Swiss immigrant Meyer Guggenheim and wife Barbara started their road to wealth in Leadville when Meyer invested in two meager mines that became very profitable. Meyer also ventured into ore processing, where he realized the most money could be made in the mining industry. He opened in Leadville the first smelter of what would ultimately become a global giant, the Guggenheim family's American Smelting and Refining Company. Meyer and his wife built this two-story, front-gabled Italianate-style clapboard home with a symmetrical design including twin bay windows framing a front door. Although Meyer and Barbara rarely stayed in the house, a distant Guggenheim relative is said to have lived here until around 1900 when it became a rooming house.

Abandoned for most of the 20th century, the house became a shambles, with broken windows and graffiti tagging it as a teenage party site. In the late 1990s, Steve and Ann Moore bought the house and approached the Leadville/Lake County Chamber of Commerce Foundation. The Moores and the Chamber matched a $1,100 SHF grant to begin the restoration, including clapboard and plaster repair, painting, and installation of a banister to make this house once again a show home.

HEALY HOUSE MUSEUM
912 Harrison Ave. NHLD NR
Built: 1878, August R. Meyer, builder; 1899 addition

Photo courtesy of Tom Noel

August R. Meyer, a mining engineer and smelting magnate, platted Leadville. He and his wife, Emma, built this two-story clapboard house. It is distinguished by elaborate roof brackets, a balustraded porch, a bay window, shutters, and pedimented lintels. After a few years the Meyers sold the prominently sited hilltop home. Daniel Healy, a local property investor, converted it into a boarding house, with a third-floor addition in 1898. Nellie A. Healy, Daniel's cousin, inherited the boarding house in 1912 and operated it until the 1930s. Nellie gave the property to the Leadville Historical Association, which in turn donated it to the Colorado Historical Society (CHS) in 1947. The CHS restored the house as a museum displaying beautiful Victorian furnishings typical in prosperous mining towns. The CHS matched SHF grant funds totaling $26,938 for structural repairs, roof restoration, chimney rebuilding, repainting, boardwalk replacement and re-landscaping with guidance from the original plan by Colorado's most notable landscape architect, Saco R. DeBoer.

INDEPENDENT ORDER OF ODD FELLOWS BUILDING
719 Harrison Ave. NHLD
Built: 1890

The Independent Order of Odd Fellows (IOOF) built this two-story brick building for both IOOF meetings and public events. Originally, the IOOF used the second floor as its lodge hall and leased the first floor for the offices of Leadville's power company. The hall remains a center for town functions, such as Boy Scout troop meetings, family reunions, weddings, and special events. The Water District and a retail business now occupy the first floor. The City of Leadville assisted in the IOOF building restoration by matching the $119,700 SHF grant for a $151,669 restoration of the brick walls and beams and repair of the metal cornice, windows, and stone window pediments. Additionally, the IOOF updated the electrical elements and installed a fire detection and alarm system. "The Odd Fellows was not a pretty sight," admits Linda Hollenback, director of administrative services for the City of Leadville, "but with SHF, we hope it will eventually look good again."

IRON BUILDING
516–522 Harrison Ave., southeast corner of 6th St. NHLD
Built: 1893

After the 1893 silver crash, Leadville's economy recovered somewhat when miners turned from silver to iron ore, which inspired Joshua Fearnley to change the name of his elegant Fearnley Building to the Iron Building. The two-story brick edifice is highlighted by stone accents, including decorative triangular parapets graced with finials. Originally, some offices occupied the building's second floor and a saloon the first. Since the 1940s, the second-floor offices have been roomy, skylit apartments. In 1999, the City of Leadville and owner Dorothy Hayes matched an $86,677 SHF grant to reroof, repoint the brick façade, and repair the chimneys and parapets.

LEADVILLE HIGH SCHOOL / NATIONAL MINING HALL OF FAME AND MUSEUM
120 W. 9th St. NHLD
Built: 1896

This four-story brick edifice, accented by pedimented dormers, started its life as Leadville's high school. Today, it promotes education in a different format. After the high school moved to larger quarters, the school district leased it to the National Mining Hall of Fame and Museum, which opened in 1989. The building "desperately needed repair," according to Sam McGeorge, museum president and executive director. The SHF assisted with a $25,000 grant toward a $50,000 facelift including the roof, dormers, chimneys, and entry façade. Some 30,000 visitors annually tour what has evolved into not only a hall of fame and museum but also into a research library and education center.

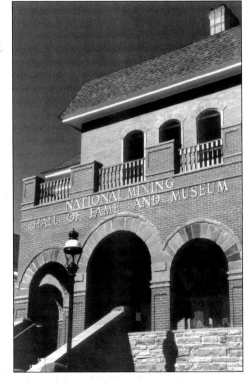

OLD FIRST PRESBYTERIAN CHURCH
801 Harrison Ave., northwest corner of 8th St. NHLD
Built: 1889; Eugène Robitaille, builder

Carpenter Gothic trim accents this Queen Anne–style red brick church. A square corner tower extends to an open belfry accented with a curved balustrade under a shingled spire. Stained glass allows colorful light to brighten the interior. When the congregation moved to a new church in the early 1970s, this abandoned and derelict structure narrowly missed a date with the wrecking ball. The Lake County Civic Center Association (LCCCA) purchased it in 1978 and began restoring it for use as a local theater and for choral productions, lectures, art exhibits, films, and community meetings. The Chamber of Commerce also used the building, primarily as a visitor center. With $96,000 in SHF grants, LCCCA completed a $114,129 restoration that replaced the roof, repaired the bell tower, repaired and painted the exterior, fixed doors and door-

jambs, and restored the stained-glass windows. After this renewal, another church began using the restored space.

OLD POST OFFICE / CITY HALL
800 Harrison Ave., northeast corner of 8th St. NHLD
Built: 1904; George King, architect

This two-story, red-brick building features a steeply pitched, hipped slate roof with flared eaves, tiny hipped dormers, and a dentiled cornice. Fanlights and decorative keystones accent the first-floor windows, and second-floor windows feature arches and keystones. Upon its 1904 grand opening, the *Leadville Herald Democrat* praised the new post office as the finest structure in town, but condemned as a waste of taxpayers' money the basement "lounging room for [mail] carriers and elegant marble wainscoted lavatory with a $600 shower bath."

After the post office moved out in 1973, the city government moved in. Much of the marble and golden-oak interior remains, as do the large interior transoms that brighten the offices of the mayor, administrative services, municipal court, and city clerk. A conference room is available for community meetings. The City of Leadville matched SHF grants of $268,949 to repair the slate roof, windows, and entryway.

SEYMORE'S NEW GROCERY
1001 Poplar St., northwest corner of 10th St. **NHLD**
Built: 1888; Charles Seymore, builder

Charles Seymore's grocery endured until 1950, then was an army surplus and sporting-goods store from 1964 to 1991. That year, KW Woodworks, Inc., purchased the building to house its general contracting, remodeling, restoration, and cabinetmaking business. The City of Leadville assisted KW Woodworks by administering a $96,940 SHF grant matched by the owner. The project included reconstruction of the storefronts and façades, installation of two new sets of wooden double doors, new wood flooring, and roof repair. KW Woodworks completed extensive interior restoration and also installed new plumbing and structural support. Linda Hollenback, Leadville's director of administrative services, says proudly, "The project looks really great. Locals can't believe it is the same building."

TABOR GRAND HOTEL
701 Harrison Ave., northwest corner of 7th St. **NHLD**
Built: 1885; George and John King, architects

Leadville mayor and silver mining mogul Horace Tabor financed the construction of this elegant four-story brick hotel with a distinctive octagonal mansard tower on the corner. Bracketed metal cornices highlight the mansard roof with its prominent dormer windows. Long touted as Leadville's finest accommodation, the Tabor had the city's first elevator, a fire-alarm system, a fireproof vault, and steam heating. It hosted the likes of President Theodore Roosevelt, Bat Masterson, and John Philip

Sousa before declining into a flophouse for unemployed miners and pensioners. After closing as a hotel in 1989, it deteriorated badly. The northwest corner had collapsed, leaving the interior exposed to the elements, causing locals to refer to it as "Colorado's largest pigeon coop."

The Tabor Grand Limited Partnership bought and restored the old hotel before it faced condemnation and demolition. In 1992, the partnership invested

$3.1 million to stabilize and restore the crumbling corner and convert the building for use as 37 units of low-income housing on the upper three floors and retail space on the first floor, including the Cloud City Coffee House, which features an oxygen bar popular at this two-mile-high elevation. The City of Leadville assisted the partnership by administering a $42,255 SHF grant, which the partnership matched, to repair and repaint the exterior masonry, wood trim, and metal cornice. Marcel Arsenault, one of the partners, says he was "quite proud to have my company come to the rescue of this precious piece of Colorado history."

TABOR HOME MUSEUM
116 E. 5th St. NHLD
Built: 1877

Photo courtesy of Tom Noel

Horace Austin Warner Tabor started out in Leadville as a merchant who grubstaked local miners. Just a year before the Little Pittsburg Mine (one of Tabor's grubstakes) made him a millionaire, Horace and his first wife, Augusta, settled into this modest little two-story clapboard cottage. Originally located at 312 Harrison Avenue, it was moved to 5th Street in 1879 to make way for the Tabor Opera House. The front-gabled, five-room home features roof cresting, long narrow windows capped with pediments, a bay window, and a side porch. The Tabors lived here for four years before moving to more elaborate residences in Denver (all three have now been demolished). A private individual restored the home as a museum in 1952 with Tabor furnishings and memorabilia. After the museum closed in 1994, the City of Leadville used a $52,800 SHF grant to restore the interior and exterior and install a new electrical system for what is now a city-owned museum.

TABOR OPERA HOUSE
308–312 Harrison Ave. NHLD
Built: 1879, George King, architect; J. Thomas Roberts
and L. E. Roberts, builders

To bring culture and respectability to the rough mining town of Leadville, Horace A. W. Tabor built this opera house. Although Tabor lost it in the 1893 silver panic, it continues to bear his name and host cultural events. The three-story, brick Italianate-style structure has a central pedimented pavilion from which a balcony projects out over a fanlighted, double-door entry. Freight wagons hauled the 800 cast-iron, plush upholstered opera seats over Weston Pass. Among the celebrities appearing here have been Susan B. Anthony, Jack Dempsey, Anna Held, Harry Houdini, John Philip Sousa, and Oscar Wilde.

Evelyn E. Livingston Furman and her mother admired and bought the old opera house and began restoration, ultimately projected to cost $5.2 million. Furman later inherited it and opened it for tours and performances. Continuing the family tradition, Furman's daughter, Sharon Furman Bland, now owns and operates the opera house for performances, tours, and special events. The Leadville Coalition assisted Bland by obtaining a $400,000 SHF grant for restoration. The project covered a roof replacement, structural wall stabilization, and repair and restoration of the masonry and other exterior features of Leadville's cultural cornerstone.

TEMPLE ISRAEL
201 W. 4th St., southeast corner of Spruce St. NHLD
Built: 1884, George E. King, architect; Robert Murdoch, builder

Much to the joy of the Jewish community, Leadville mayor and mining millionaire Horace A. W. Tabor donated a city lot to David May in 1884 for a synagogue. May, whose Leadville shop was the first of what later became the National May Company department store chain, and the Jewish Community erected a clapboard temple with stained-glass windows and twin wooden spires on the front corners. Temple Israel closed its doors and became a single-family residence, then an apartment house. During the mid-1980s, the Temple Israel Foundation formed to purchase and preserve the building. With a $19,015 SHF grant, the Foundation completed a $36,030 restoration that reinstalled the lost corner towers, rose window, and entry. This beginning, according to Foundation president William Korn, has heartened the team, who now hopes to restore the interior for use as a temple and Jewish museum despite a bad fire in Spring 2006.

Littleton _____

Littleton's landmarked 81-foot-high Columbine Grain Elevator towers over the small community that Richard Little modeled after the quiet, tree-shaded New England village from which he came. Littleton likewise has preserved its Main Street with a National Register Historic District stretching roughly from Santa Fe Drive to Court Place, and from Berry Street to Alamo Street. A series of SHF grants totaling $127,000 has gone into Main Street façade restorations. After removing 1960s-style face-lifts, Littleton preservationists found that many of the original façades remained underneath and began repair and restoration.

Littleton also preserved a spectacular Modernist home as the core of the Littleton History Museum. On the large museum grounds in Ketring Park, the museum also rescued a half dozen 19th-century relics, ranging from a blacksmith shop to a slab-log outhouse. Former Littleton mayor Susan Thornton observes, "The SHF has enabled our town to pursue first-rate preservation. We've managed to save many of our old treasures and, in partnership with the SHF, restore them for new uses."

ARAPAHOE COUNTY COURTHOUSE / LITTLETON MUNICIPAL COURT
2069 W. Littleton Blvd. Ⓗ 🅛🅛
Built: 1908; John J. Huddart, architect

At the east end of Littleton's downtown historic district is a commanding edifice built for $58,000 as the Arapahoe County Courthouse. Its hipped roof and curvilinear parapets represent a Mediterranean twist on the Neoclassical Revival style. The building housed the county jail in the basement, offices on the first floor, courtrooms on the second floor, and jury rooms in the attic. In 1987, the county courts relocated to a site farther east, and the courthouse building was abandoned except for record storage.

L

The fortunes of the building turned in 1998 when Littleton approached the county about taking over the old courthouse to use as a municipal court. "This was a true example of cooperation between levels of government," said David Flaig of the City of Littleton. The county agreed to cede the building and surrounding land to the city, as well as chip in $250,000 for the removal of a 1948 brick addition. Littleton also received a $324,231 SHF grant for exterior restoration.

"One of the greatest challenges we faced during the exterior restoration," says Flaig, "was providing accessibility for the disabled." Digging a trench leading into the basement level on the western approach to the building solved the problem. Another concern was removal of pigeons, bats, and cats that had colonized the interior. "The courthouse restoration, now showcased by external lighting, has turned out to be the real jewel of the Main Street district," concludes Flaig. "When the city did such a spectacular job on the courthouse, it spurred surrounding property owners to better maintain their properties and undertake improvements."

COLUMBINE MILL / 5280 ROADHOUSE BREWERY
5798 S. Rapp St. LL NRD
Built: 1901; Richard Little, builder

Littleton founder Richard Little built this mill as a storage and shipping center for his Rough and Ready Flour Mill Company. In 1920, the Columbine Mercantile Company purchased the property and installed a flour mill in the building. Made of stacked, flat 2-by-12-inch planks sheathed in corrugated, galvanized-metal panels, the Columbine ground barley, corn, oats, and wheat into animal feed. The Denver & Rio Grande ran a spur line to the mill, which sold its grain throughout the Denver region.

After 1974, the old mill housed several short-lived restaurants before its 1994 rebirth as Littleton's only brewpub. Grubstaked with $40,000 from the SHF and matching monies from the City of Littleton and the U.S. Small Business Administration, Pasquale Girolamo and Leo Lech spent $1 million to recycle a tired granary into a fresh brewery. "To swing the deal," Pasquale notes, "the bank said we had to keep our engineering jobs at Lockheed Martin. So we're working two full-time jobs. Our wives—and five new partners—have taken up the slack." A key partner, brewmeister Sean T. Halloran, has won awards for beers that the public can see being born thanks to large windows overlooking the brewing apparatus amid some of the original framing timbers.

Both photos courtesy of Tom Noel

COORS BUILDING
2489 W. Main St. **H** [LL] [NRD]
Built: 1905; Adolph Coors Co., builder

One of a dozen similar structures built throughout the state by Adolph Coors, the founder of the Colorado brewing dynasty, this two-story brick building on Littleton's historic Main Street originally housed several stores as well as the Arapahoe Saloon, which, of course, sold Coors beer. Over the years, various businesses and functions have been housed here, but the story of its restoration began with its purchase by Sue Carbaugh in 1993. The new owner set out, in conjunction with the Littleton Historical Museum, to restore the much modified building. Launching her investigations with a preliminary SHF grant, Carbaugh uncovered transoms, pilasters, and cast-iron columns under the boarded-up corner entry. Underneath stucco, brick arches marked the original locations of doors and windows, and Carbaugh discovered the original front door stashed in the basement.

An additional $56,250 SHF grant, plus assistance from Littleton's Main Street Historic Preservation Program, enabled Carbaugh to undertake extensive restoration. Workers found much of the original tile work and interior walls still in place. As workmen removed the stucco, the contractor found a similar brick and used it to replace bricks crumbled beyond repair. The discovery of a large skylight hidden by a drop ceiling led to its restoration.

"Prior to the Coors project, many buildings downtown were sitting vacant," recalls former Littleton mayor Susan Thornton. "The Coors rehabilitation served as the magnet to attract new owners and tenants, and has spurred interest in renovating other downtown stores."

LAMB SPRING ARCHAEOLOGICAL SITE
9752 W. Titan Rd., access through Roxborough State Park [NR]
c. 7,000–6,000 BC

"Lamb Spring is exceptional because it has well-preserved bones of Ice Age animals in the Denver metro area. Also, as one of the few archaeological sites with a street address, it provides unusual educational opportunities," says CU anthropology professor James Dixon. "The SHF-funded interpretive kiosk and tours help us to tell a story of global significance about some of the very first human activity in North America."

Excavation began in 1960 after landowner Charles Lamb discovered woolly mammoth bones while enlarging an artesian well to create a stock pond. Lamb called the U.S. Geological Survey and the Smithsonian Institution. They excavated the site and found the bones of several woolly mammoths, bison, and other Ice Age mammals dating from more than 13,000 years ago. Smithsonian Institution archaeologist Dennis Stanford found projectile points in 1981 that were evidence of people having hunted and butchered at the spring between 8,000 and 9,000 years ago, making this one of the earliest major Paleo-Indian cultural sites found in Colorado to date.

In 1995, the nonprofit Archaeological Conservancy purchased the 35-acre site with a $275,000 SHF grant and additional assistance from the Denver Museum of

Nature and Science, Douglas County, and the University of Colorado Museum. Another $100,000 in SHF funding has supported research, planning, and interpretive efforts. Of 24 woolly mammoths excavated, one had 16-foot-long tusks. Most of the remains have been reburied to prevent their rapid decay upon exposure to air. One showcase mammoth skull with intact tusks was re-excavated in 2002 and sent to the Denver Museum of Nature and Science, where a mold and cast were made for display at Roxborough State Park.

PERSSE PLACE STONE HOUSE AT ROXBOROUGH STATE PARK

1.1 miles down Fountain Valley Trail from south end of Roxborough Park Rd. (H) [LL] [NRD]

Built: 1903

Henry S. Persse, would-be developer of Roxborough Park, built this small summer cottage as a rustic show home. The New York native acquired and named this park in 1889 after seeing its huge, awesome, red-rock formations. In 1902, he and two other men formed the Roxborough Land Company to build a "splendid resort." The simple house that he constructed helped attract visitors, including Denver mayor Robert W. Speer, who suggested that the park "should be owned by the public for the free use of the people." In 1975, the Colorado State Division of Parks purchased 500 acres of the Persse family property, forming Roxborough State Park. Since then, the park has expanded to 3,319 acres and enjoys National Natural Landmark and National Register Historic District designations.

The State Historical Fund awarded Roxborough State Park four grants totaling $208,552 between 1994 and 2003 to restore the stone house. The porch and kitchen, which had collapsed, were rehabilitated, mortar was replaced in the stone walls, doors, and windows were re-created, and interpretive signs and a guide booklet were prepared. Ongoing work aims to restore two log cabins near the stone house, one of which is believed to be an original 1870s homesteading cabin. The other cabin was built by Persse in 1901 and contains philosophical sayings

inscribed on the walls. Restoration work will involve replacement of rotted sill logs, chinking, roof repairs, and the preservation of his graffiti. The SHF also enabled the park to conduct a cultural resource inventory and help train volunteer interpreters who introduce visitors to Persse's restored stone cabin and log outbuildings. Some 100,000 schoolchildren and visitors annually use the site, which is also available for special events.

TOWN HALL ARTS CENTER
2450 W. Main St. NR NRD
Built: 1920; Jules Jacques Benois Benedict, architect

Photo courtesy of Tom Noel

Until the new Littleton Government Center opened in 1977, this building served as the town hall, jail, and firehouse. It was designed by one of Colorado's most notable architects, Littleton resident J. J. B. Benedict. He drew inspiration from the Palazzo della Ragione in Vicenza, Italy, for this exuberant Renaissance Revival–style gem, but gave it local context by trimming the edifice with Colorado symbols, such as the columbine. The state flower adorning the ornate terracotta façade was restored to full bloom by the city with the help of $5,000 from the SHF. Restoration also recaptured the façade's shadow-forming molding, cast-iron ornament, and Gothic arched windows. Reborn as the Town Hall Arts Center, it hosts live performances by a wide variety of artists. The interior has been completely redone to include a spacious lobby and a 200-seat theater.

Longmont

CALLAHAN HOUSE

312 Terry St., northeast corner of 3rd Ave. LL NR
Built: 1892, James Wiggins, architect; 1908 addition

Thomas M. Callahan, a prominent Longmont retail merchant, helped his former employee, J. C. Penney, establish his chain stores and also prospered in his own business. His former residence is a two-and-a-half-story Queen Anne made of pressed red brick on a foundation of red-rock-faced Lyons sandstone. His daughter donated this stylish family home to the City of Longmont in 1938, so it never had to endure the limbo that so many historical mansions face. The result is an interior par excellence, with woodwork as crisp and unspoiled as the day it was carved. The City of Longmont matched $91,122 from the SHF to restore both the house and the gardens. Craftsman Leo Middleton, a bas-relief specialist, redid the garden fountain and benches, and Don Hildred, a blacksmith, restored the wrought-iron fence and railings while other artisans restored the gilded molding inside. The house is used for weddings, meetings, small conferences, and house tours.

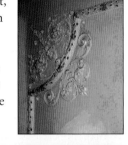

L

FOX/TROJAN/LONGMONT PERFORMING ARTS THEATRE
513 Main St. [LL]
Built: 1939; Charles Jaka, architect

Opening a theater is not easy when electrical problems short out the marquee sign. Furthermore, below the neon "Trojan" sign, an ominous crack, like something out of Poe's "Fall of the House of Usher," was making its way up the entire wall. Such obstacles inspired Cheri E. Friedman, executive director of the Longmont Theater Association, and her associates to raise $6,700 in matching funds to secure $20,025 from the SHF. The Scientific and Cultural Facilities District, Downtown Longmont Development Grants, and other resources have all helped return this Art Deco dream to use as Longmont's downtown theater and performing arts venue. "Thanks to the SHF funds," says Friedman, "we fixed the marquee, installed a new roof, repaired the masonry, and did other outside stuff to make it safe and fun to be inside."

GREAT WESTERN HOTEL / INN BETWEEN
250 Kimbark St. [LL]
Built: 1919

Reviving this prominent landmark next to the Longmont Safety & Justice Center as a home for some of the neediest members of the community was made possible by local churches, the City of Longmont, the Longmont Board of Realtors, the United Way, and Ball Aerospace. The SHF contributed $7,399 to assure that this $300,000 project had a strong preservation component. This Tudor Revival, U-shaped, red-brick boarding house was constructed to house sugar-beet workers. During World War II, it sheltered Italian and later German POWs, who helped plant, cultivate, and harvest the local sugar-beet crop.

The nonprofit Family Extension, Inc., bought the Great Western Hotel to use as a home for people in crisis and in transition—the Inn Between. Contractor Leo Pilkington replaced plumbing, wiring, and the heating system with monies from various sources, including city block grants. With the help of local inmates on day release, Pilkington began restoration. Local churches donated a playground, and each sponsored a room, to ensure that this dream became a reality. Church members, youth groups, and volunteers worked with donated materials on the weekends, doing the drywall, painting, and appliance installation. Crews repaired and resurfaced the three-quarter-inch, tongue-and-groove hickory floors and the five-panel, Douglas-fir doors with operable transoms. Inn Between now has 13 family units, 18 single rooms, and two community spaces. Residents sign two-year contracts spelling out their plans for job searches, school, or job training, and they participate in programs to help improve parenting and life skills.

Photo courtesy of Tom Noel

HOVERHOME AND HOVER FARMSTEAD
1303–1309 Hover Rd. LL NR
Built: 1909, farmstead; 1914, Hoverhome, Robert S. Roeschlaub and
  Frank S. Roeschlaub, architects

This brick mansion trimmed in terracotta is adorned with Jacobethan Revival elements. Its prominence is enhanced by large lawns and mature trees. Businessman
Charles Lewis Hover came to Longmont in 1902 to escape the bustle of Denver.
For 10 years, Hover and his wife, Katherine, lived in the house of the original
farmer, Joseph Williamson, before constructing their new estate just to the north.
At Hoverhome, craftsmen custom-built the 6,000-square-foot interior. All of the
first-floor rooms open to the outside, reflecting an Arts and Crafts penchant for
blending interior and exterior space. The interior also reflects the Arts and Crafts
movement in its built-in yellow-rose theme, showcased in the stained-glass windows, custom cabinetry, and woodwork. Hover Community, Inc., which provides
residential housing for seniors, had cared for Hoverhome since daughter Beatrice
Hover moved out in 1982.

Unable to maintain the structure as a showplace but hoping it could be preserved as a public museum, Beatrice Hover sold the estate to Hover Community,
Inc., who in turn sold the house and immediate grounds to the St. Vrain Historical
Society in 1994 for the below-market price of $500,000. The Society raised more
than $421,000 and received SHF grants of $336,280 to assist with the purchase
and begin restoring the rambling, two-story dwelling with multiple bays and
gabled wings that form a modified U plan with a porte-cochere. Hoverhome still
looks like a country mansion, although new residential subdivisions now occupy
141 of the original 160 acres. Among the frame outbuildings on the remaining
20 acres are a garage, a barn, and the original two-story frame Victorian cottage.
The SHF has funded an assessment and roof replacement.

Saving the house from encroaching development was "the biggest hurdle,"
according to St. Vrain Historical Society executive director Dale Bernard. Not only
the Hoverhome house but also the creamery, woodshed, and chicken house have
been restored, Dale adds, "as relics of Longmont's disappearing agricultural past."

LOHR-McINTOSH FARM / STROH-DICKENS BARN /
AGRICULTURAL HERITAGE CENTER
8348 Ute Rd. (CO 66) LL
Built: 1881

Boulder County Parks and Open Space spent $1.6 million to purchase this farm
amid encroaching subdivisions. The site includes the 1881 barn, the 1909 Lohr
farmhouse, and the Stroh-Dickens Barn, moved here in 1998. "We couldn't take
anybody into this complex before the SHF helped make it safe as well as historically
accurate," says Chris McLure, interpreter at the Agricultural Heritage Center. "Now
everybody can enjoy the fun interior of our Edwardian frame farmhouse, and many
surviving outbuildings." The SHF awarded $50,725 for farmhouse restoration and
$87,500 for exhibits and interpretive signage at this agricultural theme park.

LONGMONT CARNEGIE LIBRARY
457 4th Ave. southeast corner of Kimbark Rd. LL NR
Built: 1913; Benjamin C. Viney, architect

Longmont used a $183,173 grant from the SHF to restore the one-story, yellow-brick Carnegie Library. In the late 1980s, the old library was deemed too small, and the city council was considering plans to enlarge or demolish it. Protesters subsequently besieged city council meetings until their views were taken seriously. Citizens Opposed to the Removal of Public Structures (CORPS) launched citizens' initiatives, a ballot measure, and fundraising events at Longmont's Strawberry Festival, Pumpkin Pie Days, and Boulder County Fair to save the old library. Persuaded to preserve, the city obtained SHF money and advice and found that Channel 3, the local public-access cable TV station, could use the building and would help pay for its restoration and maintenance. Tim Chaffin, Channel 3 general manager, says, "The building is a fit. And tourists come by wanting to tour it, including some who claim they have been to almost all of the 600 to 700 Carnegie libraries still standing in the U.S."

Asbestos removal was followed by installation of a new roof, bathrooms accessible for the disabled, and new heating and air-conditioning. The decorative radiators were left as bookshelves and planters in the offices. The basement, formerly the Children's Library, has technologically updated studios and a video library. Today the old library still houses and perpetuates media for the community.

OLD CITY ELECTRIC BUILDING / LONGMONT MUSEUM STORAGE FACILITY
103 N. Main St. LL
Built: 1931; 1938 and 1951 additions

Founded in 1940, the Longmont Museum and Cultural Center is one of Colorado's oldest and best municipal museums, but it has desperately needed more storage space. Director Kent Brown explains, "As we collect and exhibit not only history, but also art and science, we had run out of room for the artifacts that enable us to keep coming up with new exhibits to give Longmonters a new reason to visit us."

The answer was a boxy, brick electric plant prominently sited in the heart of Longmont. It has undergone a $656,000 restoration with the help of $26,250 from the SHF. This cavernous plant served as Longmont's power supply until the 1950s, when the city took it over and used it variously for offices, storage, and a garage for garbage trucks. It now houses more than 30,000 museum artifacts, from old stagecoaches to cider presses to children's bicycles.

L

OLD POST OFFICE / OLD AMERICAN LEGION HALL
525 3rd Ave. southeast corner of Main St. [LL]
Built: 1905

City of Longmont block grants, matched by $40,000 from the Coors Foundation, a Boettcher grant of $70,000, and the SHF's $242,610, restored this two-story, yellow-brick Neoclassical edifice with sandstone trim. Lead paint was removed and 25 of the boarded-up windows were replaced. An abandoned eyesore for years, it has been reincarnated as a handsome address for small businesses and offices.

ROYAL HUBBARD HOUSE
243 Pratt St. [LL]
Built: 1873

After being moved to Old Mill Park, this frame house, once owned by Longmont's first postmaster, needed a "facelift," according to Dale Bernard, executive director of the St. Vrain Historical Society (SVHS). The exterior woodwork was repaired and repainted, and the 34 original wooden windows were restored. Hubbard's descendant, Denver schoolteacher Havis Motisher, paid for the move and first restoration herself in the 1970s, but it had deteriorated since then. In 1998, she deeded it to the SVHS, which, with the help of the SHF's $7,930, rehabilitated Hubbard House. It now sits demurely tucked under shade trees, looking as if it has been part of Old Mill Park all along.

L

SANDSTONE RANCH
3001 CO 119, 3 miles east of Longmont
Built: 1860s–1880s

The 313-acre Sandstone Ranch property is a historic showcase, which has also provided a site for a large regional park, nature trails, and wildlife preservation. Morse Coffin homesteaded this land in April 1860 and operated a sawmill before turning to agriculture. He was also the central figure in the *Coffin vs. Lefthand Ditch* Supreme Court case that established the foundation for western water law—the Doctrine of Prior Appropriation. The original log cabin was replaced in 1882 by the present house, which was built in the Second Empire style from stone that

was quarried on-site. The ranch complex also includes a barn, icehouse, tool shed, and spring house.

The City of Longmont bought this valuable property in 1998. Parks and Recreation Department employee Paula Fitzgerald managed the project. Aller-Lingle Architects prepared the plans for the complex which included rehabilitation of the stuccoed stone ranch house for use as a visitor center and as an environmental library. The stone outbuildings were also restored, drainage was improved, and interpretive panels were installed throughout the property.

This is a highly visible hilltop project featuring many recreational facilities, including links to the St. Vrain Greenway trail system in the valley where the ranch house lies. The public can enjoy the beauty of the grounds and homestead, as well as appreciate the opportunity to explore the unique history of the St. Vrain Valley. The site offers a valuable open-space buffer in the rapidly suburbanizing Longmont area. A $104,000 SHF grant enabled the city to undertake the $968,000 stabilization and restoration of the historic ranch house for use as a visitor center.

TOWNLEY HOUSE
239 Pratt St. LL
Built: 1871

This frame dwelling, the oldest house in Longmont, dates from the town's founding by the Chicago-Colorado Colony. Englishman John Lawrence Townley, treasurer of the colony, moved here with his family from Fall River, Massachusetts. Its antiquity and association with this prominent pioneer made Townley House a preservation priority, reports Dale Bernard, executive director of the St. Vrain Historical Society. By matching $87,745 in SHF funds, the Society undertook foundation stabilization and repair of the exterior sheathing, shutters, pediments, and other architectural features. The dwelling is currently rented to tenants to help fund St. Vrain Historical Society projects, although longterm plans include opening the house as a public interpretive site. The restored Townley House greatly enhances the entrance to Old Mill Park in Longmont, a pocket urban park that features two transported settlers' log cabins, an 1860 sandstone milk house, and a replica waterwheel on the old Denio Flour Mill site.

Louviers

LOUVIERS VILLAGE CLUB
7885 Louviers Blvd., off US 85 LL NRD
Built: 1917

For this company town dedicated to making dynamite, E. I. du Pont de Nemours and Company built the Louviers Village Club. The clubhouse, like this tiny town on the southwest outskirts of Denver, is named for du Pont's ancestral home in France. Douglas County used SHF grants totaling $658,609 for new roof installation, exterior repairs, window and door restoration, and paint for the Shingle-style clubhouse, distinguished by its towering end chimneys. The large meeting room has been restored to its original appearance. The two-lane bowling alley is being stabilized and restored. The owner since 1975, Douglas County hopes that the rejuvenated building will once again be a popular community center, complete with assembly hall, bowling alley, store, barbershop, theater, billiards, and reading room.

Loveland

RIALTO THEATER
228–230 E. 4th Ave. NR
Built: 1920; Robert K. Fuller, architect

Loveland chose not to demolish but to restore this star. Fronted by a creamy terra-cotta Art Deco façade with three arched storefront windows, the Rialto originally

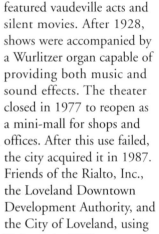

featured vaudeville acts and silent movies. After 1928, shows were accompanied by a Wurlitzer organ capable of providing both music and sound effects. The theater closed in 1977 to reopen as a mini-mall for shops and offices. After this use failed, the city acquired it in 1987. Friends of the Rialto, Inc., the Loveland Downtown Development Authority, and the City of Loveland, using $214,185 from the SHF, returned the Rialto to the limelight as a 450-seat performing-arts center. This restoration has inspired more attention to other downtown landmarks: the First Presbyterian Church, the Beaux-Arts–style First National Bank, the Top Hat Lounge, the Lovelander Hotel, the Loveland Feed and Grain Company, as well as the Bartholf Opera House.

"My father, Ken Fuller, donated to the Friends of the Rialto copies of my grandfather's original records and drawings for the theater," says Robert K. Fuller, II, a Denver architect who is the third-generation principal of Fuller Fuller & Associates, the oldest continually operating architectural firm in Colorado. "We attended that wonderful 1996 Rialto grand opening and can only congratulate Loveland, the theater, and the SHF on a first-rate renewed Rialto."

Ludlow

LUDLOW TENT COLONY SITE
End of Delagua Canyon Rd., 12 miles north of Trinidad and 1 mile west of I-25, Exit 27 NR
Built: 1913

At the first excavation of Ludlow, the bodies of 11 children were found with arms clasped. On top of them lay the burned bodies of two mothers. Thanks to new SHF-funded archaeological research, Coloradans are learning more about the bloodiest tragedy in Colorado labor history.

Striking miners erected the 40-acre Ludlow Tent Colony after being evicted from company housing during the winter of 1914. On April 20, 1914, when the Colorado National Guard attacked the village, wives and children of the striking miners dug pits under the tents to avoid the machine-gun fire. When the tents were set on fire, two women and 11 children were suffocated in one of the pits. This tragic climax to industrial warfare between the Colorado National Guard and striking miners pitted John D. Rockefeller, Jr., and his Colorado Fuel and Iron Company against the United Mine Workers of America.

To help examine and interpret this controversial historical event, the SHF contributed $762,706 toward an archaeological investigation of the Ludlow Tent Colony. Dean Saitta, University of Denver anthropologist, is leading a team of professionals and college students in this endeavor. Saitta notes, "The project had a positive cultural impact, in the sense of piquing local interest and alerting tourists to the richness of southeastern Colorado history."

The site is owned and operated by the United Mine Workers of America. As a partner in the preservation project, the union has erected a monument and preserved the pit where the women and children died. Ruins of several Ludlow town buildings linger along the railroad tracks, and a 1918 granite statue of a mining family by sculptor Hugh Sullivan marks the site of the ill-fated tent city. Those figures were decapitated and disarmed in 2005 by unknown parties. Although repaired by the UMWA and other friends of labor, that episode rekindled passionate feelings about the need to remember what happened at Ludlow.

Lyons

LONGMONT HYDROELECTRIC PLANT
1195 Old Apple Valley Rd. NR
Built: 1911–1960; C. W. Fravert, Hendrie and Bolthoff Architects

Longmont purchased water rights to the North St. Vrain to support its growing population in 1900 and also decided to harness the energy of the plunging water by building this $87,000 hydroelectric plant in Lyons. The first publicly owned power plant in northern Colorado, it still serves Longmont. Restored with city funds, private contributions, and the SHF's $45,000, this is not only a power plant but also a museum, complete with tours and exhibits. Tom Barnish, site manager, says, "This plant is a working historical landmark and a great tool for educating the public on the history and energy of Lyons."

MEADOW PARK SHELTER HOUSE
600 Park Dr., at center of park SR
Built: 1933

During the Great Depression, the WPA helped the small town of Lyons build a community gathering place: a shelter house for picnics, dances, watching baseball games, and entertaining tourists. "This simple, open-sided shelter of Lyons sandstone has been rejuvenated," says Lyons park director Kurt Carlson, "thanks to the SHF's contribution of $38,143 matched by the town."

Photo courtesy of Tom Noel

Mancos

BAUER BANK
101 Grand Ave., southwest corner of Main St. (H) (SR)
Built: 1905; George Bauer, builder

George Bauer's dedication to the community of Mancos is commemorated in this Italianate-style brick-and-sandstone edifice in the heart of the business district. A stonemason as well as the building owner, Bauer probably helped build what is now the town's oldest surviving masonry commercial building. It initially housed the George Bauer Bank, John Sheek's poolroom, the Mancos Mercantile, and the post office. In the 1990s, some wanted to tear down the teetering old-timer, but the owner, Charlie Mitchell, saw what others could not. The greatest of many problems was a leaking roof. "I walked in," Mitchell recalls, "and there were icicles from the ceiling to the floor."

Mitchell needed help and the SHF came to the rescue with an $84,643 grant toward the total $241,570 interior and exterior restoration budget. Mitchell wasted no time getting started. On the day that he purchased the bank, he hired local welder Boyd Sanders to cut off the awnings and remove signage. Bobbi Black, owner of the Bauer House Bed and Breakfast (another SHF grant recipient), showed up at the restoration site with a bucket of margaritas. Fueled by this liquid inspiration, Mitchell added new lathe and plaster. "Because I don't like to paint," Mitchell explains, he hired local people to do the painting and finish work. The chimney flues still worked, so Mitchell installed small gas heaters in each of the rooms. Today, a gift shop and bakery have replaced the bank and the poolroom. Offices are located on the second floor. According to Mitchell, "This grand old bank anchors the very heart of Mancos and speaks loudly for the vision of the pioneers. The building rents itself."

M

BAUER HOUSE BED AND BREAKFAST
100 Bauer Ave., northwest corner of N. Main St. (SR)
Built: 1889; George Bauer, builder

This stately mansion is a visual centerpiece of the community, hosting various events during the year, including an old-fashioned Christmas Victorian Ball, concerts, Mancos Day events, and the Victorian Tea Society. Owner Bobbi Black hired local contractor Brooke Builders and local brick masons, carpenters, and landscapers to fully restore the home of the first mayor of Mancos, George Bauer. One of the more challenging aspects of this project was the restoration of the balustrades on the lower front porch, which had been encased in concrete. Jacky Evans, a local artisan, had to reproduce the balustrades using the upper porch as a model. Local schoolchildren participated in the cleanup and renovation of the Bauer mansion as a lesson in community heritage. Restored with the help of the SHF's $25,115, Bauer House is the first stop on the SHF-funded brochure for a historic walking tour of Mancos.

MANCOS HIGH SCHOOL
350 Grand Ave. (US 160) [NR]
Built: 1909; W. L. Morse and David Ramsey, builders

In 1908, graduating seniors bid farewell to the old Mancos High School, as the growing town decided a larger school was needed. In 1909, the town constructed the new high school, which is today the pride of the Mancos Bluejays. During its first 10 years, the school was a victim of two devastating fires; however, the school never closed and is now listed on the National Register of Historic Places as Colorado's oldest high school in continuous use.

In the 1990s, the school had been showing its age. Eaves had rotted away because of a leaky roof, and mortar had eroded from the building's locally-quarried blocks of sandstone. School custodian Kim Bondeson urged teacher Michael Maxwell to apply for SHF funding so that the building that meant so much to the town of Mancos could be repaired. In 1997 and 2001, grants totaling $152,974 were used for roof replacement, repointing of mortar, and restoration of bead-boarding at the eaves.

Much has changed over the years at Mancos High School. Jean Bader, Mancos native and 1940 graduate, recalls, "Boys and girls went up separate stairs, but we had classes together." Another graduate, Frank Willburn, has a different spin on how the school has changed. "In 1945 there was not really any dress code—the only requirement was that you wear clothes." Today, there are more memories being made, the roof no longer leaks, and the building's ready for future generations of Mancos Bluejays.

MANCOS OPERA HOUSE
136 W. Grand Ave., northeast corner of Mesa St. [NR]
Built: 1910; Gregory Cavanagh, architect

The Opera House in Mancos is a landmark in need of major restoration. Designed as a multipurpose community center, the building has housed a variety of sporting events, graduations, dances, theatrical presentations, and motion pictures. From the front, the opera house looks like a three-story building, but the top two stories of windows all open into the high-ceilinged performance area. Unfortunately, the doors have been closed since 1968.

The Veterans of Foreign Wars Post No. 5231 acquired the building in 1953. The storefronts were bricked up and the community space began to crumble. The ceilings collapsed and bats became regular inhabitants. The Town of Mancos and the Friends of the Mancos Opera House spearheaded an effort to obtain SHF support for a study of the building and the feasibility of returning it to public use. In the course of that study, it became clear that the roof and parapets required immediate stabilization. The SHF provided $158,800 for this purpose and the Friends managed to raise a $40,000 match for a proposed future restoration. The VFW, however, is now unsure as to whether it should retain ownership of a building too large for its needs and too expensive for its budget. In the meantime, deterioration continues and Friends of the Opera House are pursuing other solutions and keeping their fingers crossed.

M

Manitou Springs

CITY HALL
606 Manitou Ave. ⃞LL⃞
Built: c. 1918

The City of Manitou Springs used a $10,000 SHF grant to repair the knobby red-tile roof that distinguishes this white stucco structure with Doric pilasters. Extensive gardens in the back include a reconstructed mineral-spring pavilion where visitors can sample the curative waters that made Manitou Springs a far-famed spa.

CLIFF HOUSE HOTEL
306 Cañon Ave. Ⓗ ⃞NR⃞
Built: 1873, Shertleff and Webster, architects; Gillis Brothers, builders; various additions

When a 1982 fire gutted the fourth floor and attic of the Cliff House, its future looked bleak. Manitou Springs city planner Michelle Anthony notes that the former

luxury hotel had become a vacant eyesore "inhabited by several raccoon families." With the assistance of $216,430 in SHF grants, the picture brightened with a new roof, doors, and windows and exterior rhyolite restoration. Because so much of the structure was lost in the fire, much of it had to be reconstructed.

Built in front of a sunny, south-facing cliff, the four-story Queen Anne edifice with ornate corner towers opened as a boarding house for miners and health seekers. Edward E. Nichols and his family, the owners from 1876 to 1948, expanded and improved the hotel, making it an elegant year-round resort with more than 200 sleeping rooms. Guests drank from and also bathed in the nearby mineral springs and took burro and buggy rides to the area's many attractions. Notable guests included Buffalo Bill Cody, Thomas Edison, Henry Ford, Clark Gable, J. Paul Getty, and President Theodore Roosevelt. For such gentlemen, the hotel hosted an exclusive club called The Cave.

In 1981, the fading hotel became an apartment complex, which burned a year later. The burned-out shell sat abandoned until California investor James S. Morley bought and transformed it into one of Colorado's oldest, most charming, and finest luxury resorts. As noted Colorado historian James Edward Fell says this $12 million reincarnation provides "a magisterial reflection of the lost, serene Victorian epoch in Colorado in one of the most thorough building rehabilitations I have ever seen."

COMMUNITY CONGREGATIONAL CHURCH
OF MANITOU SPRINGS
101 Pawnee Ave. [NR]
Built: 1880; Angus Gillis and George W. Snyder, builders

Colorado's oldest Congregational church is new again. This small Gothic Revival structure, made of Manitou greenstone quarried from nearby Williams Canyon, boasts an open belfry and a bell inscribed "I ring for God, home, and native land." The church had fallen into disrepair and even resorted to a neon cross before its architectural and spiritual rebirth.

"We could never have done it without the help of God and the State Historical Fund," says Pastor David L. Hunting. "The SHF not only gave us excellent advice, but kicked in $81,272 toward our $982,000 restoration and new community center." The SHF funded repointing masonry and repairing original windows, the cupola, the bell tower, and foundation, and helped the church protect its precious stained- and leaded-glass windows with Lexan. Inspired by the SHF, the congregation independently restored its 750-pipe organ. This "green" restoration used recycled and environmentally friendly materials to repair the roof, cupola, woodwork, plasterwork, and windows, including the original stained glass.

PIKES PEAK AUTOMOBILE COMPANY /
BUSINESS OF ART CENTER
515 Manitou Ave. **H** [LL]
Built: 1893; Wallace Gould, builder

M

Built as the Manitou Livery & Transfer Co., this horse-and-buggy-era edifice got an automobile-age rehabilitation as the Pikes Peak Automobile Company, which motored tourists to local attractions such as Pikes Peak and the Garden of the Gods. After a 1980 tornado destroyed the upper floor, the city repaired the building for use as storage, then sold it to the Business of Art Center (BAC), a nonprofit organization that promotes the arts. Due to the building's architectural and transportation legacy, the SHF contributed $227,930 to stabilize, repair, restore, and repoint the rusticated buff-sandstone landmark and to rebuild the second floor. Sculptor Harriet Lee replicated the elegant,

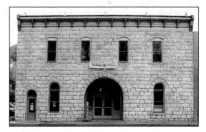

acanthus-leaf brackets and cornice. The BAC reconstructed or repaired the roof, floors, and walls. The large, round-arch entry, with its massive oak doors and matching windows, is back in place for this haven for the visual and performing arts, which also helps out other local nonprofit organizations.

RED CRAGS BED AND BREAKFAST
302 El Paso Blvd. [LL]
Built: 1889; Henry Van Brunt, architect

A fine example of the Shingle style, this house rises four stories above a Peachblow sandstone foundation and sits commandingly upon a south-facing slope overlooking Manitou Springs. Shingled walls feature large arched windows and several decks. Denver & Rio Grande Railroad vice president William Bell commissioned Van Brunt, a famous Kansas City architect, to design this show home to impress potential investors. The City of Manitou Springs and the owner of what is now a bed-and-breakfast matched the SHF's $10,000 to repair the retaining walls of this scenic hillside site.

Marble

FINISHING MILL SITE, COLORADO YULE MARBLE COMPANY
W. 3rd St. and Park St. [NR]
Built: 1907; John C. Osgood, builder

Along Yule Creek near the headwaters of the Crystal River, an outcropping of high-grade white marble was found by George Yule in 1874. Marble's quarriers exhibited their 99 percent–pure calcium carbonate at the World's Columbian Exposition of 1893, where the popularity of the Neoclassical buildings helped create a national market for this fine Carrara-like marble. Mule sleds were used to haul the stone to the Denver & Rio Grande railhead in Carbondale until the Crystal River & San Juan Railroad reached Marble in 1906.

John C. Osgood opened this mill to refine the snowy white stone. Several marble-clad ruins, including six storage-shed towers, remain from Osgood's operation. These mill sites provided stone for the Lincoln Memorial and other landmarks

Both photos courtesy of Tom Noel

nationwide. In 1907, the Colorado Yule Marble Company finishing mill began operations and by 1915 was the largest facility of its kind in the world. In 1931, a 110-ton block of marble, the largest ever quarried in the United States, was hauled from the mine, trimmed to 55 tons, and sent to Arlington, Virginia, for the Tomb of the Unknown Soldier. The memorial is inscribed with the words, "Here Rests in Honored Glory an American Soldier Known but to God."

In 1941, the quarry closed, and the structures and machinery were sold for scrap. Although much of the site above ground is gone, the SHF funded an archaeological investigation in conjunction with the Town of Marble, which owns the site, and the Marble Historical Society. Using an SHF grant of $9,891, archaeologists studied the foundations, cellar holes, and privy pits of at least 50 structures. Further excavation and artifact analysis revealed much about the workers and their families whose lives revolved around this mill. Additionally, a $3,750 SHF grant funded a Historic Structure Assessment of the deteriorated remains of the Documents House, the most intact structure remaining at this once extensive mill site.

MARBLE CITY STATE BANK
105 W. Main St. [NR]
Built: 1909

Marble's only surviving early commercial building opened with storefronts below and living quarters on the second floor. Closed in 1918 as the town population dwindled to ghostly proportions, this stacked-timber marvel is made of four-by-eight-inch planks pinned with spikes on each course and tied together with lap joints at the corners. The sturdy structure withstood a 1916 fire and a 1940 flood. It reverted to Gunnison County in 1925 at a tax sale. In the 1940s, the County Road and Bridges Operations converted it into a garage and living quarters for the county roads manager. A $105,000 SHF grant, plus a cash match of $65,903 from Gunnison County and private donors, restored the exterior and the interior. The old bank now houses history displays and visitor information and hosts public meetings, and the Marble Town Council, which uses the original concrete vault.

M

MARBLE HIGH SCHOOL / MARBLE HISTORICAL SOCIETY MUSEUM
412 W. Main St. [NR]
Built: 1910

Marble's old high school, with its marble foundation and stout porch, is the largest building in town. The open bell tower crowns a two-story, shiplap-sided building with Craftsman elements. The schoolhouse was originally built from a catalog plan by volunteers, with marble donated from the quarry. The school closed in 1948 and was sold for $1 to the Marble Historical Society, which opened a museum here in 1979. The SHF contributed $181,100 to the Gunnison Watershed School District and the Marble Historical Society for a $360,000 restoration so the structure could be used for a museum and charter school. Having a local school after almost 50 years saves the students a two-hour commute to down-valley classes and, along with the museum, creates a sense of place for the newer families in town. As Marble's only large heated public space, the reborn school hosts community and town meetings.

McCoy

WATERWHEEL RANCH
19717 CO 131, southeast of McCoy [NR]
Built: 1922; Earl Brooks, Wyman Franklin Dixon, and Jim Jones,
   builders

Early settlers used waterwheels to raise water from a stream to the level of the fields that needed irrigation. Colorado's only surviving functional waterwheel, built in 1922 by three local ranchers, lifted water 30 feet from the Colorado River by means of 35 wooden buckets. The wheel has approximately 4,000 handmade parts, most of wood, including a massive central axle.

Amazingly, none of the three men had any experience building waterwheels and supposedly worked without a plan. "When it came time to hay, we hayed," Dixon once said. "When it came time to build a waterwheel, we built it. People just took such things for granted."

Eagle County restoration specialist John Comer got an SHF grant of $35,000 with a match of $10,000 and donated all of the carpentry. With a new concrete foundation, solid uprights, a new axle, and restored fir and redwood components, this 40-foot-tall wonder will continue to astonish future generations.

Meeker

HOLY FAMILY CATHOLIC CHURCH
890 Park Ave. [LL]
Built: 1913; Aaron Gove and Thomas Walsh, architects

Prominent Denver architects designed this one-story Gothic Revival church with a commanding, crenellated square bell tower for a $125 fee at a time when they were also working for the Diocese of Denver on the Mile High City's Immaculate Conception Cathedral. The Meeker church had a leaky roof and a cracked wall until the SHF's $68,850 helped to restore the central entry tower, replace the roof, install new gutters and downspouts, and put snow brakes on the roof.

RIO BLANCO COUNTY HIGH SCHOOL/PRESCHOOL
555 Garfield Ave. (SR)
Built: 1924; Robert K. Fuller, architect

This two-story structure of rough-cut local sandstone was the county's only high school from 1924 until 1951. For its first two years, students had to play basketball on packed dirt until the school board had enough money to install a hardwood floor. In order to preserve the school, the Meeker School District raised $283,000 and another $100,000 from the SHF to rehabilitate the interior and exterior. Much of the work involved upgrading the mechanical systems to address various safety and teaching concerns. Preservation work included repointing of exterior masonry to prevent further deterioration as well as to repair and paint the interior hallways. The rehabilitation allowed for its reuse as a preschool, kindergarten, school district offices, and meeting space. The gym now hosts recreation, dances, performances, school activities, and meetings.

Photo courtesy of Tom Noel

St. JAMES EPISCOPAL CHURCH
368 4th St. [NR]
Built: 1889

The first church in Meeker and one of Colorado's oldest still-flourishing Episcopal churches is made of golden sandstone from the nearby Flag Creek Quarry. Rough

cut into blocks, the stone is used for the walls, sills, trim, and the buttresses, which peek out from under the steep, shingled roof. The corner entry is topped by a distinctive, shingled tower with a bell from the Blymer Bell Foundry of Cincinnati. This lovely little Queen Anne–style church is enhanced by a generous and well-maintained garden and lawn. St. James raised $35,000 to match $105,000 from the SHF to restore and straighten the badly leaning bell tower, stabilize the foundation, and replace the roof.

M

*Mesa Verde National Park*_____

Mesa Verde contains some of Colorado's most significant archaeological resources and architectural stabilization projects—and the first structures to be designated World Cultural Heritage Sites by the United Nations. This park humanizes the earliest Native Americans, according to former Colorado U.S. senator Ben Nighthorse Campbell. "I'll never forget a tour of one of the Mesa Verde pueblos," Senator Campbell recalled in 2003. "On one wall the ranger showed me a child's muddy handprint—the same muddy prints my nieces and nephews love to leave around today—a paw print from the past." In all, SHF has awarded 30 grants totaling more than $1.3 million that have impacted Mesa Verde National Park. These grants have helped document, stabilize, survey, and interpret sites within the park, which celebrated its centennial in 2006.

CLIFF PALACE
Built: 1200–1280 NRD

Originally excavated and stabilized by Jesse Walter Fewkes in 1909, the Cliff Palace is considered to be the "gold standard" by which all other Ancestral Puebloan archaeological sites are measured. This southwestern Colorado treasure hadn't been re-evaluated for more than 40 years and was being damaged by water seepage into the rear of the alcove, threatening two courtyard complexes and other areas of the site that had not been adequately documented. In 1996, the SHF granted the Mesa Verde Museum Association $62,809 to update the documentation of the Puebloan culture at Cliff Palace. The project examined the courtyard complexes to analyze household and network relationships. More importantly, this study demonstrated to the Native American community that archaeological studies could be done without invasive excavation, a refinement that has helped to build bridges with the Native American tribes in the area.

SPRUCE TREE HOUSE
Built: 1200–1300 [NRD]

The Spruce Tree House site at Mesa Verde receives the largest number of visitors in the park. According to archaeologist Larry Nordby, "It is a paramount example of a large, residential cliff dwelling that serves as a foil to the socio-ceremonial role played by Cliff Palace." Spruce Tree House displays a number of strategic approaches to space utilization and building practices employed by the inhabitants of these dwellings. A courtyard complex containing a kiva and 17 rooms was studied using monies from the SHF to incorporate anthropological principles in the site interpretation. Previous studies dated back to 1910, and adequate documentation of the site had never been performed. The study found that the site had been used by about 20 households. Dendrochronology (tree-ring dating) pinpoints courtyard-complex construction dates. This site contains one of the best groups of roofed rooms remaining in the park. The SHF grant continued work that had begun as part of the Save America's Treasures grant, which addressed the needs of numerous cliff dwellings at Mesa Verde. Former first lady Hillary Rodham Clinton was present at the granting of the award, which ultimately helped elevate public awareness of the value of Mesa Verde National Park.

Mogote

SAN RAFAEL PRESBYTERIAN CHURCH
4.5 miles west of Antonito on CO 17 at CR 9 (SR)
Built: c. 1895, Manuel Sisneros and Antonio Martinez, builders;
  1911 addition

San Rafael is a small adobe building that housed a Spanish-speaking congregation and represents competition between Protestant Anglo and Hispanic Catholic missionaries near the border with New Mexico. Manuel Sisneros made the adobe bricks and Antonio Martinez crafted the pews, wainscoting, pulpit, altar railing, and wooden doors. The United Presbyterian Church is matching SHF grants of $296,470 to restore this church. The grants, says church historian/caretaker Margie Garcia, are saving a church that closed in 1965 when its 30 members switched to the nearby Presbyterian church in Antonito. The adobe walls had slumped, and the shingled roof deteriorated, allowing water infiltration that cracked the walls and rotted the wooden floor. Birds nested in the belfry, since the bell never rang. Inclusion on Colorado Preservation Inc.'s "Most Endangered Places List" in 2001 focused community support and statewide attention on the church. SHF grants assessed the structure, performing asbestos abatement and restoring the roof. Doors, windows, and wooden trim were painted, an adobe wall rebuilt and the building replastered. The congregation will also restore the interior and is in the process of conveying a perpetual easement on the building. The bell rings in the bell tower, and roses and lilacs bloom again behind the repaired wooden entry gate with its arch inscription, *Dios es Amor* ("God is love").

Monte Vista

CARNEGIE LIBRARY
120 Jefferson St. [NR]
Built: 1919; John J. Huddart, architect

Designed by a prominent Denver architect in the Classical Revival style, this is one of many public libraries throughout the United States that were funded by the wealthy industrialist and philanthropist Andrew Carnegie. The library matched $175,480 in SHF funds to restore the interior and exterior. The glazed red brick with banding of glazed white brick and terracotta ornament now sparkles anew in this classy two-story landmark. A sympathetic rear addition expanded the facility, and SHF funds were used to improve accessibility for the disabled without compromising the building's architectural integrity.

CENTRAL SCHOOL AUDITORIUM
612 1st Ave. **H** [NR]
Built: 1938; Charles E. Thomas, architect

This WPA room has long hosted public gatherings in the largest auditorium in the San Luis Valley. Incorporating elements from the Mission, Romanesque Revival, and Spanish Colonial Revival styles, it is distinguished by a curvilinear parapet and a copper canopy at the main entrance. Wrought-iron chandeliers and other ornate fixtures adorn the 920-seat hall, which retains its original wood and cast-iron opera chairs. The two-story, T-shaped brick building stood between elementary and junior high schools that have both been razed. The auditorium faced an equally grim future until locals protested that it had architectural, historical, and sentimental merit and helped the Monte Vista School District raise a match for $263,260 in SHF grants to repoint the masonry and restore this treasure inside and out. Designed by a noted Colorado Springs architect celebrated for his finely detailed Southwestern-style

edifices, it sparkles again as a community center and is used as a town showplace.

M

L. L. FASSETT DEPARTMENT STORE
102 Adams St. (SR)
Built: 1898; 1906 addition

Situated on a key corner in downtown Monte Vista, Fassett's store is one of the first mercantile establishments in the San Luis Valley. In fact, the original store, built in 1881, predated the founding of Monte Vista itself. Built by Lillian L. Taylor, a widow with two children, the store housed the town's first post office and circulating library. Taylor married Charles Fassett in 1882, and the store was renamed the L. L. Fassett Department Store. The family replaced the original building with a one-story stone store in 1898, and constructed an addition to that building in 1906. Three years later, part of the store was topped by a second story. The Fassetts continued in business until 1980, when the building was sold for other retail use. A fire in January 1987 caused extensive damage, but enough of the structure survived to permit rehabilitation. Travelers' Insurance Company assumed ownership in 1991,

and donated the building to the City of Monte Vista in 1992, with the Monte Vista Urban Renewal Authority (URA) taking title. The URA started its project with the help of a stabilization and reuse study funded by the SHF. Subsequent grants accomplished a complete interior and exterior restoration. Today, the building looks much as it did a century ago. At the conclusion of the project, the URA transferred ownership to a private owner and the building returned to commercial use. The SHF's contribution of $303,500 assisted in preserving this monument to women's history and the importance of family-owned business on the western frontier.

MONTE VISTA CEMETERY CHAPEL
4927 CR 27 (SR)
Built: 1912; George F. Harvey, architect

This quaint, 34-by-24-foot temple of glazed brick with local rhyolite trim is the centerpiece of a 35-acre burial ground on the northwest side of Monte Vista. After falling into disuse in the 1940s, it became storage and maintenance shops. To correct this indignity, the Monte Vista Cemetery Association and local volunteers organized the Chapel Fund Restoration Committee to tackle the interior and exterior with the help of $82,250 from the SHF. Sally Kehler, head of the committee, reports that restoration has highlighted elements such as the Greek Revival columns and pedimented temple front for this reborn chapel.

Montrose

DENVER & RIO GRANDE DEPOT / MONTROSE COUNTY HISTORICAL MUSEUM
21 N. Rio Grande Ave., northwest corner of Main St. [NR]
Built: 1912

This Mission-style passenger and freight depot served the Denver & Rio Grande Railroad. Converted into the Montrose County Historical Museum in 1974, it houses artifacts inside and on the grounds, including a Barlow & Sanderson stagecoach, an ice wagon, a homesteader's cabin, and a cowboy line-camp. Along with Ute Indian artifacts, the museum houses farming, ranching, and mining equipment and belly-dump wagons used to build the U.S. Bureau of Reclamation's nearby Gunnison Tunnel. The City of Montrose restored the depot's unusual cinder-stuccoed exterior with the help of a $17,500 SHF grant. It was matched by the Gates and El Pomar Foundations for a $60,000 project that, among other things, replaced wire over the windows with a security system.

MONTROSE COUNTY COURTHOUSE
320 S. 1st St., southeast corner of Townsend Ave. [NR]
Built: 1922; William N. Bowman, architect

Mules hauled large blocks of local tan sandstone from the nearby Kaleway Quarry for the walls of Montrose's Neoclassical cornerstone. The stone is rusticated on the walls but smooth on the quoins, banding, entry bay, and fourth story. A sympathetic WPA-era addition and landscaping fill out the half-block site. Montrose County restored the courthouse inside and out, including replica windows, a new electrical system, lobby rehabilitation, and grand-stairway reconstruction. The $601,970 restoration was supported in part by the SHF's $165,828 grant and funds from Montrose County and the State of Colorado's Department of Local Affairs.

POMONA ELEMENTARY SCHOOL
1045 S. Cascade Ave., northeast corner of S. 10th St. (SR)
Built: 1919

This wood-frame, one-story, hipped-roof school closed in 1940 when the new school was built next door. After that, it survived as a food-storage facility for the Montrose County School District. In 1996, the structure returned to active service as a media center for Pomona Elementary School. The Montrose County School District raised a cash match of $48,480 and used $104,530 from the SHF to restore the exterior with help from the Home Builders Association.

U.S. BUREAU OF RECLAMATION / UNCOMPAHGRE VALLEY WATER USERS ASSOCIATION OFFICE

601 N. Park Ave. [NR]
Built: 1905; J. J. Kewin, architect

Designed as a foursquare in deference to the surrounding residential neighborhood, this building made hydraulic history as a hub for construction of the $3 million tunnel affiliated with the Uncompahgre Valley Project. This two-and-a-half-story office oversaw one of the earliest major projects of the U.S. Bureau of Reclamation: the Gunnison Tunnel (1909), whose portal is just off US 50, located 6.5 miles east of Montrose on CR 348 (Miguel Road). It also housed some of the first Bureau workers in Colorado. As one of the first and longest U.S. irrigation systems when built, the Gunnison Tunnel has been designated a National Historic Civil Engineering Landmark. Since 1935, the Water Users Association has occupied the old Bureau offices in a structure that has been rehabilitated inside and out, from the widow's walk to the shiplap siding and stone foundation. It took $200,000 from the SHF and $266,295 from the Bureau of Reclamation to save a landmark almost demolished for a modern office replacement. Association manager Marc Catlin says, "The SHF technical assistance and funds allowed the project to be completed. The community was, and is, very proud of the building, which we plan to maintain and keep looking like it's new."

M

UTE INDIAN MUSEUM AND MEMORIAL SITE

17253 Chipeta Dr. at US 50, 2 miles south of Montrose [NR]
Built: 1956, Dudley T. Smith, architect; 1996–1998 addition

To celebrate the Ute Indians and their culture, this classy, stuccoed museum has permanent and changing galleries, a classroom, and a large gift shop specializing in Indian goods. The museum honors Ute chief Ouray and his wife, Chipeta, who once farmed this 8.65-acre site where their adobe house stood. The property includes a park; the graves of Chipeta and her brother, Chief John McCook; and a marker for the Dominguez-Escalante Expedition of 1776. The Ouray Springs on the grounds are covered with a cement tipi (1924) donated by the Daughters of the American Revolution.

With a $29,500 SHF grant, the Colorado Historical Society upgraded the utility systems as well as programs for artifact-preservation, including conservation and interpretation of a rare and distinctive Ute residence, a stick wickiup. Curator Carole Jean "C. J." Brafford,

a Lakota born on the Pine Ridge Reservation in South Dakota, has installed a native-plants garden and wildflowers on the grave of Chipeta. "The SHF grant," Brafford says, "has complemented a $500,000 addition and upgrade to the building, the addition of the Montrose Visitor Center, and $286,000 for landscaping." Some of the improvements include new stucco skin, murals and sculptures, an Indian dance circle and tipis.

Monument

MONUMENT NURSERY / MONUMENT FIRE CENTER
3751 Mt. Herman Rd. (SR)
Built: 1907; 1930s addition, Civilian Conservation Corps, builders

Next to Cathedral Rock, the natural landmark that gave Monument its name, lies this rustic frame complex. The Civilian Conservation Corps (CCC) expanded the operation of the 1907 Mount Herman Planting Station to replenish trees in areas damaged by fire and logging. In the 1930s, the CCC renamed the site Monument Nursery and constructed its own quarters, a seed building, cold storage, a blacksmith shop, and a residence for chief nurseryman Walter Schrader.

Pikes Peak Wildfire Prevention Partners worked with the U.S. Forest Service and other agencies to update this forestry-restoration center. They used $126,100 in SHF funds for repair, restoration, and outreach. They replaced the roofs, siding, and windows on the carpenter's shop and seed building. Today, the nursery serves as the headquarters for two firefighting crews, the Pike Hotshots and the Helitack Crew. Pikes Peak District ranger William Nelson says the old nursery's new mission "shows how it's possible to live safely in a wildland area that's subject to fire, while restoring and protecting historical structures." This restoration provided a new fire-

fighting center near the area devastated by Colorado' largest wildfire, the 2002 Hayman Fire.

Morrison

MORRISON CIVILIAN CONSERVATION CORPS CAMP
300 Union Ave. and 16351 CR 93 NR
Built: 1935; Civilian Conservation Corps, builders

About 125 young men aged 17 to 26 pitched their tents here in the summer of 1935. Paid $30 a month ($25 of which went to their parents), these CCC boys found that their first job was to build the barracks, mess hall, and other buildings where they would live while constructing Red Rocks Amphitheatre. What is now one of the nation's best-preserved CCC camps consists of simple frame structures: five barracks, a mess hall, a recreation hall, a camp commander's residence, camp headquarters, a blacksmith shop, and a carpenter's shop. The camp is still used as the base for Denver Parks and Recreation employees working at nearby Red Rocks and other Denver mountain parks. As late as the early 2000s, CCC veterans maintained the mess hall and helped maintain the interiors of other camp buildings. Denver Mountain Parks superintendent A. J. Tripp-Addison reports, "We've used the SHF's $10,000 to master-plan preservation of this camp and begin restoration. For labor we're using AmeriCorps, the modern version of the CCC, to do repair, restoration, and repainting. We began with the reroofing, which the SHF helped finance."

Albert S. Coven, president of the Colorado CCC Alumni, reminisced in a 2002 interview, "We were mostly pick-and-shovel boys but did like doing the fancy rockwork up at Red Rocks." Coven added that construction crews used local stones, gravel, soil, and junipers to construct Red Rocks Amphitheatre. He also elaborated on this frugal use of free local resources by reciting the CCC's Depression-era slogan: "Wear it out/Use it up/Make it do/Or do without."

M

Photo courtesy of Tom Noel

MORRISON TOWN HALL
110 Stone St. **H** NRD
Built: 1896; Woodmen of the World, builders

Built as the Morrison Lodge of the Woodmen of the World, this building was donated as a town hall in 1950 by the ladies of the Morrison Booster Club. After the town hall moved out, it briefly was the Morrison Theater Company. According to Jamie Chambers, chair of the Morrison Planning Committee, "We had a historic building whose decay made it unusable for the town." With an $85,000 SHF grant, the town restored windows and added a ramp to provide access for the disabled, modern heating, a dressing room, and public restrooms, making it into a viable theater.

RED ROCKS TRADING POST
16351 CR 93 NRD
Built: 1931; Wilbert R. Rosche, designer

Rosche, a draftsman for Denver Parks and Improvements, designed this striking two-story Southwestern-style structure with the help of anthropologist Jean Jeançon, artist and artifact collector Anne Evans, Denver Art Museum Native arts expert Frederick Douglas, and artist Allan True. The design combines a Mission Revival parapet with Pueblo Revival vigas. Built for $18,000 as a visitor center, café, and museum, the earth-colored, smooth stucco building was the brainchild of the Denver Art Commission. They all believed that the building should reflect Native American architecture as well as blend in with the surrounding red rocks. In 1930, the *Rocky Mountain News* reported, "A pueblo of purest Indian architecture will greet the first of the summer visitors to Denver's newest and most imposing mountain playground—Park of the Red Rocks."

Over time, Denver Theatres and Arenas, which operates the adjacent Red Rocks

Amphitheatre in addition to the Trading Post, has updated the electricity and the heating and tackled the asbestos abatement. Using $48,750 from the SHF, the city repaired the crumbling stucco structure and its leaky roof, and began restoration of the surrounding nature trails and cactus garden. Today, there is a room that's dedicated to the CCC workers who built the amphitheater, and an account of historical Red Rocks performances, preserved within this extraordinary work of craftsmanship. This small, restored gem retains its casual, friendly, and funky charm.

A. J. Tripp-Addison, Denver Mountain Parks superintendent, reports, "With SHF funds we undertook a collaborative effort with Denver Theatres and Arenas, concessionaire Bill Carle, architect Noel Copeland, and landscape architect Pat Schuler. We brought the Trading Post up to code while respecting its historic integrity. We replaced the vigas and the roof, and we repaired and repainted the stucco skin a subtle earth tone to complement the natural setting."

Mosca

GREAT SAND DUNES NATIONAL PARK AND PRESERVE
CO 150, 21 miles east of Mosca
11,000 BC; Folsom People

This national monument, consisting of a 39-square-mile sand dune field with dunes up to 700 feet above the valley floor, was designated a national park in September 2004. It has a rich human as well as natural history. The SHF has contributed approximately $300,000 to help conduct a resource survey of the Native American archaeology and ethnography, document oral histories, and publish a book. This project is a partnership among the Friends of the Dunes, a nonprofit group in the San Luis Valley; the National Park Service; The Nature Conservancy; and the Smithsonian Institution. The project team includes archaeologists, anthropologists, geologists, historians, environmental scientists, and educators. This team will ensure that the human and the natural history of this unique area is included in the new national park's official story.

M

Nederland

NEDERLAND STONE GARAGE / MINING MUSEUM
200 N. Bridge St. LL
Built: 1937

The Nederland Historical Society used a $26,000 SHF grant and raised $55,000 from the Energy and Mineral Resource Group to recycle this obsolete county garage

with its barrel-vaulted roof and walls of native stone. Once a home for highway maintenance vehicles, it now houses mining equipment and exhibits. Nederland cleaned up decades of motor oil, gas, and diesel spills to make way for more than 280,000 tons of mining equipment, including four operational, 20-foot-high, 30-ton, steam-powered rock shovels. Among other mechanical marvels here are Wilfley ore-sorting tables, steam boilers and hoists, and ore wagons. "With this museum," reports local miner and historian Tom Hendricks, "we can save and exhibit our mineral heritage for future generations who might not realize that silver gave this town its start and tungsten kept it alive when most other mountain mining towns were becoming ghosts."

Needleton

NEEDLETON WATER TANK
Milepost 484.4 on Denver & Rio Grande Railroad NHLD
Built: c. 1928; Denver & Rio Grande Railroad, builder

The SHF awarded a grant of $45,000 to Fort Lewis College's Department of Southwest Studies to assist with the restoration of this historic water tank, admired by some 200,000 tourists who annually ride the Durango & Silverton Narrow Gauge steam summer excursion train. One of only two surviving water tanks on the Durango-to-Silverton run, it faced collapse in 1999.

"These fast-disappearing water tanks must be preserved now," cautions project historian Duane Smith, "or the next generation will only see them in the movies."

Olathe

PEA GREEN COMMUNITY HOUSE
3015 CO 348, 13 miles west of Olathe (SR)
Built: 1927

After the first frame schoolhouse was built here in 1887 and painted pea green, folks started calling the area "Pea Green." The school that gave focus and a name to the community was replaced by this one-story, stuccoed log building with a south-side shed roof addition that served as the social and community center of this agricultural hamlet. The school closed in 1950, but the Pea Green community continued to use the building. Rehabilitated with the help of a $35,000 SHF grant and a $23,000 cash match from the Olathe State Bank, Tri County Water District, and personal donations, it continues to serve as the community center and now boasts indoor plumbing and a fresh coat of pea green paint.

Ophir

RIO GRANDE SOUTHERN RAILROAD BRIDGE 51-A
FR 626, southeast of CO 145 [LL] (SR)
Built: 1910–1912; Rio Grande Southern Railroad

This 146-foot-long wooden bridge built over Trout Creek on a sharp 24-degree curve was constructed by the Rio Grande Southern Railroad, a narrow-gauge line. It is the largest standing bridge left by this baby railroad, which once snaked through the San Juan Mountains. As the major freight and passenger connection between the towns of Ridgway, Telluride, Rico, Mancos, and Durango, the RGS was not abandoned until 1952. Now owned by the U.S. Forest Service, the trestle is being preserved by a partnership that includes the nearby Town of Norwood, San Miguel County, the U.S. Forest Service, and the SHF, which committed $195,370 to the project. The bridge is a highlight of the Galloping Goose Trail and is also an interpretive site on the scenic San Juan Skyway.

O

Osier

OSIER SECTION HOUSE
FR 104, 20 miles west of Antonito [NRD]
Built: 1884; Denver & Rio Grande Railroad, builder

This 16-by-52-foot frame section house built for $1,800 was restored with the help of $186,600 from the SHF and the labor of the Friends of the Cumbres & Toltec Scenic Railroad. Once home to section crews working on the line, it is now used for storage of railroad tools and equipment.

OSIER DEPOT
FR 104, 20 miles west of Antonito [NRD]
Built: 1880; Denver & Rio Grande Railroad, builder

The Cumbres & Toltec Scenic Railroad was awarded SHF grants totaling $58,689 to replace the roof and restore this 16-by-24-foot frame building, now used as restrooms. Friends of the Cumbres & Toltec assisted with labor. The bunkhouse, coal house, and turntable once nearby are all gone, but the old water tower still crowns the horizon. This depot is inspected and often photographed by rail buffs who stop for lunch at Osier while riding the highest and longest U.S. narrow-gauge steam passenger train.

Otis

SCHLIESFSKY'S DIME STORE BUILDING
206 N. Washington St. (SR)
Built: 1915; W. J. Kilpatrick, builder

The Town of Otis received $24,315 from the SHF and contributed a cash match of $8,380 to restore the exterior and the pressed-tin ceiling inside this old-fashioned

nickel-and-dime store, which had suffered from a leaking roof. Originally built as a false-front, two-story clapboard commercial building, it served as a store and community hall. Schliesfsky purchased the property in 1936 and opened a "dime store." The historic building is now used as a senior center. The metal ceiling is one of the more ornate examples in Colorado, and has been beautifully repainted. Many other buildings in Otis have benefited from the SHF, including the Hoopes Drug Store building (shown in after photo) on the corner next to Schliesfsky's, as well as buildings along Washington Street on the other side of CO 34.

Ouray

Ouray is one of Colorado's best-preserved, most picturesque mountain mining towns. An active Ouray County Historical Society has gained local landmark designation for many sites in town as well as around the county. A National Register Historic District encompasses most of the town between Oak and 5th Streets and 3rd to 8th Avenues. The town's major preservation battle ended in 2004 when the Beaumont Hotel, the town's

Photo courtesy of Tom Noel

crowning achievement, was rescued from decades of neglect and restored to glory as a luxury hotel. Many other local landmarks have been restored and rehabilitated with the help of the SHF, which has also aided a coalition striving to save the adjacent and endangered Red Mountain Mining District.

ELKS LODGE No. 492
421 Main St. NRD
Built: 1905, E. H. Powell, designer; W. A. Reynolds and Gustave E. Kullerstrand, builders

After raising an $18,000 match from local members, a community support fund, and the Zanett Foundation, the Benevolent Protectorate of Elks of Ouray was awarded $30,000 from the SHF for exterior restoration of its two-story lodge. SHF funds were used to repair bricks, mortar, stone, and roofing. Additionally, the SHF helped to restore the building's windows and woodwork. This elaborate edifice of polished blond brick features a hexagonal, capped corner tower rising into an Art Nouveau finial bouquet. Second Empire dormers punctuate the mansard roof, and elaborate brick courses double as trim for the Italianate windows. Inside are an antique two-lane bowling alley, billiards hall, banquet room, and a 35-by-60-foot lodge hall. Virtually unchanged inside and out, the Elks Lodge is a stately monument to one of the fraternal orders that became surrogate families for single miners.

MASONIC LODGE No. 37 / HESS BLOCK
541–545 Main St. LL NRD
Built: 1893; John J. Huddart, architect

Ouray Masonic Lodge No. 37 used $5,000 from the SHF for preliminary stabilization and beginning restoration of the two-story, red-brick Romanesque Revival building. Constructed by Theodore Hess as the Hess Block, it housed a billiards hall, saloon, barbershop, and dry goods downstairs, with the Masonic Lodge upstairs. In more recent years, the building housed the Ouray Hotel. Ornate brickwork, exemplified by the round arches framing second-story windows, and an elaborate cornice distinguish this business block.

OURAY COUNTY COURTHOUSE AND JAIL
541 4th St., southeast corner of 6th Ave. LL NRD
Built: 1889; Frank E. Edbrooke, architect

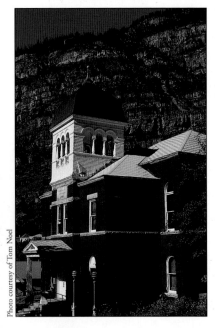

Photo courtesy of Tom Noel

Ouray County has begun restoration of its grand courthouse, complete with jail and elegant upstairs courtroom, thanks to the help of $261,604 from the SHF. Funds have been used to thoroughly assess the condition of the building, to restore the windows, and to create construction documents that will be used to guide the interior and exterior restoration project. A third-story tower above the entry portico is the building's main attraction. Its large, square belfry has triple round-arched openings beneath a bell-shaped roof topped by a ball finial. Charming inside and out, this old-time courthouse retains many original fixtures, including a jury box equipped with rocking chairs. Courtroom spectators may sit in one of 150 cast-iron chairs that once accommodated townsfolk who, before the days of television and radio, would entertain themselves by watching trials—or would watch courtroom drama when shopping for a lawyer.

RED MOUNTAIN MINING DISTRICT
Between Ouray and Silverton along US 550
Built: 1882–1893

The picturesque ghost towns of Red Mountain are still rich in head frames, jails, shacks, and boarding houses, and the surrounding Red Mountain Mining District is studded with landmarks such as the Joker Boarding House, the Longfellow Mine, the Genessee-Vanderbilt Mine buildings, and the ghost towns of Ironton and Guston.

Photo courtesy of Tom Noel

Now known as one of the major preservation battlegrounds in America, the Red Mountain mining district first became famous between 1882 and the silver crash of 1893 as one of the country's biggest silver producers. To save the mining relics from development, which are major tourist attractions, a broad coalition of preservationists, along with the Idarado Mining Company, Colorado Preservation, Inc., former U.S. senator Ben Nighthorse Campbell, the Ouray and San Juan County commissioners and their Historical Societies, the U.S. Forest Service, the Trust for Public Lands, the National Trust for Historic Preservation, and the Colorado Historical Society, have gathered to form the Red Mountain Task Force. The SHF has contributed $26,000 to restore and interpret mining sites and another $50,000 to the Task Force to purchase and protect 10,500 acres in the heart of the Red Mountain Mining District.

SILVER LEDGE MINE
20 miles south of Ouray along US 550
Built: c. 1885

The Ouray County Historical Society used $30,000 from the SHF to help restore one of the Red Mountain Mining District's finest surviving mineshaft head frames, complete with its pulley wheel. An 1883 discovery on the headwaters of Mineral Creek gave birth to the Silver Ledge Mine a mile south of Red Mountain City. When the Silver Ledge proved profitable, the owner built a mill and an office building on the site, and the town of Chattanooga sprang up nearby. Visible from US 550 and accessible by a half-mile trail starting in the ghost town of Chattanooga, the Silver Ledge is now a striking testament to the region's mining era.

St. JOSEPH'S MINERS' HOSPITAL / OURAY COUNTY
MUSEUM
420 6th Ave. LL
Built: 1887; Francis Carney, builder

The Ouray County Historical Society received $6,306 from the SHF for a museum fire, safety, and security upgrade. The community held a matching drive reminiscent of the original 1880s campaign in which editor David Day of Ouray's celebrated newspaper, the *Solid Muldoon*, raised $5,000 and St. Patrick's Catholic Church next door provided the site for this hospital. Frank Carney, a leading local stone- and brickmason, used large, rough-faced blocks from nearby Limestone Hill to erect a sturdy, two-story Italianate building with a full basement.

Inside, Mother Mary Michael Cummings and her Sisters of Mercy offered both spiritual as well as physical care, redirecting heavenward the soul of many a hardened unholy miner. Originally called the Miners' Hospital, it was renamed St. Joseph's. After the Sisters left it in 1920, it was Dr. Carl V. Bates' private hospital until 1945, when the Idarado Mining Company began operating it again as a miners' hospital. The Ouray County Historical Society purchased it in 1976 and converted it into a museum. Three floors and 27 rooms house exhibits devoted to medical, mining, and local history. Two rough-hewn log cabins have been transplanted to the museum grounds. Ouray tour guide and county commissioner Alan Staehle, who helped oversee the project, says that fire and safety upgrades were essential to protect the archives, including "some 6,000 original photos, 160,000 paper records, and a priceless collection of Colorado minerals."

WESTERN HOTEL
210 7th Ave., northeast corner of 2nd St. [LL]
Built: 1891; Francis Carney, builder

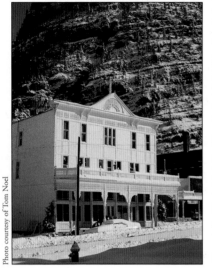

Photo courtesy of Tom Noel

A 1995 SHF grant of $20,000 supported the Ouray County Historical Society in restoring the exterior of this three-story frame hotel. The expansive plate-glass storefront has elongated transoms and ornate sidelights illuminating the old-time saloon and dining hall. The hotel became a home for many miners, while tourists gravitated over to the more elegant Beaumont. Maria "Ma" Flor, who operated the hotel from 1916 to 1961, welcomed the poorest and sickest miners and would never let anyone leave hungry. Later used as a museum and a Jeep rental business, the Western reopened in 1982 as a 50-room hotel with a vintage first-floor restaurant and saloon. The latter is a veritable museum of Old West art and artifacts, that includes a 140-pound female mountain lion stalking prey atop the bar.

WRIGHT OPERA HOUSE
480 Main St. [LL] [NRD]
Built: 1888; Francis Carney, builder

Ouray's opera house has an ornate two-story, cast-iron storefront, a design that was patented in 1887 by Mesker Brothers of St. Louis, incorporating Corinthian pilasters, a stained-glass transom window, cornice, and pediment. The elaborate design typifies the tendency throughout America at the time to combine machine-age technology with classical ornamentation. Edward Wright, part owner of the Wheel of Fortune Mine, commissioned the opera house during Ouray's flush times. First-floor stores helped support the second-floor opera hall.

The opera house has had many uses, including the Arps Brothers Hardware Store, a community center, and the high school's auditorium and basketball court.

In more recent decades, it has housed the General Ore Reduction Company, as well as a garage and a Jeep rental. Its back wall was replaced with cinder-block, a faux-rustic log façade was tacked onto the front, and cellulose insulation was applied to the walls and ceiling. Current owner Larry Leeper, in partnership with the Ouray County Historical Society, removed the "improvements" and "modernizations" to restore the exterior. He also restored the stairwell, carpentry, tin, and ironwork on the building's interior, assisted by $53,020 from the SHF.

Pagosa Springs

CHIMNEY ROCK ARCHAEOLOGICAL AREA
West of Pagosa Springs, 3 miles south of US 160 on CO 151 [NR]
c. 925–1125

Two giant stone pinnacles, as well as a modern fire lookout tower, make this spectacular site easy to find. This northeastern outpost of the Chacoan culture, once occupied by an estimated 2,000 people, has a 35-room Great House, Ridge House, and Great Kiva. Among more than 200 structures are 91 residences and 27 work camps on or just below a mesa top 1,200 feet above the Piedra River. After constructing this stone city during the 10th century, the residents, like the nearby Mesa Verdeans, abandoned it.

The first legitimate excavations were conducted in 1921. University of Colorado astro-archaeologist J. McKim Malville believes the site, which is the centerpiece of the six-square-mile Chimney Rock Archaeological Area in San Juan National Forest, is geared to lunar activity. Forest Service and Chimney Rock Interpretive Association staff and volunteers offer tours of the site and its hiking trails, fire tower, and stabilized pueblo structures. To assist the Forest Service, the Chimney Rock Interpretive Association, and the San Juan Mountain Association, the SHF contributed $50,225 to survey, document, and interpret the site, including a three-dimensional, virtual-environment tour of the magical place.

P

Paonia

CURTIS HARDWARE COMPANY / BLUE SAGE CENTER FOR THE ARTS
228 Grand Ave. NR
Built: 1902; Sidney Curtis, builder

Blue Sage, which owns and operates this building, was awarded grants of $115,222 from the SHF to pursue plans to restore the exterior, rehabilitate the high pressed-metal ceiling interior with new wiring and heating, stabilize the brick walls, and restore the front door. Originally, horses and wagons delivered the bracketed metal cornice with its central arched pediment and the cast-iron storefront, which features bay windows framed in engaged Doric columns. Embossed metal panels with classical urn designs, a fleur-de-lis first-story frieze, and other classical ornaments adorn the façade.

A hardware store occupied the first floor until 1987, after which the building's reincarnation as a performing-arts center began. According to general contractor Mose Oppenheimer, "Support for this project could not have happened if Paonia was not already a haven for artists, poets, and writers." These folks are keeping the building alive, with storytelling and children's activities as well as yoga, art, and music classes.

Parker

RUTH MEMORIAL METHODIST EPISCOPAL CHURCH / RUTH MEMORIAL CHAPEL
19670 E. Main St. LL NR
Built: 1913; William Holmes, builder

The Town of Parker matched $63,042 from the SHF for restoration of Parker's first church. George Parker donated the land, and Walter Heath, superintendent of Douglas County Schools, gave $1,000 for construction of a church named for his daughter, Ruth, who died at a young age. This Gothic Revival clapboard church, tended by Father John Dyer and other circuit-riding clergymen, has also served as a community center, library, and school. Now owned by the Town of Parker, the church is receiving interior and exterior restoration, including mold and lead-paint abatement and window and floor repair. The church is available for weddings, meetings, and other events.

SEVENTEEN MILE HOUSE
8181 S. Parker Rd. (CO 83) NR
Built: c. 1870; 1874 and 1880s additions

One of only two surviving Colorado mile houses, Seventeen Mile House sits amid one of the state's fastest growing suburban areas. Located 17 miles from downtown Denver, it was one of the pioneer way stations on the trail into the big city. Back in the 1870s, this may have been the only building in sight when Susan and Nelson Doud moved into what was then a small clapboard cabin. They and their five daughters catered to travelers passing by on the Smoky Hill and Cherokee Trails, which followed Cherry Creek to their front door. Built as a one-story, two-room log cabin, it later received an 1874 addition by the Douds on the south side.

Both photos courtesy of Tom Noel

George F. Cummings bought the house from the Douds in 1881 and owned it until 1906. He added the second story and rear bunkhouse during the 1880s.

While passengers refreshed themselves in the Seventeen Mile House, their horses were watered and fed outside. By 1882, completion of the Denver & New Orleans Railroad ended the need for rest stops such as this. From the 1880s to the 1980s, the old stop became a working farm, where ditches off Cherry Creek helped grow alfalfa, barley, corn, and wheat, as well as apple, pear, and cherry trees.

Fans of the Seventeen Mile House have battled for decades to fend off various proposals to develop the property and either demolish or move the structures to another site. In 1984, the Colorado Historical Foundation obtained a façade easement and open-space arrangement to protect the main building and the area around it. Development was further staved off by a remarkable coalition consisting of Arapahoe County commissioner Marie MacKenzie, planners Jennifer Drybread and Julio Iturreria, and Woody Beardsley of the Trust for Public Lands. Arapahoe ($1 million) and Douglas Counties ($500,000), the Town of Parker ($500,000) and City of Aurora ($25,000), Great Outdoors Colorado ($325,000), Urban Drainage ($100,000), and the Gates Family Foundation ($125,000) joined in a coalition organized by the Trust for Public Lands ($50,000) that raised $3 million to buy the 34.75-acre Seventeen Mile site. The Town of Parker bought the adjacent 72-acre Norton Farms property for $1 million to save as additional adjacent open space. Another adjoining 120 acres were converted into additional open space by the Cottonwood Community Metropolitan District. Arapahoe County added the 35-acre Southcreek Open Space to what has become a 261-acre buffer on the south and east sides of the Seventeen Mile House. The Friends of Seventeen Mile House coalition, encouraged by $135,000 in grants from the SHF, plans to restore the house, barn, silo, and other outbuildings. A reborn Seventeen Mile House and adjoining 261.37-acre nature preserve will save this souvenir of the 1860s gold rush.

P

TALLMAN-NEWLIN HOUSE
Callaway Rd. and Canterbury Trail LL SR
Built: 1866; John and ElizabethTallman, builders

Restored by the Parker Historical Society with the help of a $2,860 SHF grant, this relic retains an exposed section of the original hewn-log cabin, which had been covered around 1900 with wood siding. Relocated here in 1977 to avoid demolition, it is now restored as an exhibit of Colorado pioneer life and is owned by the Parker Area Historical Society, which obtained title in 1996. John and Elizabeth Tallman built this little three-room, L-plan home that was later occupied by William and Elizabeth Newlin, who lie in the tiny family cemetery next to the house. The only log cabin left in Parker, the Tallman-Newlin site is also memorialized in Elizabeth Tallman's essay on pioneer life in Douglas County, published in the July 1936 issue of *The Colorado Magazine.*

Pine

BAEHR DEN OF THE ROCKIES AT PINE VALLEY RANCH
16405 CO 126, 1 mile west of Pine SR
Built: 1927; Jules Jacques Benois Benedict, architect

William A. Baehr, owner of the Denver Ice and Cold Storage Company, became acquainted with this stretch of the South Platte River when he built one of his ice farms here. Enthralled with the beautiful river canyon with its ponderosa pines and fabulous rock formations, Baehr hired Jacques Benedict, the premier champion of Rocky Mountain Rustic–style architecture, to design this log-and-boulder lodge as his summer home. It later became the main building of the Pine Valley Ranch and, still later, a restaurant and special-events venue.

Jefferson County Open Space bought the lodge and 820-acre ranch in 1986 for $2.35 million as a recreational site, which now encompasses five nature trails and features interpretive exhibits. Open Space used a $15,000 SHF grant to plan reuse of the Baehr Den as a public facility. Built in 90 days by 60 craftsmen for $1.5 million, this 14,000-square-foot lodge of native stone and spruce logs has two hexagonal pavilions, massive stone chimneys, porches, and second-story balconies. It is the centerpiece of a complex that includes a barn, ice shed, observatory, pagoda, and teahouse.

Pingree Park

RAMSEY-KOENIG RANCH
16321 Pingree Park Rd. via CO 14 in Cache la Poudre Canyon (SR)
Built: 1919; Hugh Ramsey, builder

In 1893, the Ramseys homesteaded in what is still one of the least developed Front Range mountain valleys. They must have considered giving up when diphtheria, whooping cough, and other diseases kept taking their babies. Heartsick, they burned down their first family homestead house, hoping to incinerate the germs. A few years later, the family buried more children and burned their second homestead house. The tiny cemetery filled with little lamb tombstones stands up the hill from their 1919 frame house, the third try for Hugh Ramsey. The Ramsey's surviving daughter, Hazel, married Frank Koenig. Fearing her ranch might be subdivided, Hazel Koenig sold it to Colorado State University in 1974. She had found CSU to be a good neighbor ever since 1913, when it opened its 1,300-acre Pingree Park Campus as a center for forestry, natural resources, and wildlife biology students. Today that campus is run by Professor William J. Bertschy, a fifth-generation Coloradan. Bertschy says that "thanks to $195,025 from the SHF and our matching funds, we restored the ranch, installed interpretive signs, and plan to turn this homestead house into a museum."

Pitkin

TOWN HALL
400 4th St. (SR)
Built: c. 1900; Fred G. Zugelder and
   William H. Ender, builders

Receiving $70,722 in grants from the SHF, the Pitkin Historical and Community Association did a showcase restoration of the old Town Hall, which now has a new roof and new foundation, a restored exterior, and a rehabilitated interior. The stone first floor, lap-sided second story, and open bell tower sparkle anew. Volunteers donated much of the labor to a space now used for town meetings, dances, and shows.

Pueblo

From atop the Colorado Fuel & Iron Company's handsome Mission Revival–style administration building is a bird's-eye view of dead and dying buildings of Colorado's greatest Industrial Age dinosaur. All four giant blast furnaces have been demolished for scrap metal. Fast disappearing are other traces of CF&I, once the state's largest employer, with 63 company towns scattered across the state.

Janet Boyd, founding director and secretary of the Bessemer Historical Society (BHS), is the third generation of an Italian immigrant family to work at CF&I, now Rocky Mountain Steel Mills. Boyd says, "Because CF&I owned so much, built so much, and has records that many communities have lost, I knew we had to save at least the company archives."

In Pueblo's Bessemer neighborhood, the BHS was conceived. "Since our incorporation in 2001," reports BHS executive director Maria Sanchez-Kennedy, "we've raised more than $1.4 million, enlisted almost 400 members, and are planning a cleanup and conversion of the administration building into an archives and museum."

With support from Rocky Mountain Steel, the University of Southern Colorado, the City and County of Pueblo, and SHF funds, the BHS is making Herculean efforts to save a piece of history about to vanish. With the CF&I Archives and Museum, future Coloradans may know why Pueblo was called the Pittsburgh of the West, producing much of the railroad track, barbed wire, mine drills, and nails that built the West. Pueblo is preserving not only relics of its steel mill but many other landmarks, as well as Pitkin Place and Union Avenue Historic Districts.

CENTRAL HIGH SCHOOL
431 E. Pitkin Ave. NR
Built: 1882; C. R. Manning, architect

After the new Central High School was completed in 1905, this Italianate two-story edifice of rough-faced, light pink rhyolite with Manitou sandstone trim became an elementary school. A central 80-foot bell tower is topped by a mansard roof with a pediment that mimics the main entry below it.

Scheduled for demolition in 1979, it was rescued and housed the Pueblo Ballet, Pueblo Symphony, and the Pueblo Junior League. The Pueblo Housing Authority bought the structure in 1994 and restored and renovated the school as apartment housing for low- and moderate-income families. The SHF's $100,000, with a $28,000 cash match from the city, renovated and restored the building's exterior, removed a 1950 addition, and reroofed the bell tower. Pueblo architect Gary Trujillo, who oversaw contractor BAV Construction, observes, "The SHF grants and staff are the greatest preservation tools we've ever had. Without the leverage from the SHF funds we couldn't have done this project or gotten tax credits."

Photo courtesy of Tom Noel

CF&I MINNEQUA WORKS OFFICE COMPLEX / STEELWORKS MUSEUM OF INDUSTRY & CULTURE
215 and 225 Canal St., northeast corner of Abriendo Ave. (SR)
Built: 1901; Frederick J. Sterner, architect, 1921 and 1926 additions

This Mission Revival–style complex with its distinctive curvilinear parapets and stucco walls includes the Colorado Fuel & Iron Company's 1901 office building and the 1902 dispensary next door. Company president John C. Osgood wanted a genteel architectural façade for his gritty steel business and brought in the prominent Denver and New York City architect Frederick J. Sterner to design it. The three-story office building features a four-story, domed roof tower and a red Spanish-style roof with curvilinear parapets at each end. Two prominent Pueblo architects were hired to design later additions that continued the Mission style. William W. Stickney designed the 1921 addition and Walter DeMordaunt the 1926 employment office addition to the single-story dispensary.

By the 1910s, CF&I, one of America's largest steel producers, governed some 7,000 employees who produced as much as 600,000 tons of steel annually. This industrial giant was fed by CF&I coal mines, limestone quarries, and coking plants produced in CF&I's many company towns. The CF&I archives building preserves records of the steel giant, which dominated the Pueblo region during the first half of the 20th century.

In the 1990s, Rocky Mountain Steel Mills Company purchased the former CF&I complex. It helped the Bessemer Historical Society use SHF grants totaling $534,300 to leverage $1.5 million to acquire and rehabilitate the CF&I Minnequa Works Office Complex. Contributors included El Pomar Foundation, the David and Lucille Packard Foundation, Boettcher Foundation, Energy Impact Assistance grants from the Colorado Department of Local Affairs, and private donations. The Bessemer Historical Society plans to use the former steel-industry office complex as a museum and archive, a western steel-arts design center and incubator for artists, and commercial office space.

Professor Jonathan Rees of the CSU Pueblo History Department writes, "The SHF is probably the most important among an extraordinary number of public and private partners who have helped the Bessemer Historical Society make great progress toward establishing a museum and archives at a time when [the building and records] are under constant threat of disappearing entirely."

P

COLORADO FUEL & IRON MINE RESCUE CAR No. 1
223 and 301 W. B St., Southwestern Colorado Heritage Center (SR)
Built: 1882; Webster Wagner Palace Sleeping Car Co., builder

Originally a sleeper equipped with 12 upper berths and a drawing room, this was one of six cars bought in 1910 by the U.S. Bureau of Mines as an educational and rapid-response rescue station. Its first rescue mission was the November 1910 Delagua mine disaster in Las Animas County. Between 1910 and 1923, this car was called into service at numerous Colorado coal-mining disasters, including Cokedale and Leyden. CF&I purchased the rescue car from the U.S. government in 1923 and renovated and re-equipped it before putting it back into service.

In 1941, CF&I converted it into an office and then placed it on a concrete foundation. In 1994, the Pueblo County Historical Society saved the mine rescue car from demolition. The Society also got SHF grants totaling $243,685 to help with the $373,000 interior and exterior restoration.

EL PUEBLO HISTORY MUSEUM AND ARCHAEOLOGICAL SITE
301 N. Union Ave. [NR]
Built: 1842, archaeological site; 2003, museum built

P

In 1842, mountain men built an adobe trading post where Fountain Creek meets the Arkansas River. They named it El Pueblo (Spanish for "the village"). This ancestor of the modern town of Pueblo was a hangout for frontier legends such as James P. Beckwourth, Kit Carson, Mariano Medina, and Richens L. "Uncle Dick" Wootten before it was abandoned in 1854 after Chief Tierra Blanco and his Ute band attacked on Christmas Eve and killed or captured all occupants.

To help recapture that history, the Colorado Historical Society's El Pueblo History Museum, next to the Fort Pueblo site, has local history exhibits, including a replica of the original one-story trading post. The City of Pueblo, the Colorado Historical Society, and the Friends of El Pueblo, Inc., have obtained $1,300,111 in grants from the SHF and a $112,000 Intermodal

Surface Transportation Efficiency Act federal grant to complete archaeological investigation and research, acquire an adjacent piece of property, and develop physical site improvements. Consulting archaeologist William Buckles, structural engineer Loren Kilsotofte, and tensile-structure design consultant Robert Tinney also collaborated on a protective year-round structure that covers this important, exposed archaeological site.

FIRST CONGREGATIONAL CHURCH
228 W. Evans Ave, southwest corner of Jackson St. [NR]
Built: 1889; Fred A. Hale and C. H. Stickney, architects

Pueblo's oldest continuously used church has a distinctive northwest corner entry bell tower, a circular transept with arched windows, and an apse with a row of Tiffany-style-stained-glass windows. The Pueblo *Colorado Chieftain* for October 3, 1889, described the Romanesque Revival–style church as "a regular gem in church architecture, complete and perfect in every aspect. . . . The walls are built of pink stone, cut to represent the natural fracture of the rock."

The SHF contributed $66,630 to the $107,604 cost of making the venerable structure accessible for the disabled, restoring the oak and wrought iron double-entry doors, replacing the protective covers over the Tiffany-style stained-glass windows, repairing the eroding foundation, and restoring and repointing the sandstone exterior. The cash match was secured with a $17,833 Community Development Block Grant and church-member donations. Today, the church also serves as a community center, polling place, and meeting place for the Girl Scouts and the Neighborhood Watch program.

GOODNIGHT BARN
4575 W. Thatcher Ave. (CO 96) [NR]
Built: 1870; Charles Goodnight, builder

P

Charles Goodnight was the "Chuck" of the cattle drive's chuck wagon fame, and he is also remembered for having established, with partner Oliver Loving, the Goodnight-Loving Trail that first brought numerous Texas longhorns to Colorado along a route roughly paralleling today's I-25. Between 1867 and 1890 an estimated 10 million cattle trudged this historic trail to stock the ranches and butcher shops of New Mexico, Colorado, Wyoming, and Montana. In 1869, Goodnight established a ranch along the trail east of the town of Pueblo for his cattle, fruit orchards, and vegetables. All that remains of Goodnight's pioneer Colorado agricultural center is this barn constructed of rough-cut local limestone blocks.

The barn made Colorado Preservation, Inc.'s "Most Endangered Places" list after Transit Mix Aggregates of Colorado purchased it in 1997. Preservationists persuaded the firm to spare the barn and even invest $10,000 in stabilization efforts. Subsequently, SHF contributed $228,140, with another $55,000 from the City of Pueblo and other funds from the County of Pueblo, Pueblo County Historical Society, Hudspeth Family Trust, and a Frontier Pathways National Scenic and Historic Byways grant. This enabled the City of Pueblo to acquire the barn and two acres of what was once the 100,000-acre Goodnight Ranch encompassing today's City Park. "We have stabilized and hope to restore the barn," says Pueblo preservationist George Williams, "as an interpretive site along the Frontier Pathways Scenic and Historic Byway and as part of the new entrance to Lake Pueblo State Park."

LINCOLN HOME / PUEBLO COLORED ORPHANAGE & OLD FOLKS HOME
2713–2715 N. Grand Ave. (SR)
Built: 1889 and 1904

This orphanage consists of two red-brick, one-and-a-half-story late Victorian homes built in 1889 and 1904 and connected by a passageway. From 1905 to 1963, this operated as Colorado's first Black orphanage and old-folks home. In 1993, the E. M.

Christmas Foundation donated the collection of buildings to the Pueblo Dr. Martin Luther King, Jr., Holiday Commission. It is being converted into a museum that exhibits the orphanage's history and artifacts, Pueblo's Black history, and the teachings of Dr. Martin Luther King, Jr.

The Holiday Commission captured a $105,775 SHF grant with $37,095 in personal donations to rehabilitate the exterior and interior and to develop a museum exhibit plan. The project received more than $200,000 in community funding and in-kind donations. Architect John C. Hurtig directed the contractors (Cortez Construction Company), architects Andrews & Anderson, and landscape architect Don Claussen. In 1999, the commission received the "Making of the King Holiday" award from Coretta Scott King, who came to Pueblo to help open the museum. Director Ruth Steele reports that the museum showcases the Martin Luther King, Jr., statue that formerly stood in Denver's City Park. Steele notes that "the SHF grant and their technical assistance was outstanding in helping us to save the first colored orphanage in the Rocky Mountain region. Our future plans include adding a multicultural center."

McCLELLAND ORPHANAGE / THE McCLELLAND SCHOOL
415 E. Abriendo Ave. NR
Built: 1935; Walter DeMordaunt, architect

Andrew McClelland, who parlayed Pueblo real estate into a fortune, and his wife, Columbia, donated this Georgian Revival complex as an orphanage. The McClelland School, current owner and operator of the orphanage, obtained a SHF grant of $99,900 for a $184,132 restoration and rehabilitation of the original carriage house as a middle school. Project architect Gary Trujillo notes, "Without the SHF grant, the restoration would not have been done. It would have sat there underutilized and eventually neglected."

PUEBLO CITY PARK ZOO
3455 Nuckolls Ave. NR NRD
Built: 1933–1940; Civil Works Administration, National Youth
    Administration, Public Works Administration, and Works
    Progress Administration

On a 25-acre site in Pueblo City Park, New Deal–era craftsmen built this state-of-the-art zoological garden. The structures, made of sandstone, present a unique expression of the American Rustic movement. The exotic stone and unusual style are typified in the 6,000-square-foot Animal House with two large wings and a hexagonal central atrium with reflecting pool and seal fountain. Concrete animal sculptures climb and cavort atop the cupola, on the drinking fountain, and in bas-relief trees and vines within the 17 cages. Unemployed men, trained by the WPA as artisans by making sand sculptures along the Arkansas River, were hired to design and construct the sculptures and other artistic details.

P

    In 1999, the Animal House and much of the rest of the zoo were to be mothballed due to maintenance and safety problems. The Pueblo Zoological Society promptly undertook restoration and rehabilitation, securing an SHF grant of $343,425, another $88,316 from the City of Pueblo, and $4.3 million from the David and Lucille Packard, Thatcher, and Chamberlain Foundations.

    Jonnene McFarland, executive director of the Pueblo Zoological Society, beams with pride when discussing this major preservation project. "The SHF's grant and their technical assistance helped us with everything from National Register designation to master planning to specific plans and rehabilitation. The Animal House and Monkey Island will become an 'Islands of Life' exhibit featuring animals from isolated habitats around the world. In the future, the historic Monkey Mountain will be rehabilitated, and the historic Bear Pits will again house animals."

RIO GRANDE WESTERN FREIGHT HOUSE / SOUTHEASTERN COLORADO HERITAGE CENTER
223 and 301 W. B St. (SR)
Built: 1924; Denver & Rio Grande Western Railroad, builder

Pueblo's sole remaining freight station is a two-story, red-brick building with a stepped parapet located across B St. from Union Depot. Owned since 1994 by the City of Pueblo, it is managed and occupied by the Southeastern Colorado Heritage Center. SHF grants of $330,000 expedited a three-year, $1.2 million restoration for reuse as a regional museum. Major financial contributors to the project were the City of Pueblo, the County of Pueblo, and the Union Pacific Foundation. Genova Construction, among others, restored and rehabilitated the building into museum offices, a conference room, public restrooms, a research library, and museum exhibits.

P

ROOD CANDY COMPANY / APARTMENTS
408–416 W. 7th St. [NR]
Built: 1909

This three-story, red-brick manufacturing facility for the Rood Candy Company is the only survivor of what was a four-building complex. A leading candy manufacturer between 1900 and 1940, Rood employed hundreds and sold sweets throughout the West. The firm popularized candy punchboards as an advertising tool, with lucky-number winners receiving a five-pound box of chocolates. Rood ran out of luck during the Depression, when the company closed.

During World War II, Pueblo Junior College housed vocational and technical education programs here for war production. Afterward the structure went through a series of ownerships and various uses. In 1997, it was serving as a storage facility for Parkview Hospital and School District No. 60 when it was purchased by the Housing Authority of the City of Pueblo (PHA).

To convert the interior into residences, the PHA and the El Centro Pueblo Development Corporation arranged loans from the local Minnequa National Bank and the Colorado Division of Housing, and raised another $2.6 million through tax credits. The SHF provided $150,000 to fund masonry, door, and window restoration to enhance this $3,450,841 project. The former home of southern Colorado's biggest candy maker has now been reborn as subsidized loft-style apartment housing for low- and moderate-income families and individuals.

ROSEMOUNT (THATCHER) MANSION
419 W. 14th St., between Grand Ave. and Cottonwood St. [NR]
Built: 1891–1893; Henry Hudson Holly, architect

P

Commanding an entire square block on a hillside, Rosemount is a magnificent late Victorian mansion built by John A. and Margaret Henry Thatcher. John came to Colorado in 1863 where he started a general store in Pueblo. He and his brother Mahlon established the First National Bank of Pueblo in 1871, built retail stores, and invested in large tracts of land in Colorado and New Mexico for their cattle business.

Thatcher's three-story, 24,000-square-foot residence, where his family lived until 1963, is a brick building faced with rough, rose-colored rhyolite

Photo courtesy of Tom Noel

and accented by smooth stone stringcourses. The red Vermont slate roof is hipped, gabled, and detailed with eyebrow dormers, a dentiled cornice, and columned chimneys serving 10 fireplaces. The veranda has golden-oak ceilings and is accessible from inside through 10-foot-high windows.

In 1967, the mansion was donated to Pueblo for use as a house museum. The Rosemount Victorian House Museum, Inc., matched a 1993 SHF grant for $50,000 toward the $187,870 reinstallation of the historic Victorian landscaping and site interpretation development. The cash match was obtained with community block grants and Chamberlain and Jackson Foundation grants. Labor was donated by the Pueblo City Parks and Recreation Department. Under the watchful eyes of Long-Hoeft Architects and architect Gary Trujillo, City Parks workers, Don's Landscaping, and landscape architect Tina Bishop transformed the grounds. Rosemount Museum executive director Deb Darrow says, "The gardens of the Thatcher home were as important to Margaret and John Thatcher as the interior. She named the house for her rose gardens, which once again grace the grounds."

SANTA FE LOCOMOTIVE No. 2912
B St. and Victoria Ave., behind Union Station (SR)
Built: 1944; Baldwin Locomotive Co., builder

Santa Fe No. 2912, a standard-gauge, oil-burning steam locomotive, pulled passenger freight trains in southeastern Colorado until the early 1950s. This was one of the largest and heaviest steam locomotives ever built in the United States. The 4-8-4 locomotive weighed 488 tons and was capable of speeds of 100 miles per hour on the straightaway pulling a string of 15 passenger cars.

As diesel power replaced steam in the early 1950s, Santa Fe's steam power moved into retirement. No. 2912 made its last freight run in August 1955, after which the Santa Fe Railroad donated it to the City of Pueblo. It was originally displayed at Elizabeth Street and Union Avenue, across from Pueblo City Hall, but it was moved later to the Pueblo Union Depot.

Pueblo Locomotive and Rail Historical Society members have volunteered an enormous amount of labor and materials to revive this industrial behemoth. They received SHF grants of $99,375 toward the $124,500 needed to restore the exterior and steam appliances. Restoration engineer Bernie Watts oversaw the project, with

Renovation and Demolition Environmental Services, Inc., removing the asbestos and "Q" Machine Company performing the mechanical work on the boiler and cab. The major steam appliances were rebuilt, and today the locomotive, awaiting restoration, sits as a grand sentinel of the steam age and as a grand centerpiece of Pueblo's Southeastern Colorado Heritage Center.

TEMPLE EMANUEL
1325 N. Grand Ave. NR
Built: 1900; Jacob M. Gile, architect

This one-story, red-brick synagogue was dedicated with the help of former Colorado governor Alva Adams and Dr. E. G. Hirsh, a well-known scholar and rabbi from Chicago. Distinctive twin turrets flank the pedimented entry on a structure with flared eaves, gabled dormers, stained glass, and elliptical windows. The Reform Jewish synagogue matched an SHF grant of $157,269 to complete the $217,000 rehabilitation of the interior and exterior. Contractor BAV Construction supervised myriad subcontractors, including Seamless Gutters and Siding, MacIndoe Plumbing, Pueblo Window and Door for the tempered-glass overlay, Eye Dream Designs for releading the stained glass, Schrock Electric, and R&R Heating. Architect Gary Trujillo notes, "It was extremely important to stabilize the exterior, fix the drainage, then patch and paint. Without the SHF, we would probably have lost this temple."

YOUNG WOMEN'S CHRISTIAN ASSOCIATION BUILDING
801 N. Santa Fe Ave., northwest corner of 8th St. NR
Built: 1935; Walter DeMordaunt, architect

YWCA development director Liz Grutt reports that "the State Historical Fund enabled us to revive a landmark that is not only a significant glimpse into the past, but is also a shelter for homeless women and domestic-violence victims and their children."

This Mission Revival villa has a prominent four-story corner tower and sturdy, 14-inch masonry walls faced with stucco. Inside are original oak woodwork, wrought-iron fixtures, red-tile floors, a fireplace, and a swimming pool. The YWCA of Pueblo utilized $179,719 in SHF funds to help leverage more than $1 million in Packard and Coors Foundation and Pueblo City grants, Colorado Lottery funds, and donations. YWCA director Diane Porter stresses, "Colorado Historical Society staff members Joseph Bell and Holly Wilson made this project possible." Today, the YWCA houses a wide array of programs ranging from a Family Crisis Shelter to warm-water aquatics.

P

Rangely

CHEVRON CAMP HOUSE / RANGELY OUTDOOR MUSEUM
500 Kennedy Dr. at CO 64 [LL]
Built: c. 1948

This 760-square-foot cottage is a rare relic of the 1940s-era Rangely Oil Field boom. The Montgomery Ward company prefabricated this two-bedroom house, which was then installed by Chevron Oil Company over a cement basement. Some of the earliest Colorado oil wells were drilled here around 1900, but the big boom came after World War II, when thousands of people descended upon Rangely Oil Field. Most oil workers lived in tents without running water or sewer systems until the oil companies finally built camps like this one for their workers.

The Chevron camp closed its doors in 1987 and then deeded the house and recreation hall to the Rangely Outdoor Museum. With financial assistance from Chevron, the town, and Rio Blanco County, this camp house was moved to the museum site provided by the town. Sharon Wardell, the director of the Rangely Outdoor Museum, notes that, once the building was moved and designated, "we used $39,550 in grant funds from the SHF to make basic repairs. We hope to do a full restoration," including period furnishings. Together with the Chevron Recreation Center, also moved to the museum grounds, this camp house is a rare survivor of the once ubiquitous worker houses that were rented for $10 to $18 a month.

Rico

OLD DOLORES COUNTY COURTHOUSE / RICO TOWN HALL
2 N. Commercial St. and Mantz St. [NR]
Built: 1893

The SHF has invested $526,246 to help restore the exterior and complete a planned upgrade to the mechanical systems of this two-story, pressed-brick courthouse. The building has a basement red-sandstone that still contains the original jail. Its brick walls are trimmed with red-sandstone from the local Cutler Quarry, and the central entry is distinguished by a protruding square tower flanked by hipped dormers.

R

Constructed during Rico's bonanza mining days, the courthouse symbolized Rico's highest hopes. Originally built as the county courthouse, the building became the Rico Town Hall and library after the county seat moved to the town of Dolores. The courthouse, like the town itself, faltered after the silver crash. Heavy snow loads and years of neglect damaged the roof and strained the bearing walls. Ice and water damaged the building inside and out. The south wall of the building had buckled badly and by the 1980s was near collapse.

In the early 1990s, the town partnered with the SHF to save the grand old building. SHF funds went toward repairing the walls, restoring the roof, securing the sandstone entry steps for safety, and upgrading all of the building's mechanical systems. Once the restoration of the exterior is completed, preservationist Fritz Klinke and his partner Loren Lew, as well as William Grande, hope to work with the town to focus attention on the interior, where a leaky roof has damaged the plaster and the wood trim.

Ridgway

SHERBINO THEATER / SHERBINO PERFORMING ARTS CENTER

604–606 Clinton St., southwest corner of N. Cora Ave. (SR)
Built: 1915; Gustave A. Kullerstrand, builder

Louis Sherbino, a native of Montreal, Quebec, celebrated his success as a mining magnate by erecting this one-story brick theater with a large corner entrance. Opened as a movie theater, it also housed dances, school plays, a roller-skating rink, and community gatherings. For the filming of the 1968 John Wayne movie *True Grit*, the theater was given a covered wooden sidewalk. Owner Richard E. Fike, a Montrose archaeologist and historian, restored this theater with $150,578 in SHF grants. Fike provided a $24,524 match, volunteer labor, and artifacts for exhibits. "The Sherbino Theater," says Fike, "was a joint effort with SHF, the Ridgway Historic District Preservation Committee, Ouray County, the Ridgway Community, and the Ouray County Historical Society. Julie Coleman ably wrote the grants and administered the project." Reborn as the Sherbino Performing Arts Center, it has been restored, including the stage and the stained-glass windows, and reopened for community events, live bands, and theater productions.

R

Rocky Ford

CARNEGIE PUBLIC LIBRARY / ROCKY FORD HISTORICAL MUSEUM
1005 Sycamore St., between 10th St. and 11th St. [NR]
Built: 1909; Walter Dubree, architect

This single-story Greek Revival design on a raised basement of rough-faced, cast-stone block sports a cornice supported by pairs of wooden Doric columns. A total of $146,284 in SHF grants helped with a $200,000 project to replace the roof, repair

timeworn bricks and stone blocks, and restore and rehabilitate the interior. "Repairing the roof was crucial to preventing further interior water damage," says Rocky Ford city administrator Gregg Bar. "The SHF grant for the exterior restoration freed financial resources for restoring windows and their frames and fixing up the basement of what has been, since 1976, called our Rocky Ford Historical Museum."

Restoration architect Dennis Humphries reflects, "The former Carnegie library sat in the middle of the town park, like a heavily tarnished jewel in a dirtied display case. The restoration opened shuttered windows, cleaned the stone cladding, enhanced the interior lighting and finishes, replaced monumental entry stairs, and allowed access for the physically impaired." The building now proudly invites everyone to see the treasures of the Rocky Ford Historical Museum.

R

GRAND THEATER
405 S. Main St. (SR)
Built: 1935; J. C. Moresi, architect

This two-story brick theater was constructed on the site of the original 1901 Grand Opera House, which had been destroyed by fire. The new Grand featured a Mission-style stuccoed façade. The theater's Art Deco interior allowed Depression-weary Rocky Ford–area residents a respite from economic hard times. In 1950, the exterior and lobby were modernized with the addition of a large marquee and the application of colored glazed tile.

After the theater closed in 1986, Grand Theater restoration project coordinator Mike Shima notes, "The City of Rocky Ford purchased the local landmark from United Artists back in 1991. The Grand now screens weekend family movies and showcases local plays and live-music performances. The SHF technical staff was extremely helpful to us in saving our small community theater." SHF grants provided $24,000 toward the more than $35,000 needed to refurbish the marquee and restore the glazed tiles. The Grand Theater's reincarnation guarantees Rocky Ford a cultural focal point for the future.

Dennis Humphries of Humphries Poli Architects, who oversaw the project, reports, "Restoration focused on the Main Street façade and the neon-framed marquee. Through the generosity of the SHF, the marquee now proclaims events such as Melon Day Parade, held each August, with a brightly illuminated reminder." Rocky Ford citizens are now pursuing further restoration of the 813-seat theater, of which much of the original interior fixtures and seating remains intact.

Salida

NEW SHERMAN HOTEL
123 G St. NRD
Built: 1890; 1900 and 1920s additions

What started out as a Red Cross hospital in 1890 has changed functions several times and has seen both additions and neglect, culminating in a fire in 1999. The imposing red-brick structure, with its bracketed cornices, double-hung windows, and contrasting limestone lintels, anchors the western edge of the Salida Downtown Historic District. New owner Thomas Sundheim raised $3,350 to match a $10,000 SHF grant to the Heart of the Rockies Chamber of Commerce to help salvage the mansard roof in danger of collapse. The old frame rafters were sistered with new material to improve load-bearing, and plastic sheeting was installed to reinforce the original tin roof. Restored as small, inexpensive apartments, the New Sherman still sports its vintage, restored purple neon "Rooms" sign, complete with yellow hand pointing to the front door. In the beginning, miners and railroad workers roomed here; now it houses service workers, retirees, and young rafters and skiers.

R

S

SALIDA PUBLIC LIBRARY
405 E St. at 4th Ave. (SR)
Built: 1908; Thomas C. MacLaren and Charles E. Thomas, architects

Photo courtesy of Tom Noel

"Libraries are the best thing towns do for kids," says Salida scribe Ed Quillen, a noted *Denver Post* columnist. "I can't imagine life without a library," adds his wife, Martha. Thanks to such supporters, librarian Jeff Donlan reports, "Salida voters strongly approved by a two-to-one vote a $580,000 bond issue in 1996 for expansion and restoration. To help raise another $720,000, we received generous support from both the Boettcher and El Pomar Foundations and raised $180,000 on our own through garage sales, art auctions, and hike and bike races. We also sold hundreds of library tee shirts." The library strapped an eight-foot-high thermometer to the front of the building to dramatize the campaign. The Tuesday Evening Club, the women's club behind the original 1908 Carnegie library, helped get them over the top. A grant of $26,085 from the SHF helped Salida to restore its old Carnegie landmark, whose initial Neoclassical façade and distinctive entry pediment are echoed in the new addition.

SALIDA STEAM PLANT / STEAM PLANT THEATER
PERFORMING ARTS CENTER
312 W. Sackett St. [NRD] (SR)
Built: 1887

Photo courtesy of Tom No

Opened as the Edison Electric Light Plant, this brick structure beside the Arkansas River produced electricity by using steam, created from river water, to drive generators and turbines. The coal-fired plant, fed by a Denver & Rio Grande spur line, provided electrical power to the Salida region. Closed in 1958, the plant sat idle until its rebirth as an arts and cultural complex. Sited on the northern edge of the Salida Downtown Historic District and along the riverside path and whitewater park, the reincarnated powerhouse now showcases an innovative outdoor sculpture garden. SHF grants totaling $264,000 were matched by $298,282 from the owner (the City of Salida), the

S

operator (the Salida Steam Plant Council), and the Boettcher, Coors, Gates, and El Pomar Foundations.

Work started with rehabilitation of the corrugated-metal roof and the mechanical systems. Scott Hahn, the city manager of Salida, notes that the building was structurally sound even after many years of hard use. One of

the greatest challenges was the plant's "Pigeon Room," whose persistent avian residents had to be evicted so their former haunt could be cleaned, rehabilitated, and pigeon-proofed for use as a community-events space. The exterior brickwork was repointed and repaired and the foundation was waterproofed with the latest in latex technology: a liquid, cold-applied, elastometric waterproofing membrane system. The "Salida Steam Plant" lettering on the exterior red-brick walls peeks out underneath a later sign, "Public Service Company of Colorado," disclosing the plant's powerful past. More recently, the reincarnated complex has hosted melodramas, plays, dance classes, cowboy poetry readings, magic shows, weddings, lectures, and other special events.

METHODIST EPISCOPAL CHURCH / UNITED METHODIST CHURCH
246 E. 4th St. (SR)
Built: 1899

Through the efforts of preacher Father John Dyer, this congregation was founded in 1868 and by 1899 had moved into their new red-brick Gothic Revival church. Later, in the 1930s, a full basement was dug out by hand. Little has changed on the building and today many organizations use it for various events, including an annual Christmas dinner funded by local businesses. The structure needed preservation and the church raised $21,330 in matching funds to earn SHF grants totaling $96,000 to restore the interior and exterior. Restoration of the bell tower was a priority. The first seven courses of brick and a makeshift repair were removed and rebuilt. Staining from deteriorating sandstone was cleaned and the sandstone sills stabilized. A second project involved replacing the clouded plastic covering over the stained-glass windows. Since the windows had no religious images, SHF installed new safety-glass protection that allows the multicolored patterns to shine. The slab doors on the main entry distracted from the architectural integrity of the building. Replica doors were chosen to closely match the originals. Today, visitors walk under a restored tower through more compatible doors and enjoy an interior awash with light shining through the clear window covers, including a reincarnated round transom window.

S

Salina

SALINA SCHOOLHOUSE
536 Gold Run Rd. [NR]
Built: 1875

Judge Hamilton, the town founder, saw Salina becoming a growing city like its mother city in Kansas. So this small mining town built this tiny frame edifice for its 18 children. The old-style blackboards and coat hooks survive, although the cast-iron stove did not. Salina restored the schoolhouse with the help of SHF's $38,602 grant and the Salina Community Association volunteers. Today, the bell in a restored tower rings again in this one-room schoolhouse, which is used as a community center for dances, daycare, garage sales, and public gatherings.

San Luis

COSTILLA COUNTY COURTHOUSE
Main St. and Gaspar St. [NRD]
Built: 1883; Farrington and Rucker, builders

Founded in 1851, San Luis is the oldest incorporated town in Colorado. This courthouse is one of the attractions of the Plaza de San Luis de la Culebra Historic

District, which encompasses the convent and church of the Most Precious Blood, many residences, and the town's commercial core. San Luis also boasts a Vega, a communal pasture, and the San Luis People's Ditch, Colorado's oldest operating water ditch. County commissioners initially specified that the single-story courthouse with an open bell tower be built "of Chicago lumber with good substantial adobe

Photo courtesy of Tom Noel

S

walls." But over the years, as the needs of the county grew, a variety of additions were constructed. As is frequently the case, these additions damaged and diminished the original adobe building. Eventually it became unsafe, as roofs leaked and saturated adobe walls crumbled. Some urged abandoning the building completely and moving county offices into a new building on the outskirts of town. Instead, Costilla County decided to remove the inappropriate additions and return the courthouse back to its historic appearance. The county has received SHF grants of $836,465 for stabilization and restoration of Colorado's only adobe courthouse. Proposed work includes removal of nonhistoric additions, stabilization of adobe walls, and major work on the roof, followed by reconstruction of wooden floors, new utilities, and repair and replication of the windows and doors. A partner in this project was the Colorado Department of Local Affairs, which contributed cash from the Energy and Mineral Impact Assistance Fund reparations from the Battle Mountain Gold Company for 1990s contamination of Rito Seco Creek, four miles upstream of San Luis. Costilla County provided nearly 6,000 adobe bricks for use in the project. Soon, the once shaky cupola again will crown the San Luis skyline, and the old courthouse will be the new location of the combined local courts.

Sargents

SARGENTS SCHOOLHOUSE
346 Hicks Ave., southeast corner of 1st St. (SR)
Built: 1924

After the school closed in 1960, this building continued to serve the tiny town of Sargents as a community center. The Upper Tomichi Historical & Community Association matched a $22,200 SHF grant for stabilization and restoration with $10,280 in cash and in-kind donations. This sturdy rose-brick schoolhouse has been maintained by volunteers who completed

plumbing, rewiring, and furnace work. They relied on the SHF funding to install a new roof and reinstall the 1924-style stage and curtain. The building now houses the town library. Inspired by the SHF help, the community is planning to rehabilitate the interior and the outdoor playground.

S

Sedalia

CHEROKEE CASTLE AND RANCH
6113 N. Daniels Park Rd., off US 85 LL NR
Built: 1924–1927; Burnham Hoyt, architect

Cherokee Ranch and its castle belonged to noted Colorado cowgirl Tweet Kimball, who died in 1999. Always a strong woman, she rules posthumously, having saved from subdividers her castle and most of her ranch, now reincarnated as a museum

and open space. The former executive director of the Cherokee Ranch and Castle Foundation Deborah Jordy helped to raise, with more than $348,000 in SHF support, almost half of the million dollars that was needed to restore one of Colorado's most fabulous and fabled ranches. This once again shining castle, a medieval apparition, overlooks Denver and the Front Range panorama from Longs Peak to Pikes Peak. Constructed of lava stone (rhyolite) quarried on-site or nearby, the castle rises out of a craggy hillside into slate roofs, gables, turrets, towers, and dragon gargoyles.

Photo courtesy of Tom Noel

The fairy-tale building began with Charles Alfred Johnson, a Denver real-estate agent who developed Denver's fashionable Park Hill neighborhood. The Johnsons hired noted Denver architect Burnham Hoyt to design and construct the lodge on a cliff 600 feet above Plum Creek and the tiny town of Sedalia. Johnson gave Hoyt carte blanche, so Hoyt modeled the design after a 15th-century Scottish castle and hired a crew of stonemasons to fashion building blocks from the local pink, maroon, gray, and buff rhyolite. After three years of construction, the 24-room castle opened with stone walls inside and out, high vaulted ceilings with carved wooden crosspieces, Romanesque arches, stone cornices, and leaded-glass windows with massive petrified-wood lintels.

In 1954, the Johnsons sold the ranch to Tweet Kimball. She raised her two sons on the estate and introduced to the ranch Santa Gertrudis cattle, a breed developed from American shorthorn and East Indian Brahmans on the King Ranch in Texas. The Cherokee still runs a show and breeding herd of around 100 of these distinctive, dark red cattle. Kimball sold all but 3,600 of the 10,000 acres to Jack Vickers, who developed Castle Pines, the adjacent upscale subdivision named for the castle. After her death, another 460 acres were sold off to cover legal fees and expenses of setting up the foundation.

S

Restoration, aided by $348,330 from the SHF, has focused on shoring up the south wall with 40-foot-deep, concrete-reinforced steel micro-piles (6-inch-diameter rods). Anchors and compression piles keep the castle standing. With its own funding, the foundation has restored the interior, which is now showcased on tours. The castle and nearly two dozen outbuildings on the site are also open for tea parties; naturalist, birding, and photography hikes; elk-bugling concerts; and special events.

St. PHILIP–IN–THE–FIELD EPISCOPAL CHURCH
5 miles south of Sedalia on Perry Park Rd. (CO 105) LL NR
Built: 1872; Newton S. Grout, builder

The oldest church in Douglas County is a shiplap Gothic Revival antique that Newton Grout, in his diary, says he built in two months using grocery boxes and planks for pews. Parishioners restored this miniature church inside and out with the help of $106,809 given by the SHF. Father Robert Walker, the pastor, was disconcerted to find—when the hardwood floor was being restored—a rat's nest under his pulpit. Many other critters and skeletons were found under the crawl space until a Jack Russell terrier was hired to roust out rodents still living under the church. The beautiful all-wood interior features a hand-carved altar, baptismal fount, oak pews, and vaulted beadwork ceiling. "We took St. Philip apart board by board," Father Walker recalls. "Thanks to the Colorado Historical Society's fund, we've restored the oldest church in Douglas County from its rhyolite foundation to its steeple-top Celtic cross. While it cost only $200 to build in 1872, it cost $200,000 to restore."

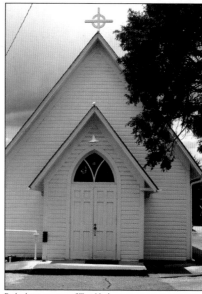

Both photos courtesy of Tom Noel

S

Silver Cliff

TOWN HALL AND FIRE HOUSE MUSEUM
606 Main St. (SR)
Built: 1882

The volunteer fire hose team stationed here fought two major fires to save Silver Cliff, but then needed saving itself. Their false-front, wood-frame hall has been rescued by SHF funds totaling $43,500, with other funding and services from the Town of Silver Cliff. The foundation, walls, windows, and façade, as well as some interior finishes, were restored. Susan B. Hutton, project administrator and clerk of Silver Cliff Chamber of Commerce, says this will enable the Silver Cliff Town Hall and Fire House to function better as the reborn Silver Cliff Museum. Prominently located next to the new town hall, this reincarnated gem recalls the silver age, when Silver Cliff shone as Colorado's third largest city.

Silver Plume

BLANTON HOUSE
461 Main St. **NHLD**
Built: 1884

People for Silver Plume, Inc., was awarded $21,500 from SHF to stabilize, preserve, and restore the façade on one of the few remaining two-story wooden buildings in the town's historic commercial district. It needed help, as it was leaning over the street propped up by a crossed brace pole.

GEORGETOWN LOOP RAILROAD
10 Mountain St. at I-70 **NHLD** **NR**
Built: 1884; Jacob Blickensderfer, engineer

The Georgetown Loop Railroad is a 1984 reconstruction of the famed Georgetown–Silver Plume narrow-gauge line. The Colorado Historical Society, which owns the

S

line and reconstructed it, used $45,000 from the SHF to remove a stressed girder narrow-gauge railroad bridge and to replace it with a replica of the original truss bridge. Besides addressing a safety issue, the new bridge is more historically accurate. A cash match of $175,000 from the ISTEA (Intermodel Surface Transportation Efficiency Act) further facilitated this replica of the 1884 truss bridge. SHF has also facilitated restoration of rolling stock. More than 100,000 visitors a year take this trip into the past, and a million more have watched it chug along while they are stuck in traffic jams on I-70. The Georgetown–Silver Plume National Historic Landmark District includes not only this summer excursion train but also an 1870s silver-mining complex, the Lebanon Mine, that is also open to the public.

LARGE TOWN HALL
487 Main St. NHLD
Built: 1885; William Clair, builder

The Town of Silver Plume used a $28,705 SHF grant along with a cash match of $39,875 from Plume Players melodrama profits and concerned citizens to preserve its large town hall. Restoration included repairing the historic façade and siding, creating new wallpaper to match the original, and restoring the interior of what is now a multipurpose hall, kitchen, and foyer used by the Plume Players as a theater.

S

MAIL CAR No. 13 AND PASSENGER COACH No. 76
10 Mountain St., Silver Plume Depot NHLD
Built: 1880/1912, mail car, Pullman; 1902, passenger coach, American Car and Foundry Co.

The Colorado Historical Society used SHF funds totaling $248,203 to restore Mail Car No. 13, including its trucks (wheelbase), and to stabilize the trucks of Passenger Coach No. 76. The project is part of a comprehensive long-range plan to protect and stabilize original railroad equipment for the Georgetown Loop Railroad. No. 13 is the only remaining mail car known to have been used on the Georgetown Loop. Originally numbered 114, it was built by Pullman in 1880 and was rebuilt in 1912 to meet new U.S. Postal Service safety and security standards. Two years after the Georgetown line was abandoned, cars No. 13 and No. 76 were displayed at the 1939 New York World's Fair and then later at the 1948 Chicago Railroad Fair. Passenger Coach No. 76 is the only remaining passenger car known to have been used on the Georgetown Loop Railroad. This 44-passenger coach was heated by a coal stove and cooled by opening windows. Quartersawn oak was used for the finish work throughout the car, which last saw service on the loop in 1927.

Inmates of the Arkansas Valley Correctional Facility did the restoration work after undergoing a rigorous training course and demonstrating sufficient skill at working on historic pieces. Mail Car No. 13 was dismantled to allow work on all sides, even the undercarriage. The roofing and the wall paneling were rebuilt, damaged floorboards replaced, and bent exterior stair railings straightened. All of the the fixtures and hardware were repaired, rebuilt, or replaced; the car repainted its original green; windows repaired; and an old-fashioned stove reinstated.

SCHOOLHOUSE / GEORGE ROWE MUSEUM
139 Main St. NHLD
Built: 1894; William Quayle, architect

One of Denver's leading architects designed this Romanesque monument to public education. After its closing as the Silver Plume School in 1959, town mayor George Rowe purchased the five-room school and converted it into a museum in 1960. Thirty-five years later, People for Silver Plume, Inc., matched $50,000 from the SHF to help restore the exterior masonry and portals, install an alarm system, update the electrical system, install a water tap, clean and repair chimneys, and repair interior water damage.

SMALL TOWN HALL
350 Main St. NHLD
Built: c. 1880s

With $51,000 from SHF, the Town of Silver Plume restored this single-story frame structure prominently that's sited at the entrance to the historic commercial district. Constructed as a store, by 1890 it had been converted into the firehouse, a court-room, and the office of the town clerk. People for Silver Plume, Inc., raised $7,000 plus volunteer labor for exterior repairs and a complete interior restoration in a building now stable and secure enough to house the town's archives.

Silverton

This silver city founded in 1874 has been preserved by its economic poverty and geographic isolation. Snuggled into a picturesque valley surrounded by snowcapped mountains, Silverton is part of a National Historic Landmark District that includes Hillside Cemetery, the Animas Water and Power District buildings and mule barn, the Polar Star Mill, and the Shenandoah-Dives (Mayflower) Mill. The antique commercial district, which has seen little new construction since 1910, includes several livery stables. Of the notorious red-light district on Blair Street, some of the former bordello buildings survive, most notably the Welcome Saloon (1883) at 1161 Blair, and the Shady Lady Bar (c. 1900) at 1154 Blair. Fines levied on bordellos, bars, and speakeasies sustained the town coffers, so Silverton did not levy the heavy property taxes, which in other mining towns led people to demolish their buildings during hard times to avoid taxes.

FIRST CONGREGATIONAL CHURCH OF SILVERTON
1060 Reese St., northwest corner of 11th St. NHLD
Built: 1881; Harlan P. Roberts, builder

The oldest Congregational church on Colorado's Western Slope boasts a steep, shingle-clad steeple with a weathervane finial. Pastor Harlan Roberts and his flock constructed this Carpenter Gothic church for $4,500. A white clapboard church that was modeled after traditional New England houses of worship, it was made famous by a 1951 Ansel Adams photograph. The walls were pulling apart, the roof was about to fall in, and shingles had disappeared from the steeple until the SHF stepped in to help this tiny congregation restore the distinctive church. SHF grants of $206,794 to the United Church of Christ enabled exterior restoration of this interdenominational community church.

S

MINERS UNION HALL
1069 Greene St., northeast corner of 11th St. NHLD
Built: 1901; Western Federation of Miners, builders

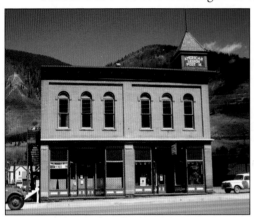

Members of the Western Federation of Miners Union donated their own labor to build this brick edifice. It has a granite basement and foundation that hold up a first-story saloon and second-story hall. The WFM was evicted during the 1903–1904 strikes. Subsequently its hall housed a store, a funeral home, as well as various saloons, while many lodges met upstairs. Thanks in part to $170,000 in SHF grants, the building has been stabilized, restored, and given a new roof, and the corner entry and flagpole have both been redone. This labor-history landmark has come back to house the Miners Union Theater upstairs, while the saloon is back in business on the first floor.

SAN JUAN COUNTY COURTHOUSE
1551 Greene St., northwest corner of 15th St. NHLD
Built: 1907; James Murdock, architect

A gold-colored dome crowns this Georgian Revival monument on a grassy square block shared by the San Juan County Historical Society Museum, Archives, and Research Center. The SHF's $1,121,925 was matched by San Juan County, the state's Energy and Mineral Impact Fund, and San Juan County Historical Society. This $2 million project was one of the first to involve a partnership of the State Historical Fund and the state's Department of Local Affairs. Cooperative funding helped install heating system upgrades; restore the building's front portico, windows, and exterior masonry; and repair the slate and lead roofs, dormers, and interior finishes. Additional work will provide access for the disabled, window and masonry restoration, and development of a maintenance manual. The bright golden dome on the San Juan County Courthouse shines again on Silverton. "We are the least populous and one of the poorest counties in Colorado," notes County Treasurer Beverly Rich. "Without the SHF, the restoration of our elegant courthouse would be only a dream. This landmark can now continue to serve the county through the next millennium."

S

SAN JUAN COUNTY HOSPITAL
1315 Snowden St. NHLD
Built: 1907; Frank E. Edbrooke, architect

On the site of the 1874 log cabin of town founder Francis Snowden, Silverton Local No. 26 of the Western Federation of Miners Union built this $35,000 hospital by holding dances and other fundraisers. Each union member also donated shifts to the hospital construction crews. During the 1918 flu epidemic, which hit isolated mining towns such as Silverton particularly hard, this hospital was overflowing with afflicted residents. After the union was broken, the hospital became the headquarters of the Standard Metals Mining Company. The SHF contributed $100,000 to the San Juan County Historical Society to rehabilitate this Renaissance Revival–style structure of Denver pressed brick with Mesa Verde sandstone trim and a beautiful distinctive cupola.

SILVERTON ELECTRIC LIGHT COMPANY SUBSTATION
1157 Greene St. NHLD
Built: 1906; Silverton Electric Light Co., builder

This 22-acre site includes a brick electric substation and a frame mule barn built by Silverton Electric Light Company. With SHF grants of $95,000, the area was regraded and the old railroad grade rebuilt to serve as Animas River flood control. San Juan County commissioner Terry S. Rhoades says, "The board feels very strongly that preserving the historic assets at this site will undoubtedly enhance its cultural, aesthetic, and economic value." With SHF aid, contractors Fritz Klinke and Loren Lew and the San Juan County Historical Society have repaired the brick, restored the windows and doors, and installed a new roof on the substation, which will also be used as a business incubator.

SILVERTON TOWN HALL
1360 Greene St. **H** NHLD
Built: 1910; Silas W. Smith, architect

On a frigid Thanksgiving weekend in 1992, tragedy struck Silverton. A faulty rooftop snow-melting device set the Town Hall ablaze. Despite the heroic efforts of the fire department, people gathered in the street, horrified to watch a favorite landmark burn to the ground. The water from the firemen's hoses froze upon contact with the building, coating the ruins in a glassy shell. Town residents brought hot coffee to the firemen, and helped them to remove and thaw out their gloves between efforts to stop the flames. Some people cried. With only about 500 year-round residents, the town had suffered from the recent closure of the last active mine and many jobs had been lost. The Town Hall, which had become a symbol of Silverton's

S

Photo courtesy of Tom Noel

achievements, now looked lost, too. So when the long night was over and they were faced with the ruins, Silvertonians decided that the Town Hall must be restored.

Local contractors Fritz Klinke and Loren Lew got the job. With quick assistance from the National Trust for Historic Preservation and the State Historical Fund, as much original material as possible was salvaged to facilitate a complete restoration/ reconstruction. Former mine employees in need of new jobs were trained as stone-masons, plasterers, and wood workers. It took four years and $574,065 from the SHF, matched by this tiny town and the San Juan County Historical Society. Every stone in the building was measured, assessed, and either repaired or replaced. The gold-topped dome with its leaded-glass skylight was replicated. Every interior feature was either restored or replicated, from the pressed-tin ceiling in the courtroom to the glass shades on the light fixtures.

"Our motivation is totally alien to the way most construction projects go," says Klinke. "We do research. We get to know the building, and the building will tell us what we need to know. You've got to spend time with it, wander through it. We felt that we're working for the building, that the building is the client, and whoever owns it is a temporary custodian."

Spencer

SPENCER SCHOOLHOUSE
Off CO 149, 10 miles south of Blue Mesa Reservoir,
*   1.5 miles west on Wildcat Gulch (149 Rd.)* (SR)
Built: 1902

Gunnison County's best surviving one-room schoolhouse sits in a remote mountain valley. It includes not only the small frame schoolhouse with its bell tower, but also the horse barn for students who rode to school, a well, both outhouses, and the teacher's house. The Gunnison County Pioneer & Historical Society restored the site with the help of $3,900 from the SHF and additional funding from the Bureau of Land Management, which owns the property. The venerable schoolhouse, closed since 1946, is used for interpretive tours by the Gunnison County school system.

Steamboat Springs

CARVER POWER PLANT / CENTENNIAL HALL
124 10th St. 〔LL〕
Built: 1901; George Slater, builder

The *Steamboat Pilot* of March 22, 1901, reported, "The deep-toned whistle of the Power House startled the natives when it was first turned loose. For miles around

the dogs barked themselves hoarse, and some of them are running yet." This simple story-and-a-half structure is made of local sandstone and bricks from Trogler's brick-yard. Norman Carver had this built as the first Routt County steam plant to supply the town with electricity. Abandoned in the 1950s when a new coal-fired plant opened 12 miles away at McGregor, the Carver became a storage facility.

When Steamboat needed new city offices, someone remembered the sturdy but neglected old powerhouse. With the help of $160,646 from the SHF, the city restored the exterior and rehabilitated the inside to house a conference room, the City Café, and city offices. Council president Kevin Bennett discovered that the restored power plant was not roomy enough to accommodate all of the city offices, so preservation architect Nan Anderson designed a compatible new addition behind it. At the reopening ceremony, the community toasted rejuvenation of the 100-year-old plant and renamed it Centennial Hall.

HAYMEADOW/LEGACY RANCH
35385 US 40 and CO 131, south of Steamboat Springs 〔LL〕
Built: 1917

As one of the most historically intact ranches in the Yampa Valley, the Haymeadow Ranch, formerly the Yampa Valley Land and Cattle Company, became a significant acquisition for the City of Steamboat Springs in the late 1990s. With a conservation

easement in place for the land and historic designation for the buildings, the preservation of open space and ranching heritage was ensured. The facility needed help, however, before it could open up for community and city use.

The City of Steamboat Springs is using more than $116,000 in SHF grants and $624,000 in city funds to help

S

rehabilitate the structures on this working 132-acre cattle and hay ranch as an interpretive center and city offices. To begin, site drainage issues were corrected so that foundation repairs could be made on several of the buildings. The modest, one-story 1917 clapboard ranch house had wood shingles reintroduced to the roof and the front porch returned to its open-air configuration. Plans include service as a museum and starting point for tours. The 1926 bunkhouse has been rehabilitated as city offices. Coal, machine, and stock sheds, as well as a barn, have also been preserved in this bucolic retreat located on the southern outskirts of fast-growing Steamboat Springs.

Kevin Bennett, former mayor of Steamboat Springs, made this his pet project. He remarks, "This showcase restoration is happening through a unique partnership of four levels of government and various private parties. We've been able to preserve 3,920 acres of agricultural land at the entrance to the city, continue a viable ranch while preserving some of its structures for future city offices, and conserve a stretch of the Yampa River Valley as a wildlife preserve. In addition, we look forward to greatly expanding our city trail system."

HOWELSEN HILL ROPE TOW HOUSE
845 Howelsen Pkwy. (SR)
Built: 1914, ski area, Carl Howelsen, builder; 1945, Rope Tow House

Photo courtesy of Tom Noel

Just across the Yampa River from downtown Steamboat Springs is a 40-acre ski area constructed by Carl "The Flying Norseman" Howelsen for downhill skiing and competitive ski jumping. Howelsen worked summers as a stonemason, and his craftsmanship still shines in the Furlong Building and the First National Bank, both at 8th Street and Lincoln Avenue. He also put Steamboat on the map as Colorado's first major ski center. Owned by the city since 1935, his hill is still used for recreational and competitive skiing and for training local skiers as part of the Steamboat school curriculum. Surrounding the old ski lift is a big city park with rodeo grounds, ballfields, tennis courts, and a fitness center. Although the Howelsen Hill outhouse was demolished in 1996, the 1945 Rope Tow House has

been reincarnated. Now restored using $117,000 in SHF grants and more than $50,000 from the City of Steamboat Springs, the log tow house, with its unusual steep, multi-gabled roof, makes Howelsen Hill one of the state's oldest operating ski lifts as well as one of the most picturesque.

MAD CREEK BARN
7 miles north of Steamboat Springs. Take CR 129 off US 40 north
5.5 miles to trailhead; hike Trail No. 100 for 2 miles ⎣LL⎦
Built: 1907; James Harry Ratliff, builder

Photo courtesy of Tom Noel

Mad Creek Barn is made of horizontal logs with a loft of vertical planks. James Ratliff used a simple hog trough–type construction with a primitive foundation of logs and stones. When President Theodore Roosevelt established what is now Routt National Forest, James Ratliff recalled, "I took the job of Forest Guard. I furnished my own horses, paid my own expenses, left my wife to run the ranch, and started to ride. I had about 24 arguments a day with ranchers refusing to pay for use of federal land and lost about half of them." With an SHF grant of $42,943 as well as $10,000 in matching funds and volunteer help from Historic Routt County!, the U.S. Forest Service has restored this unusual barn and corral as an interpretive site explaining Ratliff's roles as a typical rancher and as an advocate in the long struggle to regulate private use of the public domain.

MESA SCHOOLHOUSE
US 40, 4.5 miles southeast of Steamboat Springs ⎣LL⎦
Built: 1916

Historic Routt County! raised nearly $500,000 in cash and in-kind contributions, and the SHF added $70,000, to purchase this one-room schoolhouse, which closed in 1959 when the district consolidated. Over the years, the clapboard structure had been a gathering place for picnics, dances, and other social events. Arianthé C. Stettner, executive director of History Routt County!, notes, "Routt County had over 60 tiny schoolhouses before the statewide consolidation in 1959. We saved this beloved community landmark and restored the inside of the one-room school, while adding a modern kitchen and bathrooms. The historic bell tower has a bell and a ringing rope again." Reborn and repainted in its original red with white trim, the "little red schoolhouse" is back in session as a center for community use and a lesson in preservation, complete with blackboards.

S

PERRY-MANSFIELD PERFORMING ARTS SCHOOL AND CAMP
40755 CR 36, 3 miles north of Steamboat Springs NR
Built: 1914–1970s

Photo courtesy of Tom Noel

Charlotte Perry and Portia Mansfield, both graduates of Smith College, opened a dance school as a "haven for artistic expression" outside of Steamboat Springs at Perry's father's hunting lodge. After long and successful careers as performers and educators, the women retired in 1965 and gave the camp to Stephens College in Columbia, Missouri. But when the college planned to sell the 76-acre property in 1991, the people of Steamboat Springs decided to save what they felt was a national arts treasure. With the help of fundraising by Perry-Mansfield alumni, including Julie Harris, Dustin Hoffman, Lee Horsley, Lee Remick, and Joan Van Ark, the town made the purchase in 1994.

The campus includes 63 buildings, from small, private residences for staff to larger dormitories and the main dining hall. Most are rustic structures of slab logs on no foundations or on a few stones. SHF grants totaling $698,907 have enabled the camp to stabilize and restore the Louis Horst Studio where the floor had buckled, giving dancers vertigo, if not a twisted ankle. The Ranch Dormitory was restored, and work has begun on the Main Lodge, which serves as a studio, offices, and dining hall. Known as the "Cabeen Cabin," the original 1880 hunting lodge, with its quaint elkhorn entry arch, is also being restored.

Perry-Mansfield is one of the oldest continuously operating dance camps in America. More than 300 students, ages 9 to 21, come here annually to study all dance forms, theater, music, creative writing, and horseback riding. June Lindenmayer, the camp's executive director, explains that the tuition fees cover camp operations but not building maintenance, so they must rely heavily on grants and gifts. "After the SHF project," Lindenmayer adds, "it's safe to dance on the cabin floors again."

ROUTT COUNTY NATIONAL BANK BUILDING / REHDER BUILDING

S

802–806 Lincoln Ave. NR
Built: 1919; Carl Howelsen, builder

The Routt County National Bank Building is a two-story, flat-roofed commercial building that is made of red and blond pressed brick and locally quarried sandstone. Supported by a stone foundation, the six first-story façade bays form a double storefront facing Lincoln Avenue. Windows on the second story are grouped into three sets of three, while red brick rises vertically to form the parapet. Corbelled blond brick capped with sandstone forms a cornice of alternating blond and red brick set in vertical and horizontal courses. These elements, however, had been lost for many years. Several decades of remodeling schemes had resulted in a coat of stucco, installation of a cedar mansard roof that hung obtrusively from the building front, and the removal of many windows. This façade was beginning to fail and the owners were faced with repair or total restoration, a more expensive alternative.

Taking the high road, the Masons, Steamboat Springs Agency, LLC, Historic Routt County!, and the Yampa Valley Land Trust partnered with the SHF, which awarded $84,000 toward this $168,439 exterior restoration. In what can be a disastrous procedure, the stucco was carefully

and successfully removed and the brick elevations and stone detailing were resurrected. More historically accurate windows were installed, including a unique corner porthole window, and the storefront doors and windows were restored or re-created as needed. Today, the Masons still meet on the second floor, businesses have been reintroduced to the commercial first floor, and a former misfit now shines on this prominent main street corner.

STEAMBOAT SPRINGS DEPOT/ARTS CENTER
39265 CR 33 at US 40 and Stockbridge Rd. [NR]
Built: 1909; Frank E. Edbrooke, architect

Built by the Denver, Northwestern & Pacific (the Moffat Road) and later acquired by the Denver & Rio Grande, the depot closed when passenger service ended in 1968 on a line last run as the Yampa Valley Mail. This symmetrical, two-story, brick Beaux-Arts depot, with wooden bay windows and broad eaves supported by scrolled Craftsman brackets, seemed doomed to demolition. Eleanor Bliss helped organize the Steamboat Springs Art Council to save and recycle it for office and arts use. The council, which still owns and operates the building, restored the interior by raising $54,489 to capture $65,000 in SHF funds. The passenger waiting room is now a

gallery and the baggage room a theater and dance studio. The depot sits in a spacious park along the Yampa River, which features some restored mineral springs and a large, steamboat-shaped playground fixture.

S

St. Elmo

Fires have tested St. Elmo, one of Colorado's best-preserved and most scenic ghost towns. The 10,000-foot-high village endured fires in 1890, 1898, and 1987, and another blaze came in 2002, when the Town Hall, jail, and four other structures were destroyed. Locals, who were restoring the St. Elmo Town Hall and jail with $94,794 from the SHF, conducted an archaeological assessment of the burnt buildings and were able to do a thorough analysis for a possible future reconstruction, thanks to the gamblers who donate generously to Colorado casinos.

Photo courtesy of Elwin Arps

OSTREMAN (McKENZIE) CABIN
25835 CR 162 [NRD]
Built: c. 1885

Melanie Milam and other partners worked with a philanthropic fund established by her grandmother, the Marie R. Skogsberg Trust, to restore the exterior of this

cabin now used as the St. Elmo Information Center. The trust, which owns many St. Elmo landmarks, received $16,800 from the SHF and raised $27,404 in matching funds. This log cabin and its clapboard kitchen additions had to be jacked up after heaters were installed in the cellar to melt, in mid-June, six inches of ice. Crews excavated and then laid a treated-wood foundation with a French drain around the house—an aesthetic and less modern-looking alternative to concrete foundations. Among the historic items found near the foundation were unopened sardine tins from a packinghouse in northern Maine, a glass ladies' jewelry box with its contents, and children's marbles and wooden alphabet blocks.

Project director Milam notes that the rear shed was saved along with the old outhouse. New metal roofs were added to the main cabin and old-fashioned tin covering reinstalled over the antique outside stairway. "People may think I'm crazy," Milam laughs, "but I work side by side with the contractors. That's how you really get to know a building, to see its soul."

PAWNEE MILL BLACKSMITH AND LIVERY SHOP
25830–25838 CR 162 NRD
Built: c. 1892

Melanie Milam, local restoration organizer and savior of much of St. Elmo, notes that the Marie R. Skogsberg Trust received $9,767 from the SHF after providing $11,000 in matching funds to save these two buildings at the east entrance to town. "They would be rubble now," she says, "without the structural stabilization, new roofing, and in-filled wood siding. Thirty-seven volunteers restored the buildings with old boards and beams from St. Elmo in order to preserve the uniform weathering." The original buildings had sunk into the rocky soil, so the first task was to jack them up and add a French drain and chemically treated wood foundations to protect against rot. Surprisingly, the roof rafters on the livery were found to be sound and needed only new nails. The structures now house period carriages, horse and blacksmith equipment, and interpretive historical displays.

ROADS BROTHERS BUILDINGS
25910–25920 CR 267 NRD
Built: c. 1881; Roads brothers, builders

Restoring these two structures started with pulling out a foot of pack-rat nesting in the attics. The pioneers had used poisoned grain to keep varmints at bay, but in the intervening years, rodents had ruled the roost. Built in the 1880s on the north bank of Chalk Creek, the one-story Roads buildings were commercial at first but became residential later. Vacant since the 1950s, the buildings are perched on a gulch and exposed to the severe winter weather in 10,012-foot-high St. Elmo. Stabilization of the compact buildings required them to be jacked up and then supported by new concrete foundations.

Melanie Milam, project director and local historian, notes that "eight dedicated volunteers put in 268 hours on almost all phases of the project, from restoration to painting to cleanup. For the exterior work, we reused as much of the original wood as possible and used antique glass to replace the broken panes." The $9,903 SHF grant was matched by $17,800 raised by the Marie R. Skogsberg Trust. The old-fashioned, weathered look on the other exterior walls was maintained by putting

S

linseed oil on the new rough-sawn wood. Roofs were replaced and rear decks rebuilt; chimneys were repaired and repointed with salvaged St. Elmo bricks. As a final touch, interpretive signage and interior displays are planned for these reborn buildings. Milam adds that "there is considerably less vandalism to historical sites with interpretive signs that indicate an involved local community."

Sterling

FIRST UNITED PRESBYTERIAN CHURCH
130 S. 4th St. NR
Built: 1919; J. C. Fulton, architect

The imposing dome of this Neoclassical edifice echoes that of the county courthouse across the street. The speckled, buff-brick walls stand on a base of limestone, which is also used for the trim and the four two-story, Ionic entry columns. The semicircular golden-oak auditorium, with all of its 500 seats within 40 feet of the pulpit, has a wrapping balcony. Large, leaded stained-glass windows light the auditorium and also color the rotunda. In the choir loft, two large urns with bas-reliefs of children listening to Jesus' teachings are the work of the famous Sterling sculptor Mabel Landrum Torrey.

One of only two surviving churches in downtown Sterling, First United received $83,987 from the SHF and $44,436 from the community for restoration inside and out. The funds helped rehabilitate the church's basement, repair and refurbish the doors, and restore the dome. According to Hollis Jackson, former chairman of the church property committee, "We found that our 'solid oak' doors are actually made of seven-ply wood. You never know what you're going to find when you start a preservation project! We have also restored our spectacular, but hail-damaged, stained-glass windows." The church plays a vital part in the community, housing the Logan County Family Center, a food bank, various public and civic meetings, a countywide parenting program, as well as religious services.

LOGAN COUNTY COURTHOUSE
315 Main St. NR
Built: 1909–1910; John J. Huddart, architect

Huddart, who designed many Colorado courthouses, planned this Neoclassical gem in a tree-shaded square complete with a bandstand and miniature Statue of Liberty. Long-postponed maintenance is being undertaken by the Logan County commissioners, with the SHF's $458,140 and a county cash match. The money went to repair and restore the doors and windows and to install an elevator that would not compromise the historic integrity of this formal, three-story, beige-brick edifice with rich terracotta trim. A 1984 interior restoration addressed the stained-glass skylight that brightens the four-story rotunda, Colorado Yule marble and golden-oak trim, wrought-iron staircase,

S

and brass railings. The project also replaced 4,000 broken floor tiles with hand-cut duplicates and refinished the original golden-oak jury chairs. "We are grateful to the SHF," County Treasurer Patty Bartlett said in 2005. "That funding helped us clean up the basement vaults for our county records. We used to draw straws to see who had to go down into that dark, damp, sticky hole to fetch documents." Much more work is currently being done and will continue until the building is fully restored and rehabilitated.

Sunshine

SUNSHINE SCHOOL
355 CR 83 [NR]
Built: 1900

A concern about educating their children first drew the miners of Sunshine together as a community. They agreed to pay to help build and maintain the only stone school in the mountains of Boulder County. In this one-room school-house, a single teacher taught all eight grades at once. In 1944, the final year for the school, it had only a single student. Matching the community effort of the Sunshine Cemetery Association, the SHF provided $10,000 to help repair the granite walls and sandstone trim outside and the dark hardwood floors

inside. Today, the school is used as a community center, with a resurrected interior that is still adorned with original fixtures, such as blackboards and portraits of George Washington and Abraham Lincoln.

S

Superior

HAKE HOMESTEAD IN GRASSO PARK
122 E. William St.
Built: c. 1875–1904, Hake and Grasso families, builders

William Charles Hake, founder of
Superior, homesteaded here on Coal
Creek in the 1860s. At first he raised
cattle and crops, but after finding
coal, he began selling off his land to
miners. His homestead became part
of the coal-mining town of Superior.
John Grasso and his family purchased what was left of the Hake
Farm in 1925 and added another
house and a chicken coop. The
Town of Superior purchased the
homestead in 1994. Six years later,
the town put up $58,700 to match
$40,000 in SHF grants to restore the
decayed structures inside and out.
Now the town has one rural relic
amid the vast new subdivisions and
big-box stores that have transformed
Superior from a tiny town of 255 in
1990 to a city of 9,011 in 2000.

Telluride

FIRST NATIONAL BANK
201 W. Colorado Ave., northwest corner of Fir St. `NHLD`
Built: 1892; James Murdoch, architect

Restoration contractor Fritz Klinke says this bank is built—and will be rebuilt—like a fort. After construction, it began to crumble, the stone walls literally falling apart to bomb the sidewalk below. Maintenance was deferred as the bankrupt bank

Photo courtesy of Tom Noel

became a movie theater during the 1930s; an Elks Lodge occupied the upstairs. To stop the sandstone skin from falling off in the 1970s, the owners sprayed the outside of the building with shotcrete—a cheap and ineffective way to cover the decaying sandstone.

To the rescue came new owners Katrine and Bill Formby, who put in a lot of their own money and used $306,500 in SHF grants with matching funds from the Town of Telluride to stabilize and restore the building. The National Park Service and its Save America's Treasures program also contributed. The shotcrete was painstakingly removed by hand to resurrect the beautiful pink-purple local sandstone and the polished Pikes Peak granite entry columns. The three-story corner entry tower, lost during the 1930s, may also be reconstructed in the future as the crowning glory of this cornerstone of Telluride's downtown historic district.

LEWIS MILL
3.5 miles above Bridal Veil Falls, 7 miles southeast of Telluride `LL`
Built: 1907; W. T. Glenn, builder

The Lewis Mill exemplifies the many ore-processing mills once scattered throughout mining regions of the Colorado Rockies. It served the nearby Lewis Mine, which thrived on a rich silver-bearing lode and this state-of-the-art, gravity-concentration mill. Ten years after construction, this system was made obsolete by the introduction of the flotation recovery process. Most of the inner workings of the mill are still intact, such as the conveyor, crushers, boilers, and Wilfley concentrating tables. While iron and other scrap were salvaged from more accessible mill sites, Lewis was spared because of its remote location.

T

Preservation of Lewis Mill began with concerned private citizens and the owner, the Idarado Mining Company, which contributed $42,000 to restoration. Other partners included San Miguel County; Colorado Preservation, Inc., which listed it as one of Colorado's most endangered places; and the SHF, which granted $183,500. Because of the remote, 12,448-foot-high location, helicopters had to haul in the building materials, including wooden beams and the metal used to restore the roof. Workers camped at the site for three weeks, since travel to the location was difficult. After installing roofing, they stabilized all three stories of this high-country marvel.

MINER'S HOSPITAL / TELLURIDE HISTORICAL MUSEUM
201 W. Gregory Ave., at the north end of Fir St. **(H)** **LL** **NHLD**
Built: 1893

Miner's Hospital, also known as Hadley Hospital and Dr. Hall's Hospital, tended to Telluride residents until 1964. Harriet Fish Backus, author of *Tomboy Bride*, gave birth to her first baby in the hospital in 1901. Fifty years later, Dr. George Balderston wanted to try a new anesthetic and did with the aid of a nurse when he removed his own appendix.

After closing in 1964, this once-thriving hospital sat vacant for two years, then reopened as the San Miguel County Historical Society Museum. In 1991, the museum was deemed structurally inadequate and closed. When a portion of the west wall collapsed, the museum collection was removed and placed in storage. As chunks of sandstone fell from the exterior, the interior suffered water problems. An archivist fell through the rotting second floor but lived to suggest repairs. When

demolition was proposed, the alarmed townsfolk voted a $1.4 million bond issue to restore this building as the Telluride Historical Museum.

Restoration took seven years, using bond funds, a $214,000 grant from the SHF, and contributions totaling more than $200,000 from the town, the San Miguel County Historical Society, and private donors. Loren Lew, a stone restoration expert, along with Dick

Lippoth, a geologist, developed a mortar mix to patch and repair the soft, red-purple, locally quarried sandstone. A new wood-shingle roof was installed and adorned with a restored widow's walk, twin corbelled chimneys, and a shingled front gable with its original porthole window. The full-length front porch, designed as heliotherapy for recuperating patients, was jacked up and given a new foundation. All original doors and windows were restored. Original stenciling found behind a storage cabinet was re-created.

"We dug through six levels of flooring, including linoleum, to get down to the original," says assistant museum director Brenna Cohen. "We now have restored that plank flooring and are investigating it and other surviving clues—such as the recovered wall stenciling—to help us interpret life at this hospital where more than 600 babies were born. We are now far enough along," she reported in 2002, "that Clio, the museum cat, found the building secure and comfortable enough to move back in."

POPCORN ALLEY
121, 123, and 127 E. Pacific Ave. NHLD
Built: 1890s

A century ago, ladies of easy virtue solicited business from the doors and windows of these cribs on Popcorn Alley in Telluride's red-light district. These structures on Pacific Avenue are souvenirs of the town's "brides of the multitudes," whose brisk business supposedly created a popping popcorn-like racket from the doors opening

and closing all night long. In 1979, the National Trust for Historic Preservation acquired and sold these endangered cribs to the Town of Telluride for restoration as low- to moderate-income family housing.

The $13,285 SHF restoration grant, along with a match from the residents, helped the town repair leaking roofs and repaint. As the shingle roofs installed during the 1980s had not kept out the heavy Telluride snows, corrugated-metal roofs, much like the originals, were installed. One of the owners, Stacey Sheridan, declares that before the new roofs, she chose only tall roommates, because the snow on the old shingle roofs had to be continually swept off to prevent severe water damage to these tiny cottages. "We renters of Popcorn Alley," she adds, "are careful to close doors quietly and never go to them in our nighties."

T

SAN MIGUEL COUNTY COURTHOUSE
301 W. Colorado Ave., northwest corner of Oak St. NHLD
Built: 1887; W. H. Nelson, builder

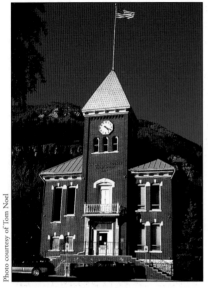

Photo courtesy of Tom Noel

The most distinctive landmark in town, the San Miguel County Courthouse has been the heart of Telluride's business district, not to mention the site of many church dinners, dances, and town meetings. The first courthouse, built in 1885, burned down within the year and was replaced by this handsome red-brick, stone-trimmed edifice.

The $384,142 in SHF grants is helping the town with this multiphase project to address long-standing rehabilitation and restoration needs to keep this a functioning landmark. A new, silvery, standing seam metal roof now covers the building, and the pyramidal clock tower also has a new metal roof in a vintage fish-scale pattern under a shiny new flagpole.

SHERIDAN OPERA HOUSE
110 N. Oak St. NHLD
Built: 1913; W. S. Segerberg, builder

The Sheridan Arts Foundation, a nonprofit organization founded in 1991 by Sandra Carradine, is using $417,640 in SHF grants and many other contributions, including $25,000 from the Town of Telluride, to restore this old theater inside and out and to upgrade the building's electrical and fire-suppression systems. Originally built for vaudeville and movies, this 236-seat theater welcomed such stars as Lillian Gish, Sarah Bernhardt, and William Russell to its stage, which has a vintage Venetian scene painted on its roll curtain by J. Erickson.

Two misguided renovations left the opera house in poor condition and by the early 1990s it faced demolition. The Sheridan Arts Foundation purchased the building, aiming to restore it for public use. As stated on its website, the goal of the Foundation is to "preserve the historic Sheridan Opera House as an arts and cultural resource for the Telluride community, bring quality arts and cultural events to Telluride, and provide local, national, and inner-city youth with access and exposure to arts education." Since 1980, the Opera House has annually hosted many festivals, including the world-renowned Telluride Film Festival, live performances, local plays and recitals, and film screenings. When not in use as a movie or live theater, the opera house doubles as a dance floor and conference center.

SILVER BELL BUILDING / AH HAA SCHOOL FOR THE ARTS
135 S. Spruce St., northwest corner of Pacific Ave. LL NHLD
Built: 1890

Previous owners Jo Ann and Bob Miller purchased the structure from the Town of Telluride and originally began the restoration process with help from the National Trust for Historic Preservation. When the Ah Haa School for the Arts purchased the building, several repairs were still needed, such as roof replacement, exterior painting, and siding repair to prevent additional damage. The Silver Bell is a reminder of the women who came out west to make money respectably or find husbands, but instead turned to prostitution. Romona and Rita, two of the fallen ladies who worked at the Silver Bell Dance Hall and Saloon, are said to haunt the building. They have a more comfortable home thanks in part to a $6,500 SHF grant to restore the shiplap siding and paint it yellow with crimson trim, suggestive of the Silver Bell's red-light days.

UNRUH HOUSE
602 E. Pacific Ave., in Town Park NHLD
Built: c. 1900

The Unruh House is the last remaining house in what was platted in 1898 as a working-class community but is now Town Park. The restored and preserved Unruh House sits at its original location on a new foundation thanks to an $87,000 SHF grant to the Town of Telluride and matching funds of $63,800 from various donors for exterior restoration. It now serves as an office for the Town Park staff and a public meeting place as well as a winter Nordic sports center. SHF support also helped to install interpretive signage such as that found at the entrance of the park.

T

Toponas

ROCK CREEK STAGECOACH STATION
FR 206, off CO 134, 11 miles east of Toponas [NR]
Built: 1880; James P. Gates, builder

James P. Gates built this two-story hewn log cabin as his family's home, then converted it into a stagecoach stop and an inn. It proved to be a convenient rest stop for travelers, particularly for those riding on the Georgetown–Steamboat Springs stagecoach line which opened in 1882. A flat-roofed porch originally extended across the entire front of the cabin. A second-floor door allowed the Gates family and guests to step out on the porch's roof and admire the view of the Gore Range. Abandoned after the railroad arrived in the early 1900s, the stage station stood empty for decades and almost collapsed.

Restoration efforts begun in the 1990s were boosted when the SHF came to the rescue with $86,382. This enabled volunteers and preservation partners, including

the U.S. Forest Service, the Steamboat Springs' Tread of Pioneers Museum, as well as Historic Routt County!, to rebuild the foundation, repair and rechink logs, and install Plexiglas windows and new interpretive signage. Project architect Jan Kaminski says, "Rock Creek is one of those rare treasures not often found,

especially out in the forest. Revitalized as of 2001, the old stage stop will now be used to display the history of Routt County pioneers and maybe even serve as an overnight shelter for recreational use."

Towaoc

PORCUPINE HOUSE
Access information available at:
Ute Mountain Ute Tribal Park, US 160 and 166,
**   15 miles southwest of Cortez** NR
c. 1100–1280; Ancestral Puebloan Peoples

Porcupine House is located in the Ute Mountain Ute Tribal Park near the southern boundary of Mesa Verde National Park. This spectacular cliff dwelling in Mancos Canyon has 60 rooms and four kivas. Badly eroding and in danger of tumbling into the canyon, it has been stabilized by the Utes, who matched more than $13,000 to draw SHF funding of $39,951 for site restoration, including foundation repair, repointing masonry joints, and improving drainage. In addition, tribal members were given training in preservation techniques for further restoration and mainte- nance of the site in cooperation with archaeological specialists. Now the Utes proudly incorporate Porcupine House into their guided tours, before which they always say a special prayer and then tourist groups are treated to one of Colorado's most unforgettable explorations.

Trinidad

Founded in 1859, Trinidad boomed between the 1880s and the 1920s, when a thriving coal industry made it Colorado's fourth largest city. The Corazón de Trinidad National Register Historic District includes much of the town. The district is noted for red-brick streets and for one of the state's finest collections of stone structures, many built with the local golden sandstone. Architects Isaac Hamilton Rapp, William Morris Rapp, and Alexander C. Hendrickson designed many prominent buildings here before moving on to Santa Fe, where they created the Santa Fe style. From its early days as a hub on the Santa Fe Trail to its current prominence as the last town on I-25 before motorists climb Raton Pass and drop into New Mexico, Trinidad has shone as a jewel worth preserving.

BACA HOUSE
300 E. Main St. NR NRD
Built: 1869–1870; John S. Hough, builder

Merchant and mill owner John S. Hough constructed this 10-room house, which was sold three years later to Felipe Baca, a rancher and state legislator. Baca House is a Territorial-style home that incorporates Greek Revival and Italianate features. A two-story adobe, it has thick walls and a hipped roof, pedimented windows, shutters, and a balustraded front porch. Used as the Baca family home until the 1920s, the residence includes a large rear courtyard and L-shaped, 12-room, adobe servants' quarters. At the rear is an adobe barn, now the Santa Fe Trail Museum. Through the efforts of Friends of Historical Trinidad and the Trinidad Historical Society, the Colorado Historical Society acquired the neighboring Bloom Mansion along with the Baca House in the early 1960s. The Colorado Historical Society

began restoration and opened both to the public as the Trinidad History Museum complex. Baca House commemorates Hispanic history, culture, and folk art, while the Bloom Mansion interprets Victorian history and lifestyles, and the Santa Fe Trail Museum showcases regional history from the Santa Fe Trail era through the coal-mining days.

A Colorado Department of Transportation (CDOT) grant of $75,940 and SHF grants of $117,850 allowed an archaeological survey, historic landscaping, and site interpretation. The CDOT and SHF grants also allowed museum director Paula Manini to add Santa Fe Trail exhibits and provide accessibility to the nearby Barglow House, which houses the Santa Fe Trail Information Center, gift shop, and offices. Manini reports that SHF funds were matched by National Park Service funding, as Baca House is an official Santa Fe Trail Historic Site. That funding helped install an underground drainage system and repair water damage to the house.

BARGLOW HOUSE
350 E. Main St. NRD
Built: 1906

This two-story brick structure featuring a Neoclassical front porch was constructed in 1906 for Dr. R. G. Davenport's office and residence. In 1943, Dr. D. R. Barglow purchased the building and moved his practice here. During the 1960s, the Colorado Historical Society acquired Barglow House as part of the Trinidad History Museum complex. A $20,500 SHF grant and a Federal Byways Fund grant helped to cover the $130,200 reconstruction, which replaced the dilapidated wooden porch with a copy of the original, replaced the boiler, and also upgraded the fire-alarm and security system.

BLOOM MANSION
300 E. Main St., southwest corner of Walnut St. NR NRD
Built: 1882

Cattle baron Frank G. Bloom and his wife, Sara Thatcher Bloom, were the wealthiest and most influential pair in Trinidad and built this mansion to prove it. As the local representative of Pueblo's powerful Thatcher clan, Frank opened the first major mines in the southern Colorado coalfields in 1869. He also operated the Thatcher Brothers store in Trinidad, as well as the Bloom Cattle Company. Frank and Sara selected their Second Empire house design from a magazine and had a local contractor build it. The three-story home bristles with restored cresting atop the roof and a fourth-story mansard tower. The red brick is frosted with white stone quoins, while the first floor is wrapped by an elegant wood-frame veranda. Inside, the house retains its elegant carpets, wall-papers, and lace curtains. Outside, the grounds feature a Victorian garden with brick path, sundial, and cast-iron water fountain. The backyard also contains a vegetable and herb garden and a *horno*, the traditional Hispanic outdoor oven.

The Colorado Historical Society has undertaken ongoing restoration of the mansion as a house museum, in conjunction with the Baca House next door. SHF grants totaling $110,650 have helped fund a new roof, stabilize the wraparound porch, and upgrade the electrical system. Museum director Paula Manini notes, "Without the SHF grant, we were being faced with closing the Bloom Mansion to public tours. Now safe public access can be guaranteed."

BRICK STREETS
Cedar St. and Plum St. between Commercial St. and Convent St. [NRD]
Built: 1890s

The SHF has invested about $2 million in projects in Trinidad, and buildings up and down the streets have been studied, restored, and interpreted. But in Trinidad the streets themselves are also historic. Few communities in Colorado have surviving brick streets; Trinidad has over six miles, lined with locally manufactured bricks, many of which are stamped "Trinidad." A study funded by the SHF indicated that many of the city's brick streets were prime candidates for restoration.

A second SHF grant of $155,000 aided a $380,187 project to begin restoration in the heart of the city's downtown historic district. Former Trinidad planning director Karl Gabrielson comments, "This project of restoring Cedar and Plum has had a tremendous impact as a pilot project to determine if, and how, we restore the rest of our brick streets." Much remains to be done, but the future of Trinidad's brick streets is brighter. Visitors strolling along the historic streetscape will be able to enjoy the many restored buildings and learn more about Trinidad's history from the interpretive signs, also installed with the help of SHF grants.

T

CARNEGIE PUBLIC LIBRARY
202 N. Animas St., northeast corner of W. Church St. [NR] [NRD]
Built: 1904; John G. Haskell, architect

This building, made of Trinidad sandstone from the nearby James Radford Quarry, has Ionic columns that echo those of City Hall across the street. This typical Neo-classical design is one of 1,679 Carnegie libraries built in the United States and one of 35 constructed in Colorado. Built for $15,000, the library has been restored with $110,650 from the SHF, matched by $77,400 from the City of Trinidad. The library features the original high ceilings, stained-glass lunette windows, golden-oak card-catalog cabinet, wrought-iron bookshelves, and restored original tin roof. Library patron and local architectural historian Ken Fletcher notes, "It is wonderful what the SHF grant did. You cannot put a price on this library for what it means to Trinidad. Many people come here for historical research and genealogy. We have recently added 40,000 Trinidad newspaper pages to our microfilm collection and now have it complete from 1879 to the present. So the library has become a source, as well as an inspiration, for other preservation projects."

COLUMBIAN HOTEL
111–119 N. Commercial St. [NRD]
Built: 1879; John Conkie, architect

Since the 1970s, this 100-room hotel has been vacant. Originally called the Grand Union Hotel, the three-story brick landmark trimmed in stone and pressed metal was renamed in honor of the 1893 World's Columbian Exposition. A tile-floored lobby leads to a Rococo ballroom, a ladies' "retiring room," and a gaming room, saloon, and smoking parlor, all of which await restoration under the original 18-foot-high, pressed-metal ceiling.

Photo courtesy of Tom Noel

T

While the marshal of Trinidad, gunslinger Bat Masterson lived here for six years. Other notable hotel guests included the humorist Will Rogers, and movie stars Mary Pickford and Douglas Fairbanks, as well as Presidents Herbert Hoover and Theodore Roosevelt. Cowboy movie star Tom Mix supposedly insisted his white horse stay in an adjacent hotel room. When the temperamental equine refused to enter the elevator, the horse had to be led up the stairs.

In 1995, Charles Albert of San Juan Columbian, Inc., purchased the structure and launched an ambitious plan to stabilize and make emergency repairs to the exterior and reopen the street-level retail shops. A $72,000 SHF grant supported a $156,000 restoration that reawakened what was once southern Colorado's finest hotel. Next, Albert plans a full exterior and interior restoration so Trinidad's visitors may once again savor a downtown grand hotel.

FIRE HOUSE No. 1 / TRINIDAD CHILDREN'S MUSEUM
314 N. Commercial St., southeast corner of Cedar St. NRD
Built: 1895; C. W. Bulgar and Isaac H. Rapp, architects

Featured in bas-relief under the second-story entry arch is a restored, brightly painted fire horn and ladder. Such flourishes exist because of SHF grants of $23,550 to the City of Trinidad, which raised twice that amount to restore the roof, bell tower, and parapet and replicate the firehouse's double doors. Since 1985, the firehouse has been a children's museum run by the Trinidad Junior Historical Society. Among the attractions are an 1880s classroom and a 1936 La France fire truck.

Sandstone quoins and banding contrast dramatically with the red-brick skin of this narrow, two-story building with its asymmetrical bell tower. The City Hall, jail, and other city offices were also housed here until the new City Hall opened in 1909. The old jail cells still occupy the catacomb-like basement.

"For the project, we turned to the Colorado Historical Society," recalls Children's Museum director of programs and tours Mary Ann Newman. "The SHF has assisted us with several grants and also with guidance. I don't see how the CHS could have been more helpful. This project began during a recession and provided needed jobs and money." Visiting children love climbing the fire truck, watching model trains run, writing on slate boards, and wearing the dunce cap in the classroom. They try out an old typewriter and adding machine and play with other hands-on exhibits.

FIRST CHRISTIAN COMMUNITY CHURCH
200 S. Walnut St. NR
Built: 1922; Isaac H. Rapp, William M. Rapp,
and A. C. Hendrickson, architects

The SHF awarded $8,000 for interior and exterior restoration of this Mediterranean-style, three-story structure. It has unusual milk-glass windows and Classical details in the entablature and main entry. Red wire-cut brick rises to a green-tile roof in an irregular composition with a setback second story. The church today offers its facility, newly accessible for the disabled, to various religious and secular organizations and graciously hosts free funerals even for nonmembers. Church pastor Cary T. Nelson says, "The SHF grant made possible a major remodeling project. Now, our church is more user-friendly, with new restrooms and a nursery."

JAMIESON BUILDING / A. R. MITCHELL MEMORIAL MUSEUM
150 E. Main St. NRD
Built: 1905–1906; John Conkie, architect

This two-story brick building housed the Jamieson Department Store from 1906 to 1986. Beneath a fancy pressed-metal cornice, this venerable edifice boasts a tin ceiling, original wood floors, and a beautiful horseshoe-shaped mezzanine. The A. R. Mitchell Memorial Museum Board purchased the store in 1989 to house the art and historical collection of artist, illustrator, and town benefactor Arthur Roy Mitchell. Trained as an artist in New York City, Mitchell returned to his hometown of Trinidad and gained fame as an illustrator who drove around in his Ford to paint the outdoors. The "Model A Cowboy" painted more than 150 covers for western magazines. In the 1960s, Mitchell helped save Trinidad's Baca House and Bloom Mansion from destruction and restored them as Colorado Historical Society museums. In 1993, a $23,000 SHF grant helped cover the $30,000 cost of replacing the roof. A 1996 elevator replacement and ventilation improvements to protect the collection were aided by another SHF grant for $100,000 toward the $126,000 total cost. Planning for further restoration is also being funded with SHF grants.

T

JOHN'S BUILDING
126–134 W. Main St. NRD
Built: 1883; E. S. Bell, builder

This commercial double storefront of 4,350 square feet was built in 1883 of native stone by E. S. Bell. The property was donated in 1991 to the Trinidad State Junior College Educational Foundation, Inc. The building houses offices and support space as a community development center in conjunction with Trinidad State Junior College, Trinidad/Las Animas County Economic Development Corporation, and the Trinidad Chamber of Commerce. The property is a keystone for the central commercial portion of the Corazón de Trinidad National Historic District. The interior was rehabilitated with a $250,000 grant from the Colorado Department of Local Affairs Energy Impact Fund. The SHF contributed $23,500 toward a $76,350 façade and window restoration.

LAS ANIMAS COUNTY COURTHOUSE
200 E. 1st St., southeast corner of S. Maple St. NRD
Built: 1912; Isaac H. Rapp, William M. Rapp, and A. C. Hendrickson, architects

This Beaux-Arts monument of buff Indiana limestone with terracotta trim was built for a cost of $250,000 on a full-block site. Beneath a rooftop balustrade, two-story Ionic columns dominate a three-story façade. Inside, white marble walls, ornate plaster trim, golden-oak woodwork, and gilded-iron stair railings still survive, as does a mural depicting local history, painted by Colorado artist Angelo di Benedetto. An SHF grant of $267,300 helped pay for a $457,300 restoration of the courthouse's 14 stained-glass clerestory windows, 15 stained-glass skylight panels, and almost all the other windows.

"This building was designed by the well-known Rapp brothers, who invented the Santa Fe style," observes Las Animas County Courthouse restoration project coordinator Constance La Lena. "This project would not have gone forward without the SHF grant. They also provided the needed extra funding for historically correct replacements. Our next priority for work should be masonry and terracotta restoration."

Uravan

JOE JR. MILL AND CAMP
206, 207, and 209 Main St. Ⓗ ⓈⓇ
Built: 1912

Uravan helped give birth to the nuclear age with a mill built to process carnotite ore, breaking it down into its base elements of radium, vanadium, and uranium.

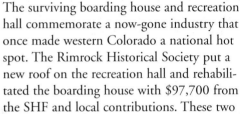

The surviving boarding house and recreation hall commemorate a now-gone industry that once made western Colorado a national hot spot. The Rimrock Historical Society put a new roof on the recreation hall and rehabilitated the boarding house with $97,700 from the SHF and local contributions. These two

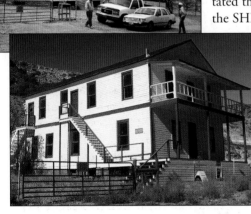

structures are the last survivors of a once thriving camp that was one of the earliest and most important ore-processing centers of America's nuclear age.

Vernon

VERNON SCHOOL/COMMUNITY CENTER
25817 Colorado St. ⓈⓇ
Built: 1927, Dan Funk, architect; 1949 gymnasium addition,
    Cliff Carson, builder

In 1927, the town of Vernon was a fast-growing farming town on the Eastern Plains when it built this school to serve all grade levels. The brick structure with a central hall plan received a gymnasium addition in 1949, which provided a full-size basketball court (the only one in Yuma County), stage, kitchen, and dining room. The school was closed in 1969 due to declining enrollment, and in 1974 ownership transferred to the community center. Though the town did its best to maintain the property, the shoestring budget and all-volunteer commitment did not allow for extensive repairs or restoration and the building's needs became pressing.

Through two SHF grants, matched by the Vernon Community Center, the exterior has been restored, masonry repaired, brick repointed, and structural cracks addressed. The large classroom windows, once hidden by a corrugated fiberglass covering, have had missing elements replaced, existing frames repainted and reglazed,

U
V

and more compatible exterior storm windows installed. New, more historically accurate doors now greet visitors. Peeling and cracking plaster on the interior was repaired. Missing tiles on the gymnasium ceiling proved to be a challenge when no duplicate material could be located. A solution was found when a pattern, duplicating the original tiles, was employed. Volunteers produced the pattern by drilling one hole at a time. On the gym's hardwood floor, loose and twisted boards were replaced with the same type of wood and the entire surface refinished in a warm, natural tone. And though the home court loose-board advantage may have been taken away, the court is ready for activity and the entire building has seen a resurgence of functions and gatherings.

Victor

"The City of Gold," one of Colorado's best-preserved mining towns, is ringed by the head frames of million-dollar mines. In the winter, Victor showcases its mining heritage by illuminating the head frames of the most famous mines: the Ajax, American Eagle, Anchora Leland, Cresson, Hoosier, Independence, Teresa, and Vindicator. Using SHF funds, Victor has restored treasures in its downtown National Register Historic District, roughly bounded by Diamond and Portland Avenues between 2nd and 5th Streets. Celebrating its golden heritage, Victor has also established, with SHF aid, hiking and biking trails to the most famous and scenic mines.

Mayor Kathy Justice notes, "Victor has appreciated SHF collaboration in reviving our past grandeur from a dilapidated state. We've restored our Victor City Building, which was in a downright dangerous condition, and thanks to the SHF we've also been able to do a first-rate restoration of city offices and the city council chamber. Not to mention we've fixed up the old fire-truck bay, so we can now exhibit our 1942 fire truck and show off the old firemen's brass pole."

CALVARY LUTHERAN CHURCH / VICTORY CHAPEL / VICTOR COMMUNITY CENTER
2nd St. and Portland Ave. NRD
Built: 1905

Robert Burns, the president of the Victor/Goldfield Initiatives Consortium for Community Improvements, reports, "The old church, unused since the 1970s, was vandalized and in bad shape. Local contractor-electrician Bob Harmes did the project and hired many unemployed locals." Car washes and bake sales, as well as pledge drives

Photo courtesy of Tom Noel

helped raise money. Burns notes that SHF grants of $108,228 were used to acquire the site, repair the foundation, fix the walls, and add a new roof. A local women's group raised $1,700 to add a new kitchen. To top off the church's rebirth, $1,400 went toward landscaping, dainty curtains for the new windows, and shiny new roof finials, all spotlighted by new exterior lighting to show off the building at night.

"We use the new Victor Community Center for all kinds of things," adds town postmaster DeeAnna Keller. "I hold my aerobics classes there. We also have the city council meeting and the AA weekly meetings. This rehabilitated church now gives Victorites a great place to get together."

TOMKINS HARDWARE / LOWELL THOMAS MUSEUM
298 Victor Ave., southeast corner of 3rd St. NRD
Built: 1899

Built as the Reynolds Block, this two-story brick edifice sports a large plate-glass window and egg-and-dart detailing. Over the years it has housed Tomkins Hardware, the Victor Mining Stock Exchange, the Victor Dry Goods Store, and, since 1960, a museum honoring Lowell Thomas, Victor's most famous resident and a onetime reporter for the *Victor Record*. The museum contains information on Victor, mining, and Thomas, who served as the voice of *Movietone News* from 1935 to 1952 and wrote more than 50 books. The famed newsman and travel writer announced his retirement in Victor and passed away two weeks after a final visit to his boyhood home in 1981. The museum has received $17,500 from the SHF for rehabilitation of the foundation and walls, with additional help from the Victor Improvement Association, Inc., and $50,000 from the Cripple Creek & Victor Mining Company.

VICTOR ARMORY / ELKS LODGE No. 367
128–130 N. 3rd St., southeast corner of Diamond Ave. NRD
Built: 1900

A well-respected architect who followed in the footsteps of his architect father in Denver, M. Lockwood McBird was commissioned by the Woods Brothers and others to reconstruct Victor after the fires of 1899. Although this sturdy, three-story, brick Romanesque Revival fortress with a distinctive stepped parapet was built for the Colorado State Militia as an armory, McBird is thought to have been involved in its design. During the labor strikes of 1903–1904, striking miners were imprisoned in it. A leaded-glass fanlight distinguishes the double-doored entry on a full-length front porch added later to make this a friendlier place after the Elks bought it in 1914. Elks and Elkettes have maintained the splendid interior, with its hardwood trim and many original fixtures. $30,980 from the SHF also helped finance a new roof.

VICTOR CITY HALL AND FIREHOUSE
Victor Ave., northwest corner of 5th St. NRD
Built: 1900

Following Victor's disastrous fire in 1899, the city built this elaborate two-story brick hall with a gilded cupola for the town bell. The brick edifice features sandstone quoins and an arched sandstone entry. Brick dentils and sandstone egg-and-dart trim embellish the exterior, as does the roofline brackets and frieze. Although the fire department has now moved out, the large double firehouse doors and an antique fire truck remain. Inside are the city offices and wall maps of the maze of mining claims, shafts, and tunnels underlying the "City of Mines."

The SHF has contributed $650,000 and Victor has raised more than $375,000 for this 11-year project. Among other things, the money paid for rehabilitation of the foundation, mechanical systems, and restoration of the interior and exterior, from a new roof to reinforcing and refinishing the hardwood floors. Victor mayor Kathy Justice, who delights in giving tours of the showcase reincarnation where she offices, claims, "Victor is a sleeping princess. We need to awaken her with preservation of our historic integrity. By restoring City Hall, we have brought this historic building back to its past beauty. We hope to inspire other people to help bring our downtown area back from a dilapidated state to its past grandeur."

This big step toward maintaining its treasured past earned Victor the Colorado Historical Society's 2005 Governor's Award for Historic Preservation. The award notes that the upstairs courtroom has been returned to its original splendor and original use as the municipal courtroom and the city council chambers, while the old firetruck bay and jail have been restored as public museum areas.

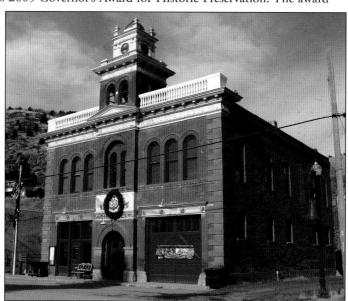

V

Virginia Dale

VIRGINIA DALE STAGE STATION
5 miles south of the Wyoming border, east of US 287 and 1 mile northwest of the post office NR
Built: 1862; Jack Slade, builder

Jack Slade, the notorious station agent (and rumored bandit), named this Overland Trail stop for his wife and welcomed thousands of visitors, including author Mark Twain and photographer William Henry Jackson. The building later served as post office, general store, and community center. Years of weather had badly deteriorated the structure, an example of piece-by-piece construction. A $35,224 SHF grant helped enable the Virginia Dale Community Club to address the repair and historically appropriate replacement of the windows, doors, hand-hewn sill logs, and foundation; removal of a shed addition and lap siding; and drainage improvements to prevent further damage. Immortalized in Twain's *Roughing It,* Slade's stage stop endures as the most intact Overland Trail structure still on its original site.

V

Walden

JACKSON COUNTY COURTHOUSE
396 Lafever St. at 4th St. [NR]
Built: 1913; William N. Bowman, architect

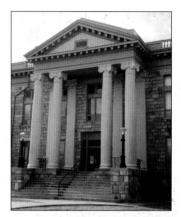

Dominating this sagebrush hamlet on a hilltop site, the three-story Neoclassical courthouse is made of large blocks of rough-faced native sandstone with dressed-stone quoins and two-story, twin Ionic columns. Inside, the original woodwork, signage, and floor plan survive. Jackson County matched $506,103 from the SHF to restore this landmark, with its grand pedimented entry portico, using replacement sandstone from the original local quarry. Restoration work included repainting the dentiled entry pediment, rooftop balustrade, and the repair of the cast-stone quoins. The grassy, landscaped, one-block site, which also includes the North Park Pioneer Museum inside a vintage 1883 cottage, is also in the process of being rehabilitated.

Walsenburg

FOX THEATER
715 Main St. (SR)
Built: 1917, Frank Yano, architect; Paul Krier, builder

This two-story, brick-and-stucco Art Deco structure, originally the Star Theater, featured vaudeville performances as well as silent movies. A special treat in 1923 was the addition of a Wurlitzer pipe organ. In 1929, Krier remodeled the façade in a Spanish Southwestern style, renamed it the Valencia Theater, and began showing "talkies." From 1941 to its closure in the late 1980s, the theater was named the Fox, as a member of the Fox Intermountain Theater chain. In 1992, the vacant structure was purchased by the Optimists Club and Huerfano Youth and Arts Foundation, Inc.

Grants totaling $46,400 from philanthropic groups such as the Helen K. and Arthur E. Johnson Foundation, the Boettcher Foundation, and the Adolph Coors Foundation stabilized the deteriorating building. A 1995 SHF grant of $92,704 provided the lion's share of the subsequent $101,733 interior and exterior restoration, including the showy neon marquee. Final restoration came with an SHF grant of

$49,450, contributing most of the total cost of $51,620 to rehabilitate the balcony and reinstall 200 seats. Interior restoration has returned the 1923 Wurlitzer pipe organ to operation and retained the rope-and-pulley system used to change scenery flats during performances. Today, the theater is used as a meeting place by various community organizations and on the weekends features first-run movies.

HUERFANO COUNTY COURTHOUSE AND JAIL
401 Main St. (US 160) [NR]
Built: 1904; Charles A. Henderson, architect

This building dominates Walsenburg's skyline with its silvery roof and rich stone detail. This two-story landmark is built from rough-faced local sand-stone that rises to a central, four-story bell tower. The adjacent jail (1896) is similarly Romanesque

Revival in style, of the same stone and with the same dominant square tower. In March 1914, the steel cells and beds housed the 84-year-old radical union activist Mother Jones, who was jailed by the state militia during the violent southern Colorado coalfield strike that culminated in the Ludlow Massacre. In 1994, the jail became the Walsenburg Mining Museum, marking a past era in southern Colorado in which coal was king. Having undergone a $568,750

restoration that used $378,310 in grants from SHF as well as funding from the state Department of Local Affairs, the courthouse and jail have received the stone repairs and restoration from Pinnacle Quarry, Inc., a new roof, heating and air-conditioning, and window repair and restoration.

W

Ward

WARD SCHOOL AND TOWN HALL
66 Columbia St. [LL]
Built: 1898

The Town of Ward matched a $17,700 SHF grant to restore the school and Town Hall as a community center and library by repairing the foundation, improving drainage, and adding a new roof. Barely big enough for full-sized patrons and a librarian, it is no wonder the library is self-service. Neat hand-printed signs urge patrons to "please reshelve books." The signs work: The library is the tidiest place in town. A tree trunk with log steps and tree branch railing leads to a balcony children's section. Most of the fiction corner is taken up by a cat-clawed, old easy chair. *Webster's Second International Unabridged Dictionary*—the biggest ever compiled for the English language, with more than 600,000 entries—has its own hand-carved stand. The front half of the old school contains the post office and a free public shower.

Westcliffe

BECKWITH RANCH
64159 CO 69 [NR]
Built: 1874–1877; Elton T. Beckwith family, builders

This collection of red-roofed clapboard buildings commemorate one of the most important ranchers in southern Colorado, Elton T. Beckwith. This son of a Maine shipbuilder prospered by driving cattle from the Midwest into Colorado to feed mining towns. The family played a very prominent role in the formation of some

W

early cattlemen's associations, supposedly endearing themselves to locals by hanging a rustler from their barn roof. Beckwith became a leading rancher and was elected to the Colorado state senate. He built Custer County's first ornate residence, a ranch house boasting a balcony, tower, bay windows, and porte cochere. By 1900, the family owned the largest ranch in the region, running 7,000 cattle and 200 horses on 60,000 acres. This vast, storied, and scenic spread was purchased in the 1980s by developers Phyllis and Paul Seegers, who donated 3.9 acres and the 10 original buildings of the Beckwith Ranch to the nonprofit Friends of Beckwith Ranch, Inc., and then began developing the rest as 35- to 80-acre ranchettes.

The Friends raised a match for the SHF's $467,842 to stabilize foundations; repair roofs; and restore the ranch house's lap siding, windows, porte cochere, and porches. Work continues on a gem that the Friends hope will become the interpretive and community center for a legendary ranch in this breathtaking setting in the Wet Mountain Valley. At the ranch, the Colorado Historical Society and Colorado Department of Transportation have erected an interpretive display, with photos, maps, text on local history, and a new concrete base stamped with local cattle brands.

DENVER & RIO GRANDE ENGINE HOUSE
West end of Rosita Ave. SR
Built: 1901; Denver & Rio Grande Railroad, builder

Westcliffe eclipsed its much larger rival, Silver Cliff, after the Denver & Rio Grande Railroad chose it as the terminus for its narrow-gauge route. The commerce that came from this decision kept Westcliffe alive while many other Custer County mining towns died. This single-stall, board-and-batten engine house served the line until its 1937 abandonment. It now houses All Aboard Westcliffe, Inc., a group determined to preserve one of the few engine houses left in Colorado. The SHF supplied $78,454 to help build a new foundation, reframe the exterior, and repair windows and doors. Tim Thurn of All Aboard Westcliffe says that community support and volunteers were essential, and that "the SHF fills the gap between caring historians and a finished, preserved project that would otherwise remain in ruins."

W

HOPE LUTHERAN CHURCH
310 S. 3rd St., northwest corner of Powell Ave. [NR]
Built: 1917; John Reininga, builder

This beautiful, ornamental concrete-block church has maintained an unchanged, traditional interior and exterior, complete with stained-glass windows of biblical scenes and a 96-foot spire. With $93,000 from the SHF, the congregation has restored the church spire, roof, and interior while rehabilitating the basement and kitchen area. Half the town turned out to see a giant crane lift the steeple off for repair, repainting, and regilding of the cross, then lift the steeple back into place. Pastor Wayne Riddering elaborates: "The town and this church have been depopulated for the past generation. Fixing up the church was beyond our wildest dreams until the SHF funds appeared. They have helped our volunteers spruce up this landmark to appeal to the new people now moving into the Westcliffe area to build second and summer homes." The next step will be to restore the church's exterior ornamental concrete-block.

KENNICOTT CABIN
63161 CO 69
Built: 1869; Frank Kennicott, builder

Photo courtesy of Tom Noel

This rare, two-story, hewn-log cabin is a picturesque reminder of the first Europeans to settle in the Wet Mountain Valley. The San Isabel Foundation used $10,875 from the SHF and volunteer labor to stabilize the foundation and repair or replace the round logs. With the help of Gertrude Schooley, ranch owner and granddaughter of Frank Kennicott, volunteers removed rotting sill logs and improved drainage around the ranch house, which is set in a lush meadow with a soaring backdrop: the 14,000-foot-high Sangre de Cristo Mountains.

W

WESTCLIFF SCHOOL
304 S. 4th St., northwest corner of Powell Ave. [NR]
Built: 1891; Archie Scherer, architect

Made of fieldstone, concrete, and rhyolite, this one-room school was originally called the "Rock School." It was later renamed Westcliff School (without the usual

final "e"). Upon closure in 1953 it was rehabilitated as a community center. It now houses the offices and exhibits of the Custer County Historical and Genealogical Society and the Valley Park and Recreation Youth Center, Inc., which raised a match toward a $13,500 grant from the SHF for new roofing, heating, and an indoor bathroom. One corner of the school has a reconstructed antique four-desk classroom.

Wheat Ridge

A tiny farming community that has become a large Denver suburb, Wheat Ridge boasts the nearly restored Richards-Hart Estate Mansion, a historical park, and a greenway along Clear Creek that has partially revived the stream's original natural setting. Since its 1974 founding to save the town's sod house, the Wheat Ridge Historical Society (WRHS) has worked with the Wheat Ridge Parks Department to create the Wheat Ridge Historical Park at 4610 Robb Street. This one-acre park boasts the first Wheat Ridge Post Office and Library, which had been slated for destruction before being moved to this location. Other relocated buildings here include a circa 1863 hewn-log cabin that is one of the earliest homestead houses in Colorado; a board-and-batten shed overflowing with antique agricultural tools; a tiny frame outhouse; and, most notably, metro Denver's only surviving pioneer sod house.

This circa 1864, three-room marvel was constructed of 5,000 square feet of native tall prairie-grass sod cut into strips. These sod bricks were turned upside down and stacked on top of each other to form the walls of a well-insulated earthen house. Claudia Worth, president of the WRHS, reports, "Without the SHF's $125,000, we never could have done all this."

W

RICHARDS-HART ESTATE
5349 W. 27th Ave. NR
Built: 1869–1890s

The 1859 Colorado gold rush lured a 20-year-old Ohio farmer named James W. Richards. After finding his fortune not in gold but in the more lucrative business of transporting men and supplies to Central City and Georgetown, Richards then purchased 160 acres overlooking Sloan's Lake, where he built this country residence. In 1926, the property was purchased by the Patrick F. Hart family, who sold it in 1977 to Wheat Ridge for use as a museum and open space. Then, according to Joyce Manwaring, director of Wheat Ridge Parks and Recreation, "You could see upstairs through holes in the walls and ceiling, and the grounds were a mess!" With the SHF's $126,991 as seed money, the city has begun restoring this treasure. Though work is ongoing, the porches are restored, the sandstone windowsills have been cleaned and repaired, and lath-and-plaster walls have been replaced, along with repairs or replacements of the windows, wallpaper, and a skylight. In Frank Hall's 1894 *History of Colorado*, the Richards Estate was listed as one of the outstanding farms in Colorado. Today, with its Italianate architecture, charming gardens, and unusual linden, Kentucky coffee, and walnut trees, this two-story, stuccoed brick house and its 3.5-acre estate are outstanding again—and available for weddings and parties, including other special occasions.

WHEAT RIDGE POST OFFICE
4610 Robb St. (SR)
Built: 1913

When scheduled for demolition at its original site at West 38th Avenue and Teller Street in 1992, this 26-by-17-by-13-foot brick building was moved to the Wheat Ridge Historic Park. This little structure encapsulates much Wheat Ridge history. In 1922, it became the first Wheat Ridge public library. With $7,285 from the SHF, the Wheat Ridge Historical Society has restored it inside and out. The large glass storefront allows visitors to peek in at the old-fashioned golden-oak counters, clerical cages, pigeonholes, brass mailboxes, the original Wheat Ridge telephone exchange, and even a drowsy mannequin posing as the postmaster.

W

Windsor

KAPLAN-HOOVER BISON BONEBED AND KILL SITE
2141 Meander Rd. (SR)
835 BC; Late Archaic Peoples

Lester M. Kaplan, president of River Ridge Development Company of Fort Collins, and partner Hoover, a home builder, developed a Windsor residential subdivision near the junction of Fossil Creek and the Cache la Poudre River. Workmen preparing to lay a house pad came across the bone bed at the bottom of an arroyo. After archaeologists had been called in, excavation revealed bones of some 200 bison, making this one of Colorado's largest known kill sites. Among their bones were nine projectile points. With the help of an $87,924 SHF grant, Colorado State University archaeologists and the Colorado Archaeological Society have worked with the River Ridge Homeowners Association and Colorado Open Land to purchase and preserve the site under a protective shelter as a field school for the general public and students of all ages. CSU anthropologist Larry Todd says the site "is a textbook example of the productive consortium between community, residents, educators, researchers, and responsible developers."

Winter Park

COZENS RANCH HOUSE MUSEUM
77849 US 40, 1.5 miles south of Fraser [NR]
Built: 1874; William Zane Cozens, builder

In 1872, Mary York Cozens, the first white woman in Grand County, and her husband, William, built this first homestead in the Fraser River Valley. They erected this hewn-log house, later covered by board-and-batten siding, which was enlarged in 1876 to include a hotel, post office, and stage stop. This site became the center of a 700-acre hay, potato, and cattle ranch, which the Cozens bequeathed to the Jesuits of Regis College of Denver. The Jesuits converted the house into a chapel and summer retreat that operated from the 1920s to the 1980s.

After most of ranch's 700 acres were sold to a developer, the ranch house was conveyed to the Grand County Historical Association, which spent $300,000 to restore and convert it into a museum, while the SHF provided a $2,400 grant toward an emergency $3,400 shake-shingle roof repair. The sensitive restoration retained the cold storage room, post office equipment, and backyard family cemetery. The rooms were painted and papered to replicate early interior design, leaving samples of the original lath-and-plaster walls and wallpaper. One exhibit is a scale model of the ranch and outbuildings at their peak around 1900. Much of that land has been developed, including the once-large green space surrounding this house.

W

*Woodland Park*_____

FARBER-IMMER LOG CABIN
1222 Laurel St. LL
Built: 1947; Joe Farber, builder

This peeled round-log cabin with saddle notches is named for the first two owners, who used it as a summer home. The Woodland Park School District later acquired it for use as a woodworking shop. The building had been abandoned when the city acquired it in 1994 and used $26,100 in SHF funds for interior and exterior restoration.

"We had to replace or restore most of the logs and the chinking," recalls city planner Sally Riley. "We rehabilitated the interior and added new electrical, heating, and windows. George Parkhurst coordinated the project and put in most of the sweat equity." The cabin is part of a complex including the Ute Pass Cultural Center and the new Woodland Park Public Library.

MIDDLE SCHOOL GYM BUILDING / UTE PASS
CULTURAL CENTER
210 E. Midland Ave. LL
Built: 1938; Works Progress Administration, builder

The WPA contributed $10,000 to build this gymnasium, in use until 1988, after which the abandoned structure deteriorated rapidly. In 1994, Woodland Park city manager Don Howell saw a diamond in the rough and made a trade with the school district to acquire the building. The city then obtained $100,000 from the SHF, which it matched with an additional $500,000.

"Restoration included total replacement of the floor and the interior stage, lighting, and sound equipment," says city planner Sally Riley, adding that new plumbing, restrooms, and heating were installed as well. The old gym now houses the Chamber of Commerce Visitor Center, the Mountain Arts Council, and the Pikes Peak Historical Society's museum, gift shop, and offices. Outside, new stucco and paint highlight the Art Deco elements of the building. A new roof and new gutters adorn the center, which continues to stage plays, musical performances, conferences, and other public gatherings.

W

INDEX OF SITES

International Standard Book Numbers
ISBN-10: 1-56579-493-1
ISBN-13: 978-1-56579-493-1
7660513

Text: Thomas J. Noel, ©2006. All rights reserved.
Photography, except where noted: Courtesy of the Colorado Historical Society's
State Historical Fund
Editors: Martha Ripley Gray, Elizabeth Train, Jennifer Jahner
Design: Craig Keyzer and Carol Pando
Production Manager: Craig Keyzer

Published by:
Westcliffe Publishers, Inc.   and   Colorado Historical Society
P.O. Box 1261   1300 Broadway
Englewood, CO 80150   Denver, CO 80203
westcliffepublishers.com   coloradohistory.org

Printed in China by Hing Yip Printing Co., Ltd.

Library of Congress Cataloging-in-Publication Data:
Noel, Thomas J. (Thomas Jacob)
  Guide to Colorado historic places : sites supported by the Colorado Historical Society's State Historical Fund / by Thomas J. Noel.
     p. cm.
  Includes index.
  ISBN-13: 978-1-56579-493-1
  ISBN-10: 1-56579-493-1
  1. Historic buildings—Colorado—Guidebooks. 2. Historic sites—Colorado—Guidebooks. 3. Colorado—Guidebooks. 4. Colorado—History, Local. I. Colorado Historical Society. II. Title.
  F777.N65 2006
  917.8804—dc22

2004027904

ABOUT THE AUTHOR

Thomas Jacob Noel is a professor of history at the University of Colorado at Denver and Health Sciences Center. He teaches, among other things, Colorado Studies,

Historic Preservation, and Western Art & Architecture. Tom has a B.A. in history and M.A. in library science from the University of Denver and an M.A. and Ph.D. in history from the University of Colorado at Boulder. He has also served as chair of the Denver Landmark Preservation Commission and is currently a National Register Review Board Member for Colorado. He conducts tours of cemeteries, churches, ghost towns, landmark districts, parks, saloons, ranches, and railroads for the Colorado Historical Society, the Smithsonian Institution, and others. Tom's other books include *Buildings of Colorado; Colorado: A Liquid History & Tavern Guide; Denver Landmarks & Historic Districts; Denver: The City Beautiful and Its Architects* (with Barbara Norgren); and, with John Fielder, *Colorado 1870-2000 Revisited.* Tom appears as "Dr. Colorado" in Saturday's *Rocky Mountain News/Denver Post* and on Channel 9's *Colorado and Company.*